# EXILES AND MIGRANTS IN OCEANIA

D1455044

ASSOCIATION FOR SOCIAL
ANTHROPOLOGY IN OCEANIA
*Monograph Series*

Mac Marshall, Series Editor

Other books in this series:
No. 1 *Adoption in Eastern Oceania*, edited by Vern Carroll
No. 2 *Land Tenure in Oceania*, edited by Henry P. Lundsgaarde
No. 3 *Pacific Atoll Populations*, edited by Vern Carroll
No. 4 *Transactions in Kinship*, edited by Ivan Brady

ASAO Monograph No. 5

# EXILES AND MIGRANTS IN OCEANIA

Edited by Michael D. Lieber

THE UNIVERSITY PRESS OF HAWAII Ⓧ
HONOLULU

**Library of Congress Cataloging in Publication Data**
Main entry under title:

Exiles and migrants in Oceania.

(ASAO monograph ; no. 5)
Consists of rev. and expanded versions of papers presented at a symposium held at the University of Washington in 1970.
   Bibliography:  p.
   1.  Ethnology—Oceanica—Congresses.  2.  Migration, Internal—Oceanica—Congresses.  3.  Oceanica—Social conditions—Congresses.  I.  Lieber, Michael D.
II.  Series:  Association for Social Anthropology in Oceania.  ASAO monograph ; no. 5.
GN663.E9      301.32'6'099      77–10756
ISBN 0–8248–0557–7

To Homer Barnett
Who began this work
And showed us what culture change is about

# CONTENTS

Maps     ix

Tables     x

Editor's Preface     xi

1. Introduction: Locating Relocation in Oceania     1
   *Martin G. Silverman*

2. Commas in Microcosm: The Movement of Southwest
   Islanders to Palau, Micronesia     10
   *Robert K. McKnight*

3. The Processes of Change in Two Kapingamarangi
   Communities     35
   *Michael D. Lieber*

4. Communities and Noncommunities: The Nukuoro on
   Ponape     67
   *Vern Carroll*

5. The Relocation of the Bikini Marshallese     81
   *Robert C. Kiste*

6. Making Sense: A Study of a Banaban Meeting     121
   *Martin G. Silverman*

7. Rotumans in Fiji: The Genesis of an Ethnic Group       161
   *Alan Howard* and *Irwin Howard*

8. Sydney Island, Titiana, and Kamaleai: Southern
   Gilbertese in the Phoenix and Solomon Islands          195
   *Kenneth E. Knudson*

9. Tikopia in the Russell Islands                         242
   *Eric H. Larson*

10. The Exploitation of Ambiguity: A New Hebrides Case    269
    *Robert Tonkinson*

11. What Did the Eruption Mean?                           296
    *Erik G. Schwimmer*

12. Conclusion: The Resettled Community and Its Context   342
    *Michael D. Lieber*

Appendix                                                 389

References                                               401

Contributors                                             415

# MAPS

1. Movement of Southwest Islanders to Palau                                        14

2. Southwest Islander settlements on Palau                                         19

3. Movement from Kapingamarangi to Ponape                                          34

4. Areas on Ponape designated for use by Kapingamarangi
   and Nukuoro settlers                                                            37

5. Movement from Nukuoro to Ponape                                                 73

6. Relocation from Bikini and Eniwetok                                             80

7. Relocation from Ocean Island to Rambi                                          125

8. Movement from Rotuma to other Fiji Islands                                     163

9. Relocation of Gilbertese to Solomon Islands                                    196

10. Destination islands: Ghizo and the Shortlands                                 216

11. Movement from Tikopia to Russell Islands                                      243

12. Tikopia settlements in the Russell Islands                                    247

13. Relocation from Ambrym to Efate                                               270

14. Mount Lamington, Papua                                                        303

# TABLES

1 Ethnic Status of Last Spouse, Ever-Married Members of
  Nukuoro Living Ethnic Population, by Location, 15
  March 1965                                                          78
2 Tikopia Migrating to Russell Islands, by Sex, Number of
  Visits, and Duration of Stay: 1949–1964                            244
3 Tikopia Migrating to Russell Islands, by Age:
  1949–1964                                                          244
4 Tikopia Populations in Russell Islands and on Tikopia:
  1964                                                               245
5 Composition of Tikopia Households in Russell Islands
  and on Tikopia: 1964                                               250
6 Comparative Advantages of Maat Ambrym and Maat
  Efate                                                              283

# EDITOR'S PREFACE

Resettled communities are ancient in human history. The Babylonian Captivity, the Romans' establishment of colonies in conquered territories, and the more recent establishment of reservations for Native Americans are three well-known examples of this time-honored practice. Despite the antiquity and ubiquitousness of resettlement, *Exiles and Migrants in Oceania* is, to my knowledge, the first attempt by anthropologists to confront the practice in a comparative effort. The comparative study of resettled communities was initiated largely through the thinking, planning, and coordination of Homer G. Barnett, to whom this volume is dedicated. The volume is, if anything, a first fruit of Barnett's vision and labor.

Like the other volumes of the ASAO Monograph Series, this is a symposium volume. With but two exceptions, the authors of the papers included here met at the University of Washington in 1970 to determine, through presentations and discussion, the significant issues raised by the study of resettled communities. On the basis of these discussions, papers circulated before the symposium convened were rewritten so that each essay addressed the same issues. It was this sort of comparison that Barnett envisioned when he established the Pacific Displaced Communities Project. This volume is, hopefully, a first step toward that end.

Chapters 1 and 12 discuss the theoretical and comparative issues inherent in the study of resettled communities. They are concerned mainly with the generalizations that can be made from comparing resettled communities and with how these generalizations fit with the larger body of anthropological knowledge. Chapters 2 to 11 present data on specific resettled communities in Oceania. Although each of these chapters concentrates primarily on a particular resettled community (often in comparison with the home island), its comparative focus can be seen in the presentation of the data.

I gratefully acknowledge the contribution of Martin G. Silverman to the organization and success of the symposium that resulted in this volume. I also wish to emphasize the contributions of Murray Chapman and David Schneider. The direction which the symposium and the volume took was profoundly shaped by Chapman's masterful exposition of the relation between local social units and the larger social systems that are their contexts. David Schneider's penetrating discussions of the shape that culture must inevitably give to the way a community regards its situation was equally determinative of the theoretical and substantive direction of the volume. My special thanks go to Sally Furecz and Emily Friedman for their editorial assistance in preparing the manuscript. Vern Carroll, the past editor, and Mac Marshall, the present editor of the ASAO Monograph Series, provided continual encouragement and advice during the long period of editing and reediting that followed the symposium.

In addition to his other considerable contributions to the symposium and this volume, Murray Chapman also directed the preparations of the maps for this volume. To Robert Campbell, the cartographer of these maps, goes my very special gratitude. His careful reading of the manuscript and preparation of maps on the basis of the often dense anthropological prose he had to read was, in my estimation, a marvel. He contributed his time and talent with patience, understanding, and consummate professionalism.

Finally, I wish to acknowledge the generosity of the National Institute of Mental Health for supporting the symposium and much of the costs of preparing the volume (PHS 1 R13 MH18376–01). I also wish to thank the University of Washington for support of the symposium and for a stipend that allowed me to organize this volume during the summer of 1971.

# INTRODUCTION: LOCATING RELOCATION IN OCEANIA

*Martin G. Silverman*

In 1961, Homer G. Barnett of the University of Oregon, with a number of collaborators, presented a proposal to the National Science Foundation for a study of relocated communities in the Pacific Islands. Through the fieldwork of students under the direction of Barnett and others, the Barnett project revitalized the study of many parts of Oceania. The project takes its place in the history of anthropology beside those other coordinated enterprises that have inspired and enabled fieldwork of extraordinarily high quality.[1]

This volume contains chapters by members of the Barnett project and others who have, at first hand, studied relocated Pacific peoples. Most of the contributors participated in a 1970 conference which not only provoked a useful exchange of ideas but also—and this is probably rare, as anthropological conferences go—redefined for the conferees many aspects of the nature of the problem itself.[2] In retrospect, the emphases developed were faithful to the original objectives of the Barnett project.

I shall not attempt to define relocation or devise a logical set of categories into which the various cases can be sorted. In each of our cases we find, at least, a number of culturally homogeneous people living in a locale which is different from the place they come from. Among the ten resettled groups described here, we find considerable variation in the composition of the moving group. There are groups who identify themselves as complete societies, such as the Banabans and the Bikinians, groups that begin as "satellites" of the home island, such as the Kapingamarangi on Ponape and the Tikopia in the Russell Islands, and groups consisting of people who had not previously lived together, such as the Southern Gilbertese and the Southwest Islanders on Palau. At the extreme end of this range are individuals from a natal community who go to a single island and, despite the opportunity to form a community there, choose not to do so. The Nukuoro on Ponape represent this end of the range. There is also much variation among these resettled communities in the types of movement that resettlement constitutes for them. For the Bikinians and Southwest Islanders, relocation was a novel experience; for the Southeast Ambrymese and Rotumans, resettlement was part of an ongoing history of movement in the area.

In addition to comparative ethnography, much of our activity at the conference was directed toward establishing contexts within which Pacific relocation could be better understood. In roughly increasing scope of generality from the Pacific area, these contexts are colonialism, mobility structures, cultural definitions and the relationships among them, forms of social organization, and the conditions under which such cultural definitions and forms of social organization are developed.

COLONIALISM

The people being considered lived in colonial systems at the time of research. The colonizer-colonized relation must therefore figure prominently in any social account of them. Speaking broadly, we may say that in these cases the colonizers, who include administration, commercial, and mission establishments, need something the colonized can yield and population movement is deemed necessary or instrumental to getting it.

The colonizers may need the land of the colonized, as on Bikini for atomic testing or on Ocean Island for phosphate mining. The need for the labor of the colonized is common in areas being exploited by the colonizers. This is exemplified by the Tikopia in the Russell Islands and the Ambrymese on Efate working copra and by the Kapingamarangi on Ponape initially working for a Japanese company and later fishing commercially. The colonizers may need production on the land of the colonized such as copra (practically everywhere) and other crops. The colonizers may require behavior that is less explicitly tied to economic interests—religious conversion, for example, in all these territories.[3]

The colonizers may require of the colonized behavior to sustain the colonizers' definitions of "good administration" or "public welfare" in general. Local mobility has been associated with this requirement in, for example, the British practice of forming "line villages." The colonizers may also require of the colonized behavior to sustain the colonizers' definition of a "crisis" deriving from natural disaster—volcanic eruptions in Papua and the New Hebrides, a typhoon in the Southwest Island dependencies of Palau, a wartime disaster such as the destruction of the Ocean Island villages during World War II, or overpopulation in the Southern Gilberts. It may seem unusual to link an administrative response to a perceived natural disaster with a land grab. I do this not to impugn (or, for that matter, endorse) the specific motives of administrators but rather to underscore the asymmetric situation within which these acts are carried out.

There is another side of the coin: The colonized usually need something that the situation created by the presence of the colonizers can offer. Furthermore, the colonized sometimes define their own needs and wants according to the colonizers' definitions.[4] Cash and consumer goods are the universal examples, followed by education, the bright lights of colonial centers, and access to hospital care for the Southwest Islanders of Palau.

The colonized, of course, can manipulate the colonizers' definitions of the situation to their own ends and for purposes not envisaged by the colonizers themselves. Examples of this are the Nukuoro on Ponape finding sanctuary away from kin at home and the South Ambrymese finding sanctuary on Efate away from sorcery at home.

It seems that an internationally familiar drama has been played out in a number of island groups and is currently being played out in others: As the colonized need more and more diverse elements of what was generated by the colonial situation, the colonizers need less of what the colonized can yield. Hanging onto the colony becomes an economic and political liability for the metropolitan power as its subject peoples' dependency on the colonial infrastructure has increased. In chapter 8 Kenneth Knudson reports that one reason why government administrators may have favored relocation of the Gilbertese from the Phoenix Islands to the Solomons was to cement relationships between the two territories as a prelude to independence.

Attention is directed, then, to a system with a scale much larger than that of the indigenous communities under direct analysis. Attention is forced to what in the conference was termed the "micro-system-macrosystem problem"—the articulation of the local structures to the larger structures of which they are part. The assemblage of individual cases of relocation documents how, in an orthodox functionalist interpretation, moving people about is a rather conventional way of keeping a colonial system going. In this regard the paucity of anthropological studies of another variety of relocated people in the Pacific is clearly underscored: We know very little of the colonizers themselves. Yet the converse is also true: Preventing people *from* moving about might also be a conventional way of keeping a colonial system going. Moreover, regulations even beyond those specifically dealing with travel, immigration, and emigration are related to the potential for mobility —regulations on the registration, exchange, and sale of land being one example.

This large-scale regulation of population mobility is not, of course, distinctive only to colonial systems. Ancient states as well as modern ones have been involved in moving communities and segments of communities from one place to another. The point is merely that the colonial context is an inescapable fact of life for a certain phase of Pacific history, and attention to that context allows one to place the several cases in a single perspective.

MOBILITY STRUCTURES

The big picture, however, does not do away with the local scene. If we focus on patterns of mobility, then what are the other instances of mobility in the populations under study? In the conference, Murray Chapman, Sterling Robbins, and James Watson emphasized this question. Chapman argued strongly that the current view of tribal peoples is much too static. Mobility is lurking out there if one looks for it, and it might make sense to conceive of these areas as areas of *people in circulation.*[5] And, for parts of even precolonial New Guinea, at least, mobility was necessary for the maintenance of the social system. Watson's description of the importance of refugees as clients for "strong men" underscores the significance of the dialectic of mobility and politics set within larger systems (Watson 1970).

Can we identify a mobility structure, as Chapman suggested, which would comprehend, for example, postmarital residence, visiting, short-term labor migration, and the more dramatic fact of relocation itself? Can these patterns be fitted into a structure which points inward to the details of domestic life and points outward to a whole region, with members of local units picking themselves up (or being picked up or thrown out) and moving somewhere else?

The attractions of such an approach are several. For example, bodies of data that are often taken as discrete (relocation, postmarital residence) could be brought together within a single framework. The dimensions of the colonial transformation could be charted more precisely. Some hypotheses about mobility in the postcolonial Pacific could be formulated. And, as with invoking the colonial context, ways could be found for linking our work to studies from other parts of the world.

## CULTURAL DEFINITIONS, SOCIAL FORMS, AND CONDITIONS

It is not unusual in the Pacific (or elsewhere) to encounter people who trace their origins to some other place in recent, remote, or mythological time. Does the folk history of mobility contain a paradigm for dealing with new situations? Vern Carroll, in chapter 4, raises this question directly. If such paradigms operate among some people and not among others, how can we understand that difference?

This brings us to culture, or "systems of meanings embodied in symbols." In raising the question of a mobility structure, one wants to know what accounts for that structure, and one must then move into the cultural meaning of spatial mobility. In cultural (semiological, ideological, semantic—there are a number of favorite words) terms, what can it *mean* to move from one place to another? What can it mean *not* to move from one place to another? What can it mean to live together and to live apart? If these meanings have to do with land, what can land mean? How can kinds of movement be defined and differentiated, if indeed "movement" is a relevant cultural category? How can different kinds of people be defined and differentiated? What can a crisis be, and to whom? Erik Schwimmer speaks directly to this question in chapter 11. How can people define the options open to them and the options closed to them, if indeed they structure the world in this way? How can people define their situation and what to do about it? David Schneider catalyzed the discussion of these issues during the symposium.

A particularly important set of problems involving the relationship between cultural and social forms concerns boundaries: How are boundaries defined, maintained, and changed as different groups interact (or do not interact) in particular contexts in a particular setting? Three aspects of the cases commend this line of investigation. First, the construction of particularistic boundaries is an intrinsic part of colonial practice, as is shown in Robert McKnight's case from Palau in chapter 2. Second, some of the relocated groups find themselves living next to populations they did not live next to before—although they may have had images of them. Third, if the relocated group is a satellite of the home group, the boundaries and relationships between the two become a significant analytic problem for the observer and a significant concrete problem for the groups themselves; this appears to be crucial in the Kapinga, Ambrymese, and Tikopia situations. Some of the ways in which these peoples define their new position, and have their new position defined for them, seem similar to what in other parts of the world is described under the rubric of "ethnicity." There are many possibilities for extra-Oceanic comparative work here.

In chapter 8, Knudson argues for the importance of studying short-term change for the development of an ecological perspective. Similarly, I would argue for the importance of studying short-term change for the symbolic perspective, for in these chapters we encounter real people struggling with real and changing situations. We can observe at first hand how meanings are transacted, how they become established through real events, how differing symbolic constructions relate to the action-dilemma of life in a changing environment. Schwimmer's contribution in chapter 11 and my own in chapter 6 are particularly concerned with this kind of question.

Schwimmer articulates a fundamental issue when he asks: "How should anthropologists study a nonrecurring event?" In grappling with the resettlement studies, in trying to make some comparative sense out of them, we of course want to know first whether or not the forces precipitating a move—and the kind of move itself—are recurring. Even if they seem unique in the history of a single group, we might find them to be recurrent as we enlarge the scale of analysis to a colonial system or a regional mobility system.

The fundamental issue remains, however, and it is often articulated as "the problem of structure and history" (see, for example, Lévi-Strauss 1966). Indeed, parts of the chapters are indistinguishable from history or the narration of current events. History is not simply a background section to most of the analyses. We find discussion of specific leaders, specific attempts at community organization, specific volcanic eruptions (the latter being "contingency in its purest form," in Schwimmer's phrase).

Perhaps there is a tendency in anthropology to regard such events as reflecting an underlying pattern, rather than as directing a pattern for the future. When confronted with a period in the history of a people when events seem to dominate and the pattern is elusive, many of us tend to regard such a period as transitional, the system grinding its gears while shifting from one set of ratios to another.

Alternatively we can view these systems as always moving, unevenly, with both internal dynamics and certain shifts of circumstance (that is, history) changing the nature of their constraints and thus changing the direction, or relative rates of change, or relative structural dominance, of the unevenly changing (see Mao Tse-tung 1965). From some of the chapters one might note in particular the appearance of communal forms of organization in early relocation periods. Is there a norm in these cultures: When in crisis, communalize? Or perhaps a form of organization that has been linked to one set of activities vastly enlarges its contextual scope in a set of unanticipated circumstances. When do we find that such shifts are themselves directed (or misdirected) through concrete events, such as discussions on land issues, strikes, political meetings—and the forms of those events might also be highly contingent—which force the issue?

Clifford Geertz described Indonesia as on the way to becoming a "permanently transitional" society (1965:152). That term may be equally descriptive of the societies described in this volume—

societies in the most recent moments of a history of resettlement that began, at least, with the settlement of the Pacific islands. One wonders whether such a characterization would not apply to a greater range of the human social experience than we generally believe. The ambiguous, the uncertain, the unstable, the testing and revision of old and new forms in new and old contexts, the rising to structural prominence of features that may have been secondary under other conditions—here may be the rule, not the exception.

## NOTES

I would like to acknowledge the assistance of the following colleagues, who made many useful comments on an earlier draft of this introduction: Vern Carroll, Murray Chapman, Robert McKnight, Erik Schwimmer, and Robert Tonkinson.

1. I might note that I was not part of the Barnett project myself, only an enthusiastic supporter.
2. The conference was the Association for Social Anthropology in Oceania's Symposium on Relocated Communities in the Pacific, held at the University of Washington's Lake Wilderness Conference Center on 10–12 April 1970. The symposium was organized by Michael Lieber and was supported by the University of Washington and the National Institute of Mental Health. The support of the NIMH, the support and hospitality of the University of Washington, and the untiring efforts of Michael Lieber are acknowledged with gratitude. The symposium was chaired by Martin G. Silverman (Princeton University). David M. Schneider (University of Chicago) and Murray Chapman (University of Hawaii) served as discussants. Papers and talks were presented by Vern Carroll (University of Washington), Carlos Fernandez (University of California, Santa Barbara), Robert Kiste (University of Minnesota), Kenneth Knudson (University of Nevada), Eric Larson (University of Connecticut), Michael Lieber (University of Washington), Robert McKnight (California State, Hayward), Sterling Robbins (University of California, Los Angeles), Erik Schwimmer (University of Toronto), Martin G. Silverman (Princeton University), and James Watson (University of Washington). Homer G. Barnett (University of Oregon), who directed the project on relocated populations in the Pacific, was unable to attend the symposium because of illness.
3. We note that some local mobility has been associated with religious group formation in the Pacific through the consolidation or formation of villages and hamlets around churches, as happened in the New Hebrides, Papua, and Rambi Island.
4. I do not mean to suggest that the colonized are passive actors in the establishment of these categories. Nor do I want to suggest that there is an identity of categories among the colonizers or among the colonized. Indeed,

it is the dialectic which produces the system of similarities and differences that is of extreme interest.

5. The point might be extended to encompass some of the larger Polynesian islands (at least), where competition for followers was an important part of the political process.

# 2

# COMMAS IN MICROCOSM: THE MOVEMENT OF SOUTHWEST ISLANDERS TO PALAU, MICRONESIA

*Robert K. McKnight*

## INTRODUCTION

In order to create a model industrial nation in Micronesia it has frequently been suggested that the small, outer-island populations should be relocated to reside on the few larger high islands. This, it is argued, will provide the proper market and labor conditions from which industrialization can emerge. A concentration of Micronesia's dispersed populations is a key recommendation in one of the recent economic surveys of the Trust Territory of the Pacific Islands, the Nathan Report or, more formally, the *Economic Development Plan for Micronesia* (Nathan 1966). Aside from the economic advantages of a labor pool and an enhanced market, relocation is advocated as a means to accomplish ethnocide and engineer Micronesian unity. The following is a typical passage in which these social objectives are associated with the economic advantage of relocation:

> The economic development advantages of being able to pull together a labor force from throughout Micronesia . . . will also be of benefit to the people—both those who move and those who stay at home. This kind of mobility can facilitate the creation of a Micronesian unity to replace the present somewhat artificial association of a dozen or so somewhat similar nevertheless distinctly different cultural, political and economic entities. Increased mobility can speed the replacement of local particularism with a cohesive Micronesia. [Nathan 1966:100]

Elsewhere the plan calls for the introduction of non-Micronesian labor, presumably Asian, and the continued long-term supervision of the developmental process by American administrative and managerial personnel in increased numbers.

The Nathan Report, one learns from various sources in the Trust Territory administration, is gathering dust, its specifics largely ignored. Nonetheless current practice, planned or adopted out of convenience, provides maximum public service (hence assorted ancillary "urban" conditions) only at the six district administrative centers in the Trust Territory, all but one located on a high island. This practice closely resembles the relocation tactic urged in the Nathan Report. The motives voiced by advocates of relocation and concentrated public services are also likely to be identical; aside from logistic convenience, the concentration of the various populations in a few locations, it is believed, will enhance Micronesian unity and, as the Nathan Report suggests, speed the disappearance of "ancient customs and traditions" (Nathan 1966: 100).

This model, whether it is a conscious adaptation from the Nathan Report or not, embodies assumptions that are theoretically unsound and are contradicted by data in Micronesia and elsewhere (for instance, the resettlement scheme for Tokelauans in New Zealand).

First, the notion that the association of Micronesian cultural, political, and economic entities is "artificial" belies the historical facts of colonial experience. Colonial systems, however contrived and arbitrary they may once have been, are in fact systems. As such they effect changes and realignments in contact and communication among the various sociopolitical systems they subsume.

Second, a well-recognized feature of colonial systems is that they tend to maintain, by implicit or paralegal policies of administration, indigenous sociopolitical units (tribes, clans, villages, castaways, or whatever) which might otherwise have disappeared through violence, absorption, or assimilation by dominant groups or as a result of their own internal processes. In this sense, colonial systems might be thought of as artificial. The colonial situation in Micronesia is not exceptional; rather than homogenization, more sharply defined ethnic boundaries are evident and may be expected to continue as a feature of population concentration.

Third, it follows therefore that it is difficult to assume that ancient customs and traditions will disappear or that changes in
these customs and traditions will in fact somehow correlate with
the disappearance of "extra-legal restrictions to individual mobility within the Trust Territory" (Nathan 1966:100). Such restrictions on movement are normative and are the consequence of ethnic boundaries regardless of the changing content of such ethnic
entities. Barth (1969) has demonstrated that the maintenance of
ethnic boundaries is quite independent of the nature of the cultures, or the changes in the cultures, of the ethnic groups involved.
Furthermore, Leach (1954) has shown that the maintenance of
ethnic boundaries is independent of the extent to which people
regularly cross such boundaries, even though the mobile ones may
elect to "change" their ethnic identity as they move between
groups.

These three points are obviously closely related. Critical to each
is a recognition that colonial administrations inhibit the emergence of various asymmetrical relations among independent social
units and impose another kind of asymmetry, the subordination of
all such units to the colonial administration itself. By assuring
peace and protecting the identity of each social unit, not only is assimilation of one unit by another highly improbable, but the former asymmetry among the various units involved is diminished.
Each group under the colonial umbrella will be engaged in a process of relatively autonomous adaptation to the colonial administration and its policies, mirroring, perhaps, the colonial power in
some respects but also reflecting its own cultural past. Ancient
customs and traditions may or may not disappear; certainly adaptive changes may be expected. However, ethnic boundaries will remain intact and the anticipated ethnocide will not occur. It follows, then, that the kind of happy homogenization portrayed in
the Nathan Report is, in fact, not possible in Micronesia as long as
the colonial administration maintains itself as a dominant system
controlling the social system it has created or, in the case of Micronesia, inherited.

This chapter demonstrates these theoretical formulations
through a study of the relations between Palauans and a resettled
community of people from the islands southwest of Palau, as these
relationships have been mediated by the colonial governments
that have controlled Micronesia.

## THE CULTURAL SETTING

> In the sea to the southwest of the Pelews there are a number of isolated small islands concerning which little is known. Their lack of importance commercially and politically is indicated by the fact that they have not even received a group name to characterize them, and their positions upon the chart are only approximate. Their individual names are North and South Sonsorol, Warren Hastings, Current and Lord North Islands, with some alternative names given them by different navigators who have sighted them. [Hobbs 1923:105]

The five islands and an atoll south of Palau in the southwestern corner of Micronesia remain almost as remote and nameless today as they were when described by William Hobbs some fifty years ago. As last known to the writer in 1965, the islands and their populations were as follows, moving generally southward from Palau: Fana, about 8; Sonsorol, about 70; Pulo Ana, about 10; Merir, uninhabited; Tobi, about 100; and Helen Reef, uninhabited. (See map 1.) Populations change, as we shall see, through the movement of people to and from Palau. Visits from island to island among the Southwest Islanders are rare.

Yet the Southwest Islanders do share a sense of commonality. Though their languages differ in dialect, they can converse with one another. Though there are evident physical differences (Tobians tend to be short and slight, Sonsorolese are taller and fleshier), they recognize a common ancestral origin. Futhermore, they are very much aware that they are viewed as a group by visiting Palauans and they can validate this view, in many respects, by common contrasts with Palauan society.

Within the range of variation characterizing Micronesian societies few boundaries are wider than that distinguishing the social systems of Palau and the Southwest Islands. To put the Southwest Islands on a more familiar cultural map, they are linguistically and, for most purposes, culturally derivative from Ulithi. Specifically, the differences between Palau and the Southwest Islands may be highlighted as follows.

Palauan political organization, with elaborate dual organizations at all levels, from the 'side-thighs' of the resident clans to the 'side-heavens' of the island groups, and with a host of specialized political functionaries, culminates in an arrangement that approaches a semistate with numerous communities bound loosely

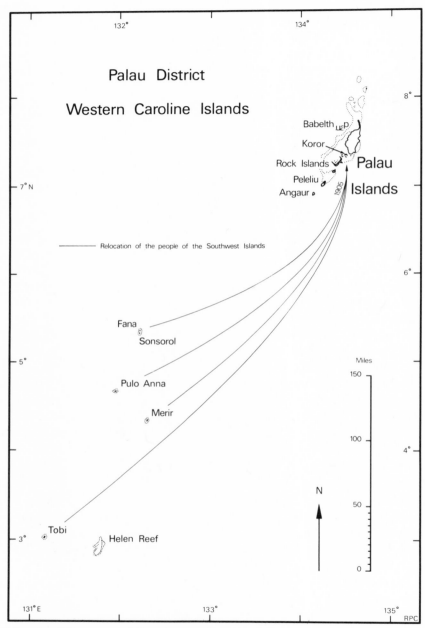

Map 1. Movement of Southwest Islanders to Palau.

together under the dominance of certain ranking villages (see McKnight 1960). If the Palauan population, prior to contact and decimation, numbered fifty thousand persons, then rather tightly controlled village collectivities (three to seven or more villages) comprehended as many as three to four thousand persons, while wider and looser patterns of political domination comprehended one-half or more of the total population.

The Southwest Island societies are best represented as communities of lineages. Each lineage maintains considerable autonomy in a network of inherited, lineage-based specializations and economic reciprocities. On each island the community is bound together loosely through recognition of a *tamol* 'head' who bows to the consensus of lineage leadership. Populations on any one island probably never exceeded three hundred persons. In contrasting the political characteristics of Palau and the Southwest Islands, spokesmen for the latter sometimes refer to the political structure of a large ship as suitable for the Southwest Islands. Debating the merits of an administered program of political development calling for the election of magistrates, a Sonsorolese spokesman pondered the propriety of electing the captain of a ship.

Of structural importance in both Palau and the Southwest Islands are matrilineal descent groups. However, Palauan matriliny extends to the inheritance of political titles while this is generally not the case in the Southwest Islands. In condensed terms, the *dui* 'title' in Palau passes from holder to sister's son and the authority of political office remains in the maternal clan. Among the Southwest Islanders the island 'head' position is inherited by the holder's son; hence the authority of political office moves from one matrilineage to another with each succeeding title generation. The Southwest Islanders have argued that their political system is more democratic than the American and Palauan systems, since the authority of a group does not extend beyond the tenure of one 'head'.

As the Western court system becomes institutionalized, with community judges bound largely to Western law, comparisons between the societies in terms of resolving civil disputes will become more important. In Palau such disputes (now more often handled by Western courts) were formerly adjudicated by a special title-holder in large communities or, in the case of small communities, by a council of titled elders. Elaborate payments of money (ceramic bracelet pieces or glass beads) were called into play as part of the settlement when violence could be avoided. In the Southwest Islands, individual disputes (adultery is the usual context) are disposed of with considerable informality (no community judges have yet been installed). The offended party is expected to attract community attention with considerable noisemaking and shouted threats, gathering a host of attention before he confronts the offender. Under these circumstances, a crowd gathers and the principals are restrained until elders of the community, through the council of lineage leaders, arrive at some solution. Payment in red ocher may occur in the resolution of disputes, but the use of red ocher is far more specialized and restricted than is Palauan ceramic and glass money.

Cross-cousin marriage, considered appropriate in the small Southwest Island communities, may be outlawed as incestuous in Palau. In one instance, Palauan courts ruled that a Pulo Ana couple could live together as husband and wife on their native island but must live separately when residing in Palau.

Marriage in Palau initiates an exchange of money and food centered on the wife, who is successful in her role insofar as she intrigues and seduces her husband and his clan into generous payments of money to her clan. A Palauan marriage to a Southwest Islander precludes the emergence of the economic cycle on which the success of the Palauan nuclear family depends. Generally speaking, a marriage in Palau to a near relative, affinal or otherwise, tends to be viewed as economically nonproductive and to a certain extent incestuous. Hence while Palauans regard some Southwest Island marriages as incestuous, Southwest Islanders view marriage in Palau as a rather exploitive economic relationship.

In Palau, the division of labor between the sexes is more specialized than in the Southwest Islands. In Palau, for example, women are the agriculturists. Palauan men may enter the taro gardens only with the consent of the women working there. Male agricultural labor in Palau is restricted to major construction or maintenance tasks associated with complex irrigation systems in the taro gardens. In sharp contrast, the man in the Southwest Islands is a competent gardener and works the crops by himself or in the company of his wife. This fact contributes to the wide cultural gap between Palauans and Southwest Islanders. Palauans do not believe that Southwest Island men can match the agricultural competence of Palauan women and consider them in general to be careless, primitive agriculturists.

The contrast between the Palauan and Southwest Island societies is most succinctly summarized as that of a large, complex, and differentiated social system opposed to small and relatively undifferentiated ones. The contrasts of scale and complexity are clearly recognized by the Palauans and have become the bases of the Palauan image of the Southwest Islanders.

RELOCATION IN PALAU

The Southwest Islanders are not strangers to the idea of relocation. Their creation myths are not tied to their present island homes; rather, the folk histories of the present populations trace various original navigator-founders back to Mogmog islet in Ulithi Atoll and to Yap. Versions of the migration story differ from island to island, though the overall impression received from informal inquiries is of a single migration that split up after arrival first at Sonsorol and subsequently at the southerly islands. At Merir, for example, the narrative recalls a separation of the founding party into one group that could not abide the heavy mosquito population and another that remained. On Pulo Ana the cult of the original navigator-founder has remained as the essence of the native religion.[1]

In more recent times most (perhaps all) of the inhabitants of Fana, Sonsorol, Pulo Ana, and Merir were brought to Palau by the German colonial administration in about 1905 in the wake of a typhoon that is said to have ravaged all four islands. The typhoon, however, was probably not the whole reason for this relocation. The islands lie scattered along a distance from Sonsorol to Merir of about 70 miles, a rather wide swath for a typhoon, particularly this far south in the western end of the Pacific. The German administrators probably viewed logistics and economy in terms similar to those of many contemporary American administrators and used the typhoon as the decisive argument for relocation. The islands are relatively flat, particularly Sonsorol and Tobi; they are small (one-half mile long at most and a few hundred yards wide); they have a fringing reef rather than a protective lagoon; thus they give the appearance of great vulnerability to typhoon damage.

Although Tobi Islanders did not figure in the original relocation, they, too, soon appeared as individual migrants in the Palau community.

These islanders were granted land defined as public on the southern coast of Babelthuap, the largest island of the Palau group. What Palauans call *chutem era buai* 'public land' comprised almost the entire island except the built-up village areas and cultivated gardens. It was viewed as belonging to the ranking clans of the local villages, held as a reserve against unspecified public and private needs. Thus, while lacking well-defined boundaries, such land was not without local "ownership." All 'public land', however, was claimed by the colonial administration for the German government.

The location selected for the Southwest Islanders was in what is now Aimeliik Municipality (map 2), where the coast is deeply forested with mangrove. The soil, red clay with bauxite and minimal pockets of alluvium, contrasts sharply with the sandy and phosphate-rich soils of the Southwest Islands. In addition, the Aimeliik coast, with its dense mangrove fringe, was "inside out," for the islanders had lived close to the shore on their home islands with the mangrove forests behind them in the inland swamps. It would be hard to imagine two tropical coastal environments with greater ecological differences. It appears, in fact, that adaptation to this new setting by the Southwest Islanders was unsuccessful. In time, according to Palauan sources, it was noted that the transplanted community was dying. Another location was sought which would more nearly resemble the home environment of the relocated islanders.

This new locus was Echol, also defined as 'public land', on the western shore of Arakabesang Island, one of three inhabited islands of what is now Koror Municipality in central Palau (map 2). This area is practically devoid of mangrove forest and has sizable, intermittent beaches and some sandy soils. The beaches face a lagoon fringed by a reef and are backed by rather steep slopes with clay soils and volcanic rock outcrops. Ecologically, the region would seem to allow a more familiar kind of adaptation, and indeed the community survived there until World War I.

Repatriation to the Southwest Islands occurred early during the Japanese mandate administration. However, a community of Southwest Islanders remained in the Echol region until World tory administrators. Though there has been no actual Trust Territory grant of use right to the Southwest Islanders for E-ang, recognition of the community by the American administration is fostered by contemporary Palauan leaders who continue to honor the original agreement made for the Southwest Islanders by the Germans. In Palauan terms, the use-right agreement for Echol has been transferred to E-ang.

Palauans realize that they have little real control over decisions regarding the use of government land. They are not, however, without some influence. In 1959, some residents from Tobi and Merir tried to gain land through the Trust Territory homestead program of government land in the region of Echol. Had they succeeded, the Southwest Island community in Palau would have achieved a permanency far beyond the present use-right concept. From the Southwest Islanders' point of view, they would have begun the process of establishing a new and separate segment of their home societies in Palau, a colony. The homesteading transaction was successfully opposed by local Palauan leaders. The Palauan reasoning is clear enough if one bears in mind the concept of clan ownership that precedes the Trust Territory concept of government land. Homesteading would alienate clan land and, in this instance, with Southwest Islanders rather than Palauans becoming the owners, the alienation would be total. Palauans are bonded to other Palauans by a complex network of relations including far more than land rights alone. Palauans who gain individual property through homesteading of government land can be relied on to conform to various social and economic constraints retaining, in most respects, their fit in Palauan society. No such constraints link Southwest Islanders to their Palauan hosts. Southwest Islanders in Palau are subordinated to neighboring villages by the fact that they reside on land that, in the Palauan conception, is owned by clans in the region. Hence the only formal control that Palauans have over the E-ang community has to do with land. No other significant structural feature mediates Southwest Islander and Palauan.

In Palauan terms the E-ang community is a use-right grant on clan land falling within the jurisdiction of the leadership of Meungs, a Palauan village on the opposite side of Arakabesang Island. The Palauan chief of Meungs village is recognized as the ranking chief of Arakabesang, including the Southwest Island community at E-ang. The Southwest Islanders contribute food to feasts held at Meungs village and there appear to be some individual patterns of food gifts from Southwest Islanders to members of the Meungs community. This kind of gift, involving garden produce, is in keeping with the ethic of reciprocity as supported by both Palauans and Southwest Islanders and expresses compensation for the use of Palauan land. Beyond this, at least in Palauan political theory, the Southwest Islanders gain representation and protection through the authority of the chief of Meungs village in transactions with other Palauan communities. It should be emphasized that this is a form of political representation that the Southwest Island minority in Palau does not enjoy in the emerging Western political system.

In this context, if the Southwest Islanders were to acquire land through the mechanism of homesteading (which is gaining recognition in Palau as a form of individual ownership), the Palauan capacity to control the Southwest Island community, in a manner consistent with Palauan ideas about assimilation, would become negligible.

The effect of all this is, of course, a general sense of transience that is not really satisfactory for either party but is viable given the presence of the American administration. Excessive exploitation of the Southwest Islanders is inhibited and, as long as Palauans exercise some control over homesteading, the E-ang community is no particular threat. In the present context, no final solution is readily apparent. The presence of the American administration diverts the migrants and hosts from one another since each relates more to the American administration. The status quo, such as it is, persists.

### THE PLACE OF THE SOUTHWEST ISLANDERS IN PALAU

Members of communities on Malakal and at E-ang return periodically to the Southwest Islands or are temporary visitors to Palau. The communities are not, therefore, fully detached from their home islands. Southwest Islanders in Palau retain the language and behavior relevant to their home communities, despite adapting as necessary to the fact of their residence in Palau.

E-ang and Malakal serve many purposes for the residents and transients. Perhaps the most evident function of the community pertains to hospitalization. As in other parts of the Pacific, patients from outer islands are seldom sent alone to the hospital in Palau. An attendant or two from the home community accompany the lone patient, bring familiar foods to the hospital, and provide necessary attention during the period of recovery. After the patient is released from the hospital, he (more often she) and the attendants stay in one or the other Southwest Island community. Because of the considerable period between field trips (as long as four or five months), this stay in Palau can become quite extended. Both Southwest Island communities provide a base for subsistence gardening and fishing.

Pregnancies constitute a large proportion of hospitalizations. Pregnant women are generally accompanied by husbands and other immediate dependents and must remain in Palau for the three or four months between field trips. This may have quite an effect on home island populations. In 1959, for example, the community at Merir had a population of six—four elderly persons and one young married couple. When the young wife became pregnant, the elders, unable to attend to their own subsistence, accompanied the couple to Palau (completely depopulating Merir). Their return depended on the young husband who, up to the present, appears unwilling to leave Palau.

Schools in the Southwest Islands, always difficult to staff with teachers, are conducted through grade six only. Intermediate and high school students must reside in Koror, in Palau, during the school term or remain the year round since field trips are so widely spaced. Hence schoolchildren form another component of the Southwest Island communities. The majority (except those from Pulo Ana) attend the Catholic mission schools. They are not formally segregated, but the Southwest Island youths form a separate social group, walk to the schools as a group apart from Palauans, and interact with Palauan children mainly in conjunction with curriculum requirements only. Separation appears to be reinforced by parental attitudes in the home communities. In the Southwest Island communities a passive, almost submissive, adaptation is fostered as appropriate to the role of outsider and guest. In turn, Palauans have stereotypes of the Southwest Islanders as a subordinate minority group. It should be emphasized, however, that the social separation of Palauan and Southwest Islander, even if it is mixed with myth and untruth, is reinforced by and has the

effect of reinforcing real cultural differences which are maintained even as both groups take on the appearance of westerniza-
tion. While they share roughly the same developmental goals (for
instance, a strong determination to provide their children with
maximum education), they approach these goals from their own
cultural perspectives and structures. In what is essentially a colonial system of administration, development has mainly to do with
the administering authority; each group relates to that authority
separately and with a distinctive style.

Two of the Southwest Island communities, Tobi and Sonsorol,
were chartered as municipalities in about 1959, with elected magistrates and with legislators seated in the Palau Legislature. The
E-ang community frequently hosts political representatives from
the home islands who must remain the several months between
field trips to attend a week or two of legislative or committee
meetings. The elected representatives are usually middle-aged
adult leaders in their communities and typically express anxiety
about the effect of prolonged absences on various home island programs: the school, the chronic drive to increase copra production,
the pressure to succeed in cultivating newly introduced crops, and
new opportunities in craft production. It may be noted here that
the role of these legislators with respect to the E-ang and Malakal
communities in Palau is ambiguous. From the standpoint of cultural identity, the Southwest Islanders in Palau are clearly constit-
uencies of the elected representatives from the Southwest Islands;
however, as we have seen, Palauan political practice tends to
designate the Southwest Islanders in Palau as wards of the
Palauan chief of neighboring Meungs village. In practice, in the
emerging Western political system the interests of these communities will be, at best, underrepresented.

Field trip vessels serving the Southwest Islands bring with them
a small assortment of retail goods for sale via Koror-based merchants, and both Sonsorol and Tobi have intermittently maintained island-based retail stores. However, special purchases or
major buying (for example, lumber to build a house) must be undertaken in person in Koror. Hence another transient at E-ang is
the buyer who must remain in Koror simply to make some complicated or major purchase. One such person was a Sonsorolese
who resided in Koror, working odd jobs with the Catholic mission

long enough to purchase lumber from the Koror mills and return to build a Japanese-style home on Sonsorol.

Aside from hospitalization, school, legislation, and purchasing, there are many other reasons for visits to the E-ang community, including a sojourn with relatives who have remained in Palau on a more permanent basis. One final category will probably become more important in the future: cash employment. A pull toward economic opportunity in Koror reflects the forecast of economic studies such as the Nathan Report. What is perhaps less apparent is the characteristic structure of this employment. Southwest Islanders are not readily employable in the private, Palauan sectors of the economy (for instance, in the many wholesale and retail outlets for imported goods), and their opportunities for employment in agencies controlled by Palauans, whether private or public, are poor.

The Catholic mission, recognizing that the Southwest Islanders are generally Catholic, has made a special effort to provide jobs for those who want to or must spend time in Palau, but the potential is small and thus far limited largely to unskilled labor. Janitorial and yard work can sometimes be obtained with the Trust Territory administration or with American families. One islander has long been employed in the government hospital as a janitor and, when needed, as an interpreter. One or two others have found employment in other sectors of government where they are disadvantaged by the fact that their supervisors are most likely to be Palauan. As long as governmental services continue to expand within the context of American administration, however, the small number of Southwest Islanders who are pursuing college degrees can probably anticipate government employment on their return to the Palau District. Recently, one man returned to Palau from medical training in Fiji and is apparently being accorded respect as a medical practitioner in the highly westernized context of the hospital program.

In the private sector, no more than one or two persons have gained employment intermittently with the trading companies that purchase copra from the outer islands. Significantly, in this kind of work they find themselves in the difficult role of cultural intermediary in frequent disputes arising between merchants and the producers and exporters of copra on the field trip visits to the islands. As employees, hence agents, of the trading companies and as members of Southwest Island societies, they are seldom able to maintain the trust of either side.

In E-ang itself some visitors and residents turn to handicraft, using Palauan hardwoods, as a source of income. The rigid ethnic boundary between Southwest Islanders and Palauans is reflected even here in the distinctive products and craft styles. In the main the Southwest Island artisans produce figures known throughout much of the Pacific as "Tobi monkey men." They do not produce, or attempt to imitate, the popular Palauan storyboard; conversely, Palauan artisans who occasionally sculpt humanlike figures, or post figures in the Palauan style, very seldom make monkey men.

In summary, the position of the Southwest Islanders' community in Palau is ambiguous for several reasons. From the point of view of the Trust Territory administration the legal status of the community is at best informal; neither the E-ang nor the Malakal settlement is formally recognized by lease, use right, or any other enforceable claim. Yet, interestingly enough, vis-à-vis Palauan society the legal status of E-ang is somewhat more explicit, as the use right of clan lands under the suzerainty of the chief of Meungs is at least recognizable within the context of Palauan custom.

Politically, the situation of the community is even more ambiguous. Given that the community is differentiated internally by island of origin and that two of the islands are municipalities, some community members may be said to be directly represented in the district legislature while others are not. This, of course, depends on whether residents of E-ang identify themselves as members of the out-island or of the E-ang community, a matter which is unclear even to the residents. At the same time, the E-ang community is considered by both the residents and the Palauans to be a political dependent of Meungs village and its chief, but whether this relation applies to temporary residents as well as the more or less permanent residents is ambiguous.

The transience which characterizes the E-ang population creates a further source of ambiguity and instability with regard to the Southwest Island populations themselves. On islands such as Merir and Sonsorol which have or have had very small populations, migration to Palau, even in small numbers, can seriously affect the home island either through total depopulation (as on Merir) or through removal of a significant proportion of residents.

This depopulation is bound to affect educational, political, and economic development programs for the home islands.[2]

The ambiguities of the situation of this relocated community are inherent in the fact of a simultaneous involvement of the community in two different systems of relations—a colonial system and the indigenous Palauan system, neither of which is totally independent of the other. Historical evidence indicates that in the absence of a colonial system, the Southwest Island commmunity could never have survived in Palau as a distinct social entity. Moreover, although the appearance of outsiders in a Palauan community was, before contact, occasional and often unpredictable, the integration of outsiders into the community was a regular, predictable process (from a Palauan point of view). In short, there is a Palauan model of assimilation of outsiders, which, although its operation as a social strategy has been curtailed by the colonial administration, continues to influence relations between the relocated community and the Palauans.

## BOUNDARY DISSOLUTION VERSUS BOUNDARY MAINTENANCE

Narratives of persons drifting in from "someplace else" are abundant in the Pacific and, in Palau at least, a fairly specific protocol for dealing with such strangers has been described by older residents. Palauan practice demanded that such persons be conducted, with no delay, to the nearest village chief. In every region of Palau, villages are part of a collection or coalition with one among them superordinate. The strangers might therefore be conducted first to the local village chief and then to the chief of the superordinate village of the collection. Such collections were themselves ranked; hence the transaction might well go on another step, terminating in one or another of the four or five historically elite villages throughout Palau. In short, the transfer of the strangers up the steps of village ranking would end when the leaders of a village were in a political position powerful enough to detain them. Several reasons can be given for this treatment of the immigrant in Palau. The factors involved demand some preliminary explanation regarding the Palauan conception of the cosmos and Palauan social structure.

Public ideology in Palau had the end of the world placed somewhere just beyond the horizon. Contradictory information made public by newcomers would pose a threat to the social order. The elite in Palau, particularly the historians of the ranking lineages, were privy to a wider scale of geographic knowledge that included information about the actual place of origin of many lineages outside Palau. Such knowledge was, however, maintained as private property among the trusted elders of the lineage or clan. As the Palauan might put it, such information was known only to those 'for whom the doors had been closed' in secret sessions of instruction by elder historians.

There were only two possibilities for dealing with strangers—they could be absorbed into the village community and, eventually, into the clan structure, or they could be put to death. Which alternative was chosen depended on the potential usefulness or the potential nuisance the strangers represented. In any case, no outsiders would be permitted to remain within or near the community and maintain their ethnic and cultural identity.

Becoming a true member of a Palauan community, with minimum qualifications for gaining a title, involves passage through three or four recognized grades of residency. The newly arrived immigrant would be designated *omengdaki* (probably derived from *omengd* 'to lean against' or *ultechakl* 'driftwood'). Whether conceived as one who 'leans against' an adopting lineage or as 'driftwood', the status implication is that of servant or slave. In time, the immigrants or their lineage descendants would be designated *beches el yars* 'new sails', would gain some access to land, and would begin to shed the stigma and obligations of servitude. The next designation would be *muchut el yars* 'old sails'. Members of such lineages would be considered long-term residents and would be eligible for lesser offices such as the leadership of their clan within the village club to which they were assigned. Finally would come the designation *techel a miich* 'core of the tropical almond tree'. The tropical almond, with its brilliant red leaves and tasty nuts, is an elite tree often prepared as a gift for elders. Persons of lineages so designated would be given public recognition as having an ancestry that reached back to the origin of the community. Generally speaking, high titled positions in a community are granted only to persons in lineages of the 'tropical almond' status of residency. Congruently, however, any individual, regardless of residency status, who gains high office in the community is publicly acknowledged to be of this elite residency designation and, publicly at least, the person so titled will carry others of the lineage to this highest residency status. Within the present century, in view of the drastic depopulation that occurred during the 1800s in Palau, upward mobility through the residency ranks has often been accelerated for capable persons, and the historical facts of residency rank have been questioned for many community leaders. But such questions are asked only in private. In public, to be elite is to be 'the core of the tropical almond tree' or at least 'old sails'.

In every Palauan community another formal ranking system exists that is more nearly ascriptive in character. In ideal terms, each Palauan community is composed of ten rank-ordered clans that, with their several lineages, make up the entire community population. The top-ranking four clans in a village constitute the local elite—the 'cornerpost' clans. Again, in ideal terms, the highest-ranking clan and four lesser clans form one house in a political balance against the second-ranking clan and remaining four village clans.[3]

Immigrants to Palau, as we have seen, are conducted to the chief of the ranking clan of the ranking regional village. Such individuals would be assigned to and, perhaps, adopted by the clan of this chief. This clan, however, might be one of the four clans allied within the village with that of the ranking clan. In any event, the leadership of the ranking clan would have a hold on the newcomers via clan membership or interclan bonds. An essential feature of this aspect of assimilation is that the actual history of migration, with whatever knowledge it might contain about regions beyond the popular Palauan cosmos, would be retained (if at all) in the archival memory of the historians of the elite with a minimum impact on the ideology of the people. We can refer to this as a cultural constraint maintaining a reduced geographic scale. Newcomers and their offspring learned that their security and status in the adopting community depended on shedding, as rapidly as possible, the stigma of their non-Palauan origin.

The rate at which newcomers, and their lineages, progress from 'driftwood' to 'tropical almond' is related to the community's need for leadership and the ability or willingness of lineage members to serve the community. The most important factor, in the Palauan conception, is the loyal service to the lineage, clan, and community—in short, recognized achievement.

A congruent feature of this assimilation process is that the immigrant, in whatever capacity he or she might prove useful, would
be immediately available to the village chief. If the immigrant had
no apparent skills, the chief or a relevant clan would gain some
additional labor. If the immigrant turned out to be hostile or a
nuisance, the chief could arrange for disposal. If, on the other
hand, the immigrant had some skill of apparent value to the community (such as medical knowledge), this skill would be available
to the chief and would be put to use through his office.

In summary, the essential features of the Palauan model of
assimilation are (1) a constricted popular conception of the cosmos, maintained by a political elite, (2) appropriation of the new-
comer, either as laborer or as innovator, by the elite, ultimately
the chief of the adopting community, and (3) the incorporation of
outsiders into the clan and community structure in a series of steps
based on their achievements within the community. Most important, the Palauan model of assimilation assumes that the category
of stranger or outsider or non-Palauan is, within the Palauan social context, temporary. The prescription of a specific mode of ethnic boundary dissolution (through assimilation or death) implies a
further assumption—that ethnic boundaries within Palauan society do not exist. Thus a permanent community maintaining a non-
Palauan ethnic identity is, at the outset, unreal from a Palauan
point of view.[4] The nature of the threat that the relocated community necessarily presented—a threat to the order of Palauan
reality—cannot be overemphasized, especially when we consider
the Palauan response to the relocated people.

The Palauans were presented with an administration demand
for land to domicile an ethnic group distinctly non-Palauan and
over whom they had no real control. Assimilation according to the
Palauan tradition was impossible within the context of the relocation since the newcomers were under German protection. Thus the
newcomers were to be a permanent ethnic community in Palau
and, as such, a challenge to the Palauan order of reality by their
very existence. The Palauan response was, predictably, stigmatization of the Southwest Islanders in Erving Goffman's sense of the
term (Goffman 1963). By characterizing the Southwest Islanders
as somehow subhuman, the threat to the Palauan social order is
minimized while a symbolic asymmetry between the two groups is

maintained. In face-to-face relations with Southwest Islanders, Palauans manifest the stigmatization by subtle condescension; in talking about them, they express overt contempt.

The stigmatization takes several forms. First, although the relocated community comprises people from several islands, Palauans ignore these distinctions and characterize the Southwest Islanders as a single group—Merir people. They label Southwest Islanders as "primitive" and "backward" and cite their "incestuous" marriage patterns, their informal political organization, and their scrupulous religiosity as evidence. Palauan children who walk barefoot are teased for walking "Merir style." Palauan children do not mingle with Southwest Island children at school, and the two groups do not speak when walking to or from school, even when going in the same direction.

In both cultures, sharing cooked food symbolizes social closeness. In Palau, Palauans will accept cooked food proffered as gifts by Southwest Islanders, but they will never eat it. After the giver leaves, the food is thrown away. On field trips to the Southwest Islands I observed that Palauans never accepted cooked food offered to them on the islands, although they would accept uncooked food such as coconut, crabs, or dried tuna. The meaning of their refusal is obvious to both sides.

On serious reflection, the Palauan will intellectualize about the differences between Palauan society and the Southwest Island communities. The much smaller populations of the Southwest Islands hardly necessitate the elaborate political and economic institutions evident in Palau. Southwest Islanders are respected as hard workers, apparently as an extension of the male agriculturist role, and on the individual level, especially between women members of the same (Catholic) church congregation, close friendships may be formed. Certain skills and characteristics are admired: Southwest Islanders are good fishermen; their dried tuna is a favored food; their canoes are readily sold in Palau; their children are recognized as quiet but capable students.

Generally speaking, however, Palauans express the same paternalistic, depreciative, and racially toned attitudes that characterize much of Western interaction with Micronesian and other non-Western societies. Young Palauans familiar with American racist stereotypes through college attendance in the United States draw a direct parallel with the Palauan attitude toward the Southwest Islander. On an individual basis, a Southwest Islander may be accepted as competent and as a friend; as a group they are viewed as childlike and naive with a few specialized skills.

CONCLUSIONS

In greater or fewer numbers, people of the Southwest Islands have resided in Palau in communities on Babelthuap, at Echol, E-ang, and Malakal for over seventy years under the aegis of German, Japanese, and American colonial regimes. Even granting that assimilation to the dominant culture in Palau may be limited by the fact that the Southwest Islanders return occasionally to their home islands, the outstanding feature of these communities in Palau has been separation and ethnic boundary maintenance with respect to Palauan society. Rather than adapting to a Palauan social environment according to the Palauan model of assimilation, the relocated communities have related primarily to the colonial administration and to the Catholic mission, remaining separate from the Palauan social structure. There is no evidence in this case study to suggest that this separation will not continue at least as long as an outside colonial administration persists. And considering that the two societies have intermixed for over half a century, it seems reasonable to argue that this separation will persist whether or not the Southwest Islanders are permitted to maintain populations on their home islands.

Without questioning the ability of competent economists to imagine developmental models for Micronesia that resemble the sort of high-density labor force market orientation that characterizes the Western and industrialized states, this chapter has explored, in a particular case study, the hypothesis that Micronesia will persist as a cultural mosaic only as long as the American administrative presence continues. A happy fusion of Micronesian societies into a harmonious national unity should not be the expected result of relocating the outer-island populations on a few high islands.

The evidence of this study suggests that a cultural mosaic, when constrained by limited space (as suggested by the economic model), will produce results in human conditions quite different from those suggested by economic models per se. Cultural particularism *and* congestion with the emergence of rigid ethnic-class structures and accelerated intergroup tension is the more likely prognosis.

## NOTES

Materials for this chapter were collected over a five-year period between 1958 and 1963 while I was in Micronesia, first as district anthropologist in Palau (1958–1963) and then as community development officer on the staff of the high commissioner at Saipan (1963–1965). Actual contact with the island communities in this study occurred during visits of about five hours on each major island (Tobi and Sonsorol), generally about three months apart. The field trip context, with myriad associated activities (copra loading, field medical services, letter writing) was not a proper one for intensive fieldwork; however, more intensive work with individuals was possible among the island passengers on the field vessel, in Palau, where many of them sojourned between field trips, and, on two occasions, through overnight visits while the ship visited other islands in the group. The need for extensive on-the-island ethnographic fieldwork persists. I hope that this chapter will encourage such research.

1. The original settler is recalled as a Yapese named Malamau who, with his Mogmog wife Iraharau, is commemorated in a museumlike house in which are maintained models of the canoe, navigational devices, and utensils used by the original couple. Pulo Ana is the only one of the Southwest Island communities that escaped the burning of its god-house in early contact with Spanish missionaries and has remained rather proudly pagan (at least until 1965). The elders of the Pulo Ana community held that performance of the ceremonies and maintenance of the commemorative house, marking the burial place of the island founders, were essential to the integrity of Pulo Ana as a cultural entity.
2. Merir, while perhaps the most bountiful of the several islands, has been plagued with hordes of voracious mosquitoes, which even figure in the folk history. Some form of biological control of these pests will probably be necessary before resettlement is possible.
3. For a more detailed account of social structure in Palau, see McKnight (1960).
4. Although relocation schemes became common in Micronesia during and after the German administration (1898–1914), the relocation of Southwest Islanders in 1905 was the first such venture in Palau.

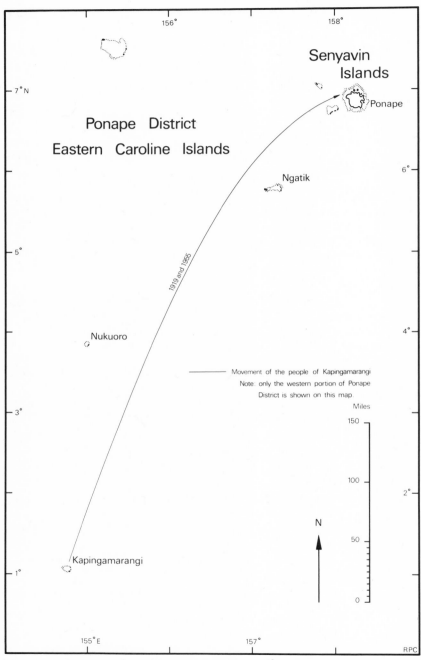

156°

158°

Senyavin
Islands

—7°N

Ponape

Ponape   District

6°

Eastern   Caroline   Islands

Ngatik

—5°

1919 and 1955

4°

Nukuoro

Movement of the people of Kapingamarangi

Note: only the western portion of Ponape
District is shown on this map.

Miles

—3°

150

100

2°

N

50

Kapingamarangi

—1°

0

155°E

157°

RPC

Map 3.   Movement from Kapingamarangi to Ponape.

# THE PROCESSES OF CHANGE IN TWO KAPINGAMARANGI COMMUNITIES

*Michael D. Lieber*

## INTRODUCTION

Kapingamarangi is the southernmost atoll in the Eastern Caroline Islands. Its thirty-three flat islets lie on the edge of an egg-shaped reef and comprise a total land area of less than half a square mile (Emory 1965:1). The Polynesian inhabitants of the atoll (the Kapinga) have made their living by planting and harvesting coconuts, breadfruit, pandanus fruit, and taro and by exploiting fish resources of the lagoon and deep sea. Ponape, a high island whose Micronesian inhabitants exploit a wide variety of plant and animal resources, lies 485 miles north of Kapingamarangi. (See map 3.) Ponape has been a center for colonial commercial, missionary, and administrative activity since the nineteenth century. Except for a very few men who migrated to Ponape after the Japanese took control of Micronesia in 1914, the Kapinga knew nothing of Ponape until two successive disasters resulted in their establishing a resettled community there in 1919.

In 1916, a drought began which was to last for two years and which would culminate in the deaths of over ninety people. As the soil dried up and staple food plants became unproductive, the threat of chaos and panic grew on the atoll. Theft of food became common, sometimes resulting in violence. As food resources dwindled, the inevitability of famine became apparent to all. No Kapinga could remember a drought of these proportions, and people were unprepared for the situation. A Japanese teacher and government local affairs officer named Huria was living on Kapingamarangi at the time. Having established a position of authority on the atoll, he was under pressure by the Kapinga to do something. Working through the atoll chief and a council of men appointed by the chief through his urging, Huria was able to institute a rationing program to conserve drinking coconuts. This was done by controlling movement from the major residential islets to coconut stands on the outer islets. Men of the council, called 'masters', administered punishments for violating these regulations. Huria also attempted to limit population growth by placing a ban on premarital sexual relations and by prohibiting many marriages, again by decree of the chief. The chief, by 1917, was a man appointed by Huria to replace the old chief, who was on his deathbed.

None of the emergency measures was able to stave off the starvation and death which finally resulted from the prolonged drought, nor were people and plants the only casualties. The ancient religion and its priesthood collapsed as years of debunking by outsiders, a growing skepticism of some Kapinga, and the obvious inability of the priesthood to alleviate the drought and famine demoralized the population. When a missionary from the neighboring atoll of Nukuoro appeared on a visiting ship in 1917, and later returned with gifts of food and offers of salvation from future disasters, the population was converted wholesale to Christianity.

Late in 1918, Huria arranged to have ninety people moved to Ponape to work for a Japanese trading company gathering hibiscus fiber for hat making. This scheme would assure adequate care for the emigrants while relieving population pressure on the slowly recovering plant resources of the atoll. The emigrants left early in 1919. Within less than a year, disaster struck again as half the emigrants died in a dysentery epidemic. The survivors were brought to the company's dormitories in Kolonia town, the administrative and commercial center on Ponape. Huria petitioned the government for a grant of land in the town for the survivors, and in September 1919 the government allowed a party of Kapinga men to select a suitable site for a village.[1] The site chosen was Porakiet ('rocky place' in Ponapean; map 4), an 18-acre tract. Half the site is a steep cliff leading to an inlet which allows access to the lagoon and the open sea.

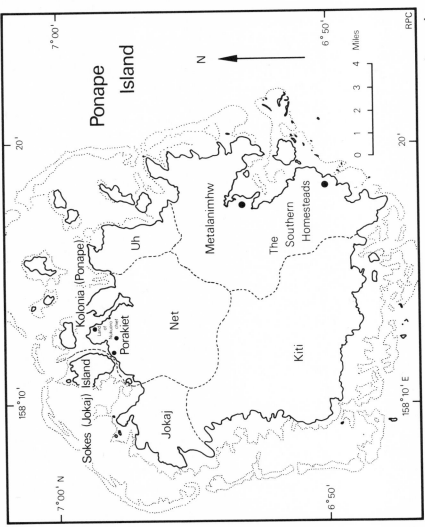

Map 4.   Areas on Ponape that have been designated by colonial administrations for use by
Kapingamarangi and Nukuoro settlers.

Clearing of overgrown land, planting of coconut trees, and construction of houses began almost immediately. As soon as houses had been built, people moved from the company dormitories into the village. The subsequent appointment of a headman for the resident population marked the beginning of the Kapinga community on Ponape. It began as a colony of transients from the atoll, a place for Kapinga to stay while visiting Ponape. Ultimate authority for making decisions for the community was the prerogative of the atoll chief.[2]

The population of Porakiet grew to eighty by the 1940s as people came to Ponape to work for the government and local Japanese commercial concerns or to engage in commercial deep sea fishing, over which the Kapinga had a virtual monopoly on Ponape. After World War II, the population of the village gradually expanded to its present size of three hundred, some of whom are permanent residents whose children have never seen the atoll. By 1961, the atoll had renounced its claim to political authority over the resettled community. At present, all the Kapinga recognize that Kapingamarangi Atoll and Porakiet are two separate, politically independent, and in many ways different communities. Both the atoll community and the community at Porakeit have changed in the years following resettlement, but the kinds of changes have been very different in each community. It is the task of this chapter to describe and account for these differences.

The traditional social system on Kapingamarangi, like those of most atolls, was relatively undifferentiated. Economic, political, and kinship relations, for example, were highly integrated rather than being clearly distinct subsystems as in Western societies. This lack of differentiation was due to the form of social relationships in the traditional atoll social system.

To be a person on Kapingamarangi Atoll was to be involved in relationships with other persons. Social relationships traditionally were and to a great extent still are whole-person-to-whole-person relationships. The whole person was presumed to be involved in every relationship to which he or she was a party. This does not mean that the Kapinga did not recognize roles or that roles did not shape expectations of behavior. Age, sex, the capacity to reproduce, and human mortality combined in different ways to yield roles such as mother, friend, expert artisan, priest, and the like.

But roles formed only part of the information that one person needed in order to interact with another. More important in structuring social relationships was information about the biographies of persons. On a tiny atoll in which each person has face-to-face relationships with everyone else, where there is little privacy, and where gossip continually supplements first-hand observation, each person brings to a relationship the more or less total biography of the other. Thus the information that comprises a social relationship includes not only role expectations but also the habits, personal likes and dislikes, personal histories, and personal styles of every participant. Personal idiosyncracies and interpersonal variability were every bit as important in the Kapinga social system as were the attributes of style and behavior that people shared.

Change in the atoll social system has been in the form of social relationships. Information about role expectations has become more important in several kinds of social relationships than information about biography. These relationships—student-teacher, customer-clerk, magistrate-constituent—are not part of the traditional social system. The result of incorporating them into the atoll social system has been the differentiation of the system into political, economic, religious, and educational subsystems.

The Porakiet social system has not differentiated, although Porakiet is located in an urban, polyethnic milieu. The forms of social relationships and the organization of the community are still those of the traditional atoll system. What has changed in Porakiet has been the life-styles of its residents. The activities in which people engage, the time and resources expended in these activities, and what people spend money on contrast with those of the atoll in many ways. While the forms of social relationships in Porakiet have not changed from traditional ones, their content has changed.

Along with these changes in the social systems of the two communities, there has been a change in the way the two communities are perceived and talked about by the Kapinga. Although Kapinga living in both communities recognize that the atoll and Porakiet are politically independent and in many ways different communities, they have come to regard both as somehow constituting a single community. The idea of a single community of people irrespective of locale represents a change in the way the Kapinga define themselves. Corresponding to this change is a change in the Kapinga view of the larger world of which their community is a part, a universe of persons and places with which the Kapinga contrast themselves. This larger world includes other island groups within a colonial government structure, and many Kapinga realize that what happens in Saipan, Washington, and New York can somehow affect them.

How is it that an atoll which has less than twelve days per year of direct contact with the outside world via ship can undergo the kind of differentiation that Kapingamarangi has, while Porakiet, situated in an urban milieu, has not? Is the change in the way the Kapinga define themselves the inevitable result of their living in two independent communities? Can the changes in social organization and culture be explained in terms of contact between the Kapinga and the colonial government? These three questions constitute the problem this chapter will address.

Although it is clear that the presence of a colonial regime and contact with other ethnic groups are associated with changes in Kapinga social organization and culture, the nature of the association is problematic. To answer the three basic questions, I begin by making two assumptions. First, the colonial government, the other ethnic groups with whom the Kapinga are in contact, and the particular islands on which the Kapinga live constitute the environment of the two Kapinga communities. Second, change and stability in the organization of each Kapinga community are to be regarded as outcomes of *relationships* betweeen the community and the natural and social systems that comprise its environment. By relationship I mean a pattern of information, or messages, exchanged by two or more systems (following Bateson 1972:275).

The central task of this chapter, then, is to identify and describe the relationships between each Kapinga community and other systems in its environment that result in change in each community. I shall begin with an analysis of change on the atoll, specifying those relationships which have resulted in systemic changes. Next I shall repeat the analytical process for Porakiet. Then I shall take up the question of the relationship between the two communities and how it has affected the Kapinga definitions of 'community' and 'the Kapinga people'. Finally, I shall draw out some of the implications of systemic change and the definition of Kapinga ethnicity to explain certain kinds of conflict on the atoll.

## CHANGE ON KAPINGAMARANGI

Systemic change on the atoll has been that of a shift from bio-graphical information to role expectations in structuring social re-lationships. The process has been a gradual one, occurring in roughly two phases. The first phase was the establishment of more or less permanent relationships with outsiders. The second phase was that of a radical shift in the content of those relationships after World War II.

Contact with Europeans began in the 1870s with European and American fishing and trading vessels stopping at the atoll. A few Europeans, Americans, Samoans, and Nukuoro left the ships to re-side on the atoll in the late 1870s (Emory 1965:12–15). These ear-ly contacts were characterized by violence on the part of the out-siders and, occasionally, on the part of the Kapinga who were allied with them. The contacts also included the introduction of imported goods and techniques of production (such as carpentry) by the outsiders. The Kapinga image of Euro-Americans and, sub-sequently, of the Japanese has been one of powerful, knowledge-able, unpredictable, and violent people. The Kapinga response to this image remains ambivalent—fear of and attraction to rela-tions with them. By the mid-1880s the high priest and the secular chief (formerly a secular functionary responsible for providing food for certain ceremonies) had become aligned with the out-siders. People left dealings with outsiders to them.

The Kapinga regard Euro-American behavior as identical to that of the ancient deities. The traditional gods were whimsical, awesome in their power to cause damage on the atoll and to be-stow abundance in the form of good weather, fruit, and whales. It is not surprising, then, that the Kapinga established a relationship with outsiders comparable to that they had with their deities. This relationship was one of subordinate to superordinate in which people showed deference to the deities, watched for omens that be-spoke their wishes, and made offerings of food and services to them (see Emory 1965:228ff.). In return, the deities would bestow favors on people or at least would be appeased enough to cause them no harm. Ordinary people avoided contact with deities. They stayed away from places that deities were known to frequent and would employ brief but proper rituals when deities were pre-sumed to be present. Relationships between people and deities were mediated through a high priest and his assistants. The priests performed daily ritual, interpreted and acted on omens, and directed community activity to satisfy the deities' wishes and protect people from their wrath. The high priest attained his position of leadership because of his knowledge of deities and omens and the ritual means for dealing with them. It was, therefore, no mere coincidence that the relationship between Kapinga and Euro-Americans was mediated by the high priest and the secular chief. Both were specialists in a special relationship. Given the pattern of attributes common to deities and Euro-Americans, relationships with both took the same form.

The relationship between priest and chief and the Euro-Americans was that of subordinate to superordinate. The priest and chief paid deference to the outsiders. They also provided the resident aliens with housing, land, labor for household help and copra cutting, and, sometimes, with wives (Emory 1965:17–18). In return, the outsiders traded copra for the priest and chief and managed their relations with visiting ships, taking a percentage of the copra money as a kind of agent's fee. They also provided the priest and chief with personal favors, such as gifts of material goods, ensuring the good favor of visitors to the atoll and, most important, identifying themselves with the interests of the priest and chief. The atoll leaders gained a good deal of material wealth from this relationship while other Kapinga continued to avoid contact with the outsiders. By the 1890s, however, other Kapinga sought to establish a similar relationship with the resident aliens. One group of men, for example, formed a trading association, using a resident Englishman as their agent with visiting copra vessels. The members of this group were to become Huria's 'masters' twenty-five years later.

When the Japanese established colonial rule in Micronesia in 1914, the Kapinga developed the same sort of relationship with them they had had with Euro-Americans. The Japanese wanted four things from the atoll—copra, labor for government projects and business enterprises on Ponape, a market for their goods, and recognition of their authority by the atoll people. In return, the Japanese provided a retail outlet for manufactured goods, cheap transportation to Ponape, occasional medical services, and, most important, support of the atoll leadership.

The breakdown of the ancient religion would have left an authority vacuum on the atoll had there not been a change before the collapse. By the early twentieth century, the secular chief, whose authority had been limited to leadership of a men's house connected ritually with the cult house and to provisioning major rituals, had become the recognized liaison between the atoll and outsiders. One reason for the chief's ascendancy in affairs with outsiders was his long tenure of office—thirty-six years. During the same period (up to 1917) there had been a succession of men to the position of high priest, some of whom were not familiar with the outsiders. That Huria aligned himself with the chief in 1915 assured the latter's position as liaison and strengthened his internal authority in new ways. During the drought Huria introduced several procedures that became permanently associated with the position of chief. Between 1915 and 1920, he introduced the promulgation of regulations and their enforcement by appointed functionaries, public hearings for violation of regulations, public meetings for discussion of atoll affairs, and public hearings of land disputes settled by judgment of the chief. The collapse of the priesthood left the chief's position and authority unchallenged, and they were enhanced even further after the introduction of Christianity. The man who succeeded Huria's appointed chief was also a deacon and regular preacher in the church. The religious and secular authority were thus united in one person until after World War II.

One of the more powerful factors buttressing the chief's authority was the unquestioned belief of other Kapinga that the government gave him its unqualified support. This belief had been an essential part of the relationship between atoll leaders and outsiders as it had developed from the 1880s onward. The chief was able to operate autocratically because he had at his disposal the implicit threat that those who opposed him would be sent to Ponape to be disciplined by the Japanese police, a threat which occasionally was made explicit. The chief and his assistants, one of whom was his half-brother, were able to maintain this belief by carefully managing the visits of government officials. Officials were always in the company of the chief or his assistants. The cordiality of their relationship with officials was always publicly displayed. All official proclamations, notices, and requests were relayed to the people through the chief.

In point of fact, the Japanese administration was totally unconcerned about atoll affairs and organization. Their interests in the atoll were limited to commerce and labor recruiting. The administration was content to deal with one man as long as its needs were met. Administrators showed respect to the chief and granted him personal favors such as material goods and free transportation to Ponape. This lent credibility to the idea of the unqualified favor of the administration for the chief's regime.

With the coming of the American colonial regime in 1946, the form of the relationship between atoll leaders and colonial rulers was maintained. The American administration is superordinate, identifies with the atoll leadership, and is regarded as granting favors to the atoll. The Kapinga are subordinate, deferential to administrators, and supportive of the administration's policies. The content of the relationship, however, changed radically and abruptly. The new colonial rulers were unlike their predecessors in that they were not primarily interested in extracting copra and labor or marketing their goods. Unlike the Europeans and the Japanese, the Americans were intensely interested in atoll affairs and social organization. Whereas the Europeans and the Japanese saw Micronesia in terms of its potential for supporting economic enterprises, the Americans have thought of Micronesia primarily as a subject population for their community development schemes. This became quickly apparent on the atoll as the U.S. Naval Administration established a school, a medical dispensary, a cooperative store, and an elective chief magistrate position by 1947. It also became apparent to the chief and his assistants that continued favor of the administration depended not on what they could supply to the administrators but on their willingness to cooperate in the development of the administration's programs on the atoll.

Several young men were selected to go to Ponape for training as teachers and nurses in 1947. By 1948, the atoll had its own school. Children began to be sent to Ponape for schooling in 1949, and by 1954 several boys had completed high school on Truk. A new medical dispensary was built in 1950. The administration provided a stock of drugs and training for two nurses. Although the copra market had not recovered from its wartime collapse, the naval administration stimulated a lively handicrafts trade. Residents were encouraged to organize a cooperative whose representatives parceled out orders for handicrafts, sold them to the naval officers, bought surplus goods from them, and sold these on the atoll at a small profit.

These early innovations were modified by the civilian administration after 1951. The atoll school was gradually expanded from two grades to six as several young men finished their education on Ponape and Truk and returned to the atoll to teach. One of the teachers was appointed principal of the school. It was his job to organize class schedules, supervise teachers, and act as liaison to the Office of Education on Ponape. The principal and teachers decided the organization of the curriculum, management of resources, and scheduling of classes, although American teacher trainers provided guidelines. Teachers were and still are taken to Ponape each summer for training. By the 1960s newly recruited teachers were being trained as specialists for certain grades.

The civilian administration began to encourage people to start their own retail businesses in 1954, when the copra market had recovered from its postwar slump. Entrepreneurs bought their stock from a Ponape cooperative and from a family of Belgian merchants that had been on Ponape since the nineteenth century. Goods were sold at the owners' homes, usually on credit against future copra receipts. There were several of these ventures, all but two of which failed. Failure always resulted from the owners' fulfilling obligations to their kin, who depleted the owners' stock without paying or bought on credit which was never redeemed. The two successful ventures survived only because the owners locked up their goods, extended limited credit, and treated everyone in the store as a customer regardless of their personal relationships. These two businessmen avoided recriminations from their kin by making periodic gifts of rice, cloth, and cigarettes from their stock. When the Kapinga set up their cooperative as a branch of the Ponape Federation of Cooperatives in 1964, the policy of limited credit was applied. People working in the store were obligated to apply credit and prompt payment rules to everyone equally. The clerk-customer relation has prevailed in the privately owned stores and in the co-op.

Political organization on the atoll also has undergone a transformation since the advent of the American administration. One of the first official acts of the naval administration was to create the elective position of chief magistrate on the atoll. The half-brother of the chief was unanimously elected. It was the policy of the administration to deal directly with the chief magistrate, relegating the chief's position to that of maintaining custom. The chief's half-brother had been his assistant since the 1920s, and his major responsibility had been that of liaison between the chief and the administrators. Election to the position of chief magistrate simply gave an official title to his normal duties. When the chief died in 1949, his half-brother succeeded him, holding both the chief and chief magistrate positions. Although there was some vocal opposition from Kapinga to the chief's policies, he managed to maintain a more or less autocratic leadership until his death in 1956.

The chief's son, who at the time was twenty-five years of age, was elected to succeed him to both offices. The young man had been educated on Ponape and Truk, spoke fluent English, and was a teacher on the atoll. His situation at the time of his election was difficult for two reasons. First, he was under pressure from the administration to create an American-style tripartite political organization on the atoll. This model of organization had been part of his education, and it was part of the curriculum in his own classroom. Second, the position of chief presumed an authority to make unilateral decisions that seemed likely to bring him into conflict with older people. Authoritative decision making was the prerogative of older people, who, having openly opposed the father on several issues, hardly seemed likely to accept the son's unilateral decisions. The young man resolved the dilemma by refusing the position of chief. Instead, he accepted the position of chief magistrate and began to lobby for the election of a legislative council and a local court judge. Several months of discussion in meetings and, informally, in the men's houses culminated in the establishment of a legislative council in 1957 and a local court in 1960. The young chief magistrate spent several months training the council in legislative procedure, and by 1960 the atoll received its charter as a municipality of the Ponape District of the U.S. Trust Territory of the Pacific Islands.[3]

In the first years of the council's operation, its members were older men who held responsible positions in the church. Much of the early council legislation dealt with moral issues with which the church was concerned. For example, the council passed bills prohibiting the consumption of alcoholic beverages, premarital sexual relations, and the like. It took the chief magistrate over two years to induce the council to pass the enabling legislation that was necessary to secure the atoll's municipal charter. Church-related issues have ceased to dominate legislative concerns over the last eight years for two reasons. First, older men have been gradually replaced on the council by younger men who are literate in English and have a firmer grasp of legislative procedure. Very few of these younger men have been church members. Second, specific issues have precipitated an explicit divorce of legislative from religious activity. One such issue concerned the request of church leaders to use community-owned roofing materials for the church in 1965. The chief magistrate and several councilors pointed out that granting the request would violate a statute of the Trust Territory Code prescribing the separation of church and state.

Of all the government programs introduced on the atoll, only the schools and the medical dispensary were actually forced on the people. The schools have been largely controlled by the Kapinga since that time. The administration maintains supremacy in its relationship with the atoll in several ways. First, the administration has been aggressive in presenting programs to the Kapinga leadership. Second, the administration maintains control over the school program through teacher training and over the medical program through periodic inspections. The administration has the power to approve or veto legislation emanating from the atoll and to grant or deny petitions for economic aid and supplies. To maintain their position in the relationship, atoll leaders have accepted many, though not all, of the administration's programs. Acceptance of a program does not imply the administration's domination of the atoll's social organization, however. The Kapinga run the programs themselves; this is a crucial feature of the relationship from both the administration's and the Kapinga's point of view. By running the programs themselves, the Kapinga control their own internal affairs—a constant feature of the Kapinga– colonial government relationship from the outset. The Kapinga, for their part, have not seemed hesitant to petition the administration for aid in atoll projects, such as materials for bridge construction and for a municipal office building.

The outcome of the relationship between the atoll and the American administration has been the establishment of several contexts of activity that are organized very differently from those of the traditional atoll system. These contexts include the atoll school, the medical dispensary, the council, the court, and retail business establishments. In these contexts the social relationships are categorical: people assume certain roles, and the roles alone structure expectations. Biographies of the persons involved in these contexts are irrelevant to the interaction. For example, people expect that a teacher will not favor his relatives in the classroom nor would a judge in the courtroom. People get angry when these expectations are not met. Each of these contexts is distinguished from the others and from traditional personal relationships. People recognize that roles appropriate to one setting, say the classroom, are not appropriate to others. The content of these role relationships has been worked out through trial and error. The forms, however, have clearly resulted from maintaining the relationship between atoll and colonial government in the form in which it originally developed in the 1880s.

## CHANGE IN PORAKIET

The Porakiet social system has replicated the major structural features of the traditional atoll social system. Social bonds are organized as whole-person-to-whole-person relationships by a combination of role, setting, and biographies of the participants. Household structure is based on the atoll prototype of a nuclear family plus relatives of either spouse. Subsistence chores are still allocated largely by age and sex. Community activity, such as work projects and feasts, is directed by a headman. The headman is also responsible for maintaining order, for the physical upkeep of the village, and for mediating relationships between the community and outsiders. Like the atoll chief, the headman has been a high-ranking member of the Protestant church hierarchy,[4] although he has never exercised autocratic rule in the community.[5] It is rather curious that the Porakiet social system has not undergone differentiation. The village, after all, is located in an urban center. Kapinga children attend schools, and adults engage in wage labor and commercial ventures. In brief, Porakiet residents assume all the roles that are characteristic of a differentiated social system—customer, clerk, student, teacher, nurse, employee, and the like. At the same time, the life-styles of the villagers are quite different from those of atoll residents. The reasons that account for the lack of differentiation in the Porakiet system also account for the differences in life-styles of villagers and people on the atoll.

The relationships between the Porakiet social system and its environment are qualitatively and quantitatively different from those of the atoll system. Seldom is the entire village party to a relationship with the outside. The only instances of such relationships are occasional feasts honoring some non-Kapinga dignitary, such as government officials or United Nations observers, and periodic petitions to the district administrator by the headman. Relationships between Porakiet and its environment involve mainly individual persons or small groups of persons of the village with outsiders. Individual villagers, for example, deal with other individuals, with business establishments, with church groups, with informal groups (such as recreational groups), and with government agencies outside the village. Small groups of villagers also have relationships outside the village, though these are less frequent than those involving individuals. The village choir, for example, sometimes holds joint rehearsals with choirs from other villages. A Kapinga family may go to visit a Ponapean family. Several Kapinga men have formed an informal yam planting group with a Ponapean neighbor. Several village men occasionally contribute labor to the Roman Catholic mission in Kolonia in exchange for use of the mission's machinery.

The systemic level at which most of the relationships between Porakiet and its environment occur, then, is that of the individual person or small group of persons. The particular parts of the environment to which villagers relate include parts of the physical environment, such as the lagoon and deep sea, and a varied range of social environments—individuals and families of other ethnic groups, businesses, government agencies, classrooms, churches, cooperatives, and recreational organizations such as baseball, track, and swimming teams. The systemic level at which relations with the environment occur constitutes a crucial difference between Porakiet and the atoll.

Kapingamarangi has been regarded as a polity by European traders, resident aliens, and two colonial governments; moreover, the atoll residents themselves have related to outsiders as a polity. But Porakiet has never been considered to be a polity by the colonial government or by other residents on Ponape. The Japanese and American administrators have never recognized Porakiet as an autonomous political or administrative entity. In fact, Porakiet has no official status whatever within the colonial system. The village has had some quasi-official recognition as an ethnic community. American tourists are regularly taken through Porakiet to see Ponape's "Polynesian village." The administration has also had to deal with periodic petitions from the chief for special considerations. The administration has been reluctant to deal with these petitions, especially since the chartering of Kolonia town, in which the village is located, as a municipality. When the Porakiet headman requested a quitclaim title or a lease for the village land in 1965 (the old lease had expired in 1961), his request was denied. The denial was based on the grounds that part of Kolonia Municipality's program was the social and political integration of the many ethnic groups living there. It would have been detrimental to the municipality to create a politically autonomous ethnic community by granting title to the land to the Kapinga.

Thus the kind of relationship which has resulted in differentiation on the atoll does not exist for Porakiet. There is no relationship between the colonial government and Porakiet as a polity. There is, however, a relationship between the colonial government and Kolonia Municipality that is coordinate to that between the government and the atoll. To the extent that Kapinga reside in Kolonia, they participate in institutions such as schools, businesses, and the like, almost all of which are located outside the village. The roles that Kapinga assume in these institutions are thus relevant to relationships outside the village. The process of differentiation characteristic of the atoll has occurred outside the boundaries of the Porakiet social system. The settings in which roles structure interaction regardless of the biographies of the persons involved have always been settings of interethnic contact for Kapinga on Ponape.[6] Information about biography is replaced in these relationships by information about characteristics of people's ethnic groups.

In their roles with outsiders, the Kapinga have used Ponapean, English, and Japanese for the language of the transaction. Every situation of interethnic contact is marked, then, by roles assumed for the interaction and by linguistic messages of ethnicity. In this manner, the relationships that result in differentiation within the atoll social system also define the boundary of the Porakiet social system. These relationships, in other words, contain information that exclude them by definition from the Porakiet social system. For this reason, the Porakiet social system remains undifferentiated.

The roles that Porakiet residents assume for purposes of interethnic contact are largely irrelevant to their personal relations with one another. One assumes the role of teacher, student, patient, or nurse outside the village, almost never within it. On the atoll, however, Kapinga assume these same roles in order to interact with other Kapinga. Although the Kapinga in Porakiet rarely assume such roles in interaction with one another, the roles are crucial to the maintenance of their personal relationships and of the community in two ways. First, because the village is small, the Kapinga community has never been self-sufficient. Porakiet residents have always depended on resources outside the community such as fish, vegetables, pigs, fowl, construction materials, and tools. Access to these resources has been necessarily through contacts with non-Kapinga. The roles that Kapinga assume in order to interact with non-Kapinga have made the interaction (and thus the flow of resources) predictable. Second, the roles and relationships that Kapinga have outside the village provide material and nonmaterial resources that are very relevant to their personal relationships within the village. What matters most to Kapinga in their interpersonal relationships is the esteem in which they are held. Deference accorded one in public, the achievement of rank and responsibility (in the church, in a men's house, in a descent group), and the accumulation of dependents are all expresssions of esteem.[7] One's esteem depends on the responsibility one can assume for the welfare of others (see Lieber 1974). The resources that enable one to assume responsibility are both material and nonmaterial—knowledge, skills, competence in making and implementing decisions.

On the atoll the crucial resources for the assumption of responsibility are ownership of land, membership in a traditionally prominent family (of the chief or the former high priests), and skill in canoe and house construction, carpentry, and fishing. In Porakiet, relations with outsiders provide villagers with resources important to their relations with one another—money, food, and construction materials. Important nonmaterial resources have been technical expertise, such as carpentry, boat building, masonry, plumbing, and mechanical skills. Another important resource has been access to powerful persons outside the community, such as the Ponape district administrator and the chiefly hierarchy of the traditional Ponapean polity. The means by which these resources are acquired are less important than the fact of whether or not one has them. More important still is what one does with one's resources. For example, one of the men in the village is a teacher with a good reputation among his colleagues and the American administrators. His reputation as a teacher is unimportant to villagers, few of whom are aware of it. This man's esteem is based on the fact that he has a steady income, supports a large household, and has access to several important Americans from whom favors might be gained.

An example of the importance of access to resources and the prestige afforded by them is the contrast between the legislative council on the atoll and its counterpart in Porakiet. The atoll council developed as a response to change in political organization. The intellectual skills necessary for its operation eventually determined its membership: younger men with schooling on Ponape and two older men who are prestigious and capable. The younger men are elected solely on the basis of their skills rather than other kinds of competence. The position of councilman is not especially prestigious.

The council in Porakiet is a response to the internal growth of the village after World War II and to the general lawlessness in Kolonia and the village at the time. The village headman faced two problems by 1952: the village population had more than doubled since 1948, and maintaining order was difficult for one man. Furthermore, with a larger population, a permanent water supply and a men's house for unmarried males to sleep in were needed. In 1952, the headman demanded that villagers elect a four-man council to serve as his assistants. The council's tasks were those of enacting legislation for the village, enforcing the legislation, and organizing major construction projects. The council functioned somewhat like the atoll chief's assistants.[8]

Council members have been elected annually since 1952, and they have been older men who have been successful businessmen, well-paid workers, fishermen, and churchmen. All the councilmen have demonstrated their ability to assume responsibility by supporting large families, by supervising construction projects in the village, by leadership of the men's house, by leadership in church activities, by success in business ventures.[9] All these pursuits have involved the men in relationships with outsiders, especially with Micronesians in the colonial administration and with Ponapean nobility. From Ponapean nobles, the Kapinga have obtained such favors as taro land for Porakiet villagers (see Lieber 1968b:84). The position of councilman in Porakiet has become a measure of interpersonal esteem. It is a prestigious position because those elected to it are responsible people.

While the kind of relationship from which prestige results has not changed in Porakiet, some of the means for acquiring resources to bring to these relationships have changed. This fact has two implications. First, those whose aspirations for prestige on the atoll are blocked by relative poverty of landholdings or, say, by lack of ties to traditionally prominent families have the alternative of fulfilling their aspirations in Porakiet. Many migrants have remained in Porakiet for precisely this reason. Second, the time and resources of individuals are of necessity allocated differently in Porakiet than on the atoll. In other words, the life-styles of individuals on Ponape are different from those of atoll residents.

The allocation of time and effort of both men and women in Porakiet is shaped by their dependence on a cash economy and on the relative scarcity of food, construction, and craft resources in the village. As of 1966, one-third of the village population over twenty-one years of age was engaged in wage labor. This requires that they spend a minimum of eight hours a day outside the village for at least five days a week. This time is spent in Kolonia working with Americans, Belgians (who own two large retail businesses), and Micronesians. More than half the population under twenty-one spends six to eight hours a day in Kolonia in schools with Micronesian children. Their teachers are American and Micronesian and the languages of instruction are Ponapean and English (Lieber 1968b:198–207). Ninety-five percent of those engaged in wage work are men. Women also spend time outside the village— working in taro pits 6 miles from the village, buying groceries, visiting relatives in the hospital or going to the outpatient clinic, selling handicrafts, and participating in church activities. The maintenance of what Sahlins (1965) calls trade friendships with Micronesians, in which both men and women are involved, necessitates periodic trips to other parts of the island (see Lieber

1968b:43–51). Young men also spend evening hours and week-ends in Kolonia drinking beer at local taverns and playing pool. Even fishermen, whose life-styles have been least affected by the Ponape environment, must spend time in Kolonia selling fish, buy-ing gear, and attending meetings of the Ponape fishermen's coop-erative.

Adult women, most of whom remain in the village during the day, allocate their time differently from atoll women. Except for periodic trips to taro plots and coconut plantations on outer islets, atoll women spend almost all their time in their household com-pounds cooking, cleaning, or doing craft work. For Porakiet wom-en, there is a good deal less work to do. Food preparation takes less time since meals consist mostly of rice and tinned food, except when breadfruit is in season. There is less craft work to do, since materials for it, such as pandanus and coconut leaves, are not readily available. Porakiet women can often be seen napping dur-ing the afternoon; this is something that atoll women rarely have time to do. Porakiet women also spend time visiting between households to talk. A few women spend a good deal of time work-ing at specialties, such as sewing clothing or tending village retail stores (which atoll women do only when they have spare time). Shopping trips to Kolonia are usually organized by several women who go together, often taking a young man along to carry groceries.

Corresponding to the differences between time allocation on the atoll and in Porakiet are differing patterns of resource allocation. Kapinga on the atoll subsist almost entirely on locally produced staples. Money earned from copra production is spent on tools, utensils, cloth, thread, tobacco, rice, and some tinned food. Im-ported food is used mainly for feasts. While dresses, shirts, and slacks are necessary for church services and feasts, few people own more than two such articles of clothing. In Porakiet, staple foods must be bought. Dresses, shirts, and slacks, both for work and for Sunday and feast dress, are worn whenever one leaves the village. Such clothing is worn more often, wears out sooner, and has to be replaced more often than clothing on the atoll. Wage workers need several sets of clothing, since washing is done only once a week. Villagers spend more than half their incomes on such necessities, although some villagers own radios, motorcycles, out-board engines, and the like. There are relatively fewer fishermen in Porakiet than on the atoll, partly because canoes are far more expensive to build in the village. Trees for the hull and gunwales must be bought. The custom of feeding the workers who help construct it requires money, since the food must be bought. A good deal of money is also spent on beer and liquor in Porakiet, whereas these were illegal on the atoll until recently.

Maintenance of the Porakiet social system, then, has required that members of that system participate in relationships outside the system. These relationships are contexts of interethnic contact whose structure consists of the rules of role performance. The Kapinga in Porakiet maintain their traditional system of personal relationships in which these roles are irrelevant. The roles do, however, constitute the means for acquiring the material and technical resources that Kapinga bring to their personal relationships with one another. To the extent that the performance of these roles requires the allocation of time, effort, and material resources outside Porakiet, the life-styles of Porakiet villagers have changed considerably from those of their fellows on the atoll. Maintaining the traditional forms of social relationships within the Porakiet social system, in other words, has required changes in the life-styles of individuals within the system.

## THE RELATION BETWEEN KAPINGAMARANGI AND PORAKIET

The most obvious sort of relationship between the atoll and Porakiet is that the Porakiet social system is a replication of the traditional atoll system. Despite its obviousness, this relation is of profound importance. The very existence of a community on Ponape whose internal social relations are identifiable as Kapinga in type has been crucial in shaping the postcontact world view of Kapinga in both communities. Since 1919, the Kapinga have had to deal conceptually with the fact that their social order has an existence within a larger universe apart from the atoll. The atoll is but one concrete manifestation of the Kapinga social order and not simply identical to it. This has become clear to the Kapinga through the process of having to debate and resolve several controversies in which the relationship between the atoll and Porakiet was a key issue (a process comparable to that described by Martin Silverman in chapter 6).

In 1930 and again in 1964, controversy was raised when some

residents wanted to divide Porakiet land into private leaseholds
(Lieber 1968b:78–79, 179). In both instances, the majority of the
residents decided that the land would be kept intact to be used by
'all the Kapinga people'. What 'all the Kapinga people' meant in
1930, however, was different from what it came to mean by 1964.
In 1930, Porakiet was a community of transients, a place for atoll
people to stay while visiting Ponape. 'All the Kapinga people'
meant residents of Kapingamarangi Atoll.

By 1964, there was a core of families in Porakiet who considered themselves to be permanent residents, claiming Ponapean
citizenship and paying head taxes to Kolonia Municipality. The
majority included people who were either staying temporarily in
Porakiet and intending to return to the atoll or people who had
been in Porakiet for some time and had not decided where they
would reside permanently. Several household heads who were permanent residents wanted to join a housing cooperative in order to
construct cement houses in the village. Because the cooperative
demanded land as collateral for housing loans, these men were unable to join. Porakiet was still public land. When one of the men
proposed in a meeting that the village land be divided into twenty
leaseholds, a long and at times bitter controversy followed. Permanent residents argued that they were the only people who cared
about the village enough to maintain it. Thus the land should be
theirs. Others, including the headman, argued that the land had
been given to all the Kapinga people. It should be maintained for
all, not just for the permanent residents. The latter's argument
that they were the major contributors of money and labor to village upkeep was granted as valid by their opponents. The headman added that all Kapinga who stayed in Porakiet were obligated to maintain the village "just as if they lived there all the time."

That Porakiet and the atoll were separate communities was
clear in the argument. That the population of Porakiet consisted of
permanent residents and transients was also made clear. Moreover, it was clear that 'all the Kapinga people' meant all the people who consider themselves to be of Kapinga ethnic identity. In
the argument, the category 'Kapinga person' included people living on the atoll, on Nukuoro, Ngatik, Ponape, Kusaie, Palau,
Oroluk, and any other place where Kapinga might reside. The
'Kapinga people' is now a category that transcends place of residence and, for that matter, one's commitment to a particular lo-

cality. The concept of 'Kapinga people' has been universalized in a manner not unlike the universalization of Jehovah and Jewishness during the relocation called the Babylonian Captivity.

In 1966, a bitter debate over the relationship between Porakiet and another relocated Kapinga community in the southern part of Ponape was resolved by interpreting it in the framework developed two years earlier.[10] Members of the southern community, who stayed in Porakiet while visiting Kolonia town, had consistently refused to contribute money toward the cost of renovating the village bathhouse. They reasoned that they had no responsibility in the matter, since they lived and paid taxes in another municipality. In a meeting called to vote on assessments for the project, some Porakiet residents (including the headman) denounced the refusal of the southern villagers to help, disregarding their reasoning. In the heat of debate, it was suggested that southern villagers who would not contribute should be barred from Porakiet facilities or from Porakiet altogether. The headman, once he had calmed down, resolved the argument. He reasoned that barring the southerners from Porakiet contradicted the proposition that Porakiet was for 'all Kapinga people'. The southern villagers, he said, would always be welcome in Porakiet because they were Kapinga people. They ought to help their fellows in Porakiet, he said, but it was up to them to decide what to do. By viewing the controversy in terms of the universalized concept of 'Kapinga people', not only was the controversy resolved but the relationship between the two villages was clarified.

The universalization of the concept of 'community' has further clarified the relationship between the atoll and Porakiet. 'Community' is used by the Kapinga to denote all the people on the island (or in the village), the organization of the people engaged in some community project, those present and eligible to vote in a community meeting, and, more generally, everybody.

A controversy mentioned previously concerning the use of communal roofing materials for the atoll church raised the issue of the application of the term 'community' in Porakiet in 1966. After the chief magistrate and council refused to allow the roofing materials to be used for the church, the atoll minister wrote to the Porakiet headman requesting a contribution of roofing sheets from the Porakiet community. He claimed that he was writing on behalf of the chief magistrate. The letter was read at a village meeting, and a debate quickly ensued. It was agreed that the villagers ought to comply if in fact the chief magistrate had made the request. Some people doubted whether the chief magistrate even knew of the letter, since church and state were legally separate. One old man replied that in the day of the former chief, such a separation was not an issue and should not be an issue now. The issue then became one of what constituted a community issue and a community responsibility, and, most important, to what extent and for what purposes Porakiet as a community was obligated to the atoll as a whole or to groups within it.

The debate was resolved by an impassioned speech by a councilman. He stated that whenever a major project was undertaken on the atoll, it was conducted by the entire community. Such was the ethic of 'love' for one another in the community. Whether the project was a church or a courthouse made no difference, he asserted. "We are all one community, and so we must help each other. Let every man decide for himself what is right, but if we are really members of the community, we will do what he [the minister] asks us." Community, in this statement, meant the social order that includes all Kapinga as its members. By universalizing 'community' and by identifying it concretely with the atoll project, his exhortation to accede to the request connected the atoll and the village in a single community. By saying that every person should "decide for himself," the councilman took the issue out of the context of the meeting and placed responsibility on the shoulders of individuals as real members of the community. The majority of those present voiced agreement with him. The impact of his speech was enhanced by the fact that the church on Kapingamarangi is Protestant whereas the councilman is a Roman Catholic.

The universalization of 'the Kapinga people' and 'community' represents an increase in the complexity of the Kapinga concepts of themselves and of their social order. That the atoll and Porakiet are separate, independent communities is recognized. 'Porakiet people' and 'atoll people' are frequently used phrases that denote the different communites. The fact that 'Kapinga people' and 'community' now denote Kapinga people in general and the Kapinga social order in general indicates two sorts of change. First, there has been an increase in the amount of information encoded in these phrases. Second, there has been a change in the organization of the information encoded in these phrases: their meanings are more abstract than before. Their present order of generality is new. The older meanings of the phrases are only part of the new, more abstract meanings.

The increasing complexity of the Kapinga image of their own society corresponds with an increase in the complexity of their view of the larger world in which they live and the relations they have in it. The Kapinga have learned a good deal about officialdom and about other ethnic groups through their experience on the atoll and through travel and schooling. People on the atoll and Ponape know about the hierarchical structure of the colonial government (the 'office'), the connection between the government and other island municipalities, and the connection between the Trust Territory and the United States and the United Nations. Children learn about these relations in school, while adults in both communities deal with the government as employees, councilmen, representatives to the district legislature, or teachers. Kapinga living on Ponape have continual contact with people of other ethnic groups—Ponapeans, Kusaieans, Mokilese, Pingelapese, Ngatikese, Trukese, Mortlockese, and Palauans. Several Kapinga in both communities have traveled to these islands, as well as to Guam, the Marshall Islands, Japan, Hawaii, and islands in the South Pacific. Information about all these groups has come from face-to-face contact and reports of such contact to others in the community. Owing to the continual movement of people between the atoll and Porakiet, information about the nature of officialdom and other islands and their inhabitants seems to be generally shared in both communities.[11] Thus, for example, one who leaves the atoll for the first time to live on Ponape already has most of the information about the island and strategies for coping with life there that he needs. His experience then fills in the details.

The universalized concepts of 'Kapinga people' and Kapinga social order and the larger world in which these concepts have their reality are all part of a growing body of information that Kapinga have about themselves. Their ideas about officialdom and other ethnic groups, about the atoll and Porakiet and the differences between them, are all part of the information that comprises Kapinga culture. The processes that have led to changes in their ideas about their world are processes of culture change. The process consists in incorporating new information, which serves to reorganize previous information in some ways but is organized by

previous information in yet other ways. Some of the most important changes in Kapinga culture, such as their definitions of
themselves as a people, are the outcomes of the increasingly complex relationship between the atoll and Porakiet.

## THE NATURE OF ETHNIC BOUNDARIES

At one time or another, most Kapinga have the experience of living in two different communities, both of which are recognizably
Kapinga communities and both of which are recognizably different in many ways. The emigrant from the atoll has a particularly profound experience in that he or she experiences both a different kind of Kapinga community and continuous contact with
other ethnic groups. The emigrant's experience is an object lesson
in what it means to be a Kapinga person. This is quite a different
experience from that of migrants to an island where there is no
migrant community. There may be contact between the home
island and the island to which people have migrated, but there is
not the kind of three-way contrast between the home island, the
resettled community, and other ethnic communities that characterize the situation of the Kapinga and, say, the Tikopia. It is the
experience of this sort of contrast that results in the universalization of island group to ethnic category and ethnic community
characteristic of the Kapinga.

What is essential to the object lesson of Kapinga ethnicity is
each individual's experience of very different contexts of interaction—those characteristic of the Kapinga community (on the
atoll and at Porakiet) and those characteristic of relations with
non-Kapinga. The very differences in the life-style in the two
communities, moreover, highlight that which is common to both:
the structure of contexts of interaction referred to previously as
whole-person-to-whole-person relations. It is these contexts of interaction that pose such a striking contrast to those of interethnic
relations.

The information a Kapinga needs to interact with other Kapinga is different from that needed to interact with a non-Kapinga.
The rules that structure the information in Kapinga relations with
other Kapinga are different from the rules structuring the information in an interethnic relationship. When a Kapinga interacts with
another Kapinga, he needs to know the other's biography and the

setting of the interaction. He also needs to know the roles that are being played, although these are often of less importance than biography and setting. This is the case because information about biography structures his expectations about how the other will play his role. It is information about biography that structures expectations of others in most situations. Biography, in other words, is the dominant information as regards setting and role. In interethnic relations, biography is the least important information. A Kapinga can interact with a Ponapean, for instance, without either knowing anything of the other's biography. All that is necessary for the relationship is a knowledge of the setting and the roles appropriate to it. Furthermore, setting and role are in one-to-one correspondence. Each role is confined to a specific setting. One plays the role of customer in stores, that of employee at the place of work, and so on. Setting and role are not in one-to-one correspondence in intraethnic relations. One can play the role of son, friend, steward, or chief in any number of different settings. The rules by which information about the relationship is put together are very different for relations among Kapinga and for interethnic relations. This is why the minimal information necessary for Kapinga to interact with one another is different from that needed for Kapinga to interact with non-Kapinga. It is this difference that constitutes the ethnic boundary between the Kapinga social system and all other social systems.

Relations among Kapinga and relations between Kapinga and non-Kapinga constitute different contexts of interaction. They are different because the rules for combining information that structures the contexts are different. The intraethnic contexts are contexts of personal relations, relationships between persons who are intimately involved in each other's biographies (cf. Hiller 1947). The interethnic contexts are those of categorical relations in which each person interacts with others in terms of the role or ethnic category the others represent.

Defining ethnic boundaries in this manner for Kapinga vis-à-vis others implies a contradiction in the atoll system with regard to the change described previously. Although Kapinga ethnicity is defined in terms of contexts of personal relations, the atoll social system includes contexts whose structure is identical to those of interethnic contexts. It is precisely this structure that accounts for differentiation in the social system. The presence of such contexts within an ethnic boundary whose definition excludes them constitutes a contradiction. Not only does this contradiction exist in fact, but Kapinga on the atoll are aware of at least some of its implications. The contradiction is manifested in several ways, the clearest of which are intergenerational hostility and an incipient church versus secularist factionalism.

Government-sponsored programs on the atoll have generated the categorical relations that have led to differentiation. These programs have been aimed at and run by younger people. Leadership and economic control, traditionally prerogatives of elders, have to some extent passed into the hands of younger people. In such settings as council meetings, retail stores, the school, and the dispensary, expectations of behavior based on personal relationships are continually being violated as role requirements take precedence in these settings. Older people respond by complaining about the incompetence, immorality, and irresponsibility of younger people, claiming that they are unfit for the positions of responsibility they hold. Older people decry the lack of respect they are shown by their juniors and the latter's disregard of their experience. Yet younger people continue to be elected or appointed to these positions by their peers and by their elders.

At the same time, younger people seem to be ambivalent about their own positions. Many younger people, both men and women, claim that the older people are right in their criticism of young people in responsible positions. Moreover, the esteem that is normally accorded to people in responsible positions has not been forthcoming to the young men who assume positions on the council, in the co-op, and in the schools, regardless of how hard they work. While the young men remain committed to these activities, they are also committed to such traditional activities as craft work, fishing, and land stewardship, in which excellence brings esteem. Those who are most involved in the council, co-op, and schools have the least time for the traditional activities. These people, mainly men in their twenties and thirties, feel this ambivalence most keenly and are among those most overtly hostile to their elders. Hostility is most often expressed in malicious gossip. A measure of just how serious the situation had become by 1966 can be seen in the council's consideration of a bill to outlaw and establish criminal penalties for malicious gossip.

The members of the Congregational church have become a quasi-political group on the atoll, often voting as a bloc in community meetings. Although 'church people' are thought of as older people, almost a third of the church leadership—the Christian Endeavor Society—are young people.

For about eight years, between 1957 and 1964, the island council was dominated by church members.[12] Many of the issues in which the council was involved reflected the strong ties of its members to the church. An early act of the council was to prohibit the sale and consumption of alcoholic beverages. The council fired three schoolteachers for violating this law. Another teacher was fired for introducing social dancing into the school curriculum and yet another for "illicit" sexual activity. A close look at the implications of these positions makes it obvious why church leadership is identified with older people. What 'church people' represent in atoll affairs is, symbolically, the kind of integration typical of the traditional atoll social system. Implied in the firing of the teachers for offences committed outside the classroom is the belief that the school is not separate from the rest of the community. Similarly, the issue concerning the use of communal roofing materials for the church involves the same kind of premise—that religious activity is not separate from other activities. It is a denial of the differentiation implicit in the new categories of activity.

It is significant that even though the 'church people' eventually lost on the issues of firing the teachers and using community-owned materials, they lost not by a community vote but by the intervention of outside authority. The Office of Education on Ponape made it clear that hiring and firing teachers was the responsibility of that office, not of the council. The church was prohibited from using the roofing materials because of regulations in the Trust Territory Code. Many people, old and young, were unhappy about the decision, but they felt that there was little they could do about it.

The contradiction in the atoll system thus manifests itself in intergenerational hostility and some of the conditions for factionalism which everyone feels but cannot quite understand. The commitment of people to very different and sometimes mutually exclusive contexts has produced conflicts that are painful and frustrating. They are frustrating inasmuch as no one can really point to any well-defined culprit or, for that matter, to any well-defined group as victim. Kapinga living on the atoll continue to define themselves in terms of traditional contexts of interaction as the atoll system continues to differentiate. The 'church people' continue to take positions that embody integration rather than differentiation. Although no one wholly disagrees with the church positions or their premises, the positions continue to meet with defeat. The outcomes of this process are hostility, frustration, and ambivalence—which are inevitable whenever people commit themselves to both horns of a dilemma.

CONCLUSION

We can conclude that the changes described for the atoll community and the community at Porakiet are the outcome of contact between the Kapinga and the colonial system. This conclusion tells us very little, however, since the kinds of contact are different for each community. Contact between the atoll and the colonial system involves a relationship between the atoll as a polity and the highest echelons of the district administration on Ponape. It has been the maintenance of the *form* of that relationship through historical changes in the administration that has resulted in change in the atoll system. Contact between Porakiet and the colonial system involves a relationship between individuals or small groups in the village and government agencies, businesses, groups, and individuals of other ethnic groups outside the village. Maintaining traditional social relationships within the village has required that its residents participate in relations with individuals, groups, and agencies outside the village. These relations require of villagers an allocation of time and resources which differs from that of atoll residents. The outcome has been a change in life-styles of Porakiet residents.

The changes in each community have occurred at different systemic levels. Yet in both communities change has resulted from the *maintenance* of certain relationships. These data demonstrate the validity of Gregory Bateson's hypothesis that "the constancy and survival of some larger system is maintained by changes in the constituent subsystems" (Bateson 1972:339). Bateson has also posited that such systemic change generates its own paradoxes (1972:339). This proposition also is demonstrated by the contradiction that has arisen on the atoll between traditional personal relationships and the categorical relations that have emerged from the differentiation in the atoll social system.

As the atoll community and the community at Porakiet have undergone changes, the relationship between them has changed. Porakiet is no longer a colony of the atoll. It is a separate social system that is politically independent of the atoll. The question remains whether the universalization of the Kapinga concepts of 'community' and 'Kapinga people' was inevitable given the existence of these two politically independent social systems. The answer is no: universalization of these concepts was not inevitable. The process of universalization depended on two historical contingencies: (1) the identification of a significant minority of Porakiet residents with Ponapean citizenship and (2) the raising of specific issues in the village by this minority, which called into question concepts of 'Kapinga person' and 'community'. Given that the Kapinga continue to think of 'person' in terms of relationships,[13] one might posit that the universalization of 'community' and 'Kapinga people' was inevitable once the issues were raised. Otherwise, the concepts could have been left safely ambiguous.

Finally, this chapter has dealt with the processes of social and cultural change and stability in two Kapinga communities. The processes of change have been viewed as changes in the organization of social relationships and the organization of ideas resulting from relationships between each community and other social systems that constitute its environment. The focus on relationships within which change occurs allows us not only to identify the change we are dealing with but also to account for it. The focus on relationships between social systems also forces us to identify precisely the systemic level at which change or stability is relevant.

## NOTES

This chapter is based on data collected on Ponape and Kapingamarangi during thirteen months of field research in 1965 and 1966. The research was sponsored by the Pacific Displaced Communities Project at the University of Oregon. The project was directed by Homer G. Barnett and was funded by the National Science Foundation. I would like to thank Dr. Barnett, Vern Carroll, and Martin Silverman for their help in preparing this chapter.

1. Huria was transferred to Ponape in about 1920, where he faced charges of criminal cruelty by the administration on Ponape. He remained on Ponape for several years thereafter. The outcome of his hearing is unknown.
2. Atoll chiefs occasionally made decisions for and about the village (see, for example, Lieber 1968b:83–84).
3. Ponape is one of six administrative districts. It includes six municipalities on Ponape Island and the additional municipalities of Kusaie Island and Pingelap, Mokil, Ngatik, Nukuoro, and Kapingamarangi atolls.
4. There are a few Roman Catholic families on the atoll and in Porakiet, but with only one exception they have not been prominent in either community (see Lieber 1968b:129–138).
5. There are three reasons why there has been no autocratic rule. First, the population has been largely transient, with people continually going back and forth between the atoll and Ponape. Second, the headman was subordinate to the atoll chief until 1961. Third, people easily avoid any attempt at autocratic rule by moving out of Porakiet to other parts of Ponape, by appealing the headman's decision to the atoll chief, or by simply ignoring the headman.
6. It sometimes happens that Kapinga must interact with one another in such contexts. When such interaction is public—student and teacher in a Kolonia school, for example—Kapinga feel very uncomfortable about it. When the interaction is private, roles tend to be played down.
7. By dependents, I mean people who join one's household, people who exercise use rights over one's land, people who become one's apprentices, people who borrow one's possessions, and the like. All these acts may encode messages of dependency in the sense of a relationship in which one assumes responsibility for the support or training of another.
8. The atoll chief's assistants were concerned with the enforcement of 'law' rather than with its formulation.
9. Running a lucrative business usually involves catering to a largely Micronesian clientele. The stores whose main clientele is composed of villagers usually run at no profit or at a loss. But even without profit, the people who have maintained stores have accumulated many debtors through extending credit. The symbolic dependency maintains the creditor's image as a responsible person. It is for prestige rather than for profit that the two village stores are maintained by their owners.
10. A homestead program was initiated by the district administration in 1954—sixty people were brought to Metalanimwh in the southern part of Ponape, a village was built, and a headman was appointed by the atoll chief. This headman attempted to maintain his political autonomy in his village, which had a population of twenty-three persons in 1966.
11. By way of contrast, although Kapinga on the atoll (most of whom except young children have lived on Ponape) have knowledge of the same ethnic stereotypes as do Porakiet villagers, very few of the stereotypes operate on the atoll. The distinctions employed on the atoll for occasional visitors are those of 'Euro-American' (dangada baalangi) and 'Ponapean' (combining Ponapean, Kusaiean, Mokilese, Ngatikese, and Pingelapese into one

category). It is the outsider's role that is important in his relations with atoll people, and contact is so brief and official that the two categories usually suffice for the interaction (see chapter 7).

12. Although the council is composed mainly of young people at present, one-third to one-half of the members continue to be church members.

13. For a fuller discussion of personhood see Lieber (1972).

# 4

# COMMUNITIES AND NONCOMMUNITIES: THE NUKUORO ON PONAPE

*Vern Carroll*

## INTRODUCTION

Unlike some of the other groups reported on in this volume, the Nukuoro have not formed a daughter community in some other place. The opportunities available to them have been identical to those afforded the Kapinga people (chapter 3), but those opportunities have been scorned: At present there is a Kapinga village on Ponape (just as there is for each of the other out-island ethnic groups in Ponape District), but one searches in vain for a Nukuoro village. The Nukuoro on Ponape seem to prefer not to live communally; they seem to have actually resisted all efforts to push them in the direction of forming a community on Ponape such as other ethnic groups have formed. This chapter is devoted to explaining this preference. The chapter can also be read as a lesson: History is not always dealt with most adequately by framing one's analysis in historical terms. I shall return to this point at the end of the chapter.

## THE KAPINGA AND NUKUORO ON PONAPE

As Michael Lieber has pointed out (chapter 3), the Kapinga on Ponape live mostly in a small village located on a tract of land awarded them by the Japanese colonial administration in the early 1920s. The village is organized into sections, with section leaders

under the village chief. All Kapinga who come to Ponape are wel-
comed to this village and assigned living space. The village en-
gages in many communal activities and has become a minor
tourist attraction because of its authentic South Seas charm.

There are also a fair number of Nukuoro on Ponape (about 151
in 1965—see Carroll 1975b). To be sure, most of them live in and
around the port town of Kolonia (see map 4), the only location on
Ponape where non-Ponapeans can obtain land-use rights without
acquiring long-term commitments.[1] But within the precincts of
Ponape the Nukuoro are widely scattered among members of
other ethnic groups. They do not have a community organization
—and all efforts to form one have failed. Nukuoro on Ponape, ex-
cepting those in the same household, appear not to interact with
one another more frequently than with non-Nukuoro, and most
Nukuoro agree that the relationships between Nukuoro on Ponape
are something less than ideal.

This state of affairs is surprising—when contrasted with the
Kapinga case—since the Nukuoro have had precisely the same opportunities for community development as the Kapinga have enjoyed and the two cultures—both Polynesian outliers—are as
similar, in most obvious respects, as two distinct cultures can be.
Moreover, the ecologies of their home atolls are very similar (Kapinga being more subject to drought and somewhat less well en-
dowed with land suitable for taro excavation).[2] The Kapinga birth
rate appears to have been somewhat higher in the first half of the
present century (judging from the rapid increase in Kapinga population), but population dynamics can be safely ruled out—along
with ecology—as the main factor in the contemporary difference
between the behavior of the two ethnic groups on Ponape. What
then accounts for this difference?

Historical investigation yields the following information. The
tract of land on which the Kapinga village on Ponape is presently
located was given to the Kapinga chief "on behalf of the people."
A similar tract of land nearby was given, at about the same time,
to the Nukuoro chief "on behalf of the people." The Kapinga chief
set about exercising his mandate in the Kapinga fashion—with the
results noted above. The Nukuoro chief also exercised his mandate, but in a different manner: The Nukuoro chief took possession
"for the people" and during the 1920s and 1930s he brought

groups of workers from Nukuoro Atoll to clear the land, plant coconut trees, and build houses for him and his family. The workers
who came were housed and fed generously, their incidental expenses were taken care of, and many volunteered again and again
for the work party (which was rotated every six months or so).
Nukuoro who came to Ponape on other business, and there were
very few, stayed at the chief's house as his guests. As far as one can
ascertain, there were no complaints about the chief's administration of this public trust, which continued until his death in 1953.

Although the American administration after World War II encouraged complaints against traditional leaders (and acted on several complaints directed at the Nukuoro chief by dissidents), there
was—as far as we were able to ascertain—still no outcry about the
chief's management of this land. Indeed, in the mid-1950s, after
the chief died, his eldest son—then resident on Ponape—managed
to obtain exclusive title to the land. He was apparently unopposed
in this endeavor, even though he made no promises about his future use of it.

Today the tract lies overgrown and all but deserted; a couple of
ramshackle structures are sporadically occupied. The new owner
lives elsewhere.

## HISTORY AND CULTURE

One might be tempted to explain the peculiar fate of the Nukuoro
on Ponape as resulting from nothing more than the behavior of an
autocratic chief and his greedy son. But the lack of public outcry
even with governmental encouragement to complain (and a demonstrated capacity on the part of the Nukuoro for doing so) suggests that the chief was merely doing what people wanted him to
do. It appears, then, that the Nukuoro did not want a community
(of the Kapinga sort) on Ponape. But how could this be?

A useful perspective on this problem is gained by looking at the
cultural context of Nukuoro emigration. The story begins with the
settlement of the atoll about five centuries ago.

Tradition records that a man in some far-off land (now popular-
ly thought to be Samoa) had a quarrel with his elder brother who
was a chief (or, in some versions, with a younger brother who was
their mother's favorite). The man gathered his affines and retain-
ers together and did battle with the brother. Losing the battle, he

was obliged to flee. Taking his party in a double canoe (or two double canoes) he sailed away. After many vicissitudes the party arrived at Nukuoro, which was uninhabited (or nearly so), where they established a permanent settlement. The leader of the party was now chief, and when his son grew up there was bad feeling between them. The son went off in a canoe one day and was never heard from again. But by and by, a castaway came to the atoll. After the castaway had been nursed back to health, he visited frequently with the chief. During these visits the chief noticed that the castaway was fascinated by the chief's tattoos, which covered the upper part of his body in a pattern distinctive to his family. The castaway explained that he had seen the same tattoo pattern on the torso of a man who was being roasted on a spit at an island he had visited. The chief, realizing that only his son bore the same markings, gathered a party together and embarked on a canoe voyage to find out more about the circumstances of his son's death. The party sailed and sailed but they found themselves eventually in the open sea with no prospects of a landfall. The chief asked his wife to ask her father (a diviner) to determine why they were unable to find land. The diviner, with considerable reluctance, advised that they had been bewitched and only the death of either the chief or the rest of his party would break the spell. The chief volunteered to sacrifice himself, and after leaving instructions to his party concerning their future conduct, he was swallowed up by a whale. The party soon made a landfall on Nukuoro, and after having followed the chief's instructions, they saw again the whale that had swallowed him.

One notes in this story that in both cases of interpersonal conflict, emigration was precipitated by a serious rupture—and in neither case was the rupture mended: The Nukuoro chief was a refugee from his home island; his son was lost to him forever; and the chief lost his life in a futile effort to follow his son's path. In both cases the person leaving was in the wrong.

Nukuoro emigration today has much the same character. Excluding those visiting on Ponape temporarily in connection with schooling, medical visits, church business, and the like, all the Nukuoro on Ponape are thought to have left home owing to disturbances in their close interpersonal relationships (with 'parents', 'siblings', or 'children'). Those who have emigrated return home rarely, and they do not seem to identify with the interests of their home community. Whereas the Kapinga community on Ponape has been active in advancing Kapinga interests with the district administration, the Nukuoro who permanently reside on Ponape are thought to be particularly unhelpful in this regard. If anything —it is said—they appear, as individuals, to work against the interests of the home community and appear contemptuous of their kin at home.[3] One index of the alienation of emigrants is the fact that a large percentage of married Nukuoro emigrants are married to non-Nukuoro (although most of these had been married to a Nukuoro at some time in the past).[4]

It cannot be said that the life of Nukuoro emigrants on Ponape is easy. Most do not have secure access to land and steady employment. Few Nukuoro have achieved positions of influence in the district government, and few are comfortable financially.[5] Most are living a marginal economic existence—by their own admission —in housing that is overcrowded with dependent relatives. All admit that the conditions of life on the home atoll are far superior to the circumstances in which they live on Ponape. Why, then, do they emigrate?

By and large, they leave the atoll for the same reasons they might leave their domicile on the atoll or move elsewhere in the same village or (occasionally) to an islet of the atoll other than the one on which the main village is located. The person moving will always claim force majeure—a sick relative needs help elsewhere. But although no one can criticize such a statement (since to be a good kinsman is to be a good person on Nukuoro), no one is deceived. Anyone will tell you that people leave home because they are unhappy. Once upon a time, before the coming of Europeans, one could not easily express one's alienation in this way (the Nukuoro, at contact, had no canoes suitable for ocean voyaging and no long-distance navigation methods). Until the 1960s, few Nukuoro had kin on Ponape with whom they could stay, although many people on Nukuoro expressed an interest in going there. Indeed, it seemed to me during the course of my fieldwork that the Nukuoro village was bursting at the seams—that many people felt trapped there and would be happy to emigrate if given the opportunity.

As more Nukuoro became established on Ponape (map 5) it became easier for others to find a place to stay. On 18 September 1973 the village population (245), according to an official Trust

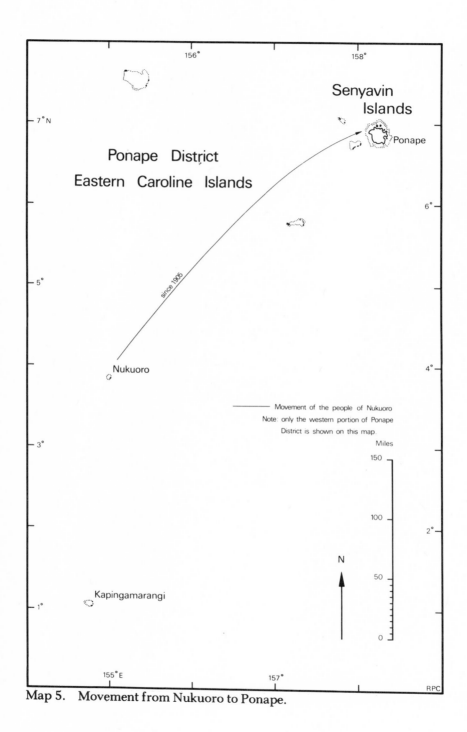

156°                                        158°

                                    Senyavin
                                    Islands

7° N                                              Ponape

Ponape   District
Eastern   Caroline   Islands                          6°

5°                                                    4°
                                          since 1905

Nukuoro                                               4°

                    ——————  Movement of the people of Nukuoro
                    Note: only the western portion of Ponape
                    District is shown on this map.

                                                Miles

3°                                                150°

                                                100

                                                      2°
                                                N
                                                       50
Kapingamarangi
1°                                                    0

155° E                         157°
                                                      RPC

Map 5.   Movement from Nukuoro to Ponape.

Territory census (TTPI 1974), was actually less than in 1965 (278), despite considerable growth in the total ethnic population.

But the question of why or how Nukuoro emigrate is not the same as the question of why they fail to form an emigrant community on Ponape—despite the obvious advantages of doing so. Here we must look closely at the *sense* of emigration on Nukuoro, once again using Kapinga as the point of contrast.

Whereas the Kapinga seem to assume that disruptions of close relationships can eventually, with patience and goodwill, be mended, the Nukuoro tend to assume that a serious rupture is irreversible. The Kapinga are quicker to explode whereas the Nukuoro continue to act as though all were well long after it is not; but when the climax is reached the Nukuoro incline to walk away from the situation and not look back. The first Nukuoro emigrant in the postcontact period (probably in the 1870s) was a middle-aged man who asked the captain of a visiting ship to take him aboard as part of the ship's crew. The man's relatives were aghast and pleaded with him not to go, bewailing the fact that they might never see him again. The man replied that he was tired of sitting in the men's house day after day munching on a piece of dead coral while his mates ate the food prepared by their devoted relatives. Despite all entreaties, the man left his relatives behind. He never sent word back to them and was never heard from again.

The Kapinga settlement story reflects a somewhat different premise about the consequences of interpersonal blowups. According to Kapinga tradition (Elbert 1949), a man's wife grew angry with him for leaving her alone frequently while he strolled on the lagoon shore, so she swam out to sea. When the man returned home he noticed her absence and was extremely upset. Ascertaining the reason, he caused a canoe to be built at top speed. Though the canoe was imperfectly finished, the party set out after her. They found her in the open sea, near death from exhaustion, and lifted her into the canoe. After many days of further voyaging, they arrived at a place hitherto unknown to them—the atoll of Kapingamarangi. Although the husband tried to feed his wife various delicacies, she was too weak from exhaustion and exposure and she died. As far as anyone knows, the Kapinga people lived on in happiness in their newfound land.

In this story the rupture is impetuous, not calculated. The estranged person (who is in the right) manages to get away only by stealth (since her husband would surely have prevented her going had he known her intentions). The wrongdoer is immediately contrite and takes quick steps to make amends. The consequences of the rupture are serious (the woman did eventually die, after all) but a reconciliation is effected. The unhappy incident does not entail a long series of similar misfortunes.

Although Kapinga may leave their home atoll today owing to interpersonal difficulties, it is rarely with the suggestion that they are leaving for good. Rather they seem to think more in terms of a "cooling-off period" or an opportunity "to get away (from certain people) for a while"—not to get away from the whole community. And, in fact, most Kapinga return frequently to their home atoll for visits (and in the absence of visits, they send presents).

The differences noted between the Nukuoro and the Kapinga premise structure can be related systematically to other differences in premises about interpersonal relations, although I shall not undertake to do so here. The differences may seem slight in comparison with the obvious cultural similarities, but the behavioral outcomes are enormously divergent. The Kapinga regard themselves (in comparison with the Nukuoro) as more cooperative, more outgoing, quicker to criticize and offer help, more good-natured, more lighthearted, more jovial, and more industrious.[6] Related to these differences are differences in childrearing, land tenure, and political organization.

Thus, although the Nukuoro and the Kapinga are very similar "culturally" (in the ways cultural difference is usually measured—language, customs, technology, and so forth), a more incisive and therefore more useful notion of culture as premise structure reveals significant cultural differences between the two communities. It is my contention that these cultural differences are sufficient to account for the observed differences in aggregate behavior and that other explanations are not required.

## ON HISTORICAL ANALYSIS

The movements of individuals or whole communities from one place to another present themselves to us (through our conventions about these matters) as *historical events*—that is, as events whose main feature is that they are located at some definable place in the passage of time. Such events are preceded, of course, by antecedent events, which are thought to bear directly on them, and are followed by consequent ones. Historical events are perceived ordinarily as such because they stand out—they are different in some interesting way from what usually happens.

By convention, one looks for the explanation of a historical event in what happened just before. A common temptation in historical analysis is to seek the explanation of a historical event not in all antecedent events but in those which are *historic*—that is, in events which are novel. Analysis in terms of antecedent "historical events" appears to make sense because, without the appearance of some novel antecedent factor, we feel, the status quo could not change sufficiently to provoke the historical event in question.

But even if all the *ordinary* antecedent events are taken into account in a historical analysis (as they always are in the better sort of history), one usually tries (again, as a matter of convention) to explain historical events mainly in terms of their *immediate* antecedents. History operates from moment to moment, it is thought, and the long arm of history does not reach out of one point in time and grab at something much later on.

Thus the conventions of historical analysis foreshorten the *context* of an event. Factors that endure over long periods of time tend, inevitably, to be given less weight in historical analysis than events that are closer at hand and more dramatic.

My contention here is that historical analysis (of the sort usual in anthropology, at least) is insufficiently sensitive to the stable features of culture and character that lie within the province of anthropological study. At best, "history" seems to relegate those enduring propositions about the nature of the world to the status of background information. At worst, they are ignored altogether.

For as long as history is concerned mainly with what does happen, there is no obvious problem with the ordinary sort of historical analysis: A (a historical event) is caused by B (an anterior historical event) or by B, C, and D—or by all these acting in concert, along with a few cultural regularities perhaps. But when, as in the present case, we try to explain what does *not* happen, there is an unexpected difficulty. If historical events are caused by (antecedent) historical events, then what causes a *nonevent*? Is it other events—or other nonevents—or is it the nonoccurrence of other events?

The most adequate description of a complex system is in terms of what will *not* happen (Bateson 1967). What actually happens in history is only a minuscule fraction of the equally plausible outcomes of anterior events. By focusing only on what has happened, we miss what might have happened—and what could not have happened. In a phrase, the ordinary sort of historical analysis is suffused with the error of thinking that *post hoc, ergo propter hoc*. Cultural analysis—dealing as it does with the central precepts in peoples' belief systems—attempts to avoid this sort of error by seeking to explain history, to the degree possible, as the ordinary functioning of a relatively stable premise system.

In the case at hand I have shown that contemporary Nukuoro emigration conveys the same meanings and is founded on the same premises as the earliest cases of emigration recorded in Nukuoro traditional history. Only in this way, I think, can we understand why the Nukuoro on Ponape have created something that, if it has any structure at all, is of the order of an "anticommunity"—or at the very least a "noncommunity."[7]

NOTES

Nukuoro is an atoll located in Ponape District, Trust Territory of the Pacific Islands. As of 15 March 1965 there were 278 persons living on the atoll, 26 of them non-Nukuoro. Further information on the population is contained in Carroll (1975b).

This chapter was first drafted while I held a National Institute of Mental Health Special Postdoctoral Fellowship during 1970–1971 at the University of Hawaii. Fieldwork (1963–1966) was supported by a National Institute of Mental Health Predoctoral Fellowship and Research Grant and (during the summer of 1967) by the Graduate School Research Fund of the University of Washington. I am indebted to the many students and colleagues who have provided valuable comments at various oral presentations of this material, and especially to the following colleagues who have provided written comments on earlier versions: Michael H. Agar, Gregory Bateson, Ivan A. Brady, Raymonde Carroll, Stephen W. Foster, Eric A. Hill, Sharif K. Kakana, Michael D. Lieber, Robert K. McKnight, Susan B. Peterson, John Rutherford, Albert J. Schütz, David M. Schneider, Bradd Shore, and Martin G. Silverman.

1. The alternatives are either to marry into a Ponapean family or to make government-owned land productive for agriculture—a homesteading arrangement (offered only occasionally) that may lead to acquisition of permanent land rights after five years of continuous cultivation.
2. Descriptions of Nukuoro and Kapingamarangi are available in Carroll (1966) and Lieber (1968a).

3. This matter may be put another way: The Kapinga, whether at home or on Ponape, seem to feel that they are all members of the same community, while the Nukuoro seem to feel that the community is coterminous with the atoll and those away from the home atoll are no longer part of the community.
4. Table 1 presents the relevant data for all Nukuoro living abroad in 1965 (see note 5 for additional information). It will be noted that 56 percent of all Nukuoro living abroad were last married to non-Nukuoro.

TABLE 1    Ethnic Status of Last Spouse, Ever-Married Members of Nukuoro Living Ethnic Population, by Location, 15 March 1965

| Status of Spouse | Location | | | | | | |
|---|---|---|---|---|---|---|---|
| | On Nukuoro | | | Abroad | | | |
| | Men | Women | Both Sexes | Men | Women | Both Sexes | Total |
| Married to ethnic Nukuoro | 28 | 37 | 65 | 9 | 8 | 17 | 82 |
| Married to non-Nukuoro | 4 | 4 | 8 | 14 | 8 | 22 | 30 |
| ALL | 32 | 41 | 73 | 23 | 16 | 39 | 112 |

SOURCE: Carroll (1975b:table 8.28).
NOTE: See Carroll (1975a) for population definitions.

5. According to a census I conducted in June 1966, there were twenty-five married Nukuoro on Ponape who were residing there permanently and an additional nine married or formerly married persons were considered to be there 'temporarily'. Of these twenty-five permanent residents, fourteen were Nukuoro married to other Nukuoro (a total of seven couples); the remainder (eight men and three women) were married to non-Nukuoro. Of the three women married to non-Nukuoro, none had jobs and only one had direct rights in land (through year-to-year lease of government land). Of the eight men married to non-Nukuoro, only three had direct access to land (one through homestead, one through year-to-year lease, and one through owning the tract mentioned elsewhere in this chapter). Two of these men did not have steady wage-earning jobs; the rest did.

Of the seven Nukuoro men married to Nukuoro women, only three had a steady wage-earning job and one (an employed person) had direct rights in land (through lease); another (unemployed) man lived on land belonging to relatives. Of the Nukuoro wives of these men, only one had a steady job (another was employed part-time as a maid); two (including the one employed full-time) had rights in land (through year-to-year lease of government land), three were living on land belonging to relatives, and two had no land rights of their own.

Thus only four of twenty-five married Nukuoro on Ponape had both a steady job and rights to land: three men and one woman (and two of these men were married to non-Nukuoro). The men who did not have steady jobs worked occasionally as stevedores or as fishermen.

6. The Nukuoro, the Kapinga, and the ethnographers who have worked among them all concur in these comparisons.

7. While the present discussion may throw some light on the question of why the history of the Nukuoro on Ponape does not much resemble the history of the Kapinga, we have provided no general solution to the age-old problem of why some ethnics abroad form communities resembling those left behind and others do not. In a curious way it does seem, however, that the Nukuoro on Ponape live much as they do on the home atoll—with the single difference that atoll life constrains the community to resemble a community in a way that life on Ponape does not.

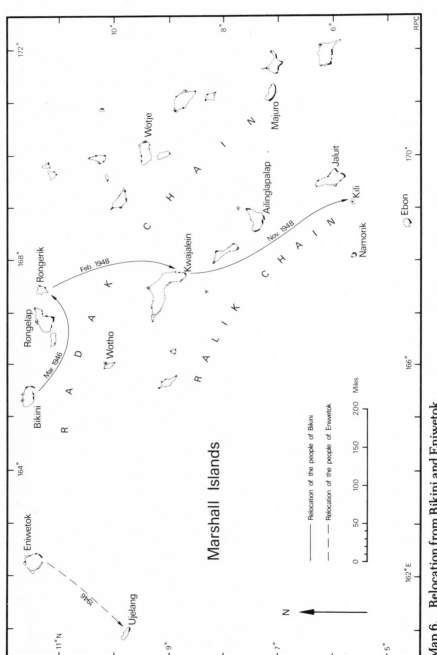

**Map 6.  Relocation from Bikini and Eniwetok.**

# 5

# THE RELOCATION OF THE BIKINI MARSHALLESE

*Robert C. Kiste*

## INTRODUCTION

In early 1946, the small community of islanders that inhabited Bikini Atoll in the northern Marshall Islands was relocated when its homeland was selected as a nuclear test site by the United States. The Bikinians did not desire relocation; they had no real alternative but to submit to the wishes of the Americans. Their first resettlement was on Rongerik, another northern atoll. Its resources were insufficient, and in less than two years the islanders suffered near starvation. Traditional forms of social organization were not effective in the crisis, and they were abandoned for a communal system in which the islanders exploited and shared their resources as a single unit. The Bikinians were evacuated from Rongerik and provided refuge at a military base on Kwajalein Atoll. After eight months, they were resettled on Kili, a small single island in the southern Marshalls. (See map 6.) After a few years, a novel system of landholding was implemented. This innovation has had numerous repercussions and has precipitated a major restructuring of their traditional social organization.

In addition to changing their community's internal organization, the Bikinians' response to relocation has also altered their relations with people outside the community. The islanders have terminated their subordinate status to the *iroij lablab* 'paramount chief', whose domain included Bikini. Concomitantly, they have allied themselves with the United States government and now depend on its agencies.

It is the task of this chapter to describe and account for these changes. In so doing, I argue that the structural changes in both the internal and external relationships of the community can only be understood in terms of a crucial continuity in the culture and society of Bikini in particular and the Marshall Islands in general. A fundamental premise by which people perceive, evaluate, and respond to the universe of human relations is that what really matters to people is their position with regard to power and influence over others, privilege, and the control of valued resources. It is, in short, the control of one's own destiny and the destinies of others that constitutes one of the most valued goals of Marshallese life. Such control is realized in certain social statuses in kinship groupings that form the corporate units of Marshallese atoll societies. It is the attainment of these statuses by which people measure their position in the social universe. These statuses are few relative to the aspirants to them, and as a consequence, much of Marshallese social life is an unending competition for statuses which entail power, influence, privilege, and the control of valued resources.

The competition has traditionally been focused on the control of land. Land is conceived of as a scarce commodity necessary for sustenance, and Marshallese, and perhaps all atoll dwellers, consider it their most prized resource. Because rights to land are held by kinship groups, competition has taken the form of struggles over land rights between such groups and struggles among individuals for leadership status within them (see Alkire 1972; Mason 1954; Spoehr 1949; Tobin 1958). Such competition has not only involved intracommunity struggles but also interatoll warfare before the coming of foreign colonial administrations. The advent of colonial powers has amplified the dimensions of the competition with the introduction of the copra trade, imported goods, and new political statuses, the acquisition of which have become new prizes in familiar struggles.

The relocations of the Bikini community and its relationship with the United States government, whose power and resources Bikinians regard as unbounded, constitute a novel context within which traditional concerns have been played out. As new opportunities for people to acquire power, influence, and privilege have presented themselves, new strategies have been devised to take advantage of them. The structure of the Bikini community has changed in consequence. Furthermore, given the Bikinians' awareness of the power of the United States government over them, it is hardly surprising that they have sought to alter their relationship with the government in order to influence its policy.

Thus the argument advanced in this chapter reflects certain realities of Marshallese culture and behavior. It is in basic agreement with the analytical stance of a number of anthropologists concerned with the dynamics of sociocultural change who have adopted what David Schneider calls the "competitive view" of society (Schneider 1970:1–6; see also Leach 1954, Mair 1965). This view assumes that people vie with one another to attain goals they hold to be of value and that the pursuit of power and influence is common to members of human groups as ends in themselves or as means to yet other ends. It is not posited here that the intensity of motivation to acquire power and influence is the same for everyone or that all are equally successful among Bikinians or in other societies. Nonetheless, it is those who are the most successful and energetic in the pursuit of such ends who chart the direction that a society follows.

I begin the argument with a description of the Bikini community's historical and environmental setting. This is followed by descriptions of the traditional social organization, the reorganization of the community during its resettlements, and the relations of the community with external authorities and other Marshall Islanders. A concluding section reviews the basic argument of the chapter, and an epilogue reports recent events that will have far-reaching consequences on the lives and futures of the Bikinians.

## HISTORICAL AND ENVIRONMENTAL SETTING

Bikini is the northernmost atoll in the Ralik (western) chain of the Marshall Islands. It consists of twenty-six islets which have a total land area of 2.32 square miles. Like other northern atolls, Bikini lies within a comparatively dry zone (Wiens 1962:154) and has a poor soil cover. Only three subsistence crops—coconut, pandanus, and arrowroot—thrive there. Like other northern atoll communities, the Bikini population was never large; it numbered only 170 at the time of relocation.[1] In contrast, the southern atolls are situated in a wetter climatic zone, have richer soil deposits, and support a larger variety of crops. The largest populations, some numbering over a thousand, have always been located in the south.

In addition to its position in northern Ralik, Bikini is also isolated from other atolls. In precontact times, sporadic intercourse was carried on with the people of Rongelap Atoll, the Bikinians' closest neighbors 80 miles to the east, and a few marriages occurred between the two communities. Bikinians had no regular contact with the peoples of other atolls, and they had developed minor variations in speech and behavior that distinguished them from other Marshallese.

Bikini's location had other consequences. Missionaries and traders were first attracted to the more favorable environment of the south, where they commenced their activities in the 1850s. The German (1885–1914) and the Japanese (1914–1943) colonial governments were headquartered at the southern atoll of Jaluit. Majuro Atoll, also in the south, was established as the Marshall Islands District Administrative Center by the U.S. Trust Territory of the Pacific Islands not long after the end of World War II.

Bikinians and other northern islanders were the last to be affected by foreign influence, and they were always outside the mainstream of events in the south. Missionaries and traders did not penetrate the north until around the turn of this century, and because of the remoteness of their atoll, Bikinians had even less contact with outsiders than other northerners. German officials made few appearances at Bikini, and the mission effort did not reach there until 1908. The frequency of the Bikinians' contact with outsiders increased during the Japanese period. A government vessel called at the northern atolls twice a year. The copra trade which flourished in the south was poorly developed in the north, however, and the Bikinians' participation in it was minimal.

Few Bikinians had ventured away from home in German times, but experiences abroad increased with the visits of the Japanese vessel. Most Bikinians limited their travel to Rongelap and other northern atolls. Two or three attended a Japanese school, several traveled to Kwajalein Atoll for medical care, and a few others also spent some time there as wage laborers for the Japanese. About half a dozen had gone to Ailinglaplap in southern Ralik to serve in one of the households of their paramount chief. Others traveled purely for the adventure of it (Mason 1954:27–33).

A small number of Bikinians acquired spouses from other atolls during their ventures abroad, but most found their travels to be unpleasant experiences. The more acculturated southerners considered them a backward people; they compared them unfavorably with their own ancestors of pre-European times and poked fun at the peculiarities of their speech. The Bikinians accepted this unflattering image and held themselves in low esteem. To some extent, they did not identify with other Marshallese but thought of themselves as "Bikinians," a people distinct and culturally inferior. Many were hesitant to journey abroad and found it more comfortable to remain at home.

Not until the war years did foreigners come to reside at Bikini: half a dozen Japanese soldiers established a weather station there. Immediately after the war, the Marshalls were administered by a naval military government, and the Bikinians received more attention from the outside world than ever before. A U.S. Navy vessel called at Bikini every third month. A modest store, an elementary school, and a medical dispensary were established on the atoll and staffed with Bikinians trained by Americans. At the Americans' urging, the eleven traditional leaders of the community formed a council which functioned as the governing body of the atoll. One of the eleven was the *iroij* 'chief' of the community; he, a man named Juda, served as the magistrate at the head of the council and community.

The initial relocation of the Bikinians was swiftly accomplished. In late January 1946, it was announced that Bikini had been selected as the site for Operation Crossroads, the code name of the first tests in the program of nuclear experiments. The military governor of the Marshalls obtained the consent of the paramount chief to relocate the people. In early February, the governor and paramount chief flew to Bikini to obtain the people's cooperation. It appears certain that the Bikinians felt powerless to resist, and they have subsequently claimed that they never wanted to abandon their ancestral homeland and understood their relocation was only a temporary measure if Bikini were not destroyed or rendered unsafe for human habitation.

The eleven traditional leaders who formed the council chose

Rongerik as the site for resettlement (Meade 1946). Rongerik was uninhabited and is only 18 miles from Rongelab and its people, with whom the Bikinians had long been familiar. Rongerik's ten islets comprise only one-fourth of Bikini's land area, and the atoll had never supported a permanent population. It was known from the outset that it would present problems of economic self-sufficiency.

In the process of preparing for their departure in late March, Bikinians witnessed the initial phase of the massive preparations for Operation Crossroads and received a great amount of attention from news media. The Bikinians were reportedly impressed at the technological achievements of the Americans, and they were flattered that the representatives of such a powerful nation felt them worthy of their attention (Markwith 1946).

Within two months of their resettlement, the Bikinians reported that Rongerik's resources were inadequate. By the winter of 1946–1947, they experienced serious food shortages. During 1947, other atolls were considered by the administration as possible sites for another resettlement. As conditions on Rongerik deteriorated, a communal system of work and food rationing ·vas implemented and directed by Juda and the council. All food resources were brought under the council's control, and the gathering of subsistence crops by individuals or traditional kin groups was prohibited. Somewhat belatedly, the high commissioner of the Trust Territory ordered a study of the Bikinians to determine "the underlying causes of their apparent discontent" (Richards 1957: 525). Leonard Mason, an anthropologist from the University of Hawaii, was engaged to conduct the investigation. His arrival at Rongerik in January 1948 coincided with the most severe food shortage experienced by the islanders. Emergency rations were provided and a decision was made to evacuate the Bikinians to Kwajalein (Mason 1954:9).

The Bikinians were given refuge on the largest islet in Kwajalein Atoll. From the debris of war, the Americans had created a base complete with streets, electric lights, movie theaters, planes, and other military equipment. The Bikinians were quartered in a tent village adjacent to a camp of Marshallese laborers. They received meals in a common mess with the laborers; the fare was extravagant by Bikinian standards and provided a sharp contrast with their Rongerik ordeal. When they were physically able, many adults were employed and integrated into the labor force during working hours. With their earnings, they bought new clothing and sampled widely from the variety of goods available at the post exchange. Their morale improved, and they reportedly were profoundly impressed with the cultural accomplishments of the United States (Richards 1957:528).

To help the Bikinians preserve the integrity of their own community, they were provided with facilities to maintain their own church, council, and school separate from those of the other islanders. The Bikinians' village was off limits to Americans other than a few officials. Inevitably, however, they had more contact with outsiders than ever before, especially with the Marshallese in the labor camp. Compared to the more acculturated laborers, they were unsophisticated with much to learn.

The administration began the search for another resettlement site by consulting the paramount chief. The choice was narrowed to Wotho, a small northern atoll which was inhabited and within the chief's domain, and Kili Island, a commerical copra plantation before the war which was now uninhabited and outside the jurisdiction of any chief. The paramount chief wanted the Bikinians to settle on his atoll, and he, American officials, Juda, and three other members of the Bikini council visited Wotho. Afterward, Juda and ten other Bikini men were taken to Kili, where they were left alone to survey the island. Kili is a single island with a fringing reef shelf which extends unbroken around its entire perimeter. It covers 0.36 square mile (230 acres), an area one-sixth that of Bikini. Because of its location in the heavy rainfall belt of the south, Kili has a rich soil cover and great agricultural potential. Well-ordered rows of high-quality palms covered 95 percent of the land. A large swampy depressed area in its center was excellent for taro cultivation. Some breadfruit trees, papayas, bananas, sweet potatoes, and taro remained from the plantation days. The Bikinians were not familiar with the cultivation of these crops, and none grew in sufficient quantity to support the population.

Kili has great disadvantages. It lacks a lagoon and other sheltered fishing areas. The long axis of the island runs almost parallel to the prevailing direction of the strong northeast trades which blow steadily from November to late spring of each year, and the winds generate heavy surf which isolates Kili except for infrequent calms. Fishing is curtailed, and ships cannot land cargo. Gaining a subsistence on Kili in winter is made even more difficult by seasonal variation in the yield of breadfruit; the period of minimal yield coincides with the trade-wind season.

No one fully appreciated the magnitude of the adjustments the islanders would have to make if they were to resettle on Kili suc-cessfully. Bikinians had always depended on the rich marine re-sources of their lagoon and had never devoted much time or effort to agriculture. Their attitude toward agricultural work was in fact quite casual. The Americans assumed that with a concentrated ex-ploitation, Kili's palm groves could yield a crop far in excess of the Bikinians' subsistence needs and that the surplus could be con-verted into copra for the purchase of imported foods. With effi-cient management of resources, it was thought, food could be stored in advance of the lean winter seasons.

The Bikini men who surveyed the island were favorably im-pressed with its palm groves, but they were distressed over its small size and lack of lagoon. They reported their observations to other members of the community, and comparisons between the relative merits of Wotho and Kili were made. In a plebiscite of all adults, Kili was chosen by a 54 to 22 margin (Mason 1954:10).

The Bikinians were moved to Kili in November 1948. Kili's lo-cation in the southern Marshalls brought them into rather close proximity to the Marshallese who had had the longest experience with foreigners. Within a 65-mile radius of Kili are the three southernmost atolls of the Ralik chain (see map 6): Ebon, Namorik, and Jaluit, the former capital of both the German and Japanese governments which is only 30 miles northeast of Kili. In contrast to Bikini's geographical isolation, Kili is on the ship route which originates at the government center at Majuro, 170 miles northeast of Kili, and services the southwestern Ralik atolls.

## SOCIAL ORGANIZATION OF THE COMMUNITY

The communal system which had developed at Rongerik was ad-vantageous during the initial months on Kili as a concentrated ef-fort was necessary for the construction of a village. In contrast to Bikini and Rongerik where houses were of thatch and timber, dwellings and other buildings on Kili were built of imported lum-ber and roofing materials supplied by the Americans. During the islanders' initial months on Kili, the first signs that a realignment of power and influence was occurring in the community became manifest. To examine these changes, it is necessary to consider the organization of the community before relocation.

Of the 170 islanders comprising the community in 1946, 164 were divided among three exogamous matriclans, Ijjirik, Makao-liej, and Rinamu.[2] The other six belonged to clans from other atolls. Thirty-five other Bikini clansmen lived on other atolls (some since Japanese times). These were islanders and their children living with non-Bikini spouses.

Each of the three clans was composed of two or more lineages between which genealogical ties were known. An islander belonged to the lineage of his or her mother and membership was permanent. The lineage was a highly segmental structure. The term for 'lineage' is *bwij*, and it refers to the entire lineage or any segment of it.

Lineage mates were ranked according to two principles: chronological age and seniority of generation. Age was expressed in the relations among siblings, who were ranked from eldest to youngest. As an extension of the same principle, the lineages of a clan and the segments of a lineage were ranked according to the birth order of the sisters who founded them. The second principle was equally simple: members of ascending generations were superior in rank to those of descending generations.

The senior ranking member of a clan, lineage, or lineage segment was its *alab* 'head'. When the senior in rank was female, the senior ranking male usually assumed the title. As implied above, the term *alab* was elastic in the same manner as the term for lineage. The ranking member of a clan with its two or more constituent lineages was head of the entire clan. The senior ranking member of each lineage of a clan and the senior ranking member of each lineage segment were heads of their respective divisions of the clan. In the event that the head of a senior ranking lineage belonged to a lower generation than the head of a junior ranking lineage, there was a structural ambiguity in the system. The principles of relative age and seniority of generation were in direct opposition, and there were no cultural norms that specified one as being superior in rank over the other.

The head of the Ijjirik clan was the traditional chief of the community. Juda, the incumbent, was head of the senior ranking Ijjirik lineage and had succeeded to the chieftainship only a short time before the islanders' relocation. He traced his line of chiefly descent and succession to a legendary chief named Larkelon who had purportedly conquered Bikini Atoll with a group of followers in the distant past.

In large measure, the identity of Bikinians was derived from the fact that they possessed rights to Bikini land, and they held those rights because their ancestors had conquered the atoll. The entire social order of their community was largely defined and structured by land rights inherited from previous generations.

The lineage was one type of landholding corporation. The typical unit of a lineage's estate consisted of a strip of land which traversed the width of an islet from lagoon beach to ocean reef. In most instances, a lineage held as its estate a number of such parcels on several islets in the atoll. The head of a corporate lineage was an *alab in brij* 'head of land' as well as an *alab in bwij* 'head of lineage'. A male who headed a segment of a lineage that was only part of a larger landholding lineage was simply 'head of lineage (segment)'.

The rights and privileges of the lineage head distinguished him from his lineage mates. He had authority over the use of the land and oversaw the distribution of its resources. He alone was privileged to a disproportionate share of money earned from copra and usually retained one-fourth of the receipts. He used some of the money for personal wants and theoretically allocated some among his lineage mates when they were in need. The headman represented the interests of his lineage in community affairs. Lineage members under his authority were *rijerbal ro* 'workers'. They had inalienable rights to their lineage's land; those rights may be referred to as 'worker rights', and they entitled the lineage member to a share of resources derived from the land and the prerogative of residing on it. The spouses of lineage members and the children of lineage males also had usufruct rights to the lineage's land. They shared in its products and could reside on it. Children often grew up on a portion of their father's lineage land. Later, as married adults, they could and often did continue to exercise their usufruct.

The estate of a lineage was clearly distinguished from two other categories of property: (1) land to which a set of siblings had received both headman and worker rights from their father and (2) land to which an individual had received all rights in exchange for a service rendered. Ideally, only a headman could make such a transfer of land rights. In the event that a headman was the sole surviving member of his lineage, he held the land with his own children, and his children inherited both categories of rights to it. If the headman was the head of a viable lineage, he supposedly obtained the consent of his lineage mates before he could set aside land for himself and his offspring. In either instance, a headman and his children who held land together constituted a patricentered landholding corporation.

The eldest male of a set of siblings who formed a corporation with their father became the headman with authority over the land upon the latter's death. (Such a male was always *alab in brij* 'head of land', but he was not necessarily *alab in bwij* 'head of lineage' or a segment thereof.) His rights as headman were equal to those of heads of the corporate lineages, and he represented the interests of his siblings in community affairs. The siblings had three alternatives as to how they could manage the land. They could hold the land as a matrilineage composed only of themselves and their matrilineal offspring (that is, the children of the female members of the sibling set). Secondly, all rights to the land could be given to the children of the males who had first acquired it from their father; that is, once land had been alienated from a lineage, headman and worker rights could be inherited through males. Lastly, siblings could employ a combination of the first two options. In any case, land that siblings received from their father was theirs and theirs alone. Neither the head of their own lineage nor other lineage mates had claim to it.

The alternative forms of inheritance provided both a certain flexibility in the land tenure system and a set of mechanisms that were manipulated as islanders attempted to maximize the amount of land to which they could claim some right. Children who established themselves on land belonging to their father's lineage and remained after his death sometimes claimed that they had inherited all rights to it. Such claims were challenged by members of the father's lineage, but such disputes were seldom resolved.

Gifts of land in exchange for a service rendered were not common. In pre-European times, chiefs rewarded allies who had supported them in intracommunity conflicts with gifts of land. In the decades immediately prior to relocation, only one land parcel was given in such payment—for constructing a canoe for a headman.

Of the eleven men, including chief Juda, who were headmen at the time of relocation, four were the last surviving members of their lineages and headed patricentered corporations composed of themselves and their own children. Five others were heads of corporate lineages. The tenth headman was the eldest of a sibling set which had recently received land from their father, and it was not yet discernible how they would manage the future disposition of rights to it. The eleventh headman was the recipient of the only parcel of gift land in recent years. The eleven headmen were not of equal rank within the structure of the several lineages, but nonetheless, having control over the atoll's land, they had power and influence and were the traditional leaders of the community who had formed the council at the suggestion of the Americans.

In addition to disputes and grievances over land, the history of the succession of Bikini chiefs before Juda's incumbency further reveals the intensity of the competition over land and the traditional relationship between control of land and power, influence, and privilege. In pre-European times, the senior Ijjirik lineage held a disproportionate share of Bikini's land, and the holdings provided a warrant for the chiefly status of its head. Before the suppression of warfare by missionaries and the German colonial government, Ijjirik males engaged in a continuous struggle for land and power. Younger brothers plotted against elder brothers; nephews conspired against their maternal uncles. Genealogical evidence reveals that no fewer than ten males were murdered in the three ascending Ijjirik generations above Juda. The last of the assassinations occurred around the turn of this century when the eldest of Juda's three maternal uncles came to power by the murder of his own mother's brother.

During the lifetimes of Juda's maternal uncles, the senior Ijjirik lineage began to decline in size, and it was evident that it would become extinct. Juda's maternal uncles had numerous children in Makaoliej and Rinamu lineages, however, and they transferred the bulk of their lineage's land to them. As a consequence, father to child inheritance of land rights was frequent in the decades before relocation. By the time of Juda's succession to office, the power and influence traditionally associated with the chieftainship were greatly diminished because much of what once was chiefly land had been alienated.

Nonetheless, the chieftainship remained a political prize, and Juda's right to succeed was challenged by males of a junior Ijjirik lineage. The Ijjirik clan was composed of three lineages. Juda, his aged mother, and his elder brother were the last surviving members of the senior lineage. (Juda's brother was quite old when the last of their maternal uncles died, and he had voluntarily declined the office in favor of Juda.) The head of the second ranking lineage was of the same Ijjirik generation as Juda.

The third and junior lineage, however, was headed by a male of the first ascending generation above that of Juda's. Given the structural ambiguity in the system of rank and succession, the head of the junior lineage was able to claim that he was entitled to succeed Juda's mother's brother because they were of the same generation and that seniority of generation took precedence over seniority of lineage. He was supported by his younger brother, who was the most vociferous and aggressive in attempting to legitimize their claim. He argued that his elder brother was not only the legitimate successor to the chieftainship, but that the land once controlled by the chiefs should never have been alienated and should revert to Ijjirik and hence to his brother's control.

The head of the second ranking Ijjirik lineage supported Juda's succession. With Juda in office, he was to become Juda's heir presumptive and serve as his immediate subordinate, executive officer, and confidant. Other details pertaining to the dispute are not known. It is certain that the majority of headmen recognized Juda as the rightful successor to his mother's brother. Juda's status as head of the community was greatly enhanced when he was named magistrate by the other headmen and was recognized as such by the Americans. Nontraditional means of securing power and influence had been introduced, and subsequent events indicate that Juda took full advantage of American support and recognition to secure his own position.

The domestic organization of the community also reflected the traditional relationship between power, influence, privilege, and control of land. The islanders were divided into eleven extended family units which constituted "households" (Spoehr 1949:103). A household was a group which shared adjacent dwellings clustered about a cookhouse. Each household was headed by one of the headmen, and in all but two instances it was situated on land controlled by him. Affairs of the household were directed by its headman, and its members contributed to a common larder and accomplished tasks associated with everyday life.

Members of the eleven households occupied a total of twenty-six dwellings, which were dispersed over adjacent land parcels on the largest islet in the atoll. The households varied considerably in size and composition. They ranged from seven to twenty-five members with an average size of about fifteen. Variability in household composition reflected the system of land rights. As an individual had rights to the land of both his or her father and mother, a married couple had the option of residing with either set of parents; there were no prescribed rules of postmarital residence. Smaller households were little more than nuclear families with one or more attached relatives. Larger units were either bilateral extended families (which included some of the headman's children of both sexes with their spouses and children) or joint-sibling units formed by siblings with their spouses and offspring. Also reflecting the latitude provided by the system of land rights, the households were flexible units which gained and lost members in a casual way as young marrieds occasionally moved between parental households.

The land parcels on which the households were situated were divided into three districts. Each was composed of adjacent parcels and was headed by one of its senior ranking headmen who had authority over district affairs.

### RELOCATION AND REORGANIZATION

The move to Rongerik precipitated little immediate change in the organization of the community. The same number of dwellings that had existed at Bikini were built at Rongerik, and the composition of most households remained relatively unchanged. Land was never divided at Rongerik, and thus the households were no longer associated with landholdings.

Juda began to emerge as a figure of prominence and influence during the initial years of relocation. At Kwajalein he played a key role in the community's line of communication with the administration. Other headmen, however, suffered some eclipse of their power and influence as they no longer controlled essential re-

sources. Others were no longer dependent on them, and employment meant an unprecedented degree of freedom and economic
independence for most adults.

The first clear indications that a redistribution of power, influence, and privilege was occurring in the community were manifest when the islanders were resettled on Kili. Houses were constructed in a compact area along a roadway which parallels one of
the island's shores. A path intersects the roadway at midpoint, and
it became a boundary between two village districts. Dwellings to
the east of it became Jitaken ('upwind') and those to the west became Jitoen ('downwind'). A total of thirty-five dwellings, nine
more than at Bikini and Rongerik, were built. As dwellings were
completed, the council allotted them to family units, and seventeen households were formed when several of the former ones became divided.

In part, the increased number of households was a consequence
of the fact that a greater number of dwellings were available and
that the population had increased (through births and individuals
rejoining the community) to over 180. Other factors, however, appear to have been more important in accounting for the increase
in households. The fission of some of the former units reflected alterations in the spheres of influence of some of the headmen. The
newly created households were headed by younger brothers or
maternal nephews of lineage heads, and that several of them established their own domestic units on Kili was an early indication
that they were acquiring some degree of independence from the
traditional figures of authority.

Changes in residential alignments were also a factor in the
emergence of Juda's subordinate, the head of the second ranking
Ijjirik lineage, to a position of greater prominence. At Bikini, he
had been subordinate to Juda for reasons of residence as well as
lineage rank. His and Juda's households were in the same Bikini
village district, and he was second to Juda in district affairs. At
Rongerik, he had emerged as an imporant figure overseeing part of
the communal system. With the Kili resettlement, he acquired
more influence. During the construction of the village, Juda took
the first dwelling completed in Jitaken. Later, Juda's subordinate
was established in Jitoen. As the highest-ranking Ijjirik male in Jitoen and Juda's executive officer, and on the strength of his own
forceful personality, he was soon recognized as its headman. Juda

headed his own Jitaken district and remained chief and magistrate of the entire community.

The tasks of clearing the overgrowth that had engulfed the coconut groves during the years that Kili was uninhabited and the planting of more subsistence crops were left to the Bikinians. The communal system of labor and food allocation that had emerged on Rongerik was initially maintained, but by 1950 it was clear that this stop-gap organization had become ineffective. People were not motivated to improve land that was communally held. Food shortages also posed critical problems. The available food resources on Kili were consumed during the first months of the settlement, and the inexperience of Bikinians at agricultural tasks resulted in failure to establish an adequate subsistence base. Moreover, rough seas frequently prevented the sale of copra and the landing of cargo. By 1950, food shortages were severe. The Bikinians became quite negative about Kili and demoralized and disaffected with their leaders. This situation continued through 1953, despite the administration's attempts to get Bikinians to abandon the communal system and divide their land. Unknown to the administration, the Bikinians had in fact been discussing such a possibility from the outset. They had kept their deliberations to themselves, however, because they did not want to make an overt commitment to Kili—they wanted to be returned to Bikini or to be resettled elsewhere (preferably on an atoll), and they wanted to force the Americans to provide more support for them if they had to remain on Kili.

An even more serious stumbling block to a land division was the problem of deciding how to divide the island. The headmen had already suffered a decline in their authority as Juda's stature rose. They had a vested interest in reestablishing their control over land, but all the old grievances over inequities in landholdings came to the fore. Those who had controlled a disproportionate share of land were intent on perpetuating the disparity. Others demanded a larger share than they had previously enjoyed, and Kili's small size exacerbated everyone's concern over land. Thus discussions of land division only resulted in deadlock.

In their debates over land, the headmen gave little consideration to what groups could be allotted land. Bikini landholding corporations could not have been reconstituted for the division of Kili. Some individuals had belonged to both a corporate lineage and a patricentered corporation whereas others had only belonged to a corporate lineage. Individuals of the latter category would not have agreed to a division of land among the Bikini landholding corporations because such a course of action would have allowed others to have membership in two groups. For a land division to occur, discrete groups of individuals had to be delineated, and reorganization of the community was inevitable. That new groups had to be formed probably became apparent to the Bikinians when eight of the headmen's younger brothers and maternal nephews made known their ambitions to become headmen in their own right. The majority of these were men who had established new households on Kili. They refused to have their subordinate status perpetuated, and a few threatened to leave the community if their ambitions were not realized.

Several events coincided in late 1953 and early 1954 to precipitate an allocation of land. The communal effort had failed completely; people wanted land of their own. The administration explored the possibility of relocating the community again, but the proposed site was rejected as unsuitable. To salvage the Kili settlement, a community development program was initiated to provide instruction in agricultural techniques, increase copra production, and develop a cooperative to manage trading operations. The inauguration of the project made a return to Bikini appear highly unlikely.

At this critical juncture, chief Juda devised a land division scheme. He proposed that each household be allotted land in proportion to the number of its members. Land was to be assigned to each household as a unit; neither lineage membership nor Bikini landholding corporations were considered relevant. Juda approached the headmen informally and individually to argue that a division was necessary because of the people's discontent with the communal system and the likelihood that they would remain on Kili. Several were reluctant, but after some persuasion Juda's plan was accepted.

Juda and the headmen directed the land allotment, but it was accomplished with considerable difficulty. Everyone wanted land near the village; not all sections of the island were of equal quality, and there were disagreements over who would receive what land. Juda negotiated a series of compromises, and with the exception of the taro swamp and village area, Kili was divided among nineteen groups. The term *bamli* 'family' was adopted to refer to the new landholding units.

Not only did Juda's scheme and the compromises negotiated during its implementation accommodate the ambitions of the eight males of junior status who demanded to become headmen in their own right. It also solved the problem of delineating discrete groupings of individuals for the purpose of dividing land. The head of each family unit was recognized as 'head of land' as well as head of his own family corporation. As in the past, each headman had authority over his land and the people who had rights to it. A clear distinction, however, was made between two categories of headmen. The eleven headmen who had controlled Bikini land were still thought of as Bikini headmen in contrast to the eight who had become headmen by reason of the Kili land division. The latter were referred to as Kili headmen.

Like Juda's subordinate, the Jitoen headman, the eight Kili headmen had seized the opportunity of relocation to achieve positions of greater power and influence. The eight were members of four of the five corporate matrilineages at Bikini, and six of them were of high rank within the structure of the lineages. The six ranked immediately below the heads of Bikini corporate lineages; that is, they were either next or second to next in rank and in the line of succession to lineage heads.[3] Thus these six males had the advantage of occupying positions of high rank and stature, and they had advanced their demands to become headmen from positions of strength and influence that were second only to the Bikini headmen in the traditional structure of the community.

The remaining two males who became Kili headmen were of more junior rank in the structure of the lineages, and they achieved their new status by other means. They had been absent from Bikini since Japanese times and were among the few expatriates who had returned to the community on Kili; both had viable alternatives to remaining on Kili if their ambitions were not realized, and as a consequence it appears that they were more aggressive in their demands than other males of comparable rank could have been. One of the two adamantly rejected any affiliation with the head of his lineage and threatened to return to the home atoll of his non-Bikini spouse if his wishes were denied. He had few close kinsmen to call on for support, and his success appears to have been a consequence of his own intransigence. The

second male was of quite junior status, but he had considerable experience as a wage laborer at Kwajalein and felt no insecurity
about returning there if his ambitions were not realized. He was
strongly supported by one of the older men who became a headman on Kili. The two were allied by a number of kin ties; further,
and more important, the elder male had been custodian of the
Bikini land to which the younger man held rights during the latter's absence from the atoll, and he had every reason to presume
that the arrangement would be perpetuated on Kili if the younger
man eventually returned to Kwajalein.[4]

As a consequence of the land division, a major redistribution of
power, influence, and privilege had occurred in the community.
The heads of the former corporate lineages were alienated from
their younger brothers or sisters' sons who had been their immediate heirs and successors within the former system of inheritance and succession, and the latter had become headmen in
their own right with control over land on Kili.

The land division was to have other far-reaching consequences,
but its immediate results were exactly what the administration
had hoped for; each family corporation began to clear its land and
produce copra, and the development project was launched on a
positive course. By mid-1954, encouraging progress had been
made (Riesenberg 1954). The manager of the Kili development
project initiated an imaginative program wherein Bikinians
manufactured handicrafts and other items for export. Profits from
the export trade and copra were substantial. As capital was accumulated, the community's small store was reorganized as a cooperative. Part of the taro swamp was cleared, and the plantings of
taro and other crops were increased. Some Bikinians were optimistic for the first time and indicated a willingness to remain on
Kili if all continued to go well.

In 1956, a second phase of the project was begun. Land was
provided on nearby Jaluit to supplement Kili's resources. The project had some success before typhoons precipitated a number of
reversals in late 1957 and early 1958. Thereafter, the Bikinians
were little better off than they had been during the early days of
the settlement. The quantity of subsistence crops was somewhat
greater than before, but this gain was offset by a continued increase in the population. Bikinians on Kili increased in number
from approximately 180 islanders in 1948 to over 240 in 1958. A

high birth rate remained unchecked during the next decade: by
1963–1964, the community had increased to over 280 people; by
1969, the Bikinians on Kili numbered 300.

During the 1960s, the pressure of the expanding population
heightened the Bikinians' concern over the small size of their Kili
landholdings. Images of Bikini's twenty-six islets were often
evoked, and the islanders recalled the time when they had a
number of land parcels and not just a single plot. The Bikini
headmen were the most outspoken in their discontent with the
small land parcels. Some claimed that they had not received an
equitable share; others regretted ever having agreed to Juda's
scheme. The eight men who became headmen as a consequence of
the Kili land division shared in the general discontent over the
small land parcels, but they were pleased with their recently acquired status as headmen. As one of them expressed it: "Here I
have *kajur* ['power']. At Bikini, only the old headmen had power,
but now I have some land here and have power."

After the land division, the Bikini headmen refused to accept
the eight new headmen as their equals, and they did not recognize
them as legitimate members of the council. The Kili headmen argued, however, that authority over land and people had always
been associated with the right of political representation. Despite
the wishes of the Bikini headmen, a few of the more aggressive Kili
headmen began to attend council meetings. By the mid-1960s, all
of them were regularly participating in its deliberations.

In addition to the creation of a new alignment of power and influence, the land division resulted in major alterations in the relations among kinsmen with reference to rights to land. Rights had
always been inherited and defined within the structural framework of the matrilineages or patricentered corporations. As the
membership of the family corporations was determined largely by
household composition at a particular point in time, and as households included various combinations of consanguineal and affinal
relatives, the former system of defining land rights no longer applied. With the exception of the headman's rights and privileges,
the rights of individuals to the land of their family corporation
were undifferentiated at the time of the land division. No thought
had been given as to how rights would be inherited or how membership in the family units would be determined in the future.

Membership in the family corporations could have continued to be defined by household membership if the units were altered every time changes in residence occurred because of marriage, divorce, or reasons of personal preference. Since the households were always in a state of flux, however, they would not have been efficient criteria for determining land rights over time (for further discussion of this point see Goodenough 1955:71).

The Bikinians have yet to devise a set of criteria for determining family membership or access to land rights over time. They are uncertain as to whether an individual who has married since the land division should become a member of his spouse's unit or have rights to its land. There is no general agreement as to how children resulting from these recent marriages are to be incorporated in the landholding units. Most Bikinians, however, persist in notions derived from the former system of land tenure and believe that spouses should continue to have access to one another's land and that children should have some right to the land of both parents.

In the absence of norms defining membership of family corporations, each headman has assumed the prerogative of determining members himself. This prerogative has provided the headmen with a new source of power, and they have used it to manipulate others and extend their spheres of influence. One headman extended membership in his corporation to his daughter's estranged husband on the condition that he return to his wife, reside with the headman's household, and contribute to its labor force. In some instances, similar pressures have been exerted on recently acquired spouses of members of some family corporations as the headmen have attempted to bring new affinal relatives under their influence. The headmen differ, however, in their decisions about extending membership in their respective units, and there is no overall consistency among them. With each marriage since the land division, the husband and wife have retained membership in their original groups. In some instances these married couples and their children are being counted as members of both the husband's and the wife's units. In other instances, individuals married since 1954 are not considered members of each other's family corporation, but in some cases their children are being included as members of both.

Thus the family corporations are expanding in size and their membership has begun to overlap. Another factor has contributed to this growth and, to a lesser extent, to the overlap of units. Bikinians who had long been absent from the community were not included in the family units for the purpose of the land division. Subsequently, headmen have begun to list as members of their units absent kinsmen and the latter's relatives on other atolls. While this practice has few immediate practical consequences, it does expand the number of people over whom headmen claim to have some influence.

It is not yet possible to ascertain what effect the overlap in membership of family corporations will have. Young islanders who belong to more than one are beginning to utilize their potential land rights, and the Bikinians are much concerned that the overlapping of family membership may create considerable problems. If some criteria for defining membership in the units are not developed, a large number of people could very well claim membership in almost every unit within a few generations.

Initially, the Bikinians were uncertain as to how the rights of headmen were to be inherited within the framework of the family corporations. To them, the major issue was whether members of a headman's family corporation were his only potential heirs or whether a headman's matrilineal kin belonging to other units were to have any claim on his rights. Decisions have been made in establishing a rule for the inheritance of headman rights and succession to the headship of most units.

Six headmen have died since the land division. In four cases, the deceased headmen's corporations included sons but no matrilineal kin; in each case, the headman's eldest son has inherited his father's rights and succeeded him as head of the family corporation. In the fifth case, the deceased headman's corporation included his sons and his sisters' sons. The latter were among those Bikinians who had been living elsewhere since Japanese times, and the headman's eldest son on Kili has succeeded. (The matter may well be disputed by the deceased headman's maternal nephews in the future.) The particulars of the sixth case are exceedingly complex and cannot be described in limited space.[5]

Of the remaining thirteen family corporations, eight include none of the headmen's matrilineal relatives and all include sons of the headmen. The members of these eight units have decided that "sons will follow their fathers on Kili"; that is, sons will inherit the rights of headmen from their fathers and succeed them as heads of the family corporations.

Several factors seem to account for the adoption of a patrilineal rule of succession and inheritance of headman rights by these eight corporations. The precedent for father/son succession and inheritance had been well established at Bikini. Further, the composition of these family units is incompatible with the matrilineal transfer of land rights: headmen's lineage mates are not included as members of their family corporations. Lastly, the precedent established by the family corporations of deceased headmen undoubtedly influenced the decisions made by these eight.

If sons succeed and inherit their fathers' rights as headmen over a number of generations in the family units described above, each will probably evolve into a corporation which will have at its core an agnatically related set of kinsmen who will succeed to the headship of the unit and inherit headman rights. It is not yet possible to discern what constellation of kinsmen will eventually comprise the rest of the membership of each unit. If the Bikinians persist in their notion that children should have access to the land of both parents, it may be that children will inherit membership in the family units of both their parents, and those units thereby evolve into some variety of cognatic descent units with succession to family headships and the inheritance of headman rights being transmitted patrilineally. In any event, precedents, and eventually rules, for delineating membership in the family corporations will probably evolve over time as the members of each unit make decisions about who they will and will not include.

The remaining five family units have not made decisions about the future disposition of headman's rights. Each includes the headman's siblings and a variety of other matrilineal relatives, and all but one also includes one or more of the headman's sons. The designation of an heir presumptive in any of these five corporations would result in disputes or ill feelings between the headman's sons and his lineage mates. For the sake of maintaining harmony, all are avoiding the issue.

Despite these profound changes in the structure of the community's landholding corporations, the traditional clan structure and land tenure system remain important, as became clear when Juda died in 1968. Juda's demise has rekindled the earlier dispute over succession to the chieftainship. The former head of the third and junior ranking Ijjirik lineage died before Juda; his aggressive younger brother has succeeded as head of the lineage and has vigorously renewed his earlier claims that Juda was never the legitimate chief, that past injustices should now be corrected, and that he should succeed because he is of superior generational standing within the framework of the Ijjirik clan. He has also renewed his earlier contention that Bikini land once controlled by the Ijjirik chiefs should never have been alienated from chiefly hands and should be considered under his control. Predictably, the head of the second ranking lineage, who emerged as the head of the Jitoen village district on Kili and is of the same Ijjirik generation as Juda, rejects such claims. As Juda before him, he contends that the head of a senior ranking lineage is always superior in rank to males of junior lineages and that he is thereby Juda's rightful successor.

The Bikinians have elected neither of the claimants as magistrate, and the offices of magistrate and chief became separated when they elected another man to the former position. The new magistrate is the son of Juda's elder brother and is a Bikini headman in his own right. Neither contestant for the chieftainship has supported him; both have their own coterie of followers, and there is evidence that one of them is actively attempting to undermine the magistrate's authority as head of the community.

The administration is either unaware or unconcerned about the dispute over succession to the chieftainship. The new magistrate, however, has the support of the Americans, and officials are dealing with the community through him as they formerly did through Juda. The magistrate is attempting to solidify his own authority by drawing on his status as a Bikini headman, the prestige of being the son of a male of chiefly status, and the support he can garner from administration officials. The community is divided into opposing political camps, and the outcome of the contest over positions of power and influence at the head of the community remains to be determined by the maneuverings of the factions.

EXTERNAL RELATIONS

Relocation ended the Bikinians' isolation, and relationships with three categories of outsiders since 1946 have emerged as distinct: relations with the paramount chief, with the United States government, and with other Marshallese. The history of these relationships is characterized by the Bikinians maneuvering to sever their relation with the paramount chief while attempting to make the Americans assume full responsibility for their welfare. Their apparent success in this venture has affected the Bikinians' relations with other Marshallese.

In precontact times, most of the atolls in the Marshalls were partitioned among the realms of several paramount chiefs. Each was the head of a chiefly lineage; he, his lineage mates, and other kinsmen constituted the top stratum of a privileged social class (see Mason 1947). A paramount chief's power depended on the amount of land and the number of *kajur* 'commoners' under his authority.

As a consequence of its isolation and small population, Bikini was of little interest to the paramount chiefs and remained outside their domains until post-European times. About 1870, a certain Kabua came into power and began to extend his domain in the Ralik chain by conquest. Shortly thereafter, he sent a subordinate to Bikini with a force of men, and the Bikinians were persuaded to acknowledge his sovereignty over them. Thereafter, they were expected to render tribute; Kabua was expected to reciprocate, and it was his obligation to protect them and provide aid in times of disaster.

The German administration recognized the paramount chiefs as the legal owners of the atolls within their respective domains. Subsequently, and with the one exception noted below, the Japanese and the American governments have respected the arrangement. The rights and obligations of the paramount chiefs were defined by the Germans and Japanese. They were guaranteed a percentage of the copra from their lands and were required to pay taxes levied on their subjects. Under the Japanese, the chiefs were also responsible for medical expenses incurred by their subjects. Toward the end of the Japanese era, the contingent of soldiers who established a weather station at Bikini informed the islanders that the rights of the paramount chief had been preempted by the Japanese emperor and the atoll was now his possession; this claim was later to gain some significance. The United States, while recognizing the paramount chiefs as the legitimate owners of their domains, has pursued a laissez-faire policy pertaining to their relations with their subjects. The chiefs have not been held responsible for taxes, and the rights and obligations between chiefs and commoners have been considered a matter of custom and left to the islanders.

Historically, Bikini was never very important to Kabua and his successors. They had their residences at Ailinglablab and other atolls to the south; Bikini's distance from the south, the paucity of its resources, and its small population made it of negligible value, and the chiefs seldom visited the atoll. With its selection for Operation Crossroads, however, it became of increased importance and concern.

The initial relocation of the Bikinians undermined the paramount chief's authority over them, and soon after relocation it became apparent that they were to seize the opportunity to alter completely their relations with him and the Americans. After the paramount chief consented to their relocation, he urged that they be settled on either one of two other atolls within his realm. Both were inhabited and both were rejected by the Bikinians in favor of Rongerik. It fell within the domain of another paramount chief; his permission to resettle the Bikinians there was secured by the Americans, and no further consideration was given to the future relationship between the Bikinians and the two chiefs.

The Bikinians' harrowing experience at Rongerik provided them with the grounds for questioning their relations with their paramount chief. They recalled that it was his responsibility to aid them in time of need, yet they had received no assistance from him. Some Bikinians believed that the Americans, particularly the navy, should become their paramount chief because it had assumed the chief's traditional obligation of providing aid in times of disaster.

Despite the fears of some Bikinians that the paramount chief might respond to such a measure with sorcery, others were convinced by the Americans' display of power and wealth of the advantages of permanent alliance with them. The position of those who wanted the United States to become a surrogate for the chief was strengthened by their experience at Kwajalein. The social milieu in which they found themselves at Kwajalein provided even more impressive evidence of the American's power and additional ideological grounds for challenging their tie with the chief. Some of the Marshallese laborers, for example, questioned the entire traditional social system which divided people into privileged and subservient classes. Such questioning of the paramount chief's status was strengthened by naval officers who encouraged the Bikinians to develop their council as a democratic institution. The islanders heard much about the concepts of democracy and the rights of individuals, and some Americans reportedly ridiculed the idea of hereditary chiefs. Within this context, the paramount chief damaged his own interests by behaving in a high-handed manner and demanding that Bikinians serve as domestics in his household (Mason 1954:494). They resented his demands and learned from the laborers that few paramount chiefs dared to behave in the autocratic manner of former times. They were advised to cast their lot with the Americans and resolved to do so.

The Bikinians implemented their resolution both ideologically and strategically. They developed their rationale for severing ties with the chief by claiming that he had not conquered their atoll by combat, he had not fulfilled his chiefly responsibility for them before or after relocation, and his chieftainship had been terminated when Bikini was claimed for the Japanese emperor during World War II. The Bikinians' selection of Kili for resettlement, which was public land and outside any chief's domain, left the United States as the only agency with clear authority over and responsibility for them.

The negative attitude toward Kili and lack of progress in clearing the land in 1950 was in large part a consequence of the Bikinians' desire to become dependent on the United States and return to Bikini. They reiterated that their understanding had always been that if Bikini was not destroyed by the bomb tests, then their relocation was to be only temporary. After their experience with the Americans, they knew that the United States could easily provide for them. They claimed: "The Navy told us we could live anywhere . . . even on a sand island. The Navy would take care of us, we were told, until we went back to Bikini" (Drucker 1950:11).

The Bikinians also had come to believe that they had suffered a great injustice and that the United States was morally obligated to them. They concluded that it would not only be advantageous but also morally proper that the Americans provide for them. Their desire to be provided for contributed to their unwillingness to adjust to Kili; their lack of effort contributed to their discomfort; and their discomfort reinforced their negative attitude toward Kili and their desire to receive aid from the United States. In their dealings with Americans, the Bikinians elaborated on the undesirable features of Kili and extolled the virtues of Bikini; the atoll came to be remembered as "an oceanic land of milk and honey" where want and discomfort were unknown (Drucker 1950). Because of the confinement imposed by the heavy surf during winter months, Kili came to be referred to as a 'calaboose', and children were taught to repeat *Kili enana* 'Kili, it is bad' for the benefit of all visitors.

Bikinians' fears and their dissatisfaction with Kili were exacerbated in 1951 as civilian personnel replaced naval administrators in the transference of the Trust Territory from the Navy Department to the Department of the Interior. They were opposed to the new administrators' attempts to persuade them to develop Kili. Their refusal to divide the land was one strategy for managing their relations with the Americans, especially while their relationship to the paramount chief remained unresolved. The chief was trying to persuade the administration to give him title to Kili as compensation for his loss of Bikini. When an agreement to this effect was drawn up, the Bikinians unanimously rejected it, countering with repeated requests for formal severance of their relationship with the chief (Mason 1954:494). Moreover, when the community did divide the land, the fact was concealed for as long as possible lest the administration conclude that the people were committed to permanent residence on Kili (Tobin 1954).

The eclipse of the paramount chief's authority in the community corresponded to an increase in Juda's authority and influence. Although he was unprepared for his leadership role in the relocated community at the outset, his experience as community spokesman on Rongerik, Kwajalein, and Kili and his representation of the community in the Marshall Islands Congress beginning in 1950 resulted in his personal maturation and esteem from the community. As his initial indecision gave way to skill and self-confidence, his influence in the community and his influence with American administrators grew and reinforced one another. Evidence of his influence is seen in his successful negotiation of the land division and the overwhelming majority of votes he received in every election held on Kili. He also played a crucial role in the administration's development project when it was implemented in 1954. He lent his support to the program, coordinated the efforts of the project manager with the council, and encouraged people to make a go of it on Kili. The project's initial success and the optimism it generated among some Bikinians were in large part a consequence of Juda's influence. Juda continued his support for the project when it entered its second phase in 1956 and Japanese prewar landholdings on nearby Jaluit Atoll were made available to the Bikinians. The administration planned that colonists from Kili could develop the Jaluit lands and enlarge the community's resource base. A sheltered anchorage was available at Jaluit, and a 50-foot vessel was provided so the Bikinians could make the short run to Kili during calms in the winter seas. The Bikinians were enthusiastic about the vessel, but they did not view the prospect of living next to the people of Jaluit with favor and did not want to divide their community to form a colony. Further, they feared that the Jaluit people would view it as an encroachment upon their territory.

The people's attitude changed when an agreement over Bikini, Kili, and the Jaluit lands was concluded. After much negotiation, the Bikinians granted the United States indefinite use rights of Bikini in exchange for monetary compensation and full and legal use rights to Kili and the Jaluit lands. Compensation amounted to an initial $25,000 payment and a $300,000 trust fund yielding semiannual interest payments of about $5,000. The paramount chief was not included in the settlement, and the Bikinians interpreted this as American confirmation of their goal to terminate the chief's claim on their allegiance and land. In their view, a major objective had been achieved; their strategy of dealing with the chief and the United States had been successful. The administration attempted to conclude a separate agreement with the chief, but he refused and has never wavered in his claim that he has been unjustly deprived of his land and subjects.

The Bikinians viewed the financial settlement as payment for their Bikini land, and it was determined that every individual who held land rights at Bikini was entitled to share in its distribution by the council. Every Bikinian on Kili received an equal sum, and those who were resident elsewhere were allotted smaller shares. Bikinians who had left Bikini before the community's relocation were counted among the absentees along with their non-Bikini spouses and children. A similar pattern of distribution was devised for the interest payments (Kiste 1968:335–343; Mason 1958).

Since the financial settlement was viewed as compensation for their loss of Bikini land, it was further determined that Bikini headmen were entitled to a larger share of the money than others because they had always received a disproportionately large share of copra receipts gained from the land. Accordingly, every Bikinian gave a small portion of his share of both the lump-sum payment and each interest payment to the head of the corporate lineage to which he had belonged at Bikini. Children born after relocation were counted as members of their mother's lineage, just as they would have been at Bikini, and paid a share of their money to the lineage head. In addition, siblings who had also held land with their own father separate from the lineage land paid their father because he had been the authority over their patricentered corporation. In short, every Bikinian paid a portion of the money he received in the settlement to the heads of the landholding corporations to which he had belonged at Bikini.

The distribution of the financial settlement and the payment of special shares to Bikini headmen were based on the system of inheritance and succession which had prevailed at Bikini, not on the new land tenure scheme and the patterns of inheritance and succession that were emerging on Kili. The Bikinians were clearly working with two systems of land rights—the family system devised on Kili and the traditional one at Bikini. The financial settlement had come to represent Bikini land; its distribution, including the payments to Bikini headmen, symbolized those networks of social relations and groups which had been delineated by the traditional system (see chapter 6).

The agreement with the United States also had a positive effect on the Bikinians' morale and attitude. The council selected colonists for the Jaluit lands who were rotated between Kili and Jaluit. Colonists varied in number from twenty to twenty-five at any one time. Development of the Jaluit lands began under the supervision of the project manager. Bikini men manned their vessel under the direction of an experienced Marshallese captain hired by the administration. The vessel sailed between the Jaluit colony and Kili, and occasional voyages were made to Majuro and other atolls. The overall progress of the entire project caused optimism among all observers, and it appeared that the Bikinians might adjust to their new environment.

The optimism ended with the typhoons of late 1957 and early 1958. Both the colony and the vessel were destroyed. Trees were severely damaged on Kili, the cooperative suffered heavy losses, seawater washed into the taro swamp, and most other agricultural development was undone. What gains had been made in increasing the quantity of subsistence crops were offset by the ever-expanding population.

The project was abandoned by the administration as its efforts were diverted to atolls which had suffered even greater devastation from the storms. Relief foods were given the Bikinians immediately after the disaster, but supplies still ran short or could not be gotten ashore because of rough seas. In mid-1958, the Bikinians were placed on a relief food program, and when cargo could be landed, they were provided with substantial quantities of rice and flour at three-month intervals over the next year and a half. The resources of their once flourishing cooperative were largely depleted, however, and it began to fail.

By 1961, most of Kili's trees had recovered, but no substantial effort had been made to reestablish other crops. The Bikinians had clearly come to prefer food subsidies over expending their energies on agricultural endeavors; from their experiences, they were quite certain that the Americans could provide for their every want if they could only be persuaded to do so.

Efforts at creating a dependency relationship upon the United States were renewed. Dwellings on Kili were in very bad repair by the early 1960s. Islanders had repaired their homes with thatch, but they made repeated requests to be supplied with more durable imported building materials. The administration encouraged them to make their own purchases with their interest payments. The Bikinians countered that the money was compensation for their loss of Bikini and it was unfair to ask them to spend it on the necessities of life on Kili. They argued that it was the responsibility of the United States to provide housing on Kili because it was responsible for their relocation.

The administration once again considered moving the Bikinians from Kili, and the possibility was discussed with them more than once. On one occasion, Juda quite eloquently stated the political stance the Bikinians had evolved over the years. He made it clear that they wished to remain free of the paramount chief and in their opinion the United States was morally obligated to assume responsibility for their welfare:[6]

I would like to give you some history of Kili Island. We were moved here by the government 10 years ago. It was not the place we wanted to go to but the government decided that we should live here. In all these years we have tried to live here but there are many things that have come up which make it very difficult for us to make a living here. Today is a good example of what has happened in the past 10 years; it is too rough to work copra, so we are unable to sell our copra and buy food. It doesn't matter how long a ship waits off of Kili, if it is rough it is rough and we cannot get our copra to the ship or bring in food. Our group of people here is getting larger every year and is increasing every year. It is difficult to take care of these people and the island is too small for them to live on. In a little while there will not be enough copra on the island to feed all the people.

The relocation of the Kili people is up to the Government. We would like to return to Bikini which is our home but realize that we cannot do this as the Atomic Energy Commission is using it for exploding of bombs. We also know that Bikini plays a big part in world affairs and we realize this importance. The government moved us and not our paramount chief. If the paramount chief had moved us then it would be up to him to find another place for us. We want to move to government land and will not move to lands owned by the paramount chief.

Bikini is larger than Kili and we had plenty of land and a big lagoon. The government moved us; therefore, it is up to the government to find us a new place which is larger than Kili and better for the people.

Now the government knows our condition, it is therefore up to the government to find us a place.

No adequate site was found, and within the year the Bikinians were told that they would remain on Kili.

The 1960s brought no relief from the discomforts the islanders have always known on Kili. The unchecked birth rate only exacerbated matters. Even before relocation, few individuals would journey to Kwajalein to spend short periods as wage laborers, but as the Bikinians grew more discouraged with their lot on Kili, people were motivated to leave the island in increasing numbers to find employment at Kwajalein. Some remained but a few months; others spent much more time at the military base. Some traveled to Majuro to complain, and their frequent appearances at the district offices became known as the "usual Kili recreation."

Those working on Kwajalein, which had become an elaborate

missile research installation, observed not only American technology but also an affluent American life-style. Bikinians saw the Americans' stores, buildings, gadgetry, swimming pools, golf courses, and, for those working as domestics, their home life. These experiences profoundly reinforced Bikinians' thinking and political strategy. The range of imported goods and the Bikinians' taste for them was broadened. Their belief that the Americans could easily provide for them was strengthened. This served to deepen discontent over their situation on Kili and to enhance their belief that they had been done a great injustice. These beliefs were intensified by developments related to their interest payments, which they used mainly to buy trade goods. First, as their population increased, individual shares of the interest payments decreased. Second, the people of Kwajalein received $750,000 for a lease on land occupied by the military. A sum of $950,000 was paid to the people of Rongelab as compensation for damages to health and discomfort caused by radioactive fallout from one of the Bikini tests. The Bikinians compared these cash settlements with their own and became further convinced of the injustice of their own treatment by the government. Their position—that the United States was responsible for their situation and its remedies —was made concrete in continued demands for additional financial compensation and their removal from Kili.

By 1968, the Bikinians' strategies appeared to have borne fruit. In response to continued pressure, the administration had Bikini evaluated for possible human habitation by the Atomic Energy Commission (AEC). In August 1968, the president of the United States announced that with the exception of a few small islets, most of Bikini Atoll was judged safe for human occupation and Bikinians would be returned (U.S. Department of State 1968:304).

The Bikinians once again received the attention of the world news media, and reporters traveled to Kili and Bikini to gather materials that appeared in magazines and newspapers around the globe.[7] In 1969, a rehabilitation program for Bikini was begun at an eventual cost of over $3 million. Scrub vegetation which had overgrown Bikini's islets, and massive amounts of debris from nuclear tests, were cleared by the AEC and military agencies. A party of about thirty Bikini men was employed to begin replanting the atoll under the supervision of American agriculturists. After its initial cleanup phase, the project was turned over to the Trust Ter-

ritory. The main body of the community remained on Kili, however, because the newly planted palms would require eight or
more years to mature. As an interim measure to alleviate the islanders' discomfort, funds amounting to about $100,000 were
provided for new housing materials on Kili.

The Bikinians responded to their apparent successes by pressing
claims for further concessions. They rejected the administration's
assumption that they would provide the labor for the housing project on Kili. The Bikinians demanded to be paid for their labor,
and the administration agreed. In December 1969, the community
petitioned the high commissioner of the Trust Territory, albeit un-
successfully, for compensation for damages to Bikini and for discomforts suffered in the amount of $100 million. During the sum-
mer of 1970, Bikinians contacted a law firm on Guam to explore
the advantages of legal counsel. At the same time, Bikinians working on Bikini went on strike, claiming inadequate working conditions and an inadequate job of clearing debris by the AEC. The
strike was settled, but the details are not available. Meanwhile,
having failed to establish a working relationship with the Guam
law firm, Bikinians obtained the assistance of the Micronesian
Legal Services Corporation, an agency funded by the Office of
Economic Opportunity, in order to press their claims for compensation and to expedite work on Bikini.

Predictably, once it appeared that the Bikinians would be returning home, the paramount chief tried to reassert his authority
over them. He gathered supporters among Bikinians living on
other atolls. These were almost entirely people (and their descendants) who had been absent from the community since before its
initial relocation, and many were the offspring of Bikinians who
had gone to serve in the paramount chief's residence at Ailinglablab decades ago. As Bikinians on Kili remained adamant vis-à-
vis the chief, further confrontations appeared inevitable.

The Bikinians also began to reevaluate Kili. Some talked of remaining on Kili to exploit the coconut groves; others, especially
young people, were questioning the desirability of life on a remote
atoll. The entire community, however, believed that they should
retain Kili and the Jaluit lands as well as having Bikini returned to
them.

The Bikinians' experiences since relocation have resulted in
substantial changes in their relations with other Marshallese.

Their negative self-image as backward, unsophisticated people before relocation was reinforced by their early contacts on Kwajalein and Jaluit and by their desire to maintain the integrity and isolation of their community. This influenced their selection of both Rongerik and Kili as relocation sites; as both were uninhabited, they eliminated the necessity of extensive interaction with other Marshallese, among whom the Bikinians were stigmatized and made to feel uncomfortable. An example of the stigmatization of Bikinians was an incident on Kwajalein when two Marshallese laborers involved with Bikini women were advised by their fellows not to marry such backward people. By the late 1960s, however, Bikinians' own self-image had changed, as had the regard in which they came to be held by other Marshallese.

The change in the Bikinians' relations with other Marshallese is due in large part to the opportunities for acquiring experience on other islands during their relocations and resettlement on Kili. As early as the 1950s, and in addition to the few Bikinians who traveled to Kwajalein to work as laborers, some went to Majuro for medical treatment and meetings of the Marshall Islands Congress and the Association of Marshallese Churches. Bikinians who worked as colonists on Jaluit in the late 1950s had frequent contact with the islanders of that atoll. By the 1960s, the increased flow of Bikinians to Kwajalein gave them even more experience with others, and many Bikinians became less hesitant to leave Kili to find work, attend meetings, and seek medical care and schooling. Since a few Bikini families had established residences on Majuro and Kwajalein, migrants had the security of kin and friends with whom to stay or gather.

The Bikinians' success in dealing with the paramount chief and the Americans has also been important in the change in their relations with other Marshallese. Establishing their independence from the paramount chief has won them the admiration of other islanders. The success of the Bikinians' dealings with the American administration has vastly increased their own self-confidence and sophistication and has also earned them the respect of other Marshallese. Thus the present ease with which Bikinians interact with other Marshallese is in part an outcome of their relations with the paramount chief and the administration.

Indicative of the changing quality of Bikinians' relations with other Marshallese is the increasing frequency of intermarriage between them. Before relocation, nine of the Bikinians living on other atolls had non-Bikini spouses. By the mid-1960s, this number had risen to twenty-four. The number of in-married spouses on Kili had increased over pre-relocation times, but only slightly, since Kili was no more attractive to other Marshallese than it was to Bikinians. Furthermore, non-Bikini spouses came from a larger number of atolls than in former times.

Another indication of the Bikinians' changing relations with others is the nature of recent immigration to Kili. Given the prospect of a return to Bikini, the possibility of retaining Kili and the Jaluit lands, and the Bikinians' present reputation, Bikini clansmen from other atolls have begun to join the community on Kili. The island's population increased from three hundred to four hundred between 1969 and 1972 as long-lost kinsmen, their non-Bikini spouses, and their children and grandchildren "returned" to the community. Because of the potential advantages involved, islanders who had formerly defined themselves as members of other atoll communities are now calling themselves Bikinians.

CONCLUSIONS

As the foregoing analysis reveals, the modifications of the social organization of the Bikini community and its altered relations with the Americans and the paramount chief may be attributed to competition over the distribution of power, influence, privilege, and control of valued resources. The motivations to gain advantage in the pursuit of these goals were traditionally focused on land and were not new with relocation. Rather, they are an integral facet of Marshallese culture and society and account for certain events of the past: intracommunity conflicts at Bikini and interatoll warfare in the Marshalls.

For the Bikinians, relocation was just another set of circumstances, albeit unique and extraordinary, that could be employed in the pursuit of traditional ends. In reference to the internal organization of the community, the necessity of reestablishing residences and allocating land on a new island provided certain males with a new opportunity. Those who occupied positions of advantage within the traditional structure of the community or were able to advance their ambitions by other means were now able to challenge the traditional authority structure and precipitate an allocation of land which restructured the entire community. The adoption of a patrilineal rule for determining the inheritance of the land rights of headmen and succession to the status of head of the majority of the family corporations on Kili represents the transformation of what was formerly an alternative to matriliny into a prevailing norm. This transformation may largely be attributed to the incompatibility of matrilineal principles with the bilateral structure of the family corporations. Moreover, adoption of the patrilineal rule was undoubtedly facilitated by the precedent set by the high incidence of father to son inheritance and succession before relocation. In any event, patrilineal inheritance and succession for headmen and the headmen's assumption of the prerogative to determine the membership of their family corporations represent a conscious rejection of the matrilineal principles upon which the traditional organization of the community was largely based.

The status of magistrate as head of the community and the recognition and support that Americans have given the occupants of that office have created a new form of political authority that is employed in the competition over power and influence. Both Juda and his successor have used the office to strengthen their own position in the community. The office has become established as a political prize. It and the status of traditional chief have become separated, and it seems certain that the office of magistrate will emerge as the more powerful and thus more sought after position in the community.

While the organization of the community on Kili differs from that of Bikini, the traditional lineage organization and its authority structure remain a viable part of the Bikinians' culture and is given tangible expression twice annually with the distribution of the income realized from the trust fund. As a consequence, the Bikinians have two conflicting models for determining relations among kinsmen and the organization of their community. While there is some conflict of interest between the Bikini and Kili headmen, islanders compartmentalize and relegate each of the models to separate spheres of reality; the new social order determines affairs on Kili, and the traditional one pertains to Bikini.

With regard to relations with figures of power outside their community, the Bikinians realized from the outset of their relocations that their subordinate status to the paramount chief offered few. if any, advantages. They recognized that they could only achieve their objectives—returning to Bikini and gratifying the wants they had acquired since relocation—by having the Americans assume responsibility for their welfare. This required severing relations with the paramount chief and manipulating the Americans into becoming his surrogate. In essence, relations between the Bikinians and the Americans have consisted of a long series of negotiations, and the Bikinians have used continual complaints of irreparable discomfort, neglect, and injustice and a reinterpretation of their own history as tactics to justify their actions and desires. These complaints have established the remedies they insist Americans must provide. Their history has been reworked to justify their rejection of the paramount chief. Portions of their revised history as well as certain undeniable facts regarding their relocations have served to place the moral responsibility for their plight firmly upon the shoulders of the Americans. By determining the locus of responsibility for their situation, the Bikinians' total history has become a political ideology that defines both themselves as victims and their current relations with their former chief and the colonial power in a single interpretive framework. The very formulation of this framework, and the fact that it has been at least partially accepted by the administration, reflects the increased sophistication of the Bikinians in their dealings with Americans. Their recent actions—the firm stances taken vis-à-vis the administration, the workers' strike at Bikini, the acquisition of legal counsel—attest that they have shed their reputation as a backward people. And the changes in their relations with other Marshallese over the past quarter century are further evidence of their growing self-confidence and sophistication in dealing with the world outside their own community.

EPILOGUE

As this volume goes to press, another tragic episode in the history of the Bikinians is beginning to unfold. It now appears that the radiological survey conducted at Bikini in the late 1960s, which resulted in the American decision to rehabilitate the atoll for its former inhabitants, was far from adequate. In August 1975, a bulletin issued by the Energy Research and Development Administration (an agency succeeding the AEC) reported that a recent survey of Bikini has determined that radiation levels on some islets, including the largest one scheduled for resettlement, are much higher than previously indicated. A population residing on those islets for any length of time would be exposed to radiation levels higher than U.S. federal standards permit (*Micronesian Independent* 1975a). The advisability of resettling the atoll is now very much in doubt, and its actual condition is far from certain. In October 1975, the Bikinians, through their legal counsels, filed a complaint in the Federal District Court in Honolulu requesting a thorough radiological investigation of Bikini and medical examinations for all those who have worked on the atoll over the last several years (*Micronesian Independent* 1975b).

## NOTES

The field research on which this chapter is based was conducted on Kili Island in 1963 and 1964 and again in 1969. The initial research was supported by the Project for the Comparative Study of Change and Stability in Displaced Communities in the Pacific, directed by Homer G. Barnett. I also gratefully acknowledge the support of the Office for International Projects, University of Minnesota, for field research conducted in 1969.

1. Only 161 islanders were actually resident at Bikini and were moved to Rongerik in 1946; 9 others were temporarily absent from the community for reasons of employment, hospitalization, or education.
2. For the sake of brevity, the Ijjirik, Makaoliej, and Rinamu descent units are referred to as clans in this chapter. Elsewhere, and more appropriately, I have called them subclans because each was only part of a larger clan in the Marshalls (Kiste 1974:37–38).
3. Four of the Kili headmen were the *only* younger brothers of the heads of three of the five Bikini corporate lineages, and two were the *only* maternal nephews of a fourth lineage head who was without younger brothers. The only brother of the head of the fifth Bikini corporate lineage had long been absent from the community and was not present to represent his own interests.
4. The elder of the two males was proved correct. Not long after the Kili land division, the younger man returned to Kwajalein and left the Kili land his family unit had been allotted in the care of his elder kinsman. The latter had in effect gained control of two land parcels on Kili.
5. The details of the new landholding system and the separate family corporations are presented at some length in Kiste (1974:155–173).
6. Juda's statement was reported in a memorandum to the district administrator, Marshalls, from the assistant district administrator, Marshalls, dated 16 April 1961 (MacKenzie 1961). As he spoke in 1961, Juda was incorrect in assuming that nuclear tests were still being conducted at Bikini. The last tests

occurred there in 1958. Further, at the time of Juda's speech the Bikinians had resided on Kili for almost thirteen years and not ten.

7. See N. Wollaston's "Return to Bikini," *Saturday Evening Post*, 16 November 1968; Carl Mydans' "Return to Bikini," *Life*, 18 October 1968; "Tomorrow and Tomorrow," *Newsweek*, 26 August 1968; and "Home to Bikini," *Time*, 23 August 1968.

# 6

# MAKING SENSE:
# A STUDY OF
# A BANABAN MEETING

*Martin G. Silverman*

What we want is *not terms that avoid ambiguity,* but *terms that clearly reveal the strategic spots at which ambiguities necessarily arise.*
—Kenneth Burke, *A Grammar of Motives*

## INTRODUCTION

The dialectic of action is the dialectic of form and content. This is, as I understand it, one of the central messages of *The Savage Mind* (Lévi-Strauss 1966). The engaging thing about form and content is how they can shift position and thus become transformed—form becoming content for other form (e.g., the "structure of a kinship system" is shown to be a special case of the "general structure of systems," or some aspects of the "structure of a kinship system" are shown to be harmonious with the "general structure of systems," or the "structure of a kinship system" is shown to be impossible given the "general structure of systems"), content becoming form to other content (e.g., the "special case" is used to interpret another "subspecial case," which interpretation might not, incidentally, fit, presenting people with all sorts of problems to work out). And on it goes, not randomly but not completely predictably either since, among other things, form can both order and open a door to content (some of it uninvited) and content (to mix the metaphor) can twist form around itself. One man's form can be another man's content and thus they literally "talk past one another." Form and content, structuring and becoming structured—most of our basic theoretical problems are implicit in the pair.

But not only *our* theoretical problems.

Even the firmest believer in the untrammeled freedom of the human intellect would probably concede that being in a situation of resettlement is something that a people, somehow, cannot fail to note. Precisely how they note it we are not in a position to predict; and we are not in a position to predict precisely how those things that we take to be problematic are or are not problematic to the local community. There are new faces and new places, perhaps new subordinations and new equalities; there is new work to be done and new food to eat.

If we are not in a position to predict how a resettled community might note its situation, neither are those being resettled. Not even with the most careful planning, site surveys, political and economic arrangements made with governments and future neighbors can people predict what vagaries of environment, of colonial governments, of neighboring peoples, or, for that matter, of their own social relationships might confront them.

We do, however, find that a resettled community may confront the unpredictable as a community. It happens often enough to be significant that these people encounter problems, events, or situations that demand decisive action as a community and that integral to the decisions is the necessity of clarifying for themselves who they are in order to determine their position. The very unpredictabilities inherent in resettlement (but not, of course, only in resettlement) make such decisions and their implications for identity likely, if not inevitable. Such decisions may be as mundane as that of determining how land clearing will be organized by the Gilbertese resettled on Sidney Island (see chapter 8) or as dramatic as the bitter debate over whether the Kapinga relocated on Ponape should divide their village land for quitclaim to a few families or maintain it for 'all Kapinga people', the definition of which was necessarily at issue (see chapter 3). In such cases, the definition of the situation, prerequisite to deciding on a course of action, demands a more or less conscious attempt at some point to define who and what the actors and their relations to each other are, have been, and might be.

It is not only in my own ethnographic case, then, that one finds events in which people are trying to unscramble some of the things which have happened and are happening to them and to chart courses for future action. I am not suggesting that people necessarily sit down and say to one another that they will do this, but rather that doing this is known to happen. There is an attempt to get some important things together in order to clarify the dimensions of action. To use Kenneth Burke's terms, definitions of the situation and strategies toward the situation are constructed (Burke 1957).[1] And this is an event not (or at least not primarily) of the recesses of the individual mind but of the processes of social action.

Clifford Geertz addresses some of these problems in *The Social History of an Indonesian Town*, which has been a major inspiration for the present effort. Speaking of Modjokuto, he says (1965:5):

> Especially the years after the Revolution (that is, after 1940), when the whirl of innovation engulfed the entire scene, were marked by an increasing ambiguity of cultural categories coupled with a growing irregularity of social behavior. And from this double observation comes the central theoretical argument, also double, of our study: namely, (1) that ordered social change involves the attainment by the members of the population concerned of novel conceptions of the sorts of individuals and the sorts of groups (and the nature of the relations among such individuals and groups) that comprise their immediate social world; and (2) that such an attainment of conceptual form depends in turn upon the emergence of institutions through whose very operation the necessary categorizations can be developed and stabilized.

Later on, writing of an election in Modjokuto, Geertz states (1965:205):

> Seen as a crystallizing field, rather than as a collection of functionally interrelated roles, the election involved a clash of classificatory principles, of categories, embodied in individuals and in factions, and its outcome was an adjustment, as much conceptual as political, of those principles and categories to one another in a given case. In one of its aspects (though in one only) the election was a symbolic, even an intellectual process. It gave specific meaning to general ideas by filling them with concrete persons, groups, institutions, issues, and events. Despite the tension it caused, the election was considered by even those who lost to have been a good thing. As they said, it 'pulled things taut, put them in straight lines *(kentjeng).*' Selecting from a set of abstract "grammatical" possibilities by means of concrete "phonetic" process, it made potential order actual.

In this chapter I present some aspects of the analysis of an event which, as it was occurring, became a symbol for a set of conceptions. The event occurred on Rambi Island, Fiji (map 7). Since 1945, Rambi has been the home of the people of Ocean Island, which is part of the British Gilbert and Ellice Islands Colony. The indigenous name of Ocean Island is Banaba, and thus its people are known as Banabans. Ocean Island is a "phosphate island." Mining activities since 1900 have progressively converted the island into a kind of mining settlement, and the Banabans into a minority in their homeland. Their lands were literally being exported away for the benefit of others. During World War II the British government purchased Rambi with invested Banaban phosphate royalties. When the war ended, the Banabas agreed to go to Rambi on a trial basis and in 1947 decided to stay, while maintaining their rights to Ocean Island lands on which the mining of phosphate continues to this day. The population of Rambi is now about two thousand.

The event which is my major concern was a ten-hour community meeting in November 1964 during which, among other things, the Banabans were trying to make sense out of their past and present and give direction to their future. This chapter is an exploration of how they did it, although only a minute portion of the meeting can be analyzed in detail. I hope to demonstrate that a significant part of this "how" consisted in the setting up of levels of form-content relations among (1) various actors and actions; (2) the delineation of the terms and relations of a problematic situation, which included the problem of how to transform that situation; (3) the building of a structure for that situation; (4) certain symbols; and (5) the course of action taken by the meeting.

The event with which I am concerned differs from Geertz's Indonesian election in several respects. But there is a significant class of dramatic events distinguished (for present purposes) by the combination of the following related characteristics: one of the businesses of the day is the coordinating of cultural categories; an action outcome is envisaged; the cultural terrain being covered is wide and its categories are multitudinous; many relationships (of a number of orders) are problematic; the levels of form-content articulations are several and complex; the process is a social process which may have a form of its own, or a form may be under construction.

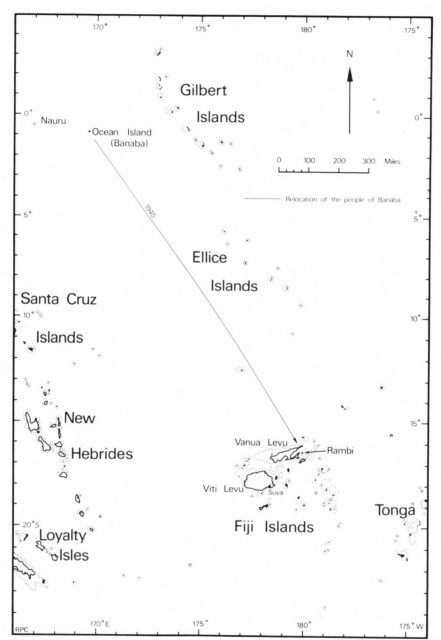

Map 7.   Relocation from Ocean Island to Rambi.

Geertz (1965:203) makes a related point when he speaks of

> the paradox of the role of culture—or, if you will, systems of ideas—in social activity. No actual event (or sequence of events) can be predicted from them, and no actual event (or sequence of events) can be explained without them. . . . Culture orders action not by determining it but by providing the forms in terms of which it determines itself.

This chapter is concerned, then, with a concrete process that may be typical of resettled communities. It is a process whereby people order knowledge, hopes, experiences, and feelings and make sense out of them. By making sense out of them, they are giving form to them, and it is through their cultural categories that form is created. Thus, in giving form, the Rambi Islanders are using their categories in a social action and pointing toward a social action; and in so doing they are creating forms that are not quite the same as before.

The analysis begins with the historical background of the problems with which the Rambi Islanders had to deal in the meeting. This discussion is followed by a presentation of the methodology used to analyze the meeting; then part of the meeting is described and analyzed. The chapter concludes with an analysis of the meeting itself as a symbol.

HISTORICAL PROLOGUE

My recent book on the Banabans (Silverman 1971) details many aspects of their history and culture. Here I shall mention again some things which are most relevant to the meeting.[2]

One of the Banabans' major public concerns is getting a just recognition of their rights to the Ocean Island phosphate and the great financial consequences of that recognition. The phosphate is mined by the British Phosphate Commissioners (BPC), which has a mining monopoly, the interests of which are held by the British, Australian, and New Zealand governments. Speaking in the ethnographic present, the Banabans have no rights to determine how much phosphate is mined, what the price per ton (which is well below market price) should be, or what amount of money they or anyone else should get from the whole enterprise. In the early phosphate days, the mining company (a private predecessor of the BPC) dealt with individual landowners, but later it began to negotiate with the Banabans on a collective basis over the leasing of land. This was important in the development of the people's political consciousness.[3] In a dispute during 1927–1931, the BPC wanted more land but the Banabans refused its offer. In 1928 the British colonial government passed an ordinance enabling itself, in effect, to force mining on lands and to arbitrate compensation when necessary "in the public interest." This it did, and the Banabans lost even more control over their land—and Ocean Island land has been and still is, among other things, one of the most powerful symbols in Banaban culture.

The Ocean Island phosphate is a critical factor in the economy of the Gilbert and Ellice Islands Colony in a variety of ways— through royalties, taxes, and wages, for example. Recently the BPC was paying out about ten times as much money to Gilbert and Ellice Islands Colony revenue as it did to the Banabans. The Banabans bitterly resent this. By the Banaban adviser's estimate, half the Banabans' cash income in 1964 was coming from the phosphate in one form or another; the other half was coming mainly from copra production. Pertinent both for the Banabans and the Gilbert and Ellice Islands Colony is the fact that the phosphate is a dwindling resource. Local estimates varied on when mining and thus the money from royalties to the Banabans would cease; some spoke of about twenty years. Uncertainty as to when phosphate operations would end may explain why there is no real sense of urgency on Rambi regarding the economic development urged by government officials. Uncertainty is one of the dominant qualities of the day.

On Rambi an island council was set up as the instrument of local government. It has eight members, two elected by each of the four villages, which are named for those on Ocean Island. The councillors elect their own chairman.[4] According to a system agreed to by the Banabans in 1947, yearly estimates of the expenditure of various island funds for the next year are prepared and sent to the Fiji government for approval. The council nominates five of its members to the Banaban Funds Trust Board, which is charged with preparing the estimates. The estimates must then be approved by the council as a whole and then by the government. The Banaban adviser, a European, is chairman of the trust board.

The position of the Banaban adviser is a difficult one. Although he is responsible to the Fiji government, he is paid indirectly from

Banaban funds and the council is consulted on his appointment. The original government conception of the office was probably something of a combination of district officer and development officer. The Banabans, however, have come to define his role as that of their advocate. He is in the classic position of the man in the middle.

The advocacy is for the related issues of securing just rights to the phosphate and the recognition of the autonomy of Rambi. Collective political action vis-à-vis the phosphate has its chronological roots in confrontations with the phosphate company and the government while the people were still on Ocean Island. It has its cultural roots in the centrality of land in the Banaban symbolic system. As far as one can tell, political action on Ocean Island was designed more to achieve recognition of individual rights (to land and thus to money) than to achieve something material for the collectivity as a collectivity. The situation on Rambi crystallized the individual/collectivity contrast into a dilemma for which the Banabans were culturally unprepared. The reasons why they were unprepared and why it was a dilemma are interlocked.

On Ocean Island the government and the BPC had provided equipment and services the Banabans valued.[5] These things were part of what modern life means and what Rambi lacked. If they wanted to recreate the accoutrements of modern life on Rambi, the Banabans had to do it for themselves. Since these conveniences had been provided on Ocean Island, the islanders had not had to contemplate the institutionalization of their newly developed values. Rambi, an undeveloped island, was a new situation. Individual action could not provide transportation, electricity, and new buildings; some kind of collective action was necessary. This articulated the "individual/collectivity problem."

In the Banaban view, the financial proceeds from the phosphate are the output of Banaban lands, and Banaban lands are owned individually, not collectively. The right and proper fate of the money is thus to go to individuals. The money equals land equation is shared by the government, which (not uncommonly in colonial structures) put itself in the position of arbiter of Banaban custom. The government for a long time insisted that from the payments for surface rights individuals should receive only the interest from the invested capital, since the lands had to be maintained for future generations and could not be alienated by an individual's own will. Since the government asserted that there was no real indigenous custom regarding the ownership of undersurface mining rights, whatever money the people derive from undersurface mining should be paid to the community as a community, ideally to be used for community purposes. Whether the people have a right to such proceeds or whether they are given by the grace of the crown is ambiguous. There was also the usual asserted fear that individuals would fritter away large sums of money if they got them and that the continuity of large individual payments would reduce the people's industriousness and make them dependent on the BPC. Hence most of the income the Banabans receive from the phosphate is not in the form of individual payments but payments to the Banaban community (which, on Rambi, includes resident non-Banabans).

The Banabans have drawn on information from Nauru to form their own case. Nauru, to the west of Ocean Island, is now independent, but at the time of my research it was an Australian-administered trusteeship. Nauru is also a phosphate island; for a long time it was worked by the same phosphate company that worked Ocean Island. The Nauruans are reported to receive large individual phosphate returns and to live a comfortable modernized life—and they organized a successful campaign of confrontation with the Australian government. The Banabans see their own basic situation as similar to that of the Nauruans, compare what they get with what the Nauruans get, and have been taking action on the Nauruan model.

The individual/collectivity problem is thus situated in the way the Banabans' returns from the phosphate are paid out. Another closely related dimension of the problem is that while the people recognize that some form of collective action is necessary to get their due, the island council has had a hard time establishing its legitimacy as a decision-making entity.[6] Furthermore, the "development" activities conducted by local authorities are considered far from adequate by local people.

Since most proposals for developing Rambi involve money, and since the Banabans believe they are being cheated out of money that is rightfully theirs but could be obtained if the right course of action were found,[7] a number of issues are inextricably intertwined for most people: the phosphate issue in general; what to do with the funds in hand; how to get more of the money which belongs to the people; how to organize and govern the new island and secure its autonomy. The money from Ocean Island lands— all of it—already belongs to the Banabans but is being fraudulently held and used by others, given the premise that money equals land. It follows that Rambi is properly autonomous because it was purchased with invested phosphate royalties, which derive from Ocean Island lands, which are owned by Banabans. Given these cultural premises, each issue logically implies the others. All the issues involve Ocean Island, which by the same logic is a symbol that can give form to the individual's sense of himself, his kinsmen (past, present, and future), village and community, morality, wealth, and the relationship of the community to the outside world.

To take one aspect salient to the meeting: a person is a Banaban by having Banaban blood or being adopted by a Banaban. Being adopted by a Banaban entails receiving some Ocean Island land from him. When the two are contrasted, blood symbolizes kinship identity and land symbolizes kinship code for conduct (see Schneider 1968). Blood and land structure both kinship and nationality. In the kinds of political discourse most closely related to the matters we are considering here, "Banabans" and "landowners" are used interchangeably.[8]

All these issues were articulated during the meeting to be analyzed. Three matters were frequently cited as central to the meeting: whether certain individual money payments should be made; whether the Banaban adviser should be retained or dismissed; and the alleged unequal treatment (by the Banaban adviser among others) of employees who had damaged certain facilities. The third issue merged into others which developed.

In 1937, while still on Ocean Island, the Banabans were granted annuities of £8 per adult and £4 per child and a yearly individual bonus based on size of landholdings (up to a certain limit).[9] In the 1947 agreement, when the Banabans voted to stay on Rambi, the continuation of this system was mentioned. The Rambi Island Council, however, for some years decided not to distribute either the annuity or the bonus, but rather to use the money for building cement block houses and other projects.

The question of distributing the annuity and bonus was part of the controversy which culminated in the calling of the meeting by the council. The meeting was a *maungatabu*, a community meeting the decisions of which were binding. Those who were instrumental in calling it, operating through Methodist church channels, wanted the annuity and bonus reinstated. The adviser had said that this was not a wise course. His position was that additional grants—for example, matching contributions for building roads and houses—had been given by the BPC after their officials had seen that money was being used for development and after the Banabans had agreed it would not be distributed. The land on Rambi, the adviser and others argued, was poorly developed and money should be used for improvements before that money stopped. The trust board prepared the 1965 estimates without the individual distribution. The full council refused to approve the estimates and said the annuity should be included. The adviser said the full council had no authority to amend the estimates. An impasse had been reached.

The council had recently approved the renewal of the adviser's contract, but various people remained dissatisfied with him, not only because of his opposition to the distribution of the annuity. Some councillors and others had circulated reports that he was acting in a high-handed manner by ordering rather than advising and by not showing proper respect for the council. Favoritism was also alleged in his relations with employees. Moreover, he had incurred the ire of a number of influential Methodists because of his attempts to disentangle the use of trust board money and paid time for activities which seemed to be more in the service of the Methodist church (which has the largest membership) and the supporters of the council chairman than of the community as a whole. There were those who at times saw the whole matter as a contest between the adviser and the chairman. The chairman had suggested that of the money the Banabans received collectively from the phosphate, two-thirds should be distributed among the people and one-third kept for public projects. Matters had recently come to a head betweeen the two over a specific issue which many believed was behind the machinations leading to the meeting.

The chairman is an important figure in the church and has been the most prominent Banaban leader since before the resettlement. He has impressive religious, descent, kinship, political, economic, and age credentials. He also has what one might term reality credentials through his involvement in various disputes with the government and the BPC at least since the 1927–1931 affair. He is generally assumed to know more about the intricacies and deceits of the phosphate history than anyone else. Some question his knowledge, and some are also opposed to him precisely because of his credentials. But for many, the chairman's information on crucial political and economic matters is nearly all the information they have. He has the authenticity of one who can say "I was there." He also has important rhetorical credentials. This analysis will try to specify some of them.

I cannot give the details of how the positions of various people on the issues of the money and the adviser were interpreted by others before and after the meeting. Often—and this is certainly not a pattern unique to the Banabans—a person claims to be motivated by principle and accuses the opposition of being motivated by kinship, descent, religion, village, friendship, self-interest, personal grudges, factional alliances, backroom deals, or ignorance.

A brief discussion is in order on Rambi's employment pattern, since it was deeply involved in what came up in the meeting. A preliminary analysis of 1965 census figures shows that over 80 percent of the full-time or part-time salary or wage earners on the island are males between eighteen and sixty years of age. Of males between eighteen and sixty, roughly 32 percent hold full-time jobs, 21 percent hold alternate-week jobs, and 46 percent are copra cutters, gardeners, and fishermen only, except a few who are small-scale entrepreneurs or mission personnel. The number of households directly affected by the salary and wage pattern is greater than these figures might indicate. In roughly one-third of the census households there is no regularly resident member with such employment. Two-thirds of the remaining census households have at least one person on alternate-week employment but no person employed full-time.[10]

The largest employer on the island is the combination of the Rambi Island Council and the trust board. The cooperative society and the Fiji government account for most of the rest of the jobs. The alternate-week pattern spreads wage labor around more widely than would be the case if all jobs were full-time. Most of the council and board jobs with which I am familiar have to do with public works and public services: house and road construction, equipment operation and maintenance (including transportation), and office work. All the board members have relatively high-paying jobs. Many of the other jobs pay no more per week than what an enterprising copra cutter could earn in a good week. But there are not always good weeks, and if there were more enterprising copra cutters, the enterprising copra cutter might earn less.

What is also at issue, however, is the cultural construction of "work" and "working." Unfortunately, I did no systematic cultural analysis of this domain while in the field, so the following discussion is after the fact and impressionistic. At one level, "work" includes wage earning, copra cutting, gardening, fishing, and the like. In some contexts, however, "workers" means public employees, in contrast with those who are primarily identified with work on land and sea. "Workers" are generally considered to be far better off than others, and those in skilled higher positions have a certain prestige. Many of the latter are centered at the island's "capital" at Nuku, where they occupy concrete block houses that go along with their jobs.

The chairman and others have often made statements such as, "We did not come to Rambi to be workers on the land." At one council meeting, the chairman said, "We did not come here for work, but for freedom on our money." The chairman avers that one reason why the resettlement proposal was approved in the first place was that the people, once resettled in Fiji, would be closer to the high commissioner for the Western Pacific, who was at that time the same person as the governor of Fiji. The high commissioner for the Western Pacific is the next step up the colonial bureaucratic ladder from the resident commissioner of the Gilbert and Ellice Islands Colony. Rambi was to be 'the land of grievance stating'. Working on the land carries a negative value in the sense that grubbing about in the bush for enough money to get by on is a compulsory way of life. This should not be the case, and may not have been expected to be the case. In this regard one must point out that on Ocean Island many Banabans and now Rambi-resident Gilbertese were BPC employees in positions of some skill and responsibility. What they are doing now is considered an inferior activity.

In the meeting it soon became apparent that discussions of the employment and public works patterns (which became fused) were being used to articulate a number of dilemmas.

## METHODOLOGY

We need terms to sort out what the Banabans were sorting out in the meeting and how they went about it. To this end I have modified and added to some of Burke's (1962) terminology in a manner that seems suited to the ethnography of the meeting.

Trying to sort out something means that something is acknowledged as problematic. The kinds of things that can be problematic are, of course, numerous: some feature of reality (what did the adviser do?); the implications of doing something (what will happen if the annuity is distributed?); how to bring about a change (how can the adviser be persuaded to distribute the annuity?); and so forth.

We begin with the *character* of the problematic situation[11]—a state of affairs that seems to point outward to the larger community in that doing something about it arises as a community problem. Doing may involve thinking about the situation, discussing it, or cooperatively enacting measures to change it. Examples in the Rambi situation are poverty, lack of control over Banaban funds, the breakdown in relations between adviser and chairman. The character of the problematic situation is something that people may be arguing about. In other words, the character of the problematic situation (like everything else) may itself be problematic.

Second is the *subject* of the problematic situation: the who or the what responsible for the situation being in the shape that it is— for example, the government, the people, the adviser, the council, the workers.

Third is the *object:* the who or the what on the receiving end— for example, the people, old people, members of a religious group, specific individuals.

Fourth is the *instrument* (the "how"): the intermediary, if any, between subject and object—for example, the council between the people as subject and the people as object or the adviser between outside authority and the people.

Fifth is the *means* (the "how to"): the device through which the situation is being made problematic—for example, using funds for public works projects rather than distributing them to the people.

The definition of the problematic situation requires that a transformation of it is in some fashion part of the situation. The same pentad can be mapped onto the question of transformation: its character (perhaps getting more money), its subject (the people or the council), its object (say, the people again), its instrument (perhaps the council), and its means (distributing the annuity). I use the term "delineating" to denote the making of all these connections.

Part of the delineating process is establishing what gets assigned to which term of the pentad. In the course of delineation, people may adopt various stances. For example, they may name (it is the board that is the trouble), contradict (it is not the board but the council), query (what does the board do?), or make problematic (how is it that distributing the annuity would bring in less money from the outside?).

This delineating activity is not, of course, a purely abstract exercise removed from people's actual experiences. It is, in part, the nature of their experience that people are attempting to work out through delineating. In clarifying for themselves the adviser-council relation during the meeting, people pointed out specific actions in the past which they considered to be typical of that relationship, such as the adviser's stopping the council visit to the governor and the council's decision not to distribute the annuity. The outcome of the delineation of this relationship is a recognizable structure of the relationship. Once worked out, the adviser-council relationship gives *structural form* to historical incidents (incidents which touch a variety of people in a variety of ways). The incidents cited become instances of a general pattern—that is, the historical incidents give *tangible content* to the structural form. Then that form and its historical incidents (contents) become *tangible forms* themselves and, thus, may be tangible content for other forms. The adviser-council relation and its historical contents, for example, interpreted as one in which the council is victimized by the adviser, becomes the tangible content of a higher-level structural form—the relation of subject victimizing object or the relation subject (victimizer)–object (victim). Thus a form may become content for another form. Integral to this transformation is the use of the "special case," where one thing is presented as a special case of another. For example, the adviser's stopping the council from visiting the governor is a special case of the pattern of action of the adviser victimizing the council.

The terrain covered in the delineating process (the number of subjects, objects, and so forth) is extensive. The delineation becomes complex if something of a comprehensive order is to be approximated. In delineating the problematic situation we observe the sorting out of a number of terms and the relations between them (how the adviser relates to the people, how the government relates to the people). "Something of a comprehensive order" in this case would be characterizing both those relations, at a higher

level, as relations of victimization. Victimization gives structural
form to those relations as the relations give tangible content to victimization. Victimization as now defined becomes a tangible
form, and thus tangible content for other forms at even higher
levels.[12]

This structure which interrelates terms and relations of the
problematic situation is itself given form by certain symbols at a
higher level. I use the term "symbol" to mean a vehicle for conceptions, a vehicle people may use to connect the unknown with
the known (see Turner 1970:48). Certain symbols in Rambi Island
culture are extremely powerful in their ability to order wide domains of objects, relationships, and actions. Land, freedom, the
person, and progress are examples. Thus the symbol "freedom"
can give structural form to other forms. For example, victimization becomes a special case of the absence of freedom, just as the
adviser's stopping the visit becomes a special case of victimization. Since the problematic nature of the situation is construed in
terms of such symbols, the symbols themselves are made tangible
and thus are structured in a conjunction.[13]

An example of such a conjunction would be as follows: "The
annuity and bonus are the money of your lands." The annuity and
the bonus may become tangible content for many things other
than "your lands," and "lands" may give structural form to many
things other than the annuity and the bonus. The conjunction is a
structuring, and "land" is made tangible in that structuring.

By speaking of a conjunction in this way, I do not mean to imply that one set of meanings (those of "lands") and another set of
meanings (those of "the annuity") are simply added to one another, nor that a structure is formed simply by putting together the
meanings of the higher-level symbol which are harmonious with
the meanings of the lower-level symbol. I am suggesting, rather,
that symbols such as "lands" and "the annuity" (or any symbols)
have *ranges* of possible meanings. In the conjunction, constrained
by the context or other ways, certain features of each symbol become stressed such that the meanings which may be given to each
can be organized in a hierarchical form. In the "special case,"
categories are juxtaposed and structured in such a manner that
contextually stressed features of some categories can be shown to
be concretizations (actualizations, instances) of contextually
stressed features of other categories (patterns, structures, symbols).[14]

To our list of delineation we must now add "concrete actors and actions." For we are dealing with a case in which "something happens in the end." At the end of the meeting an action was taken (voting was part of it), and that action gave structural form to what had been built up before (the links through certain symbols). What had been built up before it gave tangible content to the action, the action becoming a tangible form itself (and, of course, tangible content for other forms after the meeting).

The form of the final action, however, did not come magically out of a script book. That form itself became the problematic situation, and a number of levels of form-content articulation occurred within it. What happened in the end was giving form to what had been mapped out for what might happen in the end, which itself was giving form to what had been mapped out during the previous phase of the meeting, and so on.

Recall that this is not a model designed for a case where everything follows from everything else as night follows day. Various "stances" apply to the establishment of form-content relations, too. If an action is presented as a special case of a pattern of action, for example, somebody may say it is not a special case at all. If a means of transformation (distributing the annuity) is being linked to a general form (freedom), it may be made problematic whether distributing the annuity and freedom are really related in that fashion. This may be a product of different constructions of "distributing the annuity," different constructions of "freedom," or a host of other factors.

Two final and related points. First, various interventions in the meeting were related more or less directly to setting out the terms of the problematic situation or the terms of the transformation, but the distinction is an analytic one. This has an important implication both theoretically and ethnographically. The extent to which various constructions of reality can be implemented by actual behavior must constantly be borne in mind. In fact, I would suggest that the losing side in the meeting might have fared better had they borne this in mind.

Second, some segments of the meeting were developing a structure for the problematic situation and its transformation; this structure was one of *victimization*. Victimization by some outside authority is an understood feature of the Banabans' situation. Here the victimization is turned inward as well which, among other things, makes the structure more actable or transformable.

That structure also allows for the introjection of accumulated grievances, personal and collective. The very issues made this likely and (to speak with risk) it may have its own compelling form which itself articulates the various levels of form-content relations: name the crime (the problematic situation—not having enough rightful money); name the victim (the object—the people) and the victimizer (the subject—the workers, the adviser); name the weapon (the means—using the money for work); consider redress; invoke specific evidence and precedent (concrete actions out of the past); construe, direct, and legitimize the case in terms of powerful symbols; deliberate and take the appropriate action.[15]

## THE MEETING

Before going on to an annotated extract from my minutes of the meeting, a strong caveat must be introduced. Initially, I estimated about two hundred people in the island's central meeting hall at Nuka and many others listening outside. It was a ten-hour meeting. As people began to speak more rapidly with emotion or speech was indistinct to me from distant parts of the hall, my knowledge of the local language failed me. I can vouch neither for the completeness nor the accuracy of my minutes. Even in the quotations cited below, half the information may have been lost. I can only represent them as my best effort, hope that the outcome of the exercise justifies the use of such inadequate data, and carry on as if the problem did not exist. In these extracts a series of dots (. . .) indicates the omission of material because of lack of understanding, the desire to save space, or the speaker's own stylistic indication that the sentence was incomplete. This may be an important rhetorical device in itself, signaling a common understanding and allowing the listener to fill in the gap. Sometimes I fill in the gaps myself in brackets; remarks in brackets are my own observations. Remarks in parentheses are paraphrases of things said.

A brief note on the setting: the meeting hall itself is a modern form of the *maneaba*, a meetinghouse with important traditional meanings (see Silverman 1971). A meeting in it is serious business. The Union Jack adorned the front of the hall. The councillors, scribe, and adviser were literally on stage at the front, "the people" thus being seated apart. Some internal divisions were manifest in who was sitting with whom. Now, then, to my annotated extracts:

1. *Adviser:* We ask for the truth. The adviser has no power; the path [to the government] is from the council to the governor [of Fiji]. These years are our chance for success.

2. *Chairman:* The Tabwewa [one of the four villages] councillors raised the question of the meeting to me. They wanted to meet with the people [literally, 'the inhabitants of the surface of the land'] regarding the desire for the annuity, and whether your adviser will retire from among you. [The chairman then alluded to two other issues which he said were settled: a specific dispute between himself and the adviser and the handling of the case of a worker who had damaged some equipment, which the chairman said was settled by vote of the board.]

3. *Adviser:* I have worked for three years and asked regarding an additional three years. Talk to the governor if you want me to retire. [Notes unclear on a statement about the nature of the bonus, the distribution of which he was told would create difficulties with the BPC.] The annuity was stopped long ago by the council. My work on this was just advice.

4. *Chairman:* The annuity and the bonus are the money of your lands. In the 1930s the government agreed that they should be distributed. The money is your money. Here we used it for work. The old men said there was no money. I said: "We will use it for work, for one or two years. If you want it we will give it. If you want the money to work, then it will work. If you want the money, then you will get it."

5. *A Councillor:* The chairman said we would talk about the annuity, not the bonus. First, with regard to the houses. We asked the BPC for money. The [BPC] commissioners came and saw that we were suffering [in difficulty, poor]. We talked about the road, schools, and other things. We met in the house of the adviser. The BPC board has to meet, the commissioners said. After a few months the word came: they agreed. Also, with regard to the adviser: he has done nothing wrong.

6. *Another Councillor:* I am unhappy too about not having an annuity. I am also unhappy about the distribution of two-thirds of the money. The adviser said: "The distribution of the annuity may prevent the arrival of big things from the outside."

We want the bank statement [showing Banaban funds]. Maybe things are hidden there. I am the one who goes outside. If I say that two-thirds will be distributed, they have me. [This councillor is also the Banaban representative on Ocean Island. On his return to Rambi he was said to have circulated reports of having learned that £14 million was due to the people in accumulated interest from a certain fund.]

7. *Adviser:* The answer of the government regarding the money is

well known. [A man interjects from the floor, "That isn't worth anything." Speaker C rises and says he wants to talk, but the adviser says:
"The chairman first."]

8. *Chairman:* Freedom under the money of Banaba. Who is the person in whose hands it has been received? [People from the floor
answer, "No one!"] With regard to our accord on the annuity, we
cannot know how much money will go to each person. It is the people's money. The annuity is the only path open.

The company wanted to give a good price in the 1930s, but the
government objected. [This refers to the 1927–1931 land dispute. The
chairman had said at other times that the BPC had been on the point
of making an offer closer to Banaban demands, but the resident commissioner had intervened against the Banabans.] If you do not complain all the time . . . [you get nothing]. If you want the money to be
divided, it will be divided.

Regarding the adviser: there should be one person [European] here
who is not paid by the government. The first adviser (who came with
the people in 1945) said: "In Fiji we can state our grievances better.
The land of grievance stating is here. Here, we want to see the governor, and the adviser stops us. . . . Yes, we did agree to the extension of
the adviser's contract, but the decision is your decision."

9. D [one of the oldest Banaban men]: We need money for the old
people. The worker eats the money.

10. C [a middle-aged man who works for the cooperative socie-
ty]: . . . We are free under the money. The council held it for our dwellings. Regarding the adviser: did he behave badly in the council? If
one or two hold the money, that is bad.

11. E [a middle-aged copra cutter]: The money is held for the houses.
But there are copra cutters. You [workers] live on the money of the
community. There are two ways for making a living: copra cutting
and wage earning. If I ask for work, will I get it? You say that there
are £14 million. We are *filled to overflowing* with your words! Distribute the annuity!

I stand for the adviser. It is the board [that is the trouble]. What is
the value of the walkie-talkie, people say? [A set of walkie-talkies had
been purchased which many people thought was of dubious value.]
[From the floor: "Finish it!" F, a young man, says: "I support him."]

12. G [a young man employed by the Fiji government]: Whose error
is the error? It is yours [the people's]; the election was your election.
Their errors are your errors.

13. *Chairman:* Perhaps we are finished stating our opinions. Write
down whether you want the annuity or not. If there is an objection
from the government, we will have a record. As for the adviser, we
are free after three years.

Let us start with the chairman's first remarks (statement 2). He begins in a low key by referring to the question of "whether your adviser will retire from among you" rather than saying "whether the adviser will be sacked." These words are appropriate for an elder and attempt to give an aura of neutrality, although the chairman's true position was generally known. He names a problematic situation as involving the annuity and the adviser and indicates two other issues as nonproblematic (issues which it might have been assumed would prejudice him against the adviser). The softness, however, might be rhetorically double-edged, the "you" and the "your" suggesting the proper decision-making entity.

The adviser (statement 1) had situated the question vis-à-vis truth and success, indicating (statements 1 and 3) that the council (and its relationship to the governor), not he (and perhaps not this meeting either), was the significant instrument. The council, not he, was the subject of the problematic situation in stopping the annuity, and the distribution of the bonus might not be a means of positively transforming the situation but of increasing its problematic nature. He introduced the government and the BPC as elements which had to be sorted out.

Indeed, in general terms or through concrete incidents, the major categories of secular agents which superintend the Banabans' fate were named quite early in the meeting and, as the meeting progressed, most of their possible combinations appeared. The functions of one vis-à-vis the other were often problematic, with people trying to sort out what they are and to indicate (when they were the subjects of victimization) how they might be transformed.

Historical incidents are retrieved to justify the position being taken, but in the process they become part of something larger than those incidents taken separately. Just as the discussion of transforming the problematic situation relates the present to the future, the citation of these incidents relates the present to the past.

In statement 4, the chairman gives form to the elements of his own interventions when he says that "the annuity and the bonus are the money of your lands." The nature of the construction was adumbrated earlier. The bonus and annuity are given structural form by, and give tangible content to, land. The annuity and the bonus are also money, a necessary means to gain European goods and services (this is made more explicit in later statements). Land thus enters as a resouce and as something that belongs to these people. A frame is set for structuring the problematic situation and its transformation—especially as the government itself had on Ocean Island approved the distribution of this money.

The chairman begins to develop a structure in terms which are critical—the contrast between using the money (of your lands) "for work" and giving it to "you," the people. Two elements must be elaborated here: the "work" element and the "you" element.

People had said that if the annuity were distributed, it would have to come out of the money *presently* used for work (the two-thirds–one-third plan). But the contrast is more powerful than the fact might imply. The organization of the various activities involving construction and labor into the category "the work" is a cultural organization itself. There is no a priori reason why the category should exist in this form. Nor is the suggested contrast with "the people," which explicitly recurred several times during the meeting, an a priori necessity. This structuring suggested the evaluation placed on it, if not the concrete course of action necessary to transform it. Quite clearly, things for and to the people are superior to things that are not. What is disputed between some and problematic to others, however, is what "things for and to the people" are.

Given the historical incident about stopping the money in the first place, it is ambiguous whether the council was the subject of the problematic situation in that it stopped the annuity or whether the council was the instrument of the people who were the subject. This was played out later. But the people were the object (in being denied the annuity), and the means was using the money for work rather than distributing it to them.

The chairman elaborates further. In statement 2 he spoke of the councillors wanting to meet with "the people." In statement 4 he speaks of "your lands" and says that the money is "your money." The emphasis now is on "you": "If you want it . . . if you want the money to work . . . if you want the money, then you will get it." The "you" refers to the Banaban people in general (not the Rambi people in general, which includes non-Banaban residents) and to the people at the meeting (later specified as the landowners). In some way (later made problematic and elaborated), the people at the meeting are a tangible form which "is" the Banaban people and, furthermore, they can make a decision one way or another.

What is now being set up is this: the *objects* of the problematic situation (the people) can transform it by becoming the *subjects* of the transformation (telling the council what to do). The council (the position of which was unspecified earlier) then becomes the *instrument*; the *means* is then giving the money to the people rather than to the work; the *object* (as the subject) of the transformation is the people themselves. The now more highly structured problematic situation (not having more of the money of their lands) links to a set of relations which is both a *delineation of reality* (what the people can do, what the council can do, what happened in the past) and a *proposal*. This is achieved by means of at least three transformations. First is the transformation of the present or possible subject, the council, into an instrument. The council's position is ambiguous in any case, since whether it was acting as a subject or instrument by holding onto the money is itself problematic. By transforming the council into instrument (having it distribute the money), the ambiguity is resolved for the future. Second is the transformation of the object (the people) into subject (the final arbiters). Third is the transformation of the means into their antithesis: money for work versus distributing the annuity. The bonus and annuity are tangible content for "the money of your lands" and the land (money) belongs to the people, who can decide what to do with it, and so forth.

This definition of the situation is contradicted and made problematic by the two councillors (statements 5 and 6). Using the money for work rather than distributing it to the people has already been a means of transformation (rather than an element to be transformed): more money in the form of matching funds had been granted by the BPC, and an understanding had already been reached that the money would not to be distributed (who reached the understanding is not made explicit here and became problematic later). Thus the people could not become the subject of the transformation and, continuing as now, more money might be forthcoming in the future. Note that the first councillor addressed the question of the people's "suffering, poverty," but not the question of the people's lands. The second councillor began by placing himself on the horns of a dilemma.

The chairman (statement 8) gives further form to the problematic situation and its transformation. He asserts "freedom under the money of Banaba," thus linking the whole affair to freedom, with a stress on freedom as something which belongs to the community (which can make a decision) and the money as something which belongs to the individual.[16] Then he performs one of his feats of rhetorical brilliance which is conceded even by his opponents and which contrasts with his low-key beginning: "Who is the person in whose hands it has been received?" Having stated or closely implied some of the most general symbols and meanings, having raised the discussion to a high order of generality, he then takes the whole thing down to the actual person.

The chairman has done a number of things here. First, "the person" (closely linked to "freedom") is in context a symbol with a special character: its tangible content is the actor himself. And the actor himself becomes form for the problematic elements which had become tangible in that—literally—he holds or does not hold them in his hands. In the succeeding statements (to be described), the chairman deals with many relationships in a manner so persuasive as to be mesmerizing. What bears underscoring is how the chairman, through the progressive transformations of levels of form and content, set the whole thing up.

In the development of the discussion, the statement "in whose hands" has a special role. The challenge to the chairman's earlier construction was made on the grounds of an agreement having been made, the fact that more money had been received, and the likelihood of even more money being received. But here the chairman is asking which individuals have the money as opposed, say, to having seen the products of the money in houses or roads. The individual/collectivity problem is thus brought into the argument. To project to future interventions, no one has "it" in "his hands," even though some are receiving money from wages, because the "it" here is the money of Banaba which can be construed to be *all* the money distributed in freedom, unmediated by things like employment. That these two constructions are possible should not be surprising. It is one of the ways a persuasive argument is built up. Furthermore, one must "complain all the time" to get more, and the demand for the annuity could be interpreted as a special case of complaining against the existing situation.

The chairman broached another matter which was portentous in terms of the meeting and events after it. Observe closely the paragraph in statement 8 regarding the adviser. Until this point, although making a definite construction of the situation, the chairman had actually avoided coming out directly for the annuity or directly against the adviser. Here he enters the fray in an interesting way. In our terms, it is ambiguous whether the adviser is the subject or the instrument of the problematic situation defined by the people's and the council's relationship to outside authority. The adviser stopped the people from going to the governor, but this is placed in a more generalized context: "There should be one person here who is not paid by the government." Note how this ambiguity could structure a number of antiadviser positions— being against the man but not the role, being against the role but not the man, or being against both.

The delineation of the resident European's position is given structural form by something that might have had great resonance at least because the chairman had made statements like it before. Alluding to a statement of the first adviser (and thus an adviser can say something like this, just as the government could approve the annuity), the chairman pointed out: "In Fiji we can state our grievances better. The land of grievance stating is here."

In his statement the chairman defines a relationship between the presence of an adviser paid indirectly by Banaban monies (the adviser is actually responsible to the Fiji government) and Rambi as a place where grievances can be stated. This relationship is not the only one possible between these elements, nor is it the only relationship in which either the adviser or the stating of grievances can be major components. The relationship as stated does, however, have its place in the meeting as a further structuring and clarification of the problematic situation in the following manner: the relationship posited by the chairman is a structuring of two other relationships—(1) Banaban–European (government) and (2) Ocean Island–Rambi. Banaban nationality is, in an important sense, a product of the Ocean Island–Rambi relationship; therefore, one of the Banabans' most critical problems is that of arriving at a consensus on that relationship. The meanings of both Ocean Island and Rambi can be given structural form by the symbol of Ocean Island land, since Rambi was purchased with phosphate royalties derived from that land. Certain things in one place are seen in terms of certain things in the other place. Rambi things affect Ocean Island things and vice versa. Implicitly here and explicitly elsewhere, Ocean Island and Rambi relate in what we might call a "transitive metonym."[17]

The question remains: What are the "certain things" that affect each other implied by the chairman's statement? Ocean Island affects Rambi in that phosphate royalties, which purchased Rambi, maintain Rambi public works projects and pay its workers. But land also symbolizes in Banaban kinship (which is closely tied to Banaban nationality) its code for conduct. Land is what connects the Banaban–government and Ocean Island–Rambi relationships in a single structure. The actions suggested by "grievance stating" involve phosphate, which is something in Ocean Island land. Rambi is therefore related to Ocean Island (affecting Ocean Island things) in terms of action.

The revised status of a resident European is a special case of this structuring. A European responsible to the Banabans alone, rather than to the government, becomes the advocate of Banabans, the instrument of Banaban action. Having thus structured the problematic situation and having suggested an instrument for its transformation, the chairman brings the transformation back to the people: "The decision is your decision." He has made a construction in which action is inherently possible.

By the time we reach statement 9, the chairman has given the meeting a frame. When the people begin to speak, the money to the people/money to the work contrast begins to be elaborated.

One of the oldest men on the island (statement 9) rose and said, "We need money for the old people. The worker eats the money." The wage earners were using up the money which rightfully should go to the people. The contrast money to work/money to the people as a means was now transformed into workers/old people as subject/object. The workers were, in effect, victimizing the people; just as it had been suggested by the chairman that the Banaban adviser (in role or in person) had wronged the council or the people (statement 8), the people may have been wronged by the council (statement 4) and by various outside authorities (statements 6, 7, 8). In statement 10, after reaffirming the reality of situating the matter vis-à-vis freedom, speaker C asks whether some on the council (including the adviser) may be holding the money and thus, following the theme as I decipher it, be victimizing the people. The issue brought up by the old man was put more forcefully by speaker E (who has a way of putting things forcefully) in statement 11, when he baldly stated that there were two modes of livelihood, copra cutting and wage earning; the workers "live on the money of the community," and not everyone might be able to get work.

One may say that speaker D was presenting himself as representing the interests of the old people whereas E was presenting himself as representing the interests of the copra cutter. Moreover, one may say they were relating the position and experience of old people and copra cutters to both the problematic situation and the meeting itself. It seemed to me that in their highly charged remarks they were doing this, and something more, in a very critical way. The chairman had retrieved the historical incident of the old men saying there was no money (statement 4), and here was an old man saying old men had no money and stating the reason. In his giving of form he was presenting himself as tangible form. Similarly, the copra cutter injected another element into the problematic situation—copra cutters. The elaboration of the money to people/money to work contrast as a structure proceeded by constituting classes of victims (old people, copra cutters) who were there at the meeting and victimizers (workers) who were also there. The elements of the structure were not the invisible behind the visible but the made-visible organizing other meanings.

Although the frame given the meeting by the chairman is elaborated by the people, there are counterproposals and contradictions of that frame as well. Speaker E contradicts the delineation of the adviser as subject of the victimization: it is, rather, the board. And Speaker G (statement 13) contradicts the indictment of the board by suggesting that, through the election of their councillors, the people are the subject as well as the object of their own dilemma. Perhaps as a response to this, the chairman then calls for a vote, which will be a record in case the government objects. The chairman might have been hedging his bets on whether the people are totally free on the matter after all, and (with no massive movement yet against the adviser?) he notes that the people will be "free" after the three years of the adviser's contract are up.

The counterargument regarding money to work/money to the people, introduced in statement 5, was elaborated later. It was proposed that the workers had been serving the community as a whole and as individuals. Here the alleged means of victimization are depicted as a means of transformation—that is, the transformation of the island into a more modern, comfortable place to live and work.

The statements of speakers E and G—that the board or the polity responsible for placing the board in office are the subjects of the victimization—both imply that the councillors (from whom the board is selected) are vulnerable. The chairman, indeed, began with a kind of public confession that something had gone awry with the council. Later he suggested that the younger generation could carry the burden which the elder generation (his own) was having trouble with. But the councillors were workers, too. One woman articulated part of the problem later when she stated, "You councillors are landowners [too]." A councillor who spoke little articulated his own dilemma and the general dilemma:

> There is the problem of the council and the board. We didn't want the bonus and annuity because of the money from outside. There is the question of freedom under the money. Some people complained about the annuity. They said: "You do not like it because you are on salary." No. We look at the future. From the side of the board, I think: hold it. From the side of the council: give it. About the adviser, there is trouble knowing what is right. We agreed for three years. If I say I like him, you will say it is because he feeds me. We agreed for three years.

Another councillor, also an office worker, articulated a similar dilemma but resolved it:

> I have worked with the adviser for three years. He is helpful in my work, yes. But for the people ['the land'], no. If he stays you will be unfortunate. The adviser is not worthwhile. . . . He is good in the office. But we still have not seen the money on the ground. We just eat cassava. We will not be fortunate quickly. . . . There is a side that he cannot deal with. . . . For the Banaban race. There is just money for housing and the road. Our group just salts cassava. If we are fortunate, we will all be fortunate; if we have misfortune, we will all have misfortune. A Banaban who does not work is not fortunate.

The councillors were put on the defensive and were vulnerable on several counts. They had in fact voted for years to withhold the annuity and bonus. They were also receiving salaries from the money being withheld. Yet at the same time no one could deny that the policy of "money for work" had in fact resulted in some houses and a road where there had been no road before—tangible contents for the argument adduced in statement 5. Nor could one deny that the adviser was in part responsible for those results. The adviser as victimizer was not, then, all that unambiguous.

The dilemma is resolved by the position that although the adviser had accomplished good things, those accomplishments were beside the point. This is a definite construction of the situation: of the range of desirable things to get done, one was singled out, and by this singling out, an ordering was achieved.

By saying "we still have not seen the money on the ground," the councillor meant in individual hands. (Thus the collectivity is invoked—we, the people, our group, the Banaban race—but it is defined in this context as an aggregate of equal individuals.) Later in the meeting a man contrasted "work for the money" and "work on the ground" (the latter in the sense of the works projects in which the adviser was so personally as well as ideologically involved), stating that the former was more important than the latter. In the closing segment (analyzed below), the issue was stated as that between getting more money and keeping the adviser. Here may have been a way in which the problem of "the work" was resolved in a manner which was actable in terms of the process of the meeting. The "work" pattern was rehabilitated, as it were, by stressing some of its features to construe two kinds of work: one was oriented to getting more money from the phosphate and into individual hands; the other was selective in its benefits if not downright wasteful from the people's point of view. The island's senior officialdom (including councillors) is properly involved in "working for the money" (as contrasted with giving "money for the work"), and thus their own positions are not essentially threatened.

The "carry on as now" position was essentially a general restatement of the people as victims, outside authority as victimizer, the means of victimization as money being denied by outside authority, the problematic situation as not having enough money, and local authorities (the adviser, councillors) as the means of transformation.

But when the matter was raised in the meeting, even those arguing for the "carry on as now" position could not guarantee that the additional money would be distributed. Some, indeed, were inclined toward a "development centralism" and (more forcefully outside the meeting) argued that position. There are fundamental differences in the conceptions of how the community should go about conducting its business and what that business is. Those differences are not, however, in the presence or absence of certain elements (there should be more money, there should be some planning) but in their structuring vis-à-vis one another. Some people have not achieved a structuring of these features vis-à-vis one another; this is what confusion means.

The increased money might go for more "work" and thus not to the people as a community of individual landowners, the position of the individual landowner being linked to land, freedom, and the person. The people might not be getting individual payments, which would also be individual returns from the lands they individually own, and would assert freedom on their property. Besides, there was the "promises, promises!" sentiment expressed in statement 11.

The "carry on as now" and development centralist positions, then, could not be articulated with the higher-level symbols (land, freedom) in as many ways as the position for the distribution of the annuity. They were symbolically unproductive.

After the proannuity sentiment had been expressed, the adviser himself said that using the money for the distribution of the annuity would not stop "the work" entirely. Thus individual workers may not have construed the situation as an absolute choice between agreement to the annuity's distribution (loss of their jobs) and maintenance of the status quo, even if they did not agree that more money would be forthcoming anyway. The proannuity position, then, was more in line with the "maximize your options" principle of the Banaban value system (see Silverman 1969).

The counterargument was weak in another respect, one which was crucial to the process of the meeting itself. The counterargument did not spell out in any elaborate way a means of victimization or a means of transformation having anything approaching the power of the money for work/money to the people contrast. The means, of all the terms in the pentad of delineation, has the highest structuring potential because once the means is given tangible form, it clearly implies all the other terms. Thus a wide field of possibilities is opened up for identifying and structuring actors and events as subjects, objects, instruments, and so forth (including actors and events particularly meaningful to different people for different reasons).

The identification of money for work as a means of victimization encompasses relations between Banabans and the outside—

the outside in general, outside public opinion (which held that Banabans were well off), the government, and the BPC. Money for work also encompasses relations of internal victimization—the old people and copra cutters by workers, the people and council by the adviser and the board, a religious group by the adviser and the council, and even the people by themselves. Money to the people is an equally powerful relational term, since it defines the transformation of the problematic situation while encompassing precisely the same wide net of relationships as the means of victimization. These relationships could be identified and structured vis-à-vis one another or they could be left safely ambiguous for the moment. Lacking an elaborated means, the counterargument lacked the relational power inherent in the money for work/money to the people contrast.

## THE CREATION OF A SYMBOL

The details of what went on during most of the meeting are, of course, beyond the scope of this chapter. It is sufficient to say that there was a "movement" and a "filling in" among the various elements of this paradigm, with a good deal of questioning and uncertainty. A consensus on the annuity developed and was both questioned and spelled out. The pace of antiadviser interventions increased toward the end in a form that crystallized what had been prefigured earlier. The adviser was more or less in the witness box as defendant, and those who felt particularly aggrieved by his actions acted as public prosecutors, judge, and jury. After these exchanges, the adviser left the meeting.[18]

It was not long after the adviser's departure that one thing became quite clear. The people were not only collectively constructing various symbols and meanings; they were also in the process of creating a symbol—the meeting itself. Actions as well as words and objects can be symbols.[19] The notion of a symbol as a vehicle for conceptions can be sustained here only if we insist that the vehicle and the conceptions are in a dialectical relationship—that in the flow of action their forms may be problematic and their boundaries elastic, and that vehicles and conceptions are not simple things but structures. In their statements, movements, and feelings, the people were struggling to give form to a vehicle for a number of conceptions. They may have recognized this at the outset, but toward the end of the meeting their struggle assumed a quite explicit reality.

One context for understanding the symbolic nature of the meeting itself may be that it was not just any meeting but a *maungatabu*, an event which may have a special status because of its infrequency.[20] The calling of a *maungatabu* may be a structured part of a social drama (see Turner 1957) or a social-conceptual drama in which the number of problematic elements in the people's lives has become great. In the simplest interpretation, the whole thing may be seen as an attempt on the part of some leaders and would-be leaders to get a public mandate that would strengthen a council case with outside authority. But even on those grounds there would be a major bind in internal relations, external relations, or both.

Not every member of the Banaban community was present at the meeting—or, rather, not every Banaban landowner was present (and it was only Banaban landowners, Banabans by birth or adoption, who spoke). But if one were to compare this assembly with political meetings in the United States, it is clear that the meeting was one of a significant proportion of a group of people who think of themselves as a total community. There developed an "in-touchness" with the total community, and the history and future of that community, which is lacking in many meetings elsewhere. (By this I do not mean to suggest that the Banaban meeting was a unique event from a cross-cultural point of view. Far from it.) The people were putting themselves in touch with their own history and their own future. There was very much a feeling of being part of Great Events. How was this symbol construction finally realized?

Toward the end, the meeting reached a new dialectical phase, although elements of that phase had been broached earlier. Now the focus shifted to the form that the final action in the meeting would take. The creation of that form was now the problematic situation, and the content included what had gone on in the meeting before.

For the sake of brevity I shall not treat this material in sequential detail. The alternatives presented and discussed were not all mutually exclusive; they involved the issues of what should be done inside and outside the meeting. Alternatives for action inside the meeting included nothing more than signing papers on either side of the argument, dividing the house, and raising and counting hands. Alternatives for action outside the meeting were to have a plebiscite conducted, presumably by the council; to communicate the results of a vote in the meeting to the governor and the BPC; and to send the results of a vote to the council for its consideration.

The chairman, it seemed, was first calling for a plebiscite or at least the taking of signatures. Speaker H, a young man prominent in the affairs of church and state, made the critical interventions in this latter segment (as he had done earlier by "cross-examining" the adviser). Speaker H argued as follows: "On a paper for the decision: this is the *maungatabu*. The heads of families are all here. If the *maungatabu* is called, it is decided. [Next sentence unclear; probably: As you, our old men, have done from the past to the present.] . . . Who else is there to call? Are the people here valueless? . . . Then it will go to the council."

Another man echoed the point: "What is worth more? The heads of families or the council?"

And later, speaker H said: "How many Banabans are there? The government can see how many. When this man [that is, someone] comes, he speaks for his spouse and children." And later, "We call people here to sign for their families."

The chairman then shifted his own position: "Ask the community of Banaba. Stay on the *maungatabu* of Banaba." And further on: "It is the decision of the *maungatabu*. Make worthwhile the decision of the *maungatabu*. . . . Pray that the governor is guided [by God] in his decisions."

Speaker H used Banaban tradition to give form to the *maungatabu* as the *maungatabu* gave tangible content to Banaban tradition. He stressed the continuity of that tradition and the unique potential of the *maungatabu* for producing decisive action. The *maungatabu* became a tangible form which structured the transformation of "the people" into the "heads of families," the powerful images of kinship perhaps now becoming content for the *maungatabu*. While some role for the council was maintained, action in the meeting itself was presented as critical and historic. That action would then give form to the other structures.

One well-known supporter of the adviser and opponent of the annuity argued for a plebiscite or a paper vote (which one was unclear to me) in the meeting: "The word can be changed. The paper cannot. This is not the time for unenlightened thoughts ['thoughts of darkness, ignorance']. The light ['electricity', pointing to the fluorescent light above] is lit." The 'time of darkness, ignorance' and the 'time of light, understanding' are often used to indicate the contrast between the Banaban way of life before and after missionization or, more generally, as a contrast between ancient and enlightened times.

Later, speaker H came back to the issue by making of the *maungatabu* a "special case" of modern political thought. He said that the people were acting in a "democracy," that the *maungatabu* was called so that people's ideas could be made known, one after another, and that each person is precious in this system. The *maungatabu* thus became tangible content for both the continuity of Banaban tradition and political advancement.[21] Here is the artful rhetorician situating the *maungatabu* at the interface of two conceived systems, the relations of which are often quite problematic to the people—'tradition' and 'progress' (or, more generally, the nature and demands of the modern world)—and stressing the actability of both. Here a relationship can be made through action, through *that* action. As a young man said with great feeling, "We want to see the power of the community of Banaba!"

The chairman had put two papers on the stage and a few people went up to sign, but there was hesitancy. The proposal for a count of hands won out; perhaps the raising of hands on each side was a more collective and momentary act. And hand counters from both 'the council' and 'the people' joined together in legitimizing the act. The vote was read as 110 against and 18 for the adviser.

The winning side at the meeting, crystallized through the 'heads of families' route, made the Banaban community tangible by constituting the people at the meeting as the Banaban community who by a concrete action could give form to such tangible symbols and meanings as freedom and land, the worth of the person and the sanctity of kinship, the preservation of Banaban tradition and the commitment to progress.

During the course of the meeting, many relationships had been set out as the problematic situation and its transformation were elaborated. The people explored various definitions, subjects, objects, instruments, and means, which were given form by various symbols and meanings and which gave form to various events. Toward the end of the meeting they had the problem of building

the structure for the transformation (action) which would be accomplished *now*, a structure which could operate on the wide-
ranging sets of relations which had emerged.

There was obviously an "audience present" which included
outside authority, and many ambiguities remained as to the role of
the council—what power lay where, and so forth. But the position
that "the *maungatabu* can do it" meant essentially that the
Banaban community, in their action, could become the subject,
object, instrument, and means of their own transformation, giving
form to and being formed by themselves.

The symbol which was constituted by the action of the meeting
might be termed a "reflexive symbol," since the symbol and much
of the universe to which its referent applied were simultaneously
present and identical. The people were both the instances of the
Banaban community and the components of the symbol in that
they were participants in the action. Thus what in other contexts
are general symbols are given form by every individual, and every
individual becomes more than an individual by becoming the
component of a symbol.

This is not to suggest that specific grievances, alliances, and
hostilities were irrelevant to the meeting, that the meeting concerned only matters of policy and practice. Insofar as it was successful, the ordering represented by the meeting was successful
because a diversity of concerns, complaints, and strategies—a noble concern for the future of the community, a grandstand play for
position, an intense grudge against the adviser—could be given
form by that ordering. This is what any politician knows. The
commanding problem is not why certain people did what they
did, but the creation of the set of forms which enabled them to do
what they did, for whatever reason. All was not enthusiasm and
harmony at the end of the meeting. Far from it. Those opposed to
the position that "the *maungatabu* can do it" were profoundly
unhappy with what was going on and questioned its legitimacy.
Others were not sure how they felt about the outcome of the
meeting. The meeting did not resolve fundamental conflicts; it articulated them. But whether people voted one way or the other, sat
it out, made a dramatic exit, quietly slipped through the side door
—or did not attend in the first place—something was going to happen and something did happen, out of a multiplicity of events and
apart from a multiplicity of events. As Althusser (1969:126)

observes: "What makes *such and such* an event *historical* is not the fact that it is *an event*, but precisely its insertion into forms which are themselves historical."[22]

ETHNOGRAPHIC EPILOGUE

Just before the voting began, one man suggested that there should be a film showing afterward. After the chairman called the meeting to a close and said that people were free in their opinions, there was a discussion on the availability of a film. The suggestion on the film was not out of place, because films are shown there from time to time. In fact, a film was shown that evening but some people, including myself, left before it. I eternally regret that my exhaustion compelled me to withdraw from the scene.

With the people (or what was left of them) now collectively in the same position vis-à-vis an outside entertainment, they demarcated the end of the previous form. The Banabans are often quite energetic film-goers, talking and commenting. The film may have provided some kind of release from a trying event filled with hostility, latent and manifest. Perhaps the performers in the action unwound, or rewound, themselves into an audience involved in something entirely different: the medium (the meeting) had become the message, bracketed itself by the final action, and having accomplished this feat, further bracketed itself by the introduction of another medium.

CONCLUSION

Every analysis has its black boxes. Something goes into the box, something comes out of the box. But what goes on inside the box— a "how," a process—remains essentially unexplored. The analyst may consider the "how" to be understood, irrelevant, somebody else's business, perhaps describable in the future. One can easily label the box without opening the lid but thinking that one has, and then confuse product with process (for instance, some uses of "self-interest" and "adaptation").

One "how" becomes illuminated or even restructured (Lévi-Strauss on how a myth means, Peacock on how a drama works, Schneider on how kinship articulates, Turner on how a ritual works) and others are created.

My own analysis has its black boxes, too, many of them of noble antiquity. How do symbols really symbolize? What really goes on in the conjunctions? What are the operations and rules that specify how one thing can lead to another and how one thing cannot lead to another? How does what I have described articulate precisely with local social relations and with larger structures?[23]

If this chapter has any theoretical utility, it may help to delineate certain aspects of the how of events like the meeting, events which are, if you will, macrocosms of the symbolization process, where forms are under construction which enable (or, to play it out, restrict) the—quite literal—making of sense.

Ethnographically, the chapter documents the microsystem-macrosystem problem, discussed by several other contributors to this volume, as one with an urgent reality to a people struggling to become themselves and struggling to restructure at least one aspect of the world they live in.

## NOTES

I would like to thank Stephen A. Barnett, Vern Carroll, Michael D. Lieber, James L. Peacock, David Schneider, Peter Seitel, and Victor Turner for their extraordinarily useful comments on a previous draft of this chapter. A theoretical dialogue with Barnett has been particularly critical to the present effort. Lieber labored mightily and sympathetically to make the chapter more readable, rewriting some of the more obscure sections, and in so doing contributed substantively to it. I must alert the reader to the fact that the details of the methodology of the analysis were formulated after the conclusion of the fieldwork. I offer deep apologies for being able to find only rather obscure and convoluted ways of stating many of my fundamental points. Many of these points are simple, well known, and even commonsensical, but I have felt the need for a certain degree of formal abstractness to enhance the chapter's possible utility for those interested in the comparative analysis of symbolic actions. My apologies are deepest to the Banabans themselves.

1. One can also approximate Peter Berger's terms: people are, collectively and simultaneously, "externalizing" fields of meanings, asserting a "shared facticity" by objectivating meanings, and "internalizing" the objectivated production. The element of ambiguity, however, complicates the picture. See Berger (1969).
2. Much of the material in this section is repeated from Silverman (1971).
3. I note especially for comparative purposes that "direct dealings" with phosphate company and government personnel continued on Ocean Island in several respects.
4. The four centralized villages on Ocean Island were apparently consolidated

in the early colonial period from five village districts (composed of many hamlets) which were in effect maximal units (beneath the level of the island itself, which was relevant in some contexts) in the ritual, descent, and territorial systems.

5. Certain services are listed in old records as being paid for by deductions from Banaban funds. I know nothing of how this process occurred or what role the Banabans had in it. I am operating on the assumption that the role bears no real comparison to the Rambi structure.

6. A "radical" suggestion was made early on Rambi that much of the phosphate money should be distributed to the people and that the council would obtain what additional funds it needed through taxation. I do not know how general the sentiment was in favor of this proposal, but apparently it was not well received by the government.

7. The "right will inevitably be done" attitude has been losing ground recently.

8. These connections are explored in detail in Silverman (1971).

9. There was a complex set of rules about the distribution of the annuity and bonus, discussed in Silverman (1971). For "full-Banabans" (the regulations were somewhat different for others), there was recognition of the equal identity of Banaban individuals (since individuals received the same amount of money, qualified by age) through the annuity and also recognition of the differentiation of Banabans as individuals with different amounts of land through the bonus—or all Banabans are landowners, but some own more land than others. Had there been no upper limit on the bonus, the case would be much nicer: the annuity going to the person (but one, of course, whose status was partially conceived in terms of his being a landowner) and the bonus going to the land. The setting of the upper limit, however, does not preclude the presence of that conception. Indeed, it suggests it. Which features of the rules were initiated by the government and which by the Banabans is obscure, although it is reported that a committee of Banabans approved the rules.

10. The figures are presented to be suggestive. Consideration of the household as a social unit is a very tricky matter for Rambi. The full-time job category is somewhat deceptive since some of these people, too, engage in agriculture, fishing, and entrepreneurial activity.

11. The term "problematic situation" is borrowed from Laura Thompson, who uses it in applied anthropological contexts.

12. The connections being made may overlap with an anthropologist's description of social organization or social structure. I want to recognize but not explore an extraordinarily important theoretical problem here: the similarities and differences between the anthropologist's delineating activity and the delineating activity of the people he is studying.

13. The point recalls Geertz's distinction between the "model of" and "model for" functions of symbols (Geertz 1966). I refrain from adopting that language here because of complications which are provided by the elements of vagueness and ambiguity for the "template" notion and my (admittedly uneven) stress on structure in use. A solution might be to look for the principles of template construction, some clues to which are given in Geertz (1964).

14. These points draw upon Dumont (1970) and Black (1962), although I am not using "stressed" in the same sense as Dumont and do not want to situate this discussion vis-à-vis Dumont's encompassing/encompassed distinction. Although I schematize the process of conjunction as if only two things are being conjoined, that is, of course, a gross simplification. The point may appear to be vulnerable in that it says nothing more than that B meets C on the street and they talk about what they have in common. Two responses: first, "what they have in common" is not given a priori, given B and C; second, I stick to the special case since I do not want to bring up the question of change, which is really the most interesting question. For example: what happens when B meets C and one or both are not what they used to be? I hope to develop these matters in future publications.

15. Without knowledge of other *maungatabu*, it is impossible to know whether one can write a generalized scenario (or a limited number of scenarios) for a *maungatabu* of which this one would be an instance. I was struck at several points by the search for forms—the procedures to be followed were themselves problematic. The mode of the search, however, might constitute a form in itself. If there is a *maungatabu* form of which the meeting is an instance, then one would also have to demarcate that form vis-à-vis other forms in order to understand the Banaban's behavior in the *maungatabu* itself. Serious attention to matters of this kind is given in Peacock (1968). The literature on judicial proceedings also provides a clear line of comparative and methodologically illuminating inquiry. But I do not want to expand what is already a lengthy chapter, and I am not familiar enough with the literature to enter that fray at this point. The exclusive attention to verbal communcation in my analysis is a serious deficiency.

16. Aspects of 'freedom' are treated in Silverman (1971). It is a cultural label for the "maximize your options" principle. It is through events such as this that its meanings may become established.

17. Other contributors take up the question of the specific mapping of presettlement structures onto the post-resettlement situation. The mapping, of course, goes the other way, too, and it is the dialectic between them that is really interesting. The construction of the bonus and annuity, as well as land subdivisions, settlement patterns, and electoral rules, are all part of the mapping problem, which is treated in detail in Silverman (1971).

18. One ciucial feature of the intervening exchanges must be mentioned but remain undocumented here. The explicit bringing forth of the structuring symbols discussed, and the spelling out of form-content relations of the several kinds, tended to come from the protagonists in the debate—the councillors and some of the people known before the meeting as strong partisans. One would have to situate this point in terms of Banaban rhetorical action in order to interpret it. Some strong partisans were important figures in their churches. Perhaps there is some relationship between this practice and prominent organizational activity. Which comes first—whether there is an ability which selects people for such activity, or whether such activity encourages the development of the ability or marks out some people as those who should publicly symbolize in this way—is a question I cannot answer. If the rela-

tionship is not with prominent organizational activity in general, it may be with church activity. Although my notes on them are pitifully incomplete, I suspect that sermons constitute the paradigmatic continuing form which articulates things so completely. Perhaps we are dealing with a feature of most Banaban persuasive discourse, discourse in a problematic situation, or both. Many have noted, but not explored in detail, the elaboration of rhetoric in Oceania. This neglect may result from a preconception that style is an embellishment of what really matters rather than being constitutive of it.

19. I recognize a problem here which is important at the theoretical level. It is appropriate to speak of acts as symbols and objects as symbols (as in Geertz 1966), but if one is trying to specify the nature and relations of symbolic systems, a good deal more careful thought is necessary on the implications of a symbol being an act, an object, or whatever.

20. My only other reference to an event being called a *maungatabu* was a general meeting of the cooperative society on which I have sparse data. There was a real problematic situation there, but it might have been called a *maungatabu* even if there were not. The *maungatabu* may be a label for "general meetings of the membership," some of which are temporally regular and others of which are part of a social-conceptual drama sequence. I also note that the first adviser on Rambi got into many difficulties with the people, and one of the local interpretations is that the people (or certain groups) were instrumental in his departure. The whole affair regarding the adviser may thus be a replay, and there may have been a *maungatabu* in the earlier case. This does not, however, qualify the historical nature of the event. More data would answer some of these questions. For a meaning of *maungatabu* in the Gilberts, see Maude (1963).

21. It is interesting to note here that both speaker H and the man who made "the light is lit" statement were arguing in the same terms. If the discussion had been carried further, some of the terms (such as 'progress') may have turned out to be "essentially contested" concepts (Gallie 1962).

22. The quote is, evocatively and provocatively, being lifted out of context. James Peacock suggests that the actions of the viewers of the film shown immediately after the meeting may have carried forward and given new power to the actions-meanings constructed during the meeting by encoding, elaborating, and displacing those meanings through another medium.

23. I had intended to include a detailed analysis of the articulation of what occurred in the meeting with the social relations of the participants, but found that a book-length treatment would be necessary. While the omission is a serious one, I believe the content of the chapter raises enough questions of general interest to be justified.

# 7

# ROTUMANS IN FIJI: THE GENESIS OF AN ETHNIC GROUP

*Alan Howard*
*Irwin Howard*

## INTRODUCTION

In his introduction to *Ethnic Groups and Boundaries*, Fredrik Barth points out that even a drastic reduction of cultural difference between ethnic groups in culture contact situations does not correlate in any simple way with reduced relevance of ethnic identities (Barth 1969:32–33). The point is well taken, and there is considerable evidence to support his contention. One can go farther and assert that without regular and persistent contact ethnicity is socially irrelevant, for, as Barth cogently argues, the existence of ethnic groups depends less on the sharing of a common culture than on the maintenance of social boundaries. For social boundaries to be actively maintained, they need to be continually validated, and this requires regular interaction with members of outgroups.

Given these premises, the effects of European colonization on ethnicity in the insular Pacific are of particular interest. Prior to European contact, many Pacific islands experienced very little interaction with peoples of a substantially different cultural background. An occasional canoeload of other islanders might make a landfall from time to time, but as a rule they were either driven off, killed, or absorbed into the local population through interbreeding (see chapter 2). Particularly within the large culture areas of Polynesia and Micronesia, such immigrants were likely to exhibit only slight differences in language and customs from the host population.

The arrival of Europeans in the area, and the subsequent establishment of colonial regimes, radically altered this situation. Not only did the Europeans inaugurate regular firsthand contact, but they also initiated and institutionalized boundary-maintaining mechanisms designed to distinguish ethnic groups. Furthermore, social privilege in many instances was allocated on the basis of ethnicity. In the early contact period this resulted in what was primarily a European-native dichotomy, but as time passed different indigenous groups were brought into regular contact with one another and immigrant laborers were brought from outside the region (from India, China, and elsewhere) into the crucible of plantation, mining, and urban communities. Additionally, interbreeding between Europeans and indigenous populations gave rise to a half-caste or part-European group. The result has been the development of polyethnic societies and an opportunity for social scientists to study ethnic groups in the making.

One such group is the Rotumans, who currently form an ethnic enclave within Fiji (see map 8). The processes by which Rotuma developed into a hinterland community to Fiji's urban centers have been documented elsewhere (Howard 1961). Our focus in this chapter is on the adaptation of Rotumans to the social milieus of four such urban areas. Here we are concerned with the degree to which they have formed viable ethnic communities, the organizational forms that have developed, and the extent to which ethnic consciousness has been created under varying conditions. Special emphasis is given to an analysis of the Rotuman community in Vatukoula, since it is there that the processes germane to our thesis have been most intense.

THEORETICAL CONSIDERATIONS

Although a substantial literature has developed over the years dealing with such topics as race relations, minority group studies, and ethnic studies, most research and theory have focused on relations between groups whose boundaries were clearly defined or treated as unproblematic. Few studies have centered on the processes by which a people who share a common history are transformed into an ethnic group within a larger social system. Accul-

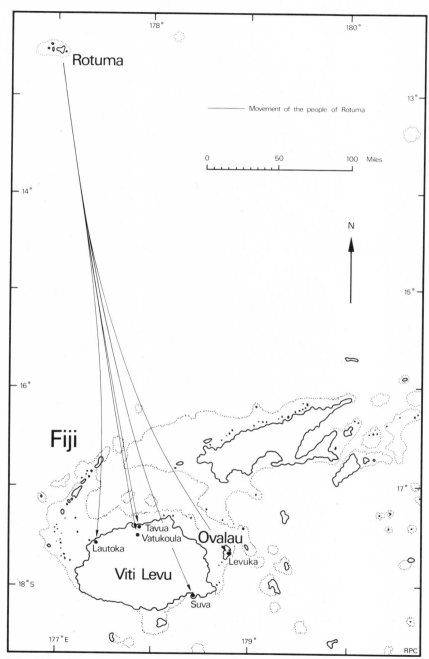

Map 8.   Movement from Rotuma to other Fiji Islands.

turation studies in anthropology, while dealing with processes of change, have generally dealt with alterations in culture content, social transformations within a group, or the significance of change for acculturating individuals. Barth's recent effort provides some promising leads, but it falls short of projecting a theory of ethnic group development. In this section we attempt to build on Barth's formulation; specifically, we postulate a set of processes that lead to the development and crystallization of ethnic boundaries and, by implication, to the formation of ethnic groups. After presenting data from the Rotuman case, we conclude the chapter with a consideration of specific variables that hasten or retard the relevant processes.

The theoretical paradigm we are advocating begins with two distinct populations who are unaware of each other's existence. Initial awareness may occur either through direct contact or indirectly through intermediaries, but in either case the first bits of information provide the basis for the development of ethnic categories. If information flow is slow and irregular, these categories may remain vague for a time, but with regular contact information input is accelerated, generating preliminary stereotypes. Barth points out that the features taken into account in generating ethnic stereotypes are not necessarily based on "objective" difference, but that "some cultural features are used by the actors as signals and emblems of differences, others are ignored, and in some relationships radical differences are played down and denied" (1969:14). He suggests two types of information of relevance to the establishment of ethnic dichotomies: one consists of the diacritical features that people look for and exhibit to show identity, such as dress, language, house form, and general lifestyle; the other involves evaluative criteria for judging behavior and the products of behavior. Barth's basic message, however, is that "ethnic categories provide an organizational vessel that may be given varying amounts and forms of content in different sociocultural systems" (1969:14). As such, their social existence is independent of culture content but depends instead on the maintenance of social boundaries.

Ethnic boundaries may not emerge with clarity as soon as categories develop, however. In the early stages of contact such boundaries may include extensive "shadow areas" in the form of ambiguous situations, role discrepancies, and obtuse or overlapping diacritical features. During these stages social relations may involve the two populations more as ethnic aggregates than as ethnic groups. Such is particularly likely to be the case when there are no clearly demarcated geographical boundaries between the populations. The distinction between an ethnic aggregate and an ethnic group is that with the former, ethnic designation is subordinate to other identity principles in the organization of a population's social life while with the latter it is superordinate. Barth's comments concerning polyethnic social systems (1969:17) are what we have in mind in considering ethnicity as superordinate:

> Common to all these systems is the principle that ethnic identity implies a series of constraints on the kinds of roles an individual is allowed to play, and the partners he may choose for different kinds of transactions. In other words, regarded as a status, ethnic identity is superordinate to most other statuses, and defines the permissible constellations of statuses, or social personalities, which an individual with that identity may assume.

The crucial question from the standpoint of the development of ethnic groups can thus be phrased: Under what conditions does ethnicity become the superordinate symbol of identification within a social system? Our position is that the fundamental conditions underlying the transformation of an ethnic aggregate into an ethnic group are (1) the development of an *ethnic community*, that is, a localized interactive network consisting of individuals of the same ethnic designation who are emotionally committed to the symbols of their common heritage and formally organized for the purpose of pursuing common goals; and (2) the formation of *ethnic consciousness*. Ethnic consciousness may be defined as a special case of ethnic awareness, that is, a recognition by an individual that his ethnicity is a significant factor in ordering his social relations. When ethnicity assumes a position of primacy for the individual in structuring his interactions, whether with others of his own ethnic category or outside it, his awareness may be said for our purposes to have become consciousness.

Ethnic consciousness may develop on an individual level in response to a number of circumstances: these include overt discrimination by others, a sense of superiority or inferiority, or status ambiguities that can be resolved by giving primacy to ethnicity. Collectively, ethnic consciousness emerges as a result of repeated messages circulated throughout networks of kinsmen, friends, and neighbors to the effect that other identity criteria are less significant for structuring interpersonal relations than ethnic differences. The redundancy of these messages serves to structure both social interaction among ethnic cohorts and an ideology of "we-ness," the sharing of a common social fate. The structural manifestations of these messages are the extension of close personal bonds characteristic of kinship and friendship to all who are members of the same ethnic category and the restricting of one's personal relationships to people within that category. That one member of the category is shamed, offended, or honored implies shame, anger, and honor for all vis-à-vis nonmembers. To the extent that nonmembers of an ethnic category view members as interchangeable, the redundancy of the relevance of ethnicity is likely to be reinforced. For example, when the message that an individual lost his job or was abused because of his ethnicity circulates through a network of people of the same category, indignation and emotional solidarity are more likely to be engendered than if other identity variables are acknowledged to have played a part. The notion of sharing a common fate, if accepted by members of an ethnic category, takes on the character of an ideology by which people interpret their relationships within and without the network of ethnic cohorts. At this point, we can say that an ethnic group has emerged.[1]

The content of the unifying ideology may vary from group to group, but it always involves a common symbol or set of symbols. The key symbols may be racial features, religious practices, a monarchy, or common acceptance of some kind of charter myth, for example. Inasmuch as symbols and ideology are involved, we regard the formation of ethnic groups as very much a cultural process as well as a structural one, although we agree with Barth that once a group is formed its culture content may change drastically without the boundaries of the group being affected. For Rotumans, the dominant symbol of their shared ethnicity is the island of Rotuma itself: any person may claim to be a Rotuman if one or more of his known ancestors was born on the island and shared in the core social and cultural life that characterizes the society.[2]

As reported in an earlier article on conservatism among the Rotumans, the emergence of a consolidating ideology is rooted in the bicultural experience of nontraditional leaders, that is, in-

dividuals whose prestige accrues from success in Western occupations and professions (Howard 1963a:73–74). These leaders are
people of influence because they are educated Rotumans among
uneducated Rotumans; their success in the outside world is acknowledged by other Rotumans as significant. Their influence and
high status are located within the Rotuman community and depend on its existence. Moreover, they are leaders because of a
demonstrated commitment to Rotuma, a commitment that has
become highly conscious as a result of European education and
experience in a Europeanized society. Having learned the
mechanics of European culture, they have also learned to evaluate
their own society in abstract terms as, for example, these terms are
used in school to describe models of law and social organization
(such as the government of Great Britain). Possessing an intellectual idiom for perceiving a society, educated Rotumans have often
been struck by the inconsistencies between ideology and behavior
in Western societies, as compared to a far greater consistency in
Rotuman values and behavior, and between Western (particularly
Christian) ideology and Rotuman behavior. Their education has
therefore tended to foster an idealism about their own society
while their experience has provided means to implement their
ideas in community action.

Before describing the circumstances that have generated a Rotuman ethnic group in Fiji, we present in the following section
some aspects of social life on Rotuma that are relevant to our basic
discussion.[3]

## ROTUMA

From Cession in 1881 until Fiji was granted independence, Rotuma was administered by Great Britain as part of the Colony of
Fiji. The decision leading to this arrangement was based on administrative convenience rather than on any existing ties between
Rotuma and Fiji. In language, culture, and physical type Rotumans are clearly distinct from Fijians, resembling more closely
than the latter the Polynesians to the east. Administration of Rotuma (which lies some 300 miles north of the Fiji group) was in the
hands of a district officer who was responsible to the commissioner and, ultimately, to the governor of Fiji. In addition to his
administrative duties, the district officer had the power of second-

class magistrate and presided over the Council of Rotuma, which
was composed of the paramount chiefs of the island's seven traditional districts, an elected representative from each district, and
the senior medical officer on the island.[4]

The traditional social organization is based on a system of bilateral kinship. A key concept is *kainaga*, which in its broadest
sense refers to kinsmen and in a more restricted sense to the bilateral descendants of an ancestor holding rights over a particular
parcel of land. *Kainaga*, in the restricted sense, are the major
landholding units. In each traditional district, a limited number of
*kainaga* hold the right to a chiefly name, some being eligible for
paramount chieftainship within the district, others not. Districts
are divided into *ho'aga*, which comprise from three to seventeen
households (with an average of ten). *Ho'aga* are essentially work
units, whose members have an obligation to assist one another in
times of crisis and on ceremonial occasions. The most basic socioeconomic unit in Rotuma is the *kau noho'ag* 'household' (essentially persons sharing a common hearth and comprising a common
consumption unit, since food is easily the most important con-
sumable commodity). The modal 'household' consists of a nuclear
family with one or more relatives of either spouse (39.3 percent) or
a nuclear family by itself (29.6 percent). Persons who are not
members of a nuclear family (widowed and divorced persons, or-
phans, offspring of unwed mothers, unmarried adults) tend to
have a high rate of residential mobility, moving from household to
household. Almost every Rotuman man is an agriculturist, at least
while living on Rotuma. Even those engaged in wage labor maintain gardens to provide their families with food. A man is judged
primarily in his role as provider, and to be a good provider means
to bring home more than enough food for his family's needs. With
the exception of wage earners, this means being a competent and
industrious farmer and harvesting available copra. The women on
Rotuma have as their major tasks the care of children, keeping the
household clean and presentable, and supplementing the family
food supply by fishing on the reef. This sexual division of labor is
not rigid, however, and cooperation between husbands and wives
on domestic tasks is the rule rather than the exception.

The traditional kinship-based socioeconomic organization is
crosscut by geographical divisions. Within Rotuma the sharpest
in-group/out-group distinctions are essentially territorial. We

found it rather striking that stereotypes held by persons of each district paralleled those between ethnic groups elsewhere. These stereotypes typically focus on alleged behavioral differences; for example, the people of one district are ridiculed as being like chickens—that is, marrying with kinsmen who are genealogically closer than deemed appropriate. For each district (and in some cases for each village) it is possible to elicit a stereotype that has currency and is essentially shared. Furthermore, it soon became clear to us that territorial proximity plays an extraordinary role in structuring social relations on the island. It is a general rule that people who interact frequently as neighbors, especially as 'work unit' mates, manifest a strong solidarity; correspondingly, clashes between neighbors often precipitate a residential move by one or the other. Even close kinship ties are rarely strong enough to overcome long-term geographical separation.

Two other organizational principles crosscut those of kinship: one is religion and the other is the formation of voluntary associations. Voluntary organizations are formed mainly for the purpose of playing such European sports as soccer, rugby, and cricket. They are generally ephemeral organizations, lasting only as long as interest in a particular sport is salient. As a matter of convenience they tend to be strongly influenced by territorial patterning. For all practical purposes the only religious groups represented on the island since Cession have been Methodists and Catholics. The division between these groups largely coincides with a pre-European political division and, therefore, also has a strong territorial patterning. Rivalry between the two religious groups was intense enough to provoke a war just prior to Cession, and religion has remained a significant factor in ordering social relations on the island to the present day. Cross-religious marriages are frowned upon, and when they do take place one of the partners usually is required to convert. Even here, the power of territorially based solidarity is manifest: it is the person who takes up residence in the spouse's village who changes religion.

Ethnicity is another factor considered by Rotumans in accounting for behavioral differences on the island. The obvious cases are when Europeans, Fijians, or Indians are involved. Attitudinally, there is a hierarchical structure of stereotypes for these three groups. While Europeans are regarded as superior and are afforded deference (although they are also seen as an enigma), Rotumans regard Fijians and Indians as of lesser status than themselves and sometimes treat them with mild disdain. Because the number of such cultural aliens on Rotuma has always been very small in the past, Rotumans have not been under pressure to differentiate themselves as an ethnic group while confined to the island. Although they developed relatively clear conceptions of other ethnic categories, their conception of "Rotuman" remained vague. In large part it remained vague because the great majority of people on the island rarely if ever interacted with non-Rotumans, and so the interfaces between ethnic groups remained shadowy. It was only after people gained a sense of what it is like to be treated as a Rotuman (rather than as a farmer, a man from the district Oinafa, a chief) that a sense of ethnicity crystallized. Our argument is that this did not occur until substantial Rotuman enclaves developed in Fiji. In recent years, as the circulation of people between Rotuma and Fiji has increased to the point that most adults on the island have spent some time in Fiji, awareness of Rotuman ethnicity has spread throughout the population. Even so, such ethnic identity is salient only in Fiji as a basis for self-identity and for ordering social relationships.

ROTUMANS IN FIJI

Rotuman emigration to Fiji in substantial numbers has been relatively recent. The census of 1921 shows only 123 Rotumans, or 5.5 percent of the total Rotuman population, residing in Fiji (Fiji Legislative Council 1922). Fifteen years later the figure had risen only to 273 persons, representing 9.7 percent of all Rotumans. Since 1936, however, the rise has been rapid—to 569 persons in 1946 (17.2 percent) and 1,429 persons in 1956 (32.3 percent). The biggest Rotuman concentration in 1956 was in Ba Province, the site of a large gold mining industry. Most Rotumans living in Ba reside in Vatukoula, where the mine is located, or in the nearby town of Tavua. In 1956, when the Fiji census was taken, the Rotuman population of Ba totaled 669. The second largest concentration was in Suva city, with 372 Rotumans. Third came Lautoka township with 71 Rotumans, then Levuka township with 56 Rotumans. These four locations accounted for 81.7 percent of all Rotumans living in Fiji at the time. Vatukoula not only contained the most Rotumans in absolute terms during 1956 but also showed the highest ratio of Rotumans to others (103 per 1,000); next came Levuka (37 per 1,000), then Lautoka (10 per 1,000), and finally Suva (1 per 1,000)(McArthur 1958).

By 1961, when we conducted our census of Rotumans in Fiji, the overall number of Rotumans in Fiji had swelled considerably. Increases were taking place selectively, however, with Suva and Lautoka absorbing almost all additional migrants and Vatukoula and Levuka remaining nearly constant. Thus the 1966 Fiji census shows 986 Rotumans in Suva, an increase over 1956 of 165 percent, and Lautoka shows an increase to 187 Rotumans for an increase of 163 percent (Zwart 1968). These were, in effect, open towns from the standpoint of Rotuman migrants. The Rotuman population of Levuka, on the other hand, decreased by 14 (−25 percent) and that of Vatukoula decreased by 3 (−0.6 percent). These were closed communities from a migratory viewpoint. During the same period the population of Rotuma increased by 7 percent. We shall refer to Rotumans in each of these urban areas as constituting an "ethnic enclave"—that is, members of an ethnic category who are residentially embedded in a sociopolitical unit dominated by others.

Before going on to a comparative analysis of Rotuman communities in Fiji, it is important for our argument to describe briefly the social structure of ethnicity in Fiji at the time of our study. One may gain a good initial picture of ethnic divisions from the dominant European perspective by referring to the census categories used. The 1956 census lists seven categories: Chinese and part-Chinese, European, part-European, Fijian, Indian, Rotuman, and Other Pacific Islander. Broadly speaking, and again from a European point of view, these groups may be arranged in three major status categories with Europeans at the top, part-Europeans intermediate, and native populations (including Indians as well as Fijians and Rotumans) at the bottom. The Chinese are generally less visible socially and their rank is less clearly defined. There are, however, refinements within these groups, one being that the Polynesian Rotumans are generally regarded as more advanced than the Melanesian Fijians.[5] The key population from the standpoint of ethnic mobility within this system is the part-European group. Because they are racially mixed, social entry into this group is less rigidly bounded than those based on "pure" race. Thus an educated Fijian remains just that, unless he happens to have a European ancestor and shows at least some European racial features; he can then pass as a part-European and probably increase his social privilege. It is significant for our purposes that Rotumans enjoy a distinct advantage over Fijians and Indians with regard to this mobility channel. As Polynesians, they were favored as mates and mistresses by European men, so a high proportion of Rotumans have a European ancestor. But apart from that, their physical type is closer to that of the stereotypic part-European, making it easier to gain acceptance without resorting to genealogical credentials. This circumstance probably has retarded the consolidation of a Rotuman ethnic identity within Fiji in some respects. It was easy enough, while numbers were small, for Rotumans to pass for part-European, particularly since a high proportion of early emigrants were in professional roles such as teachers, and medical officers. The situation in Levuka during 1960 was probably indicative of this early phase.

## LEVUKA

Levuka, on the island of Ovalau, was the original capital of Fiji when the colony was formed. After the capital was shifted to Suva, Levuka remained an administrative center (the location of the eastern commissioner, who holds jurisdiction over Rotuma), but its importance slipped as a commercial and trading town. The population of Levuka in 1956 was 1,535, including 56 persons registered as Rotumans (McArthur 1958).

At the time of our study only six fully Rotuman households existed in Levuka. Three of these were headed by men of professional status. A fourth was headed by a physician, Dr. Kautane, who ranks as the senior assistant medical officer on the island of Ovalau.[6] The other two Rotuman households were headed by a clerical worker and a postman. In addition to these, there were two Rotumans (living with non-Rotuman spouses) and two Rotuman men, each of whom had a Rotuman mother and a European father. The community was rounded out by seven student boarders and five Catholic nuns.

A significant feature of the Levuka enclave is that most of the residents were assigned to their positions; they did not opt to go there in search of employment or to be with relatives. In fact, most of the residents are functionally nonkinsmen. This distinguishes

Levuka from the other communities to be discussed, in which kinship has played an important role in expanding and organizing the enclave. As a corollary to this, Rotumans in Levuka are geographically scattered instead of being clustered in a neighborhood.

The Rotuman enclave in Levuka has no formal organization, and no exclusively Rotuman clubs have been formed. Dr. Kautane is the unquestioned leader of the enclave, but strictly in an informal fashion. He is the one to whom people go for advice regarding things Rotuman, and he serves as a critical link with the home island by transmitting and receiving information. It is to him that Rotumans outside the Levuka enclave look when mobilization of resources is required. His primary credentials are extraordinary prestige within the broader community and relatively lengthy residence in Levuka as well as compelling personal characteristics. He is one of three native members of the Masonic lodge in Fiji and a member of two primarily European clubs; his closest friends are European and part-European. He owns his own well-furnished and spacious home, which serves as a hostel for Rotuman schoolchildren studying in Levuka. Dr. Kautane is fluent in English and Fijian, although Rotuman remains the predominant language within his household.

Socially, then, the Rotuman enclave in Levuka forms a loosely knit network with Dr. Kautane as the major node. Interaction is most frequent among the professional men and their families, although there are occasions, such as births, when most members of the network are present. But these occasions are rare, and what is more important, most persons include in their intimate network several non-Rotumans. Also of relevance is that Levuka is a small town, and, particularly among the professionals, people are placed socially more by their positions than their ethnicity. As a result, the ethnic boundaries circumscribing Rotuman ethnicity in Levuka are permeable. Whatever centripetal forces are generated by a common language and sense of kinship are more than balanced by such centrifugal forces as professional association, interethnic organization, and neighborhood scatter.

## LAUTOKA

Unlike Levuka, Lautoka was a rapidly expanding town during our period of research. A new wharf had just been completed, and in addition to being the commercial and administrative center for one side of Viti Levu, Lautoka was beginning to serve as a major international seaport as well. Previously, the town centered mainly on the Colonial Sugar Refinery and had served as a market town for the sugar plantations which occupy much of the land around it. The 1956 census showed a population of 7,420 for Lautoka, including 71 Rotumans (McArthur 1958); but by 1960 the population had climbed above 10,000, and the number of Rotumans had more than doubled. Our questionnaire on residential mobility revealed that the Rotuman population in Lautoka includes few short-term visitors, particularly very few of those from Rotuma who intend to return to their home island. In this respect it contrasts most with Suva, where a high proportion of households include short-term "guests." As in Levuka, the Rotumans in Lautoka are residentially scattered, but the Lautoka community does contain a core network of closely related families.

Although there are no formal Rotuman organizations in Lautoka, the level of Rotuman-oriented activity is higher and the formalization of leadership is somewhat greater than in Levuka. A monthly service is held in the Rotuman language at the local Methodist church with the two Rotuman preachers in Lautoka presiding. Unscheduled meetings of the entire Rotuman community in Lautoka are called every month or so by Mekatoa, the acknowledged leader of most of the families in Lautoka. Very little business is discussed at these gatherings according to Mekatoa, but he believes they are necessary to keep the Rotuman community together. Because of the larger population, and owing to the greater degree of kin relatedness than in Levuka, there are more births, marriages, and funerals to bring people together and reinforce their sense of Rotuman identity, but these still occur at irregular intervals and with much less frequency than in Rotuma proper. In an attempt to perpetuate Rotuman identity among the children growing up in Lautoka, a night school was organized some years ago to teach them the essentials of Rotuman custom, but the venture did not take and dissolved from unknown causes.

Mekatoa has resided in Lautoka since 1939 and is employed as a fitter for the Public Works Department. He is acknowledged by all but three families to be the informal leader of the Rotumans in Lautoka. The three families who do not recognize Mekatoa's leadership broke with him after an incident involving kinsmen in

Vatukoula and now look to one of their own for leadership. Mekatoa also serves as coordinator of the Rotumans within the Methodist church. As a leader, he enjoys neither the legitimacy of Rotuman chieftainship nor the charisma of Dr. Kautane in Levuka. His main credentials, in fact, come from his long-term residence in Lautoka and familiarity with the local scene. Whenever a new Rotuman family comes to Lautoka, they are expected to inform Mekatoa of their arrival and intentions; he then keeps them informed about Rotuman affairs.

Discussions with Mekatoa indicated that keeping the Rotuman community together in Lautoka takes a strong conscious effort on his part; without it, he says, the community would dissolve and Rotuman custom would be neglected. The factional dispute mentioned above is only one indication of the tenuousness of group solidarity. Although the Rotumans in Lautoka are more organized than those in Levuka, they do not form a cohesive group. Ethnicity there has not yet clearly emerged as the primary basis for structuring social relationships, although it is clearly of significance.

## SUVA

Suva is *the* city of Fiji. It is the center of government, commerce, and entertainment and by far the most cosmopolitan of Fiji's urban areas. The population of Suva in 1956 was 37,371, of whom 372 were Rotumans (McArthur 1958). Residentially, Rotumans concentrate in a few clusters in different parts of the city; generally the clusters are formed around acknowledged kinship ties. The range of occupations represented among Rotumans in Suva is greater than in any of the other communities, and the degree of residential fluidity is greatest there. Persons coming to Fiji from Rotuma are most likely to spend their initial time in Suva, either because it is the center for services they are seeking (medical, governmental, educational) or because it offers the most by way of urban contrast with Rotuma. The entire picture, reflecting that of the general urban milieu, is one of considerable social, economic, and residential fluidity. Suva is the place where Rotumans come to seek their fortune, so to speak, and for many this changes on a daily basis.

Whereas the Rotuman enclaves in Levuka and Lautoka could be considered as singular loosely knit networks, in Suva it would be more accurate to characterize the social arrangement as consisting of several closely knit networks within a rather open-ended system of relationships. For one thing, class differences based on Europeanization and educational and occupational differences are more pronounced in Suva than elsewhere in Fiji and they are reflected in contrastive life-styles. There are also several Rotuman clubs to be found in Suva, some of which are exclusive to district of origin in Rotuma and help newcomers adjust to the city, although others are open to all Rotumans and serve as sports clubs as well as fraternal organizations. Both the Methodist and the Catholic churches in Suva regularly perform services in the Rotuman language, and each sponsors Rotuman-oriented activities such as bazaars and bingo.

Leadership within the Suva community is essentially informal, as in Levuka, but it is multiple. Several Rotuman men with high positions in the professions or in government reside in Suva, and each is looked up to by a portion of the enclave. They are asked for advice on issues pertaining to their competencies, but none is acknowledged by all to be their spokesman. Several attempts have been made to organize the entire community, but all have been short-lived. It seems that internal differences of interest are too great, and the pressures from outside too little, to sustain solidarity. Nevertheless, it is far easier for an immigrant to remain wholly within a Rotuman social world in Suva than it is in either Levuka or Lautoka since the variety of Rotuman-held jobs encompasses the entire range of services available without going beyond the boundaries of the ethnic enclave. This is made possible by the larger size of the Suva enclave and by residential clustering in parts of the city.

Suva thus seems to provide conditions conducive both to opening and to closing ethnic boundaries. Among the Europeanized professionals and white-collar workers, it is often expedient to minimize one's Rotuman background and pass as a part-European or to leave the whole question of ethnicity unspoken. Some minimize their affiliation with other Rotumans, including kinsmen, in order to reduce the drain on their accumulating resources. For these individuals Rotuman ethnicity plays a minimal role in structuring their social life. For others, however, the fact of "Rotumanness" becomes paramount. They are aware that the vast majority of people in the city are ethnically different from themselves and

speak languages they do not understand. They confine all significant social relations to the Rotuman enclave and come to see the
contrast between Rotumans and non-Rotumans as the most significant ones in their social worlds.

## VATUKOULA

Vatukoula grew up as a result of a gold mining operation begun in
1935 by three mining companies owned by overseas European interests. Initially it was assumed that the mining operation would
be short-term and so it was based on open-cut work, but later on
the lodes were found to have depth and underground shafts have
sustained a commercially profitable operation. Two of the companies ceased operations in 1959, leaving the Emperor Gold Mining Company in complete control. At the time of our study the
EGMC's management formed the effective government for the entire community in the classic style of colonial enterprise.

The mine management explicitly divides its employees into ethnic categories as follows: Europeans, part-Europeans (actually
limited to Euronesians, or mixtures between Europeans and Pacific Islanders), Fijians, Rotumans, and Indians. Each ethnic
group has been allocated living quarters supplied by the management. The quarters allocated to Rotuman workers are insufficient
for their needs, and many are forced to reside 10 miles away in
Tavua until additional housing is made available by the mine
management. Unfurnished houses in Vatukoula are assigned to individual workers and their families; the worker is responsible for
the upkeep of the house and pays a modest rent. A worker is not
permitted to sublet his house, and when he leaves the mine's employment he is obliged to vacate. The house is then reallocated by
the mine's management. Thus, although residence itself is quite
stable in Vatukoula, there is an aura of impermanence within the
community.

Although wages are the main basis of support, land for cultivation is made available by request to the company. Despite the per-
petuation of subsistence activities by almost all the Rotuman
households, a fundamental alteration has occurred in the relationship between people and capital in this new environment. In Rotuma, a person's descent group has use rights over his land and
can make legitimate claims on it for copra cutting and residence

sites. In Vatukoula, on the other hand, the sole criterion legitimizing control of capital goods (house and cultivated land) is merit
with the company. A result of this altered situation is that kinsmen, including parents, may be considered parasitic in Vatukoula
if they stay in a household to which they do not materially contribute. The critical distinction is that wages do not involve prior
capital, and they can be accumulated. Traditional rights are
therefore not involved in the same way, and the provision of support is likely to be interpreted by a wage earner as an act of bene-
volence rather than one of obligation. Nevertheless, Vatukoula
had the lowest percentage of nuclear households and the highest
percentage of expanded households of any of the Rotuman enclaves studied.[7] This follows from the traditional Rotuman rule
that those who are well off ought to nurture those who are not, and
since employment in the mines is tantamount to being well off for
Rotumans in Fiji, relatives are drawn to them. The net result is a
high degree of intrahousehold conflict and strains on relationships
that are more severe in Vatukoula than elsewhere. At the same
time, some informants believe that wage earning tends to reduce
disputes *between* households that stem from the system of land
tenure on Rotuma. They point out that on Rotuma, when a man
needs money he must take coconuts for copra off family land,
thereby creating competition for limited resources, whereas in
Vatukoula, as one man put it, "We earn our money by our own
sweat and it is clean money." When asked what he meant by
"clean money," he explained that it was free of the dirt of land
problems and the potent curses that accompany family disputes.

Within the mining community itself, internal residence change
is most often the result of house promotion. Thus whenever a
house becomes vacant within the Rotuman allocation, workers
with less desirable homes are given an opportunity to occupy it in
order of merit with the company. This generally starts a chain
response—a worker vacates his house in order to occupy another,
someone in an inferior structure moves into his, and so on. Ultimately, this may result in someone who has been residing outside
the company town in Tavua obtaining a company house. One
consequence of this system is that job status within the company is
directly translated into a highly visible form of social rank. This
contrasts with Rotuma, where there is far less congruence between
social status and quality of housing, and herein lies what may be a
fundamental metaphoric distinction between the two communi-

ties. On Rotuma, social status often is symbolized in acts of social deference; in Vatukoula, it is the kind of house one resides in that conveys one's social standing. Correspondingly, on Rotuma social merit is judged largely in terms of the degree to which a man uses his resources in the service of relationships and for community benefit; in Vatukoula social merit is very strongly (though not unequivocally) tied to the position a man holds in the mining company.

These shifts in perspective are part and parcel of an adjustment to a wage-oriented market economy and away from an economic system based on subsistence and ceremonial redistribution. Although Rotuma itself is involved in the money economy of Fiji and the rest of the modern world, on the island money has been adapted to the traditional system rather than having transformed it (see Howard 1970). In Vatukoula Rotuman custom has been adapted to the pressures of a capitalistic society; this is particularly evident in the way ceremonial events are handled. The most relevant social aspect of such events on Rotuma, the ritualized redistribution of food, mats, and other items, is precisely the feature that came under heaviest attack in Vatukoula. On several occasions known to us, persons in Vatukoula refused to participate in ceremonial (redistributive) exchanges at weddings and other events involving close kinsmen and insisted on giving a cash gift instead. The motives behind such deviations from custom seem to be based on a growing economic conservatism oriented toward maintaining a life-style commensurate with one's rank in the company and a cautious but nevertheless intense desire on the part of some leaders to raise the Rotumans' standard of living and esteem vis-à-vis other groups. Characteristically, every leader or would-be leader has a scheme of some sort for improving the economic well-being of the Rotuman community. Rather than being aimed at accumulating more goods, these plans are calculated to save money. This preoccupation appears to characterize Rotuman attitudes when dealing with collective assets, not only in Vatukoula but on Rotuma as well. The Rotuma Development Fund and the Rotuma Cooperative Association, for example, both have accumulated substantial assets which, despite prodding by the colonial government, remain unspent. In neither case are the Rotumans willing to eliminate the copra taxes and high prices on goods, despite the fact that these are genuine burdens on the population.

One can only speculate about the reasons for this disposition.

Perhaps it has to do with pride. We believe that to Rotumans the accumulation of money is symbolic of a capacity to master the socioeconomic system that has been imposed on them. The metaphoric power of the symbol lies, we suspect, in the measure of independence that is predicated on having capital reserves.

The concern of Rotumans for retaining independence and control over their own affairs has been expressed in several ways in Vatukoula, often to the dismay of the mine management. This feature of Rotuman coping tactics is evident in the view held by Mr. Carson, a European, the mine's welfare officer. From our field notes come Carson's observations.

> Mr. Carson feels that one of the problems in his relations with the Rotumans is that they tend to allocate themselves more power than they actually have. An example of this problem is that the Rotumans believe they should have the power to allocate housing. The mine management assigns housing facilities on the basis of seniority of merits. The Rotuman community has various other criteria of seniority that the mine management does not recognize, and this is the basis of the conflict. Mr. Carson states that the heads of the Rotuman community approached him once and wanted their native minister to have a house better than he deserved by his other merits. After a good deal of consideration, Mr. Carson pulled all available strings and got him the house in question. This was all done with the recognition by Mr. Carson that the minister was a man of great value to the community as a whole. He confides that he is still feeling the dissatisfaction of his superiors from that move. The Rotumans have come to him recently and not only told him who should go into a given empty Rotuman house, but have declared that a vacant European house across the field should be let to a Rotuman family.

This concern for housing, incidentally, suggests that although Rotumans have accepted the symbolic significance of housing for social status they are unwilling to yield completely to the mine's unilateral right to assign that status.

Another illustration of this desire to control their own destiny is the Rotuman mess hall, which is run exclusively by Rotuman shareholders. Each worker has a card that is punched every time he has a meal. At the end of each month, the cards are totaled and a list is sent to the company. The company then subtracts that amount from the individual's wages and turns it over to the Rotuman mess; profits are then distributed to the shareholders. What is significant about this is that the Rotumans are the only ones in Vatukoula who take care of their own food. The part-European and European mess are run by contract to a Chinese caterer; the Fijian mess is taken care of by the company. The advantage enjoyed by Rotumans in their arrangement lies not only in profits but also in the capacity to allocate jobs within the mess to Rotumans.

This ability of the Rotumans to organize, and the attitudes underlying their quest for control, can be better understood in the perspective of the way leadership has evolved within the community. The first *pure* 'headman' (a person with the right to make decisions for a collective) was Tafaki, who was also the first Rotuman to be employed at the mines (in 1939).[8] He had a reputation in 1960 for having been too weak in his dealings with the mine management. Tafaki's headmanship ended with his discharge from the company after he left his wife and family and ran off with another woman.

After a brief interval, Riamkau, an electrician with the company and a man of strong character, was chosen as 'headman' by the Rotuman employees. In a short time he had gained a commitment from the company for better housing, but his aggressive manner also generated some antagonism within the community. Then Chief Tausia, one of the seven paramount chiefs from Rotuma, visited Vatukoula in 1950 and appointed another man, Vai, as 'headman'. Our informants claimed that this move was unpopular but encountered no overt opposition. Vai remained 'headman' until his death in 1960. He was described as a weak leader, somewhat like a Rotuman chief whose concern is more with ritual honor than with the instrumental exigencies of leadership. It seems evident that despite Vai's formal role as 'headman', Riamkau, who assumed a chiefly title in the mid-1950s, retained a great deal of influence in the community and was the dominant political force. Thus when Vai returned to Rotuma in 1959 to discuss the effects of an ill-fated land commission, Riamkau took over in his absence and immediately introduced some dramatic structural changes. He appointed a committee composed of one man of chiefly descent from each district on Rotuma and then held a meeting of the entire community and obtained a confirmational vote.[9] Upon Vai's return, Riamkau turned the role of leader back to him, but the committee remained operative.

Interestingly, the resultant structure very nearly duplicated the social structure on Rotuma. Thus the 'headman' in Vatukoula was put in a very similar position to the district officer on Rotuma, and the committee corresponded to the Council of Chiefs. Even the monthly meetings, which rotated among committee members' households, paralleled the Rotuman custom of rotating host districts. After Vai's death, a meeting of the entire community was held in the Rotuman hall (built by the mines for the exclusive use of the Rotuman community) for the purpose of selecting a new 'headman'. Riamkau was elected. Acting on a proposal by one of the defeated candidates, the committee then passed a motion limiting the term of the 'headman' to two years. The inference was that Vai, who had been in the office for ten years, would have been replaced under such an arrangement.

The committee arrangement created some problems for the mine management in their dealings with the Rotuman community. Many of the problems that arose in relations between Rotumans and the mine management required, in the latter's opinion, more rapid decision making than was possible under the new arrangement. Furthermore, whereas Vai had been employed in Carson's department (a position virtually ensuring subservience), Riamkau is an electrician and works in a different part of the mine's operation. As a solution, Carson proposed that Sosefo Holt, a young, rather Europeanized Rotuman, be appointed clerical assistant in his office to act as a liaison between himself and Riamkau. This proposal was rejected by the Rotumans, in large measure, we were told, because the Rotumans regarded Sosefo as a man who was strictly out for his own interests and would not adequately represent the community. It is likely, of course, that the mine management was well aware of the potential such an arrangement would have had for diluting Riamkau's leadership and Rotuman solidarity in general. Riamkau had made it clear in his election platform that he was not afraid of the management and would try to push for the welfare of the Rotumans even if his position with the mine would be jeopardized. As the following passage from our field notes makes clear, he was tapping a basic Rotuman attitude:

Tomasi says that Vai was fine for dealing within the Rotuman community itself, but he was too *masraga* 'shy', 'respectfully deferential' to present Rotuman views forcefully to the European administrators. Riamkau, on the other hand, will go all the way to the general manager if he sees fit and is not afraid to deal with the management on even terms. Tomasi expressed in his conversation that the Europeans are always trying to buy out Rotuman leaders.

Rotuman suspiciousness of Europeans as being clandestine manipulators out to get around the Rotuman people seems to be one of the Rotumans' big leadership problems. The Rotuman leader who is well aware of European mannerisms and customs, and displays them publicly, is often suspected of lacking allegiance to the Rotuman community. Another problem, leading to misunderstandings between Rotuman leaders and European administrators, is the reluctance Rotumans show in passing vital information to the Europeans for fear it will be used to their own detriment.

Despite expressions of overall solidarity, including firm dealings with the management and the refusal of Rotumans to work on a day following the death of one of their number, lines of cleavage do exist within the Rotuman community. These are generally kept out of the management's view. In addition to district of origin on Rotuma, recognition of which has been made explicit in the formation of the committee, kinship and religion remain powerful organizational principles among Rotumans in Vatukoula. Kinship figures prominently in recruiting for jobs and in structuring informal relations, but it can also be divisive in that leaders are under pressure to favor their kin in decisions requiring impartiality. Also, as previously reported, the expectations of visiting relatives concerning extended, dependent visits is frequently a cause of intrafamilial conflict. The Catholic-Methodist dichotomy also remains potentially schismatic but thus far has not resulted in factional conflict. In general, it was our impression that church-oriented activities are somewhat less central in people's lives than on Rotuma. For example, the Catholic group had not held a *katoaga* 'large-scale feast in honor of a notable event' for nine years, the last time being upon completion of a new church. On Rotuma, during our year of fieldwork, two such feasts were held.

Despite these lines of cleavage, the overwhelming impression we received in Vatukoula was one of community solidarity and ethnic pride. In the mines, being a Rotuman seemed to be more important to people's sense of identity than being from Oinafa, being a Catholic, being so-and-so's kinsman, or being a winder-driver. People spoke of "Rotumans" in reference-group terms far more often in Vatukoula than elsewhere, including Rotuma, and were concerned with their reputation as an ethnic group in more active ways. They had clearly extended their idea of personal relationships to include any person who could be identified as Rotuman.

The development of firm ethnic boundaries that has taken place in Vatukoula has resulted in sharpened ethnic stereotyping and a crystallization of intergroup attitudes. Let us now consider Rotuman-other relations in this context.

If there is any dominant quality governing attitudes of others toward Rotumans and vice versa, it could be characterized as ambivalence. On the whole, the Europeans at the mine and elsewhere in Fiji have high regard for Rotumans in comparison with other native peoples. This is reflected both in the high proportion of Rotumans employed in the mines and in their overrepresentation in positions of responsibility. European managers of various mine departments were nearly universal in their praise of Rotuman employees. Despite such praise, it was our feeling that the general attitude of Europeans was somewhat condescending, that the praise had an implicit (if not explicit) condition—in comparison with other *native* peoples. It was as if their assumption is that native peoples are generally rather hopeless and that Rotumans sometimes surprise them.

Rotuman pride is something of an anathema to many Europeans precisely because Rotumans refuse to conform to the docile, childlike native of the European stereotype. Thus Mr. Dawson, the stock manager for the mines, openly dislikes the Rotumans. "They haven't an ounce of brains, and besides, they hate Europeans," he commented. When asked how they show their hostility, he could not pinpoint any specific actions, but his analysis made it clear that he equates hostility with refusing to accept European dominance unconditionally. The reasons he gives for the failure of Fijians to perform better at the mines is instructive. He attributes their lack of success to the refusal of most Europeans to join them in their work. Too often, he claims, Europeans tell the Fijians what to do and then go away, as if to show that they would never do that kind of work themselves. In his own dealings with Fijians, Dawson says that he gets right in there with them, "even if it means getting mud on my boots and getting my hands dirty"; as long as he is with them, "I'd match *my* Fijians against any group in Vatukoula" (our emphasis). He adds that he would rather have a not-so-smart fellow who is willing to learn as best he can than a smart one, because the smart ones are those who will fight for themselves and are not "behind you." Mr. Carson's complaints about Rotumans allocating too much authority to themselves, reported above, also illustrate the irritation caused to Europeans by Rotuman pride and self-respect.

The Rotumans, for their part, acknowledge the social superiority of Europeans only inasmuch as it is associated with standard of living, education, and occupation. They do not acknowledge racial superiority, nor do they accept everything culturally European as superior to those practices that are culturally Rotuman. In short, they perceive no insurmountable barriers in their Rotuman ethnicity to achieving an acceptable position in the modern world.

One manifestation of the fluidity with which Rotumans perceive racial boundaries is the ease with which they slip into the part-European category after gaining an education and when it suits their purpose. The advantage of passing for part-European rather than Rotuman stems from European rather than Rotuman ethnic conceptions. In general, the Rotuman stereotype of part-Europeans is unfavorable; they are seen as pretentious, particularly since the behavior of several of the more familiar models is less than exemplary. But being a part-European provides the possibility for entrance into the European social world in a way that being a Rotuman does not. There are six such people in Vatukoula, and their attempt to pass as part-European signals not only an aspiration to move up the ethnic hierarchy but also an alienation from the Rotuman community.

Relations between Rotumans and Fijians are likewise marked by strong ambivalences. In general, Rotuman attitudes toward Fijians parallel the attitudes of Europeans—a mixture of mild disdain with patronizing condescension. They see Fijians fairly much in the mold of indigenes quite a bit more primitive than themselves. Yet Rotumans hold Fijian chiefs in high regard and show them the ritual courtesies they would show their own chiefs; in this sense they see themselves more as part of an indigenous world in which mana and other aspects of Malayo-Polynesian supernaturalism are significant considerations. Since Rotumans do not practice sorcery whereas Fijians do, the latter are a source of awe

if not fear. In general, though, Rotumans in Vatukoula have come
to see themselves as competitive with Fijians. In charitable ventures in Vatukoula, for example, Rotumans attempt to outdo Fijians (and other groups) in a massive, public presentation of their
contribution.[10]

The prevailing attitude of Fijians toward Rotumans appears to
be one of resentment. Thus it was reported to us by several sources
that incidents of hostility between Rotumans and Fijians were not
unusual and were caused in large measure by Fijian resentment of
privileges enjoyed by Rotumans in the mines. During the previous
year, following a massive layoff of personnel, Fijian antipathy to
Rotumans reached a boiling point. The general consensus was that
this occurred because only one Rotuman was among those dismissed. Apparently the matter cooled after a ceremonial presentation of kava by the 'headman' of the Rotuman community to the
head of the Fijian community. The headmaster of the local school
also stressed Fijian resentment of Rotuman achievement. He
stated that Rotuman children appear to be much brighter on the
average than Fijian children and this results in jealousy. Fijian
teachers are unnecessarily harsh with their Rotuman students, he
maintains, and will assign them all the unpleasant jobs, such as
cleaning lavatories, while assigning the pleasurable ones to the Fijians. They never put a Rotuman child in charge of Fijians, but
always do the opposite. Rotuman teachers are discriminatory in a
reverse fashion, he says, but with somewhat less vigor.

Before concluding this section on ethnic relations it may be appropriate to comment on language use. In general, most Rotuman
men learn to get on well in both English and Fijian. English is
necessary to comprehend information passed down from managers and is clearly the status language in the overall community.
Fijian, on the other hand, is frequently necessary to communicate
with Fijian workers whose command of English is poor and who
cannot be expected to learn Rotuman. Most Rotuman women
learn Fijian, but they are less likely than the men to be accomplished in English. This is because they are able to deal with
shopkeepers, service suppliers, and in some instances servants in
Fijian even if exchanges are with Indians, but they have less interaction than men with Europeans or other exclusive English-
speakers.[11]

RESETTLEMENT AND ETHNIC CONSCIOUSNESS

We believe the evidence we have presented demonstrates that the development of ethnic communities and ethnic consciousness varies markedly within the different social milieus in which migrants live. In this concluding section we discuss some of the variables that appear to have had significant effects on these processes for Rotumans in urban Fiji. What we would like to account for by reference to these variables are (1) the degree to which individuals from a given ethnic category (in this case Rotuman) confine their meaningful social relations to persons of a like background, (2) the degree to which ethnicity provides a basis for formal organization, and (3) the degree to which ethnic identity becomes salient in ordering social relations with persons who do not share the same background. Loosely speaking, we believe our study suggests a rank ordering of the four communities with regard to the importance of Rotuman ethnicity. In Levuka it has the least effect, in Lautoka and Suva it is intermediate, and in Vatukoula it is a dominant principle.[12]

The variables affecting ethnicity can be classified into three types, demographic, social structural, and cultural. We have already mentioned the prime demographic variable required for the formation of an ethnic group in the sense we are using the phrase —the existence of an out-group, a people sufficiently contrastive in diacritical features to create a sense of in-group identity. For ethnic boundaries to be formed and actively maintained requires, as we pointed out in the introduction, regular contact with at least one other group. When Rotumans were confined largely to their home island, opportunities for interacting with non-Rotumans were highly restricted, thereby limiting the kinds of experience upon which a solid sense of ethnic identity could be based. In Fiji, however, Rotumans are in regular interaction with several distinctive out-groups.

The absolute and relative size of an ethnic enclave appears to have a significant effect. If the number of individuals in a group is small, the possibilities for organizing along ethnic grounds may be too restrictive, given a minimal number of roles that must be played in a viable organization. If all are kinsmen, of course, they may in fact form a tightly organized group, but chances are that

ethnicity will play a salient role, especially if nonkin are required
to fill crucial organizational positions. From the standpoint of
other persons in the town, ethnic stereotyping becomes a convenient means of ordering social relations only when a sufficient
number of persons become socially visible to provide a consistent
set of expectations. If this is correct, there is probably a "critical
mass" or threshold required for ethnicity to become salient. Thus
we believe it is no accident that the boundaries around Rotuman
ethnicity roughly follow size of Rotuman population in the four
towns, being least distinct in Levuka and most pronounced in
Vatukoula.

Relative size of population also may exert an influence, inasmuch as it affects overall visibility. Even though several hundred members of an ethnic group may dwell in a city, if they are
scattered and form an insignificant portion of the population they
may be absorbed without their ethnicity becoming salient. One
way in which this sometimes happens is for such people to be incorporated into a more inclusive stereotype—as Scandinavians
rather than Swedes or Norwegians, as Orientals rather than Japanese or Chinese, as Polynesians rather than Rotumans or Samoans.
Scattered residence patterns may not only diminish ethnic salien-
cy by making a group less visible socially; it also reduces interaction among members of the group and makes organization more
difficult. It likewise increases interaction with members of out-
groups who are neighbors or who perform localized services, generating friendships and cooperative relationships across ethnic
lines. Contrariwise, condensed residential patterns are likely to
facilitate organizational potential and diminish meaningful external contacts. Stability of residence is likely to be another factor,
since the crystallization of ethnic identity is probably facilitated
by feedback within fixed communication networks. Also, if personnel are continually changing, organizational potential may be
hampered and leadership rendered more problematic. It seems
clear that both the nucleated residence pattern and the relative
stability of residence in Vatukoula have greatly increased the capacity for organization of Rotumans there in comparison with
those in Suva.

One further demographic variable seems worthy of mention although its effects are far from obvious—the degree to which a
community is growing or declining in size. Our hypothesis is that

growth through immigration tends to increase ethnic consciousness because of the continual need to socialize newcomers, a process frequently requiring the explication of boundary mechanisms.

With regard to social structural variables, one must distinguish between those that are imposed by sources outside the ethnic community, particularly those prevailing in dominant sociopolitical groups, and those endemic to the ethnic enclave. To the extent that the dominant society makes ethnicity a major criterion for defining social roles and social privilege, one would expect ethnic consciousness to be fostered. As we have already pointed out, in Fiji ethnicity has been the major criterion for allocating privilege, with the gold mining community in Vatukoula epitomizing the situation. Thus the Rotumans coming to Fiji stepped into a social structure that sought to classify them by race from the very beginning. The process was fostered by their distinctiveness from Fijians in racial type (closer to Polynesian) and language; it was probably furthered by European favoritism for Polynesians (with whom Rotumans are generally classified by Europeans) over the darker Melanesians (including Fijians). It was to the Rotumans' advantage to accept if not nurture the distinction. However, the presence of the part-European, or Euronesian, group probably has had a reverse effect. What is significant about this ethnic category, in addition to the fact that it is second in ethnic rank to European, is that its boundaries are fuzzy; it is therefore easily permeated by those who look like they might have some European blood, speak English reasonably well, and display appropriate decorum. On looks alone, it is easier for Rotumans to pass into this category than any other ethnic group in Fiji. Rotumans who have acquired an education, and particularly those who are in professional or quasi-professional roles, have often elected to pass as part-European.

Social structural variables internal to an ethnic enclave may be equally important for the crystallization of ethnic identity. We might begin by considering a major point of articulation between the ethnic community and the larger structure—the allocation of jobs. It seems clear that in wage-earning, market-oriented societies, one of the primary bases of shared interest is comparability of position in the occupational structure. Men who work together in parallel roles tend to identify with one another and share common concerns. This was particularly evident in the gold mines, where the work is frequently dangerous and where safety and well-being are directly in the hands of one's work mates. In Lautoka, Suva, and Levuka, by contrast, Rotumans are unlikely to be working together in such teamlike efforts. Our hypothesis is that the sharing of work roles greatly increases male solidarity and in turn fosters the development of ethnic solidarity.

Another variable favoring the development of viable ethnic communities is effective, legitimized leadership. Migration may create some difficulties on this score. Thus, on Rotuma, chieftainship is essentially localized and related to the land; Rotumans in Fiji are deprived of these criteria. If a man assumes a Rotuman title while in Fiji, which is possible, it will be a title from Oinafa or Pepjei or some other Rotuman district. Other members of the enclave are from other districts, and although they may pay appropriate ritual deference, they are unlikely to accept his secular leadership as legitimated by the title. Legitimation of leadership in Fiji has therefore become associated with elections, and competency with political effectiveness in the larger community. Whereas effective leadership appears to have a strong centripetal effect on ethnic solidarity, ineffective leadership tends to produce factional disputes along lines of existing cleavages. These may be along kin lines, as in Lautoka, prior locality in the homeland, or religion and occupation. We would therefore advance the proposition that the creation of ethnic solidarity is inversely related to the number of salient divisive criteria within the community as well as the effectiveness and legitimacy of leadership.

There are undoubtedly many features of culture that bear on degree of solidarity among ethnic enclaves, and to complicate matters they may operate at different levels in communication systems. For example, the degree to which a people perceive their customs to be compatible with those of other cultural groups is obviously relevant: if the enclave regards outsiders' customs as repugnant, or vice versa, this is likely to inhibit assimilation and lead to rigid ethnic boundaries. But at a broader conceptual level, the very way in which cultural formulations about differences in custom are arrived at may be significant. In short, variations in epistemology of cultural difference may be of greater importance than the differences themselves. Whereas one group may postulate crucial differences to be racial (this seems to have been characteristic of colonizing Europeans), another may hold supernatural belief systems, language, or custom to be crucial. Clearly, these different views have different implications for the formation of ethnic boundaries. A people may be able to change their language but they cannot readily change their physical characteristics.

Another significant variable has to do with the importance of being a member of a culturally cohesive community. Some cultural systems produce individuals who feel personally immobilized unless they are part of an integral community, or at least they derive great pleasure from being part of one. Those reared in such a tradition tend to form compact ethnic communities even when they are few in number. Other cultural systems place a premium on independence and the maintenance of social distance from others; individuals from a background of this type may self-consciously avoid forming close ties with other members of their ethnic category. The Rotumans are intermediate between these extremes. They seek neither to converge with nor to avoid other Rotumans with any pronounced motivation.

At an even broader level, cultures may vary in the degree to which they emphasize abstract formulations of cultural differences. We have already proposed that Western-educated Rotuman leaders are likely to be more conservative than chiefs without Western education precisely because they have learned to make abstract contrastive judgments about social systems and cultural styles (Howard 1963b). The point is that the very concept of integrity of a cultural system may be of major significance. For the Rotumans, then, Western education has provided the cultural equivalent of a concept of tribal integrity in strongly unilineal societies. It has helped to provide clear criteria for inclusion in a social unit of a higher order despite the fact that the traditional system was characterized by groupings with highly permeable social boundaries.

It would seem, then, that in addition to the demographic and social structural variables that foster the development of ethnic communities, the emergence of an ethnic group is facilitated by the presence of individuals for whom ethnic identity not only becomes problematic but is of ideological import. Although such individuals may develop within an ethnic community, we believe it is more often the case that they are the products of isolation from their native cultural systems, with the very isolation heightening their ethnic awareness. Western schools are breeding grounds of such individuals by virtue of the degree to which they render one's identity problematic (particularly for non-Occidentals) and the degree to which ideological solutions to identity problems are encouraged. But ideological solutions are apt to remain idiosyncratic unless they feed back into communication networks like those provided by ethnic communities. The Vatukoula community and its leadership exemplify this process. When this occurs, and an ideology gains acceptance, conditions are optimal for transforming an ethnic aggregate into an ethnic group.

CONCLUSION

We have argued in this chapter that the development of an ethnic group from an aggregate of individuals who are members of the same ethnic category is primarily dependent upon the development of an ethnic community and ethnic consciousness. Ethnic communities are defined as localized interactive networks consisting of individuals of the same ethnic designation who are emotionally committed to the symbols of their common heritage and formally organized for the purpose of pursuing common goals. Ethnic consciousness is defined as a condition in which ethnic awareness assumes a position of primacy in structuring social relations. For a collectivity, ethnic consciousness is assumed to emerge as a result of repeated messages circulated throughout the network of an ethnic community to the effect that other social differences are less significant for structuring interpersonal relations than ethnic differences. The combination of these conditions generates a critical mass, or threshold effect, leading to the extension of individuals' integrity circles to include all members who identify themselves in terms of the relevant ethnic category (Howard and Howard 1964). This process results in the development of a secondary community in which the "we-feeling" characteristic of primary face-to-face groups is extended to other members of the ethnic category on the basis of an ideology.

We hypothesize that the major variables responsible for the transformation of an ethnic aggregate into an ethnic group are demographic, social structural, and cultural. For Rotumans in Fiji the major demographic variables favoring the development of ethnic communities have been numbers of individuals and residential contiguity. Only in Vatukoula have these variables produced a cohesive community. Social structural variables also have favored Vatukoula as a location for the genesis of Rotuman ethnicity, in large part because the management of the gold mines has used racial criteria as the primary basis for organizing labor. Demographic and social structural variables have therefore combined in Vatukoula to make it the primary place in Fiji for a critical mass to be reached, allowing for the crystallization of Rotuman ethnic identity. The cultural variable of prime significance has been the development of an ideology of cultural contrast, introduced by a Western-educated elite. Although the birth of the Rotumans as an ethnic group has taken place in Fiji, we expect that the ideology which gives it substance will eventually be accepted by all Rotumans and that a general consolidation will be the result.

The Rotuman case may contain some unique features, but we believe that the processes analyzed here may provide the basis for a universal theory of ethnic group development.

NOTES

Support for the original research was provided by the National Institute of Mental Health. The National Science Foundation and East-West Population Institute provided additional support for the analysis of data and writing up of the material. We are grateful to all three agencies. We also wish to acknowledge the excellent editorial suggestions of Michael Lieber and the secretarial assistance of Helen Takeuchi.

1. Like E. K. Francis, we conceive of an ethnic group as a kind of "secondary community" in which the we-feeling characteristic of a primary face-to-face group is extended to others on the basis of an ideology. An ethnic group is, in Francis's conceptualization (1947:399), "the most inclusive, cumulative, and realistic type of *secondary* community."
2. It is of some interest that several Rotuman clubs in Fiji are named for prominent geographical features of the home island.
3. For more extensive treatments of Rotuman society, see Howard (1963b, 1964, 1970).
4. This and what follows reflects the situation during the period of fieldwork in 1960–1961.
5. The category "Other Pacific Islander" is further differentiated for census purposes into Polynesian, Melanesian, and Micronesian, suggesting that these distinctions have a social significance for Europeans in a formal as well as informal sense.
6. Pseudonyms are used throughout this chapter.

7. In Vatukoula 21.7 percent of the Rotuman households are nuclear, with 65.2 percent lineally or laterally expanded; comparable figures for Suva are 23.3 percent and 63.3 percent, for Levuka 25.0 percent and 33.3 percent, for Lautoka 33.3 percent and 40 percent, for Tavua 45.0 percent and 45.0 percent.

8. The term used on Rotuma for 'chiefs' or 'subchiefs', who would ordinarily hold ritually assumed titles, is *gagaja*. The term *pure* on Rotuma, in addition to being used to designate the informal leader of a work group, is used to designate the steward of a landholding *kainaga*.

9. Tafaki, who had subsequently been rehired by the mines, was one of those appointed.

10. This sort of competition is also practiced among church parishes and among districts on Rotuma. In Vatukoula it is other ethnic groups that are the outgroups, but they are structurally isomorphic with the church parishes and districts in the competitive context.

11. This, incidentally, is another manifestation of relatively high Rotuman social status; quite a few Rotuman women have Fijian servants, but we know of no instances of the reverse occurring.

12. Our concern here, it should be made clear, is only with the *development* of ethnic organization and consciousness. The variables that maintain ethnic boundaries in established social systems over the long run may be of quite a different nature.

# 8

# SYDNEY ISLAND, TITIANA, AND KAMALEAI: SOUTHERN GILBERTESE IN THE PHOENIX AND SOLOMON ISLANDS

*Kenneth E. Knudson*

## INTRODUCTION

This chapter is concerned with the analysis of cultural change in a community of Gilbert Islanders relocated at Titiana Point in the Solomon Islands (map 9). This community dates back to the 1930s, when the government of the Gilbert and Ellice Islands Colony initiated a program to alleviate incipient overpopulation in the Southern Gilbert Islands. This was to be done by resettling volunteer families in the virtually uninhabited Phoenix Islands, some 800 miles to the southeast. The first settlers arrived in the Phoenix group in December 1938 and began the task of creating new and relatively self-sufficient communities for themselves on three islands they named Manra (Sydney Island), Orona (Hull Island), and Nikumaroro (Gardner Island). This chapter is concerned specifically with the Sydney Island community. After a period of enforced isolation brought about by World War II, it was discovered that the Phoenix Island area was subject to repeated and lengthy intervals of drought. In the early 1950s the male elders of Sydney Island petitioned the colony government to find a new home for their people. They were eventually offered a site at Titiana (pronounced see-see-AH-nah) Point on Ghizo Island in the Western District of what was then known as British Solomon Islands Protectorate.[1] After a survey party of Sydney Islanders

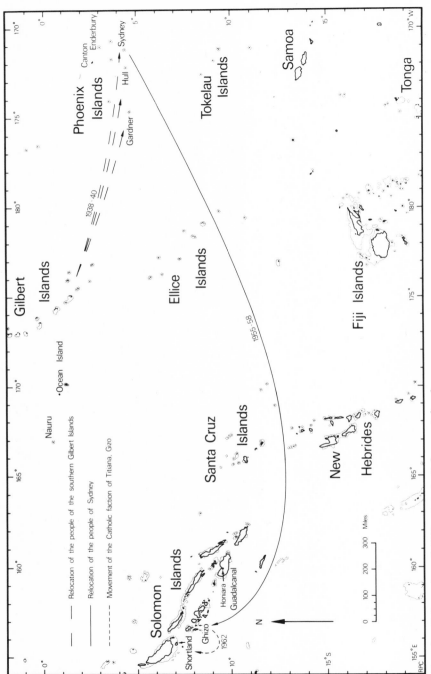

Map 9.   Relocation of Gilbertese to Solomon Islands.

viewed the site and deemed it acceptable, the new relocation began in 1955. The last remaining families left Sydney Island in 1958.

In the Solomons the settlers faced new problems of adjustment, not only to the terrain and climate but also to the presence of culturally distinct neighboring communities and a different pattern of government administration. Adjustment continues, but the principal features of life in the new setting were well worked out by 1962, when a fieldwork period of fourteen months in Titiana was begun. The trends evident at that time were still apparent in 1975, when three more months of fieldwork were completed. The recorded history of the community (Knudson 1965; Maude 1952) and the data collected during the two field periods form the basis for the analysis presented here.

The history of the Titiana community can be seen as a sequence of adjustments to environments that were themselves in a state of flux. The analytic framework best suited to this view is an adaptational one. This framework has a long history in anthropology, in which studies of ecological and evolutionary change have been intimately related (Sahlins and Service 1960; Steward 1955; Watson and Watson 1969). With very few exceptions, however, the adaptational approach has not been used extensively in the analysis of short-term change in studies of single communities (see Harding 1971; Murphy and Steward 1956; Sahlins 1957; Sharp 1952). If the culture of a community is viewed as adaptive for that community, as is generally accepted in anthropological theory, it follows that the analysis of change in any community ought to be conducted within an adaptational framework regardless of the time period being considered.

At this point let me clarify what I understand by "environment," since definitions of the term and statements of what it comprehends are rarely, if ever, explicit. For purposes of this chapter the environment of a social system includes three distinct categories of phenomena: the *physical environment*, which includes such matters as terrain and climate; the *biological environment*, which includes the flora and fauna of the area; and the *social environment*, which includes the cultures of the other societies with which the community is in contact. In examining the history of the Titiana community it will be seen that the initial relocation on Sydney Island involved primarily small-scale differences in physical and biological environments, while the later relocation to the Solomons involved some differences in physical and biological environments but a major change of social environment.

Thus a transplanted social system may be viewed as adapting to a new environment. It follows that an analysis of this kind must begin with a description of the system that is transplanted, since it is this system that adapts to new social, physical, and biological settings. The circumstances of relocation must also be described, for it will make a difference whether an entire community is relocated or whether people from somewhat different communities are brought together to form a new social system.

In the following sections of this chapter the traditional culture of the Southern Gilbertese is briefly described in its environmental setting, along with a summary of the changes known to have occurred in the historic period. This sets the stage by providing an overview of the cultural background of the people who were resettled in the Phoenix Island group. The relocation program itself is then described, followed by a history of the adaptive changes that took place on Sydney Island and in the Solomons.

### THE SOUTHERN GILBERTS

Like almost all the islands of the Central Pacific, the seven islands of the Southern Gilberts (Nonouti, Tabiteuea, Beru, Nikunau, Onotoa, Tamana, and Arorae) are coralline in structure and include both reef island and atoll forms. They are rather large as coral islands go, averaging about 7 square miles in land area. Elevation above sea level rarely exceeds 20 feet. The climate is characterized by a minimum of seasonal variation, due to the islands' proximity to the equator and distance from large bodies of land that might alter the moderating effect of the sea. Temperatures are warm, but rainfall is comparatively low by oceanic standards, ranging between 35 and 60 inches per year. The large size of the islands undoubtedly aids in storage of subsurface water, a factor that lessens the effects of the considerable annual variations in rainfall; droughts are frequent and may persist for several years. Soils are poor throughout the Gilberts, and there is little surface water. Water for horticultural, household, or other uses is generally obtained by digging down to the underlying freshwater lens.

"Fresh water" is something of a misnomer, since the available water is more or less saline depending on locality. Gilbertese horticultural activities depend on trees and other plants that are adapted to semibrackish groundwater rather than to fresh water. During long drought periods the groundwater becomes increasingly saline, but production may not be affected markedly for several years. Rene Catala visited the Gilberts in 1951, when the region had experienced two consecutive years of severe drought conditions, and noted that even then most trees appeared healthy and some were actually producing new growth (Catala 1957:iv, 31, 49–55, 61–66). It is probable that personal habits and preferences of Gilbertese are related to the general scarcity of fresh water: bathing is usually done in the sea with only a quick rinse of fresh water, and the Gilbertese do not like to drink fresh water since they consider it tasteless and insipid.

Although life on these islands might appear precarious, the available data do not bear out this conclusion. It is true that famine and scarcity are themes that appear in Gilbertese folklore, but there is no evidence that these themes are more frequent or intense there than elsewhere in the Pacific. Severe storms are virtually absent from the area, and the combination of large islands (with concomitantly large subsurface storage capacity for water) and dependence on plants adapted to brackish water added up to dense populations that were rarely affected by the considerable local fluctuations in rainfall. Indeed the available population statistics indicate nothing in the way of abrupt changes that might be associated with famine conditions (Knudson 1970:89–90).

The Gilbertese traditionally depended on both the sea and the land for their subsistence and daily needs. Interisland trade in the area was almost nonexistent. There were (and are) two major resources on the land: wet gardens and orchards. Wet gardens were located in the center of the larger islands. These plots were made by digging down to the subsurface water and planting *Cyrtosperma chamissonis* (the Gilbertese name is *babai*), and the plants are mulched with leaves and other organic material to create a small area of very rich soil. In the Southern Gilberts the produce of wet gardens was not a daily staple in the diet, and it should more properly be considered in the category of festive or special occasion foods. The production of large tubers had competitive aspects, and much prestige accrued to the man who grew a very large one.

Orchards included two kinds of trees. The Gilbertese bread-fruit, a variety that is somewhat tolerant of brackish groundwater, is found in the interior of the islands close to the wet gardens. Coconut and pandanus trees, having greater tolerance for salinity, usually are located closer to the shore. Pandanus fruit was the staple in the Gilbertese diet that helped make possible the area's dense population, since pandanus grows practically everywhere, rendering the entire surface area of an island productive.

The surrounding waters appear to have been exceptionally rich because their local temperatures were cooler than those of island groups further west. They were exploited by many techniques, including the use of nets, traps, hook and line, and spearing. Shallow-water areas appear to have been most important and provided the most consistent catches. The lagoon and open sea were of somewhat less significance, but sometimes provided spectacular catches. On a few islands fry were raised in special ponds, but these do not appear to have provided continuous production; harvesting them was a festive occasion (Maude 1963:55–57). As might be expected, canoe making was a valuable skill and Gilbertese men prided themselves on the qualities of the canoes they sailed. Canoes were far too difficult and expensive for most individuals to construct; hence they were usually sponsored by a group. Large fishing traps built in the shallow waters were also group-owned, as were fishing and gleaning areas in the lagoons and on the reef flats.

The groups exploiting these resources are of four distinct types at increasingly inclusive levels of organization (Knudson 1970: 98–106, 287–288). The smallest unit was the household, averaging about five or six persons in size. Households usually were formed about a nuclear family consisting of a man, his wife, and their young unmarried children, but there were also many exceptions to this pattern. The men of the household fished and did most of the garden and orchard work; the women were concerned mostly with keeping house and caring for the children.

Several households were grouped into a kawa 'household cluster', the average population of which was twenty-seven persons, equivalent to about five households. The men of a household cluster cooperated in tasks that required more than one person, such as housebuilding and some fishing operations, and the lands exploited by the members of a household cluster were usually located nearby; frequently such lands came close to comprising a single large block.

Although there were probably a few large independent household clusters, in most cases two or more household clusters constituted a *kainga* 'estate group'. Such groups averaged about thirty-eight persons and usually were made up of one large and one small household cluster. The household clusters of an estate group were not necessarily contiguous. In fact, they appear to have been rather widely separated so as to exploit resources located some distance apart. One of the household clusters served as the administrative center of the estate and was the site of a meetinghouse and the canoe sheds used by members of the estate. The estate group also provided the organizational basis for the construction, operation, and repair of canoes. An estate was an organizational unit in district administration, and its members cooperated in the construction and repair of the estate buildings.

Aboriginally and in the early contact period a district (or "village") in the Southern Gilberts averaged 500 to 800 persons in population. There were at least two districts per island and on Tabiteuea, the largest of the Southern Gilberts, there were nine. Thus the islands were densely populated, averaging on the order of 200 persons per square mile of land area. Districts were politically autonomous, being ruled by a council composed of the elder male leaders of the estate group encompassed by it. On the average, there were about twenty estate groups per district.

The existence of a district was marked by a *maneaba* 'meetinghouse'. A meetinghouse had a large gable roof enclosed at the ends, the eaves extending to within 5 feet of the ground. There were no interior partitions, and the center was left clear during district gatherings. The space under the eaves and just inside the ends was divided into traditional *boti* 'sitting places' assigned to the various estate groups of the district. At district meetings the elder men of the estate groups sat on the inside, toward the center of the building; young men, wives, and children sat behind them. Only elder men were allowed to speak.

The people of the Southern Gilberts were at a tribal level of organization (Sahlins 1968; Service 1962). Chiefs were absent even at the district level, although there were rules of precedence among the assembled male elders (Maude 1963), and from time to time individuals did manage briefly to exert strong leadership over a considerable region (Knudson 1970:104–106). Chieftainship may therefore be said to have been incipient in this area, although it was well developed in the Northern Gilberts (Lambert 1966). Small-scale wars and feuds seem to have been common.

Goodenough (1955) was the first to comment on the flexibility of Gilbertese rules of descent and to point out the adaptive consequences of this system in an area of limited resources. Descent was traced from the ancestral founders of the estate groups, who were thought to have been the earliest settlers of a given island district. Descent might be traced through either male or female links, and demonstration of descent was regarded as establishing a claim to part of the lands of the ancestral founder. Descent was most often claimed through male links, however, and Gilbertese themselves tend to describe the system in terms of patrilineality and patrilocality; sometimes only after considerable discussion does it become apparent that the tendency represents a preferred pattern but not an exclusive one.

Estate groups, therefore, approximated patrilineages with in-marrying females, while household clusters approximated minor patrilineages or patrilateral extended families. A man could, however, choose to live in his mother's estate group, or his grandmother's, or even his wife's, so long as he or his wife was entitled to some portion of the original land of the founder. Because descent was traced through either male or female links, an individual could lay claim to many different plots in the ancestral estates of many early settlers of a given district or island. In fact, not many generations had to elapse before an individual could claim membership in nearly all founder estates. Such potential claims had to be kept current by making contributions to life-crisis feasts (births, first menstruation for girls, marriages, deaths) and other important occasions in the families of those who actually occupied and worked the claimed land. After such contributions ceased, a claim to membership was likely to be challenged. In practice, genealogies were challenged frequently when claims to land were tenuous or when those who actually used the land wished to retain it or allocate it to someone of their own choice.

The Gilbertese system of land tenure was, therefore, intimately bound up with the kinship system and choice between alternative residences. The ancestral founder of an estate divided his holdings among his descendants at his death, and this pattern of inheritance has continued. Land was held by individuals, and a person inherited from both his mother and his father. As a result, a person's inheritance was likely to consist of a number of widely scattered parcels, and exploitation of all of them plus exploitation of a spouse's parcels was difficult. A selection was made, and parcels that could not be put to use were entrusted to others, usually close kinsmen. With time, and with continued use by others, claims to such parcels became tenuous and eventually were only vaguely remembered. When this occurred, attempts to activate the claim would almost certainly be challenged by the occupants.

Aside from the inheritance pattern there were numerous ways of adding to one's holdings. These included fosterage of children, concubinage, and care for the ill or elderly. All these were rewarded by gifts of land. Finally, confiscation of land was the typical punishment for theft, murder, and adultery. Only when a man was without land would he be punished by death, and even this fate was unlikely; a man without land was usually forced to work for others as his punishment if he committed a crime.

In view of the density of population and the low level of productivity of these islands compared to other areas of Micronesia, it is not surprising that access to resources such as land and fishing rights was valued by the Gilbertese. To be without land was equivalent to being a slave. The Gilbertese were also aware that they lived quite close to the population limits of their islands and consciously maintained a nominal rule that no woman should be allowed more than three living children. Adoption, abortion, and infanticide were recognized processes for adjusting the population in accordance with the available resources, and adoption in many cases was merely nominal, serving primarily to extend the choice of possible residence sites. The behavior of young, unmarried girls was strictly regulated with an eye toward eliminating opportunities for sexual intercourse, and the definition of adultery was extended broadly to include such nonsexual acts as speaking to male nonkinsmen. Again the effect was to reduce the opportunities for intercourse and hence control population numbers.

CHANGE IN THE HISTORIC PERIOD

The preceding summary describes Southern Gilbertese culture and its environmental setting as it was during approximately the first two decades of the nineteenth century. At that time contact with the world beyond the immediate horizon was just beginning, and during the years up to 1930 the Gilbertese experienced a great change in social environment.

In terms of political life, when the resettlement program for the Phoenix Islands was proposed, by the mid-1930s, the Gilberts had become part of the Gilbert and Ellice Islands Colony. The colony was under British administration and a uniform governmental system had been instituted, each island having its own administration and government center. Religious change had been considerable; Christian missionaries had been at work for several decades and had succeeded in converting most of the islanders to either the Catholic or Protestant faith (the London Missionary Society was the major Protestant organization represented), although a few adherents of the native religion remained scattered throughout the island group. Finally, the Gilberts had entered the world cash economy; both wage labor and the export of copra had become important sources of money income.

The major features of Southern Gilbertese life in the 1930s are quite well known (see, for example, Catala 1957; Goodenough 1955; Grimble 1921; Knudson 1965:11–13, 25–27; Lundsgaarde 1966, n.d.; Luomala 1965; Maude 1950, 1960, 1963, 1967; Maude and Maude 1931). As a result of nearly a century of political change, the apparently continual precontact outbreaks of small-scale wars and feuds had been suppressed. Each island had its own government, staffed with local people. The administrative structure included a magistrate and court, an administrative staff, a council of legislators, a police organization, a jail, and a hospital. Cooperative trading stores were beginning to appear throughout the Gilberts, displacing the numerous independent traders who were mostly of Chinese descent. The cooperatives were supervised by personnel from the colonial government headquartered at Ocean Island, some 250 miles west of the Gilberts proper. The central government staff was made up almost entirely of British personnel. These administrators toured the islands at intervals during the year, reviewing the activities of the local island governments. For the most part, then, the island governments operated without day-to-day supervision by nonislanders.

Most villages had both a Catholic and a Protestant school, and the colonial government was beginning to actively foster a program for the improvement of education. An alphabet closely paralleling Gilbertese phonemic forms had been worked out by a missionary during the 1860s, and by the mid-1930s a growing literature was being produced by government and mission printing presses. Education was primarily in the hands of native Gilbertese ministers and catechists, who acted as both church leaders and teachers.

Subsistence activities had also changed, and by this time Gilbertese men were being recruited to work for two or three years mining the phosphate deposits on Ocean Island. The mining operations were controlled by the British Phosphate Commission, a quasi-governmental organization that also recruited a few Gilbertese for their operations on Nauru. Some Gilbert Islanders also found employment in the copra plantations of the Line Islands to the east of the Gilberts. Most Gilbertese, however, obtained a small but steady income by producing copra from their own orchards and marketing it through the cooperatives or other local trading stores.

The average populations of districts and islands had changed little by this time, although local populations had become more clustered into villagelike forms. The average size of a district remained at about 500 to 800 persons. Traditional district boundaries were more or less preserved, although on each island the creation of a government center altered the precontact situation somewhat. Representation on the island council was by district, and the island government center was spatially distinct from any of the "villages." Districts remained nearly autonomous on a day-to-day basis, and district affairs continued to be the concern of the male elders of the community, who debated matters in their traditional meetinghouse.

The average size of a household at this time seems to have been about 4.3 persons (Maude 1963:31), a slight decrease from the 5.5 persons of a century before. The household cluster and estate levels of organization persisted, although as distinct population groupings they were not always visibly apparent because of village centralization. The marked bias toward patrilineality in descent and patrilocality in residence also persisted, as did the alternatives for reckoning ancestors and residence. Gilbertese population control and sexual practices such as abortion, infanticide, concubinage, and display of the nuptial sleeping mat had come under political and religious attack. A special land court had been instituted to deal with disputes in tenure and inheritance. The association of estate groups with traditional seating sites along the edge of the district meetinghouse went unchanged, however, and the elders of each estate continued to speak for its members in discussions and to act as their leaders and representatives in all district matters.

Kinsmen in household clusters still cooperated when numbers of people were required, but for the most part the literature indicates that the members of each household lived from day to day on the products of its lands and the surrounding waters. In fact, households were considerably more independent than they had been a century before, and the difference in average household size, if significant, probably reflects a declining need for larger numbers of people to cooperate. The increasing independence of households seems to have been due to changes in fishing operations that were in turn due to the effects of the new social environment (Goodenough 1963:337–343). Cash and the ready availability of new tools and new materials had resulted in a large increase in the number of canoes in the Southern Gilberts, because it had become easier for an individual to sponsor canoe construction. Furthermore, new types of fishhooks, nets, and lines meant that lagoon and open sea waters had become more important fishing areas, while dependence on the shallow waters and the large, fixed fish traps had decreased proportionately. The result was a decline in the significance of household clusters and estates as the basis of cooperation in the construction, operation, and maintenance of canoes and fixed fish traps. Undoubtedly, the availability of new tools for garden and orchard work plus the salability of copra (for which little or no cooperative work was necessary) contributed to the emerging significance of household-level economics and the declining significance of inclusive kin groups such as the household cluster and estate.

RESETTLEMENT ON SYDNEY ISLAND

It is clear, then, that a century or more of contact with the outside world had influenced every aspect of Gilbertese culture; from social and political life to economic and religious patterns, the changes that had taken place as a result of the new social environment were considerable. The administrators of the colonial government were particularly concerned about the effect of these changes on family life and individual welfare (Maude 1952). It was pointed out that the outcome of (1) the removal of population control techniques such as abortion and infanticide, (2) the introduction of Western medical techniques, and (3) the increased economic reliance on individual family holdings was likely to be cumulative. Specifically, the combined effect of these changes throughout the Gilberts was likely to result in an overpopulation problem (brought about by increasing birth rates and decreasing death rates) plus a land fragmentation problem (brought about by the distribution of land to large numbers of children). The ultimate result would be poverty and a lower level of subsistence throughout the islands. The administrators also believed that the problem was imminent and that its beginnings were already being felt in the southern part of the archipelago. There was in fact evidence that on many islands, particularly in the Southern Gilberts, fragmentation of landholdings had become extreme and some people were already living dangerously close to subsistence level.

The resettlement program was intended to relieve the situation by taking a large number of volunteer families from among the poorest Southern Gilbertese and settling them on the environmentally similar, though rather more barren, Phoenix Islands. These islands, in the mid-1930s, had no indigenous inhabitants. There was a total population of about fifty persons on the eight islands in the group (including Canton and Enderbury, which lie to the north of the other six and are sometimes considered as distinct from them). Almost all these people were engaged in operating the commercial copra plantations on Sydney and Hull Islands.[2]

The motives of these administrators may have been more complex, although definitive data are lacking. It has been pointed out (Hilder 1961:213) that the Phoenix Islands lie almost exactly halfway between Hawaii and Fiji and a trans-Pacific airline route was almost certain to be established shortly. The aircraft of that day were limited in range, and therefore control of the Phoenix Islands as a refueling stop would give effective control of the entire route. It was also known that one of the few reasons the United States would recognize as substantiating a claim to an uninhabited region was colonization (Maude 1961:69). In any event, the opportunity may well have been seen as a chance to secure two goals at once, one humanitarian and the other political.

A survey party which included a number of Gilbertese men aware of Gilbertese subsistence needs and practices was led to the Phoenix group by H. E. Maude, then a member of the colonial administration and well acquainted with Gilbertese culture. After its tour the party returned to the Gilberts to discuss the projected resettlement with Gilbertese at village meetings. Earlier talks had convinced Maude that there was considerable enthusiasm among Southern Gilbertese about the opportunity to improve their lot. The results of the survey and the reports by the Gilbertese participants at the village meetings were positive (though, of course, not entirely without drawbacks and negative response). The decision was therefore made by the colonial government to proceed with the program.

Three islands in the Phoenix group were selected for settlement: Sydney, Hull, and Gardner. Gardner was to be given a smaller number of settlers than the other two islands because its undeveloped resources were insufficient for a large population. Canton Island was selected as the headquarters of the Phoenix Islands administrative district, which was incorporated into the Gilbert and Ellice Islands Colony as part of the resettlement program. The plan was not intended to effect culture change; it was expected that Gilbertese culture would be replicated in the Phoenix Islands. Volunteers were to be taken as family groups, and each individual was to be allocated plots of productive land. Island governments and schools were to be established, trading cooperatives were planned, and native mission personnel were allowed for.

The volunteers were told that they must agree to be treated according to Gilbertese custom as castaways, which meant they would have no further claim to their lands in the Gilberts. The rights over these plots were distributed to close kinsmen of the emigrants. Finally, in seeking volunteers, the quality of their prospective life in the Phoenix Islands was consciously played down by the administration, emphasis being placed on the fact that the work of development would be hard and long and the life one of isolation. Despite the emphasis on the rigors of the resettlement program, it did not prove difficult to find volunteers. Those in charge of selecting emigrants were surprised both by the numbers of people who responded and by the severely limited resources on which many had been forced to rely. Selection was on the basis of quality and quantity of resources available, and those who seemed to have the least to draw on were chosen. It seems evident that many of the Gilbertese saw that their situation might become difficult within a short time, although motivations for volunteering differed from person to person and family to family. Informants stated that some participants actually had considerable resources but concealed this fact and took part primarily for the adventure. While a large percentage of migrants were land-poor and probably on the young side, given the preference for people in excellent health the population of migrants did represent a cross section of Gilbertese society vis-à-vis social status and knowledge of Gilbertese culture.

The first party of forty-one Gilbertese landed on Sydney Island on Christmas Day, 1938. The arrival of the last boatload of emigrants in September 1941 brought the total population to 302 persons. Large numbers of settlers had also been established on Hull Island, but Gardner received only a few in accordance with the resettlement plan. Canton Island came under development as an airbase just before the outbreak of World War II in the Pacific in late 1941. It continued to serve as a regular refueling point until the advent of long-range jet aircraft in the late 1950s. Canton, with its important airfield, eventually was placed under a joint American and British administration but continued to be the headquarters for the Phoenix Islands District of the Gilbert and Ellice Islands Colony.

Like the islands of the Gilbert group, Sydney Island is low-lying and coralline in structure. The maximum height above sea level is only 20 or 30 feet. The island is shaped somewhat like a doughnut when seen from the air, being oval in shape with an average diameter of about 2 miles. In the center of the island is a highly saline lake which lacks an opening to the sea. The lake is somewhat more than a mile in diameter, so that the width of the surrounding rim of land varies from about one-third to just over one-half mile. Annual rainfall on Sydney Island appears to vary considerably, as it does in the Gilberts. Furthermore, the rainfall appears to average only about 40 inches per year (Knudson 1965:42), lower than the average for most of the Gilberts. The small land area and the saline lake in the center of the island imply a small subsurface lens of fresh water. This in turn probably accounts for the fact that although the flora and fauna of the Phoenix group are very similar to those of the Gilberts, the total number of plant species in the

Phoenix group has been estimated at only twenty to thirty, or approximately half that of the Gilberts. The marine life of the area is apparently even richer than that of the Gilberts; however, the absence of an extensive fringing reef limited fishing activities to some extent and led to the construction of small canoes that could be launched and landed easily despite the difficult surf.

The early settlers on Sydney Island attempted to grow cyrtosperma by digging wet gardens, but the subsurface water proved too saline and the gardens were abandoned. Pandanus was also a failure when introduced in the early years of the settlement, but it was introduced again about 1950, this time successfully. Portulaca, an edible plant that grew wild over much of the island, became a mainstay in the diet (Turbott 1954) and was gathered in day-long excursions involving entire households. There were, then, some differences in subsistence activities because of the differences in resources on Sydney Island.

The migrant population of three hundred people was divided into two contiguous village areas and a government station. A complete island government headed by a magistrate was established. In 1940 an island meetinghouse was erected to serve all residents and immediately became the center of a dispute over traditional sitting places. Meetinghouses in the Southern Gilberts differ in details of construction and also in the seating arrangements assigned to estate groups. Since the island residents included household groups from all islands of the Southern Gilberts, the argument over who should sit where seems to have been intense and apparently lasted several days. It was finally resolved with the advice of the British administrative officer in charge of the developing Phoenix Island communities. He suggested that each household should be assigned a spot, with no one being allowed to occupy the location he had been accustomed to in the Gilberts.

The decision to ignore traditional seating patterns in organizing the Sydney Island meetinghouse represented a break with tradition. Yet older men continued to be the only people with the right to speak at community meetings, although this rule was probably stretched somewhat, since not all household heads were elderly. The result was therefore a kind of "least common denominator" of pan-Gilbertese custom and demographic reality stemming from the fact that the units of emigration from the Gilberts were households rather than extended kinship units.

A similar process of change can be seen in the organization of life-crisis feasting, events that were attended in the Gilberts only by kinsmen of the celebrant. On Sydney Island one of the earliest such events to be celebrated was the wedding of the daughter of the island magistrate. The magistrate invited all island residents to the feast he sponsored, and this became a general pattern for all life-crisis feasts thereafter. We may be sure that not all the three hundred or so residents attended each feast, but they were entitled to, and each household probably sent a representative, bearing, of course, the contribution of food, clothing, or whatever custom demanded.

The single most important event in this formative period of the Sydney community was a dispute between two groups that culminated in a permanent schism in the community. One group, perhaps best referred to as the "collectivists," argued that development of the island would proceed faster if it were done cooperatively. They suggested that when difficult tasks arose everyone should help without regard to locale or land ownership; thus, they reasoned, the entire island would benefit from the marshaling of as much help as possible for any task that might arise. Another group, the "individualists," argued that such a system would make it possible for the lazy to live through the efforts of the energetic; they suggested instead that development of the island would best proceed if each family were to do its own work. The collectivists outnumbered the individualists, but they could not force cooperation on an island-wide basis. One of the two villages did work on a collective pattern, however, so that this classic divergence in ideologies differentiated the two villages on the island.

The schism, though permanent, did not eliminate the occasional need for cooperative labor. After World War II an American visitor to Sydney Island suggested that young men form a service club which would make the labor of its members available to all who might request it, the only requirement being that meals be served while the task was in progress. There were also social aspects to the club, which had its own meetinghouse, and it proved to be a great success, drawing members from both the collectivist and the individualist groups.

Not only did the two groups maintain their social schism, but they also elaborated it even further through religious sectarianism. The first group of settlers on Sydney had all been at least nominal adherents of the Protestant faith. They asked that all later arrivals also be Protestant; the colonial government agreed, hoping to avoid the schisms between Catholics and Protestants that were so disruptive wherever they broke out in the Gilberts. As it turned out, it seems that some settlers on Sydney had previously been Catholics but became at least nominal Protestants because they wanted to settle on Sydney. Early in the 1950s a Catholic missionary arrived on the island and immediately succeeded in obtaining converts. Later a catechist arrived to lead the new, though small, congregation. Interestingly enough, a considerable number of the Catholic converts were members of the individualist faction, and it therefore appears that differences of opinion on the island were great and tended to diverge into strongly opposed philosophies. The schism between Catholics and Protestants grew continually wider, ultimately leading to the formation of a separate Catholic community after the Sydney Islanders arrived in the Solomons.

In spite of differences of opinion and lines of cleavage that appeared in the Sydney Island community, there was a genuine esprit de corps and a pride in the island that developed quickly as the inhabitants settled in. The war years served mainly to isolate the Phoenix Islands (other than Canton) from the rest of the world. Imported luxuries and manufactured goods became scarce or unobtainable for a time, but the settlers either did without them or, when possible, resumed making the traditional objects that had been displaced. Thus the isolation does not appear to have severely disrupted normal life.

Eventually, Canton Island became a place of employment for men and even a few women from Sydney and the other Gilbertese settlements. There was employment in a wide variety of occupations, including domestic servant positions in the homes of European and American administrative personnel, work in the island hotel, at the military and airline facilities, and with a commercial fishing company. Later some men worked in the copra plantations of the Line Islands and a few even traveled to the islands of Hawaii, Midway, and Wake in the employ of one of the airlines. The economic function of Canton Island relative to the Phoenix Islands was therefore much the same as that of Ocean Island relative to the Gilberts. As in the Gilberts, the opportunities for full-time employment on one's home island were few (limited almost exclusively to mission and island government personnel), and the work on Canton involved life on another island for a considerable period of time.

The total population of Sydney Island appears to have increased gradually over time, with the original number of 302 prewar settlers growing to 369 permanent residents who were relocated to the Solomons in the middle and late 1950s. In spite of Canton's modern airport and overseas services, Sydney and the other islands of the Phoenix group were more remote from the world economy than were the Gilberts. In the years 1949 to 1952, the period during which off-island employment was at its highest, only about 10 percent of the Sydney Island people were working on other islands. Copra production on Sydney seems to have been low compared to Gilbert Islands levels, although sales of handicraft items to airport personnel and travelers on Canton provided an added source of cash. On the whole, Sydney Island is remembered by its former inhabitants as a delightful place to live and one where money, though still necessary, was relatively unimportant in life.

RELOCATION TO THE SOLOMON ISLANDS

During the early years of the Phoenix Island relocation program, the plan appeared to be an unqualified success—so much so that Gardner Island was settled by a full complement of Gilbertese a few years after the end of World War II (Laxton 1951). In the late 1940s, however, about a decade after the arrival of the first group of settlers on Sydney Island, there were several years of low rainfall, and drought conditions prevailed throughout the Phoenix Island area. There is some evidence to show that drought periods occur on approximately a seven-year cycle in the Phoenix group, and it is probable that these recurring periods of low rainfall are responsible for the absence of an indigenous population. The droughts also vary in intensity; those of the late 1940s were endured by the Gilbertese without undue difficulty, but those in the early 1960s forced the colonial government to abandon the resettlement program entirely.

The administrators of the Gilbert and Ellice Islands Colony were concerned about the effect of the droughts on the Phoenix Island settlers, but a doctor who visited Sydney Island in 1950 was surprised at the general level of good health in the community. The settlers were found to be existing on a well-balanced though monotonous diet, and later in the Solomons my informants from Sydney remarked frequently that they had felt very well there and that children were especially strong and active.

In spite of these reports, the elder leaders of the Sydney Island community eventually sent a group of representatives to colonial headquarters at Tarawa in the early 1950s, asking that the government find a new home for their people. It had not been easy for the island leaders to reach this decision; they thought the island should be abandoned whereas the adherents of the newly founded Catholic mission expressed a desire to stay on the island even if the remainder of the population were moved elsewhere. But gradually most people came to agree with one of the non-Catholic elders who, during a community meeting attended by a visiting colonial administrative officer, remarked that while the island was certainly a healthy place to live, it held little prospect for future development. Their children, therefore, could look forward to little more than mere continued existence at the same level as then obtained.

According to informants in the Solomons, the availability of fish on Sydney was not changed by the droughts, and when the settlers' wells became brackish a rationing system was put into effect for dispensing water from a rainwater cistern in the government center. But the long periods without rain killed many young coconut palms, and during periods of heavy rains the level of the lake in the center of the island rose, inundating planted areas and killing all growth touched by its saline waters. Therefore the island offered little in the way of improvement for the future and the decision was taken to request relocation elsewhere.

The colonial government decided that the effects of the droughts were indeed severe, that Sydney Island had been the most seriously affected, and that the settlement there should ultimately be abandoned. Having made this decision, it was not easy to find a new home for the Gilbertese settlers. Return to the Gilberts was clearly out of the question, and there were no other unpopulated islands suitable for habitation. After much deliberation, the colonial government decided to offer the Sydney Islanders an opportunity to relocate their community in what was then called the British Solomon Islands Protectorate. The Solomons differ from the Gilberts and Phoenix in many respects, but both areas were and are under British administration. This would obviously simplify the relocation considerably, and it was felt that since the Solomons seemed to be underpopulated, the Gilbertese could easily be accommodated as new settlers.

There may have been other factors in the decision, just as there may have been other factors involved in the Phoenix Island resettlement program. In the mid-1950s, the initial steps were being taken toward eventual independence for both the colony and the protectorate. Elsewhere in the world, in the West Indies and the Rhodesias, British administrators were attempting to bring culturally diverse peoples together under single, independent governments. They may have thought that establishing Gilbertese settlers in the Solomons would be a step toward a similar unity between the Gilberts and the Solomons. If such a plan ever existed, however, definitive information about it is lacking.

Both the protectorate and the colony were under the jurisdiction of the high commissioner for the Western Pacific. At the time, the high commissioner's purview also included Fiji and the British government of the New Hebrides Condominium (administered jointly with France). The offices of this inclusive government organization were located at Honiara on Guadalcanal in the Solomon Islands. A joint relocation program was worked out between the protectorate and the colony, the first measure being to take several representatives from Sydney Island on a tour of possible sites in the Solomons. Representatives of several islands in the Gilberts were also included in the touring party, since it was hoped that the Solomons would prove able to take settlers not only from the Phoenix Islands but from the Gilberts as well, thereby helping alleviate new population problems there.

The Western District of the Solomon Islands was selected as the probable relocation area, since it was the least populous part of the Solomons. Several locations were examined by the survey party, and, although they expressed a preference for places that resembled their coral island homelands, they finally stated that a site at Titiana Point on Ghizo Island would be acceptable to them. (See map 10.) On their return to Sydney Island they enthusiastically reported their experience at a community meeting, and the elder leaders of the island agreed that this would be their people's new home.

The site at Titiana was preferred by administrative officers over

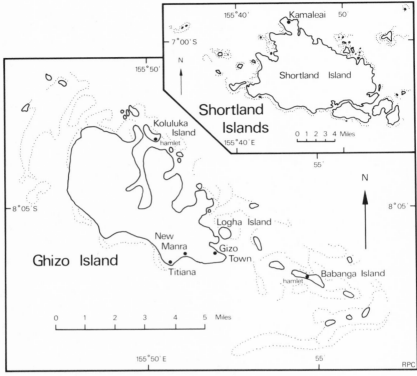

Map 10.    Destination islands: Ghizo and the Shortlands.

other locations because of its proximity to Gizo town and because of the availability of mature coconut groves that could be used by the settlers. Gizo town is the administrative center for the Western District of the Solomons, and government officers could readily monitor the progress of the new community and help avert crises that might arise in this new and different environment. Since the settlers would have to begin from scratch, clearing the dense tropical forest from the village location and planting new gardens and orchards, the mature coconut groves would provide a needed resource until the community became self-sufficient.

Ghizo is one of the smaller islands of the Solomons, being only about 6 miles long by 4 miles wide. It is roughly oval in shape, and the northern coast is deeply indented by two inlets that cut nearly across the island. Ghizo is low in relief but rugged, since the interior consists of steep hills forming an amoebalike backbone that renders land away from shore difficult to use. The maximum elevations of these interior ridges are only 400 to 500 feet, but since the area has an annual rainfall of about 125 inches, the land away from populated areas is covered by dense tropical forests.

There are a number of smaller, lower islands just offshore to the north, east, and southeast of Ghizo. These islands are connected to one another and to Ghizo by an intricate reef system which makes travel between them time-consuming, even by so small a conveyance as a canoe. Some of these islands were cleared and planted with coconuts before World War II; others retained their natural cover of trees and brush.

Gizo town is located at the east end of Ghizo Island, and in 1962–1963 it numbered about two hundred permanent residents. The town area was relatively clear—most of it planted with aging coconut palms. Not only was it an administrative center with government offices, a hospital, post office, police headquarters, agricultural offices, and public works center, but it was also a trading and distribution center. Ships from overseas entered its sheltered harbor as frequently as twice a month to unload cargo and take on copra. This cash crop was collected and stored in government warehouses while awaiting shipment overseas.

The town and the island, though small, are surprisingly diverse culturally. In addition to the European community with its nucleus of government officers, planters, missionaries, and a businessman or two, there was a sizable Chinese community associated with the many small and large trading companies in the town. There was also a heterogeneous Melanesian community of civil and business employees and a sprinkling of Polynesians from islands such as Rennell, Sikaiana, and Ontong Java. Finally, there were a few Fijians and also some Japanese businessmen. Several Christian religious denominations were represented in the town, and there was a large Catholic mission station on Logha, a small island just across the harbor.

Titiana is located on Ghizo Island's south shore about 2 miles west of Gizo town. There are two Melanesian villages on the island: Pailongge is located about 2 miles further west of Titiana along the same shore, while Sagheraghi is on the remote northwest point of the island. Both these villages are small, numbering about a hundred persons each. All four settlements are located on narrow coastal plains that are rarely as much as a quarter-mile wide.

As in the case of the Phoenix Islands program, the resettlement at Titiana was not envisaged as a culture-change project, although it was realized that some change was inevitable. The Solomon Islands Protectorate at the time was in the process of changing from a "headman" form of local administration to a system of local councils. In contrast to the Gilberts, where islands had had their own local governments for several decades, in the Solomons the headman had been a local leader who served as the focus of contact between a community and the protectorate's district administrative officers. The officers of the protectorate administration were primarily British, though a scattering of other nationalities was represented in fields such as agriculture and public works. In the local council system, a council represented a region including a number of distinct communities; this system was still in its formative years and local councils were in no way as nearly autonomous as the Gilbertese island governments. The Sydney Islanders, it was clear, would no longer constitute a distinct governmental entity: they would now be subsumed within the administration of one of the local councils.

The new settlement was to be led by a resettlement officer who was to be a Gilbertese; this role came to parallel that of a local headman in the protectorate organization. The relocation was to include settlers direct from the Gilberts as well as from Sydney Island; this decision was made because it was thought that the Sydney Islanders were likely to be dispirited and physically weakened by their drought experiences, and the inclusion of a nucleus of settlers direct from the Gilberts would provide a strong and vigorous cadre. The protectorate's agricultural department would provide instruction in local gardening techniques as well as seeds and cuttings for planting. Ultimately each household head was to be provided with clear title to a 4-acre block of land.

The first party of settlers, numbering thirty persons, arrived on Ghizo on 26 September 1955. It included settlers from both the Gilberts and Sydney and was led by the resettlement officer, who came direct from the Gilberts. This party began clearing the village site and garden areas, and its members were allowed to take occasional stevedoring work in Gizo town to vary their routines somewhat. Over the next three years small groups of new arrivals gradually increased the size of the community. Settlers continued to arrive from both the Gilberts and from Sydney Island, until by the early 1960s those from the Gilberts comprised approximately 20 percent of the Titiana population.

Adjustment to the new setting took place gradually and with little difficulty. A representative was selected for the local council having jurisdiction over Titiana, and a local court was established in the community subject to the higher district court in Gizo town. The London Missionary Society, which was not represented in the Solomons, handed over care of its adherents to the Methodist church, while the Catholic Gilbertese affiliated with the local Catholic mission. The early arrivals constructed a community meetinghouse, celebrating its completion with a feast to which the village elders invited all Gizo Europeans. This became an annual event for the community. A Methodist church building was also erected next to the meetinghouse with services conducted by Gilbertese church leaders and Melanesians trained in the Methodist mission; these Solomon Island pastors also conducted the local school until the establishment of a government primary school led by a native Gilbertese. Masses for Catholics in the community were conducted in the meetinghouse by a priest from the Catholic mission on Logha opposite Gizo town.

The slowly expanding community had filled nearly all the available space at Titiana Point by early 1958. Therefore when the decision was made by the protectorate and colony governments to remove all the remaining settlers from Sydney Island, it was necessary to construct a subsidiary village about a half-mile nearer Gizo town; this site came to be called New Manra. More than two hundred newcomers were settled into houses there in late September 1958 when the move finally took place. These included most of the Catholic faction, who had continued to hold out the hope that they would be left to occupy Sydney by themselves. After this large and sudden increase in the size of the community to approximately five hundred persons, a few settlers were added in small numbers direct from the Gilberts, but this flow had ceased almost entirely by 1962.

## THE TITIANA COMMUNITY

In mid-1963 the Titiana community numbered 436 persons living in four distinct residence areas. In Titiana proper lived 298 persons, while 86 Gilbertese resided in New Manra. A further 25 members of the community lived in Gizo town, while 27 persons lived on Logha Island, near the Catholic mission station. The Catholic members of the Titiana community had continued to differ with the Protestant faction over many issues of village politics as well as religion. In the late 1950s the island of Logha had been purchased by the Catholic mission, and in 1959 the Titiana Catholics were offered wage-labor jobs constructing the mission buildings; later they were given the opportunity to live at one end of the island and work the coconut groves as a source of income. Most of the Catholic population took advantage of this opportunity. In mid-1962, however, land was made available to the Titiana community at Kamaleai Point in the Shortland Islands about 150 miles northwest of Ghizo. This was the first instance of land allocation to Gilbertese from Titiana. Land in the Ghizo area was not made available until the following year. The opportunity to settle in the Shortlands was given to Catholic members of the Titiana community because the Shortlands were and are a predominantly Catholic area. By mid-1963 some eighty-five persons lived at Kamaleai, most of them Catholics who had moved there from Logha. In addition to the two communities of Titiana and Kamaleai, in mid-1963 there were some twenty-five Gilbertese affiliated with the Titiana resettlement program who lived in Honiara, most of them either attending school or in government employ.

Subsistence in the Titiana community rested on three major sets of activities. Fishing and gardening were traditional techniques for obtaining needed goods. Both techniques were, or course, modified somewhat in accordance with local conditions. Titiana is protected by an offshore reef. The beach is therefore free of rough surf, and canoes constructed locally could be made larger to take advantage of these conditions. Divers equipped with goggles and spear or knife obtained various kinds of marine life, including shellfish. Gardens were not irrigated, but the abundant rainfall made this unnecessary, and a variety of plants were cultivated in small plots of flat land.

A second subsistence strategy actually encompassed a number of different part-time cash income enterprises. An important opportunity here was stevedoring at the port of Gizo, a job that paid comparatively well for the few days each month that overseas ships were in the harbor. Another source of cash was the sale of handicraft goods and souvenirs, such as mats, model canoes, baskets, and so on. There was always a small but steady, demand for such items among the Europeans in Gizo, and at Christmastime the market was considerable. Another source of cash was the sale of copra. Several of the islands near Ghizo had been acquired by the protectorate government from their former owners and given to the Gilbertese for use as resource areas. The members of the community were divided into six copra sections for exploiting these resources, two sections being at work at any given time and remaining at work for two weeks. These sections were not cooperative groups; each household worked on its own to harvest coconuts, open them, and dry the inner flesh. Quotas were set by general agreement, each family keeping the money it earned. A third major activity was full-time employment. There were a number of opportunities in the government offices, businesses, and homes in Gizo town.

Given these activities open to the Titiana people, three distinct modes of subsistence had developed, and with them different household types. The multigeneration extended family remained important and usually involved two adult males. One was typically employed full-time at an unskilled job such as laborer. He provided the family with the money for necessities while the other was busy at gardening and fishing, providing the staple foods.

Among smaller, nuclear families there were two modes of subsistence. In some households an adult male had a garden and did some fishing but also engaged in stevedoring when a ship was in port. This income, combined with copra and handicraft sales, was about equal to that of a laborer, and there was the additional advantage of having adequate time for traditional subsistence pursuits.

Finally, other nuclear families depended almost entirely on the cash income of the family head, who was employed full-time. Most of these family heads were skilled workers holding jobs such as teacher, powerhouse mechanic, nurse, or plumber. The income from these occupations was sufficient to enable their families to buy their necessities, offsetting the disadvantage of full-time employment which left very little time for gardening or fishing.

The organization of the Titiana meetinghouse was similar to that on Sydney Island, each household having its own seating area along one of the sides. The addition of new families from the Gilberts meant that the Sydney Island meetinghouse could not be duplicated, of course, and the departure of a number of families for Kamaleai changed the number of households represented. Membership in the Titiana community was dependent on participation in meetinghouse activities, such as the annual feast and dance commemorating its completion and the New Year's Day dancing competition. Those who did not participate or contribute to these activities withdrew, in effect, from the community. In one such case a Gilbertese woman who married a Melanesian man from Pailongge took up residence with him in Gizo town, granting control of her house and plot to a near relative. She no longer participated in meetinghouse activities, nor did she make contributions to them (such as food or mats for the floor) when the elders required it; she was not considered to be a member of the community. In the opposite case, however, a Melanesian man from Pailongge moved in with his Gilbertese wife and participated in community affairs to the best of his ability; he was considered at least nominally a member of the Titiana community.

Membership rules were therefore clearly defined in the community. The actual conduct of meetings was somewhat less rigorous than reported for Sydney Island or, certainly, for the Gilberts. Younger men did speak, as did women on occasion. This practice reflected the structure of the community, in which not all families had elder representatives to speak for them, but it also reflected the emergence of smaller, nuclear family households as a significant and viable unit in the local economy. Informants spoke of the meetinghouse as a "free *maneaba*" where anyone could speak his mind, although usually only male elders did so.

The community was arbitrarily divided into halves for competitive purposes. The two divisions were called North and South, and formerly the Catholic residents of Logha constituted a third group. These divisions practiced separately for the New Year's Day dancing competition, which aroused great interest and attracted many spectators from Gizo and local Melanesian communities. The anniversary of the completion of the meetinghouse was celebrated in August. For this event a fish drive was held in the lagoon and the elders directed each household to contribute equal amounts of specific local foodstuffs. The entire European community from Gizo town was invited to the feast each year and treated to a display of Gilbertese dancing. The north/south division was not an important organizational feature for this event; instead the feast demonstrated to government officials that the community was self-sustaining.

Formal relations with the protectorate administration were the concern of a six-man committee; a seventh man served as principal contact with Western District officials. It was the resettlement officer's retirement in 1962 that led to the establishment of this committee. Its powers were undefined, however, and its sphere of authority was unclear, so that in 1962–1963 most community affairs were actually being handled by the elder men. The community also had a representative on the local council that had authority over the area, but because of the proximity of Titiana to the protectorate offices, the people of Titiana participated but little in local council activities.

Relations between the Gilbertese and members of other communities were neither intensive nor hostile. There had been a few intermarriages, mostly involving Gilbertese women and Melanesian men. Liaisons and marriages between Gilbertese men and Melanesian women were very rare. On the whole, the Gilbertese did not feel close to their Melanesian neighbors, although there were many individual exceptions and several friendships. Early attempts at mixed stevedoring crews of Gilbertese and Melanesians proved unsuccessful, and segregated crews had become the rule. There had been some minor altercations in Gizo town between Gilbertese and Melanesians, but no large-scale fighting. The Gilbertese tended to view the Melanesians as somewhat backward, crude, and uncivilized. The Melanesians, on their part, felt that Gilbertese were noisy, slightly immoral, and lacking in culture. In addition, there were feelings of resentment on the part of many Melanesians, who viewed the Gilbertese as having taken land and jobs that ought to belong to Melanesians.

The Titiana Methodist church, virtually the only religious organization in the community after the departure of most Catholics for Kamaleai, was gradually being integrated into the local Methodist mission organization. It was headed by a Melanesian pastor, but most were services led by Gilbertese members of the church organization. In 1963 exchange services with Melanesian congregations were being held, and the church was emerging as an important cross-cultural link with other local ethnic groups. Within the Titiana population the church was the focus of one of the most important community events, the Christmas Day singing competition between the northern and southern halves of the village.

One major problem for both the community and the government was that of how land was to be allocated to the immigrants. The government had maintained at the outset of the relocation program that each household in Titiana would receive clear title to a 4-acre plot of land. There were several stumbling blocks to land allocation, however. The government had to decide what constituted a household and a household head (since title was granted only to household heads) and whether very large households were to get one or two plots of land (as some eventually did). The land had to be surveyed and recorded before legal titles could be issued. In the process, the government discovered that there was not enough productive land in the Titiana vicinity for all the households. To make up the deficiency, many of the small islands near Ghizo, which had been used as communal resources for copra production, were subdivided and included in the lands to be allocated to households. The islands were from 6 to 10 miles from Ghizo and accessible only by canoe. Land in the Shortland Islands, 150 miles north of Ghizo, was purchased by the government for distribution to emigrant households. All families retained their rights to house plots in Titiana and New Manra.

The allocation of land took place in 1963. The government, in order to be fair in distribution, used a random selection procedure to match households with land plots. Regardless of the fairness of the procedure, many households were enraged at being placed far away from Titiana. Others were furious at having spent years clearing and cultivating plots only to have them allocated to other households. By making land exchange possible, the government was able to alleviate some, but by no means all, of the discontent over the allocation. To make matters worse, it took another ten years for the government to issue the deeds of title. In the meantime, government agriculturists in the Solomon Islands determined that a 4-acre plot was too small for household subsistence; 10 acres was deemed to be a reasonable minimum.

The land allocation program has had several outcomes. First, it has forced a dispersion of the community, which now has people living in Titiana, New Manra, Gizo, Mbambanga (a small island southeast of Ghizo), and on Alu and Laomana in the Shortland Islands. Second, it has resulted in considerable tension between the community and the government. Third, it has provided the community with another problem which has yet to be resolved: how to reallocate land at the death of a household head.

The dispersion of the Titiana community began in mid-1962 with the creation of a village at Kamaleai Point in the Shortland Islands. The Shortland Island group is a complex of large and small islands, and Kamaleai is located on the most northerly point of Shortland Island (map 10), the largest of the group. Shortland Island is called Alu on some maps, and Alu is also the name for the native Melanesian inhabitants and their language. Kamaleai is situated on a small bay facing Bougainville Island, the nearest point of which is only about 6 miles away.

Shortland Island is larger than Ghizo, being about 20 miles east to west and 10 miles north to south. The interior of the island is hilly and rolling, but the maximum elevation is only about 650 feet. Rainfall in the area averages about 160 inches per year, so that the island is covered with dense tropical forest. The coastline is low and much of it swampy; extensive areas of mangrove are common. The mountains of Bougainville, which dominate the northern skyline from Kamaleai Point, are the scene of moderate but continual volcanic activity, and earthquakes are frequent.

As is the case in most of the Solomons, human settlement in the Shortlands is in coastal regions and the interior is uninhabited. The greatest concentration of people is found at the southeast tip of Shortland Island. Here a number of smaller islands lie just offshore and the sheltered channels separating them are frequently less than a half-mile wide. A large Alu village is situated in this area, as is the Catholic mission station, a small trading store, and the government station. In 1962–1963 there were no government personnel posted permanently in the Shortlands; the government station consisted of a single building used as a rest house by touring officials.

The Catholic mission is located at a site called Nila. The mission operated a small boarding school that provided several years of education for both boys and girls. Every six to eight weeks a mission ship brought mail and supplies from Gizo, and the mission operated a small motor vessel for local transportation. This converted sailing craft was also used for frequent trips to the town of Buin on the south coast of Bougainville, where weekly airmail service was provided from New Guinea. Since there were no other missions in the area and visits by government ships were irregular and infrequent, the mission at Nila was a primary focus of Short-land Island life and the major point of contact with the outside world. There are other settlements on the eastern and western coast of Shortland Island, but Kamaleai, about 12 miles from the mission station and 8 miles from the nearest Alu village, was re-mote and isolated. There were virtually no overland roads or trails on the island and travel was undertaken by boat or canoe.

Kamaleai's isolation was in marked contrast to Titiana's setting near Gizo town. The sole means of subsistence of the eighty-five residents were fishing and gardening. The sale of copra provided a source of cash income; the crop was produced on the mature trees of the plantation which had been subdivided for the settlers. Households at Kamaleai received a total of 8 acres each in con-trast to the 4-acre plots allocated at Titiana. The copra was sold to small trading ships that visited the area occasionally. These ships operated out of Gizo, and their Chinese owners acted as middle-men, selling the copra at the government storage facilities in Gizo town. The ships were in fact small floating stores and provided the major source of rice, flour, tobacco, cloth, and other purchased items.

The creation of the new community represented the attainment of a major goal for its basically Catholic population: separation from Protestant-oriented Titiana. A few adherents of the Protes-tant faith lived in Kamaleai, but the small Catholic church that had been erected was the community center. Masses were occa-sionally said in it by the catechist who had originally led the Syd-ney Island converts. An effort was begun to establish a local school in 1963, but a number of children continued to be educated at the Nila mission school.

The community was led by its traditional leaders, the male el-ders. The catechist acted as community spokesman in relations with the mission and the government. A meetinghouse had not been erected, though one was planned, and in the meantime the church building served for village meetings. The community was a close-knit one, and the Sydney Island pattern of general par-ticipation in life-crisis feasts was followed (in contrast to Titiana, where such feasts had become mainly the business of the kindred of those sponsoring the feasts).

The Kamaleai residents plainly enjoyed their new surroundings and contrasted them favorably with Titiana. In particular they liked the escape from what they regarded as the money orientation of life on Ghizo. They found their reliance on self-production congenial and said it allowed them more freedom and leisure. The strait of water separating them from Bougainville served as an excellent, easily accessible fishing ground, and they saw this as an added advantage over the Titiana area, where fishing might involve several miles of canoe travel.

In mid-1963 more Gilbertese arrived in the Kamaleai area to begin new communities. One of these was at Harapa Point about 3 miles to the west, where a group of immigrants direct from the Gilberts began constructing a new village. The other was at Laomana about 6 miles to the west, where more people from Titiana had been granted land under the allocation program. The land at both these sites had been part of the same plantation purchase that led to the Kamaleai resettlement and therefore there were mature coconut palms to provide an economic base. The establishment of these new communities within easy reach of one another had important implications in that a sizable Gilbertese ethnic enclave was taking shape, although in 1963 only a beginning had been made.

## POSTSCRIPT 1975

By mid-1975 the community at Titiana had been in existence for nearly twenty years, a period of time equal to the total history of the Sydney Island settlement. The most visible manifestation of the incorporation of Titiana into Solomon Island life was the greatly increased frequency of contact between the Gilbertese settlers and Gizo town. By 1975 Titiana was essentially a suburban outlier of the bustling little urban center.

In about 1964 and 1965 a logging company had worked the forested interior of the island, constructing a road system to facilitate removal of the timber. In the late 1960s this road system was extended to points on the coast to reach the three villages on the island. It is now possible to drive from Gizo town to Sagheraghi at the northern end of the island and also to Pailongge, which lies about 2.5 miles west of Titiana. The road to Pailongge passes through both New Manra and Titiana, occupying what was once a broad central pathway in each community.

From Pailongge to New Manra the road follows the coast, turning inland at the end of New Manra to cut across the interior of the island to Gizo. A few people occasionally still take the path along the beach from New Manra, which offers beautiful panoramic views of the sea, the reef, and the nearby islands. The road, however, is the scene of a continual flow of traffic to and from the town. Seven or eight families in Titiana and New Manra own motorcycles, used mainly to commute to full-time jobs in the town. In June and July of 1975, there were two automobiles and a small pickup truck in use, also owned by Gilbertese families. The pickup and one of the automobiles served as taxis, driven continually between Gizo and the Gilbertese villages. If there were sufficient passengers or other demand, service was also provided to Pailongge or Sagheraghi. Though unscheduled, this motor transport was frequent and inexpensive. Particularly in the early morning and late afternoon hours there was a steady flow of people along the road, going to and returning from work or shopping.

Patterns of employment and subsistence activity had not changed fundamentally, but there were noticeable differences. Many families still supported themselves by fishing and gardening plus part-time employment, cash cropping, and handicraft sales. There were no longer any Gilbertese sailing canoes in the Ghizo area—Solomon Island dugout canoes had replaced them, and a number of families owned outboard motors. The canoes were purchased from Solomon Island craftsmen, who had adapted their traditional design to include a square stern on canoes intended for use with outboards. Fishing activity was much less common in 1975 than in 1963, and the canoes were used mainly for transportation of people and goods. The garden areas near Titiana and New Manra had been greatly extended and a tarolike plant was much in evidence. (The Gilbertese referred to this plant as *babai*, but I was unable to verify its identity; the plant was not present in 1963 and apparently was acquired in the Solomons rather than being imported from the Gilberts.) In spite of the expansion of garden areas, purchased food items were clearly more commonly used in 1975 then in 1963, and a cooperative store serving Titiana and New Manra was well stocked and busy.

About 40 to 45 percent of the families in Titiana and New Manra included a person who worked full-time for wages. This is about the same proportion as in 1963, but there was a marked difference: no longer was there a sizable number of unskilled or semiskilled laborers; almost all the jobs at which the Gilbertese worked in 1975 required considerable skill and training, such as accountant-clerk, wireless operator, outboard motor mechanic, and medical assistant. Stevedoring work was still available and provided part-time income for many men. Opportunities for this work actually had expanded since 1963; timbering had become a major industry and because much of the lumber was exported, casual labor was recruited to load the ships.

Gizo itself had grown into a busy town of perhaps a thousand people. Ships were seen much more frequently in the harbor unloading oil and other fuels, bringing cargo from Australia, and loading copra. Nusatupe, an island just across the harbor, had been leveled in the late 1960s to serve as an airport, and every day except Sunday an airline service provided mail, cargo, and passenger transport to other points in the Solomons including Honiara and Munda, where connections with international carriers could be made. There were also other means of local transportation, including a scheduled weekly ship from and to Honiara. Government, mission, and trading vessels as well as the air service provided frequent transportation to and from other points in the Western Solomons.

In 1975 the local council system of government was well established. The Solomons were near the point of self-government, and expatriate administrative personnel served mainly in an advisory capacity. There had been many changes in the council system, however, and there was a single council for the entire western area. Its headquarters and administrative offices remained in Gizo, but because of the frequency of local ship and aircraft movements there was regular contact with subdistrict offices and personnel in outlying areas.

A government primary school had been established in Gizo, replacing the one that formerly served the Titiana community. Most students in Titiana and New Manra continued to attend classes in Titiana, however, for the existing building had been taken over by the United (formerly Methodist) church and operated as a mission school. The school also served the community of Pailongge. In mid-1975 four teachers were employed in the school and a new classroom building was under construction to replace the aged thatch structure. Catholic students from Titiana and New Manra traveled to Gizo to attend the mission school there.

The Titiana community was geographically dispersed. About

315 people lived in Titiana itself.[3] In New Manra there were about 115 residents, and in the village that had been created on Mbambanga in 1963 there were about 35 persons. Perhaps 50 or so additional people affiliated with the Titiana community lived elsewhere in the vicinity of Gizo, including 35 to 40 persons living in Logha, where the Catholic mission station continued to employ Gilbertese adherents in producing copra from its plantation.

The composition and dispersion of the Titiana population has been significantly affected by two developments elsewhere in the Western Solomons. In 1962 the Gilbert and Ellice Islands Colony administration decided to terminate the Phoenix Islands resettlement program entirely, because the severe drought that began about 1960 had brought genuine hardship to the settlers remaining on Hull and Gardner islands. In 1963 the Gilbertese living on those two islands were also relocated in the Western Solomons, this time on Vaghena Island off the southeastern tip of Choiseul Island. Vaghena is about 75 miles from Ghizo and remote from centers of population. The Gilbertese at Titiana retained many ties with the newly arrived settlers, of course, stemming from the years on Sydney Island when the people of Hull and Gardner were in continual contact with them. Titiana has therefore come to serve as a point of entry for families and individuals from Vaghena who wish to live and work in the Ghizo area. In 1975 five households in Titiana, three in New Manra, and one on Mbambanga were comprised of people who had come from Vaghena, relying on ties of kinship or friendship to become established near Gizo town. Another seven or eight households from Vaghena were to be found in or near Gizo itself.

The other major development that influenced the Titiana population was the lumber industry, which had become an important economic factor in the Western Solomons. In 1975 the major center of timbering operations was at Ringgi Cove, on the southern coast of Kolombangara Island about 20 miles from Ghizo. Up to seventy-five Gilbertese men were employed there, and many had brought their families to live with them. Most of the families were from Vaghena, but there were several from Titiana as well. Employment in the lumbering operations resulted in a flow of households out of the Titiana area, while the creation of the settlement on Vaghena resulted in a flow of families into Titiana and the Gizo area. Furthermore, in 1975 Titiana was no longer the only Gilbertese community in the Ghizo area. There were perhaps 300 or more Gilbertese at Ringgi Cove, while about 800 remained on Vaghena.

Thus the population affiliated with the Titiana community was not only scattered but also fluctuating and heterogeneous. There was a continual movement of individuals and families into and out of the community according to work opportunities. It was also increasingly heterogeneous in that individuals and families moving into the community were often kinsmen or friends rather than long-time residents.

There had also been increased intermarriage with Melanesians by 1975. Although such marriages are still infrequent, at least some of the younger people thought that intermarriage with Melanesians was desirable and would hasten assimilation of the Gilbertese into Solomon Island life. There were a number of other Melanesians resident in Titiana, either as friends of Gilbertese residents or relatives of Melanesians married to Gilbertese. Some of these were children enrolled in the Titiana school. A number of other Melanesian children traveled from Pailongge each day to attend school. The school itself was headed by a Melanesian, and the committee responsible for school affairs (including the construction of the new school building) included several Pailongge residents.

Community organization in Titiana has changed markedly since 1963, and it is not difficult to identify the factors associated with the changes. Given the greater frequency of contact with Gizo exemplified by the morning and evening commuter traffic, the increasing significance of money in the local economy, the scattered and fluctuating population, the increasing effectiveness of the local council system of government, the organizations such as church and mission which cut across ethnic lines, the slowly growing number of non-Gilbertese residents, and a younger generation born or raised in the Solomons who regard themselves as Solomon Islanders, it is not surprising that leadership no longer resides primarily with the elder males of the community. They retain the respect traditionally accorded them, but their influence is no longer what it was.

A new meetinghouse was erected in 1964–1965 of permanent materials (a corrugated iron roof replaced the former traditional thatch). There were no meetings of the elders in it in June and July of 1975, but there were two dances featuring a local band that used electronically amplified instruments. There was 24-hour electrical service in Gizo town, but this had not yet reached Titiana, so a small portable generator provided power. The community was led by an eight-man committee, whose members were debating in private whether or not a fee should be charged for use of the meetinghouse by private groups. One of the dances had been sponsored by the youth group of the United church; the other was promoted by an individual as a money-making venture. The committee had appointed a headman to serve as its leader and contact man for other communities. The powers of the committee and its headman were uncertain. They were unpaid and served primarily to assess public opinion and discuss alternatives in community-wide affairs, tasks traditionally the domain of the elder men.

There were other indications of the declining authority of the elder men in 1975. Traditionally, these leaders were responsible for organizing hospitality for village guests and for feasts and dances. In 1963, for example, the first settlers for Harapa in the Shortlands visited Titiana for several weeks awaiting transportation to their new village site. On that occasion the elders divided the community into groups of households, each responsible for feeding the visitors on a given date. The new settlers ate and slept in the meetinghouse according to Gilbertese custom, and many of the elders stayed there also, entertaining the guests with cards, dancing, and conversation for the entire period. In 1975, however, guests were hosted by families or by the church.

The elders were also traditionally responsible for village feasts and dances, including the anniversary of the completion of the original Titiana meetinghouse and the New Year's Day dancing competition. By 1975 the anniversary in August had not been celebrated for some time, and no plans were in progress for that year. Enthusiasm for the New Year's Day dances had also declined, and participation had been decreasing for several years. Practice for that event usually began in late October, but it was reported that in spite of the exhortations of the elders attendance was low.

The fragmentation of the community was also apparent in changes in attitudes of village identity and affiliation. By the early 1970s the Gilbertese living in New Manra had apparently developed a considerable feeling of identity separate from Titiana. In

1973 they constructed their own meetinghouse and gave New Manra another name: Ribono. This feeling of separate identity had been apparent in 1963, but to a much lesser degree.

Titiana and New Manra had formerly been divided into two arbitrary groups for singing competitions at Christmas and dancing competitions at New Year's. The two groups were approximately equal in size: one consisted of about two-thirds of the Titiana residence area while the other consisted of New Manra plus the remainder of Titiana. In 1963 the land allocation led to a dispersal of population, and later the competitive groups were reorganized. Again there were two groups, one consisting of Titiana as a whole, the other of New Manra plus Mbambanga and the other scattered residents in the Ghizo area. The new grouping probably contributed to the ultimate separation and renaming of New Manra. During the 1974–1975 holiday season there had been three competing groups because the Gilbertese at Ringgi Cove on Kolombangara had indicated an interest in participating. Despite this added incentive, enthusiasm in Titiana, Ribono, and Mbambanga was not sufficiently raised; the Ringgi Cove group was apparently superior in both singing and dancing.

There were other signs that Titiana was undergoing a gradual transition from a homogeneous, subsistence-oriented cultural enclave of Gilbertese to something quite different: a suburban community with a particular ethnic and historical background. In 1963 travel from Titiana to Gizo was much less frequent than in 1975; in the evening families gathered at their homes for the principal meal of the day. The main path was quiet; children and young people stayed with their parents as the day's events were discussed and next day's plans made. In 1975, however, late afternoon was a time for soccer and volleyball games by the youth, and crowds of children were at play along the central road. On some evenings dances and other entertainments in Gizo attracted numbers of young people. Traditional life-crisis feasts were still in evidence, though attendance was ordinarily by kinsmen only. Birth and marriage were important events, but the occasion of a young girl's first menstruation was quietly celebrated by the immediate family only. No wedding took place in mid-1975, but people stated that the virginity of the bride was not so widely publicized as before. There appeared to be increasing sensitivity to criticism from outside the community and a growing feeling that visible celebrations of first menstruation and of bridal virginity were undesirable.

Given the rapidly changing social and economic conditions in which the Gilbertese in the Titiana area found themselves, land tenure and inheritance practices were not clearly established. In cases where a landholding household head died leaving only one heir, there was no difficulty; but where there were several living heirs, the evident practice was for them to come to agreement among themselves about the exploitation of the holding if the deceased had not made clear his or her wishes. The final technicalities of land allocation and issuance of title were not cleared away until 1974, and it remains to be seen how quickly clear-cut rules will develop.

Titiana was a predominantly Protestant community in 1975. Religious factionalism was not a major feature of village affairs, although the Baha'i church had gained some converts, particularly on Mbambanga, where this may foreshadow the formation of another organized community sometime in the future. The Methodist church in the Solomons had been reorganized as part of the United Church of Papua and New Guinea. The former Methodist church building standing next to the meetinghouse had been replaced by a building of permanent materials adjacent to the school. As has already been mentioned, the school was operated by the church. Financial assistance was provided by the Solomons government, however, and the new school building was being constructed with the aid of a government grant.

The United church, with its youth and women's groups, was also a social center, drawing its membership from Ribono (New Manra) and more distant areas as well as Titiana itself. A small church meetinghouse had been constructed across the road from the church itself, and in mid-1975 bazaars, bingo games, and auctions were being held in it to help finance the new school. The women's group held monthly meetings in the church meetinghouse, where they auctioned off handicraft and food items. At each meeting it was decided what was to be auctioned at the next month's gathering. The proceeds of the auction were put into a common fund with the church taking a share. Anyone who did not bring an item previously agreed on could make a cash contribution in its place. The fund was divided in equal shares among the member women at Christmastime.

It is interesting to note that the auctions seemed to function as a cash redistribution system. Women from affluent families were likely to contribute cash and to pay higher prices for auctioned goods. Women from families with low incomes were likely to contribute goods they had made and to pay lower prices for auctioned goods. All shared in the cash fund that was accumulated, however.

The men of the community had their own cooperative work group, although details of its organization were not clear to me. Anyone who wanted a specific task accomplished quickly, such as construction of a house, could pay for the work and the materials at set rates. The materials and labor were contributed by members and the funds were pooled. A member of the group could draw his share at any time, and there did not appear to be an annual division as in the case of the women's church group, although there could be if the members wished. This cooperative group was apparently rarely activated, but it appears to have been a development stemming from the former Sydney Island young men's club. Early in the history of Titiana there had been an effort to reconstitute that organization, but enthusiasm was lacking and the club itself was no longer active by 1963.

A final comment should be made regarding the growing evidence of significant economic differences in Titiana. In 1975 some households were visibly affluent relative to others. There had been some signs of differences in 1963, but they were restricted to one or two households. By 1975 a number of families had considerably more in the way of material goods than others; radios, motorcycles, outboard motors, and houses built of permanent materials were much more common than in 1963, but not all or even most households had them. This trend runs counter to the strongly egalitarian values of Gilbertese culture and perhaps will act in the future as an added stimulus to education and training for highly paid positions.

In 1963 the Gilbertese themselves commented on the contrast between the rural, subsistence-oriented life of Kamaleai and the gradual inclusion of Titiana within the social and economic life of Gizo town. The contrast was greatly accentuated by 1975, even though Kamalaei had come to experience much more frequent contact with other communities.

By 1975 the government station at the southeast tip of Shortland Island had been expanded to house a number of permanently stationed personnel. Government shipping from Gizo was on a regular schedule, stopping there at least once a month before continuing on to Shortland Island villages. The government ships carried cargo for the network of village cooperative societies that had been established, so that Kamaleai and the other nearby Gilbertese communities had regular communication links with the rest of the Solomons.

A large-scale malaria eradication program had been set up throughout the Solomons during the 1960s, and personnel connected with the program visited Kamaleai at least once a week to administer antimalarial drugs. Blood samples were taken regularly to detect the presence of the disease, and there was periodic inspection and spraying of all buildings (the same program was also in effect in the Ghizo area including Titiana). There was regular travel to Bougainville from the Shortlands.

Kamaleai was therefore no longer isolated to the degree it was in 1963. Furthermore, the village had become part of a more inclusive Gilbertese community that included Harapa and Laomana. Each of these three villages had its own meetinghouse. The population of Harapa was about 200 persons, that of Laomana about 100; Kamaleai was perhaps the smallest of the three, with 96 residents in July 1975. The three villages formed competing groups for singing (on Christmas Day) and dancing (on New Year's Day). The villages took turns in hosting the competitions. Each village also had its own cooperative society, but only Harapa had a school and health clinic due to its central location about midway between the other two communities. Kamaleai was still isolated, but it had become part of a Gilbertese cultural enclave numbering about 400 persons and spread over three village sites.

The community was still subsistence oriented and retained much of the characteristic life of a Gilbertese community. The elder men of the village were still its leaders. When the residents gathered for some purpose, such as greeting important visitors or discussing village matters, the elders took their accustomed places and dominated the discussion, as tradition dictated. Catholicism remained the dominant religion, and the catechist was still the spokesman for the community in its relationships with the administration and the mission. The former church building was no longer standing, however, and Sunday services and occasional masses were held in the meetinghouse.

Extensive gardens had been planted in the swampy area west of the village site. Much of this was what they called *babai*—the same plant that had been introduced at Titiana. Fish were still plentiful in the waters nearby; Solomon Island dugout canoes were the usual means of transportation to the fishing grounds. There were still a few Gilbertese sailing canoes, but they were used only infrequently, mainly for trips to Buin on Bougainville. At Buin there was a weekly market at which the Gilbertese sold fish. The Kamaleai cooperative society also owned an outboard motor and a large dugout canoe. Both were used for "official" trips to nearby villages, but fuel was expensive and difficult to come by, so that such trips were infrequent.

The village cooperative also participated in a government cattle ranching project, which provided subsidies for clearing and fencing land and made cattle available for stock. By 1975 the Kamaleai cooperative had cleared about 20 acres of land and had seven head of cattle in the enclosure. The project was still in its beginning stages in the Solomons, however, and facilities for processing and marketing the final product were still in planning by the government.

A women's group and a men's cooperative group were in existence in Kamaleai operating on lines similar to those in Titiana. There was also some mission activity by the United church; the people of Laomana were predominantly Protestant and were helping in the construction of a church building in Kamaleai. There were two Protestant families in Kamaleai itself. Protestant services were held at the new church site, led by a Gilbertese missionary from Titiana who also lived there. This location was about a half mile from Kamaleai proper; the missionary and his family did not otherwise participate in the life of the community, although the Protestant residents of Kamaleai thought that they should be included.

In spite of the increased frequency of contact and the extension of government and mission projects, Kamaleai in 1975 was much as it was in 1963, and its traditions were reinforced by the proximity of other Gilbertese communities. Enthusiasm for the singing and dancing competitions was high, life-crisis feasts were major community events, the leadership of the elder men was followed, the community as a whole acted as hosts for visitors, and only two buildings (a house and the cooperative store) were constructed of nontraditional materials.

Thus while there were undoubted pressures for change in Kamaleai, and while new pressures can be expected to appear as the frequency of contact continues to grow, the actual extent of change has been minimal compared to Titiana. It seems obvious that the reason for the differential rate of change between the two communities lies in their different settings: the isolation of Kamaleai in contrast to the proximity of Titiana to Gizo town.

## CONCLUSIONS

The nearly forty-year history of the Titiana and Kamaleai communities reveals a series of adaptations and experiments in adjustment to new and varied circumstances. When the community first took shape on Sydney Island, the major differences in environment were physical and biological. Sydney Island was small and lacking in extensive reef areas. It also had a highly saline central lake and, correspondingly, less capacity for subsurface freshwater storage than the islands of the Southern Gilberts. This meant that some of the traditional subsistence foods of the Gilbertese could not be cultivated. A local substitute was found which came to be a staple in the diet, but no change other than reorganization of household subsistence activities seems to have resulted.

The other factor influencing culture change on Sydney Island was the selection of households as the unit of resettlement. This was an obvious choice in formulating the resettlement plans. Households based on nuclear families had become increasingly independent economically in the Gilberts since the inception of the colony; furthermore, if household groups were the unit of relocation more families remaining in the Gilberts could be aided. Taking sets of closely related families would have meant a smaller number of numerically larger units. Fewer such large units could have been taken from each island, and there would have been a magnification of the administrative problems of reallocating their lands to those who stayed behind.

Because small family units were taken from different islands and localities in the Southern Gilberts, many specific local traditions were represented among the new residents of Sydney Island. The immediate result was a "least common denominator" approach to solving questions of the interpretation of tradition. The community meetinghouse organization is an obvious example of this. The concept of specific seating places was retained, but no family sat in the same location it had occupied in its home meetinghouse and no permanent allocation of order of precedence in meetings was made. Another manifestation of this generalizing approach was in life-crisis feasts, where participation was extended to all island residents rather than being limited to kinsmen as in the Southern Gilberts.

The selection of household groups meant that cooperation based on kinship to accomplish a specific task could enlist only a few individuals. The problems of initial development of the island (and, once this was accomplished, maintenance and subsistence) seem to have required more people, though perhaps at only infrequent intervals. The debate over how this was to be accomplished resulted in a gradually widening schism between the collectivists who favored group effort and the individualists who opposed it. There does seem to have been some need for collective effort, however, and the later formation of a young men's club for this purpose was the outcome. Nevertheless, the schism in the community grew deeper and led to acceptance of a new faith, Catholicism, in the previously Protestant community. Later the gap grew into a desire for separation—a desire that appeared as a wish to remain on Sydney after the rest of the community had been relocated in the Solomons.

The growing independence of nuclear families in the Southern Gilberts prior to resettlement was a trend that was probably carried to Sydney Island, but it was reduced in intensity there by the isolation of the island and the apparent need for cooperation of larger numbers of people in at least some tasks. A foundation for the potential assertion of independence of sons from their fathers was present in the fact that land on Sydney was allocated to individuals. In the Gilberts the fact that land was inherited from one's parents created a sanction that tended to make young people think twice about deviating from parental guidance; everyone had land on Sydney, however, so that the impact of this traditional sanction was reduced. The potential was never seized upon, however, and elder men retained their prestige.

In spite of the marked differences in physical and biological environment presented by the setting at Titiana when relocation to the Solomons took place, culture change resulting from these differences was minimal. This statement must be tempered, however, in the light of the features of the program that resulted in resettlement at Titiana Point. A certain quantity of land was promised to the settlers in the form of an allocation to each household head. As it turned out, the physical setting proved to be too small in area to make such an allocation possible at a single site. The result was the dispersion of the community in the Titiana area and the creation of another community at Kamaleai. At Kamaleai one religious faction achieved its goal of separation from the other. In the Titiana area the dispersion of the community resulted in an assertion of independence by residents at one site, New Manra. There are also early signs that this pattern may be repeated by the residents of another site, the village on Mbambanga Island.

The marked difference in social environment between Sydney Island and the Titiana area has had a marked effect on culture change. The proximity of Gizo town with its administrative center and employment opportunities has resulted in a decline of the prestige of the elders as community leaders, and the life of the Gilbertese in the Titiana area has been markedly adapted to that of the town. Titiana has also become a channel through which other Gilbertese gain employment and the attractions of town life. Urbanization is therefore the major process of change in Titiana.

The interpretation of change in Titiana as a process of adaptation to a new social environment is supported when a comparison is made with Kamaleai. Although Kamaleai is set within the same general Solomon Island administrative and economic framework, its remoteness from any urban center has resulted in greater continuity of Gilbertese tradition, and this continuity of tradition has been reinforced by the establishment of similar subsistence-oriented Gilbertese communities in the same vicinity.

A concept of adaptation to differing social as well as physical and biological environments has been used in this chapter as a framework for discussing culture change. The utility of the framework is evident, even though the history of the community spans less than forty years. Of course the process is an ongoing one, and adaptation continues in Titiana and Kamaleai. The Solomons in mid-1975 were nearing self-government, with independence in the foreseeable future. Both Titiana and Kamaleai were therefore part of a changing setting rather than a static one, and the younger members of the two communities are certain to find that their cultural traditions provide guidelines but not necessarily solutions to the new situations they will face.

## NOTES

The first period of field research was conducted as part of the Comparative Study of Culture Change and Stability in Displaced Communities in the Pacific (Barnett 1961), a project directed by Homer G. Barnett of the University of Oregon and funded by the National Science Foundation. Additional support in the form of two faculty research grants from the University of California at Berkeley made possible further analysis of the data between 1967 and 1969. The second period of field research was funded by a grant from the Research Advisory Board of the University of Nevada, Reno.

Although responsibility for the analysis presented in this chapter is my own, the work has benefited from the stimulus, criticism, and assistance of many people. The list is too long to give here in its entirety, but I am grateful to them all. I owe four special debts: to David Aberle and Homer Barnett, who were both members of the anthropology faculty when I was a graduate student at the University of Oregon; to Mary E. Knudson, who saw me through much of my life including the first period of fieldwork; and to Mary L. Moran, who took part in the second period of field research and provided valuable insights from a woman's perspective. I am also particularly obligated to the people of Titiana, Ribono, Kamaleai, and other Gilbertese villages in the Western Solomons for their continuing friendship, hospitality, and helpfulness.

1. The spelling of place-names in the Solomon Islands has been standardized since the appearance of the first description of the Titiana community (Knudson 1965). The spellings in this chapter are based on the new standards.
2. During the 1950s and 1960s the population problem feared by administrators some twenty years earlier became a reality and is now a serious issue. To a considerable degree the population increase stems from the economic significance of the phosphate deposits on Ocean Island, which provide income for the colony itself and wage labor for the Gilbertese. These deposits are exhaustible, of course, and when they cease to be economically exploitable, it is difficult to see any resource or activity that will replace them. The exportation of surplus population is only a temporary palliative, however, and in the late 1960s population control techniques centering on contraceptive methods began to be actively sponsored by the colonial government.
3. The population statistics for 1975 are initial results from censuses taken during the second period of field research. Further review of the census figures may result in some differences from the figures presented here, but any errors can be expected to be insignificant (less than 5 percent).

# 9

# TIKOPIA IN THE
# RUSSELL ISLANDS

*Eric H. Larson*

INTRODUCTION

Success in any venture, so folk wisdom tells us, almost always carries with it problems that the successful never dreamt of before embarking. So it is with the relocated Tikopia community in the Russell Islands. (See map 11.) Like other relocated communities described in this volume Tikopia emigrants had to cope with the inevitable problems of recreating an infrastructure and a social system in a novel environment. They appear to have been more than reasonably successful in dealing with these problems. Yet their success in adjusting to life in their new environment has brought with it a great deal of frustration and insecurity that seem to permeate community life. This chapter is primarily concerned with the nature of this frustration and insecurity, how these feelings came to be, and how the Tikopia have attempted to deal with them.

Although Tikopia have been emigrating from the home island since 1904, the patterns of migration have changed considerably since 1956, when the resettled community of Nukufero was established (Firth 1931; 1936:42;1954). Prior to 1956, it was mainly single males who left Tikopia to seek work or a change of scenery in the Central Solomon Islands. Since the resettlement of Tikopia in the Russell Islands, it has been larger groups, mainly nuclear families, that have emigrated. By 1964, approximately one-quar-

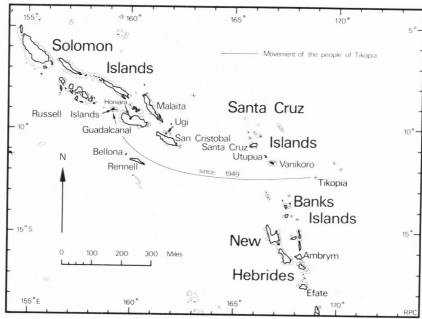

Map 11.    Movement from Tikopia to Russell Islands.

ter of the total Tikopia population resided on Lever's Pacific Plantations and in the resettled community in the Russell Islands (see tables 2, 3, and 4).

A basic reason for Tikopia emigration is the scarcity of resources on the home island. Tikopia measures only 2.5 by 1.5 miles in size and is physically isolated from main lines of communication. The distance from major population centers and the lack of marketable goods with which to establish trade cause the Tikopia to depend almost entirely on local resources. Given the small size of the island, population increases and natural catastrophes compound subsistence problems. Firth (1959:51–53) notes an increase in people from 1,300 in 1929 to 1,750 in 1952, a gain of about 35 percent in twenty-three years. He also describes the effects of a hurricane that swept Tikopia in 1952, causing extensive damage to fruit-bearing palms and flooding of the sea onto gardens close to shore. The hurricane brought near famine to the island, and the British government was forced to provide food to offset shortages. The anthropologist James Spillius estimates that possibly seventeen of the ninety deaths in 1952 and 1953 may

TABLE 2    Tikopia Migrating to Russell Islands, by Sex, Number of Visits, and Duration of Stay: 1949–1964

| Duration of Stay in Years | Males Number of Visits | | | | | Females Number of Visits | | | | |
|---|---|---|---|---|---|---|---|---|---|---|
| | 1 | 2 | 3 | 4 | 5 or More | 1 | 2 | 3 | 4 | 5 or More |
| 7+ | 22 | 0 | 0 | 0 | 0 | 17 | 0 | 0 | 0 | 0 |
| 6 | 7 | 0 | 0 | 0 | 0 | 5 | 0 | 0 | 0 | 0 |
| 5 | 36 | 0 | 0 | 0 | 0 | 21 | 0 | 0 | 0 | 0 |
| 4 | 51 | 31 | 3 | 0 | 0 | 31 | 15 | 0 | 0 | 0 |
| 3 | 87 | 62 | 23 | 0 | 0 | 62 | 51 | 18 | 0 | 0 |
| 2 | 123 | 147 | 93 | 63 | 36 | 92 | 102 | 72 | 41 | 18 |
| 1 | 110 | 172 | 87 | 51 | 23 | 84 | 111 | 63 | 36 | 10 |

NOTE: The table shows individuals who have gone once or more to the Russell Islands and who may have remained for varying periods depending on the visit. Thus a given person may be represented in several of the cells shown in the table, since some people make more than one trip and stay for different extended periods.

TABLE 3    Tikopia Migrating to Russell Islands, by Age: 1949–1964

| Age of Migrants in Years | Total Migrant Population (%) |
|---|---|
| 0–9 | 20 |
| 10–19 | 19 |
| 20–29 | 28 |
| 30–39 | 25 |
| 40–49 | 5 |
| 50 and over | 3 |
| TOTAL | 100 |

NOTE: The percentage in each age category is computed on the basis of the chronological age of persons living in the resettlement and the duration of the stay for each visit. For example, if a person migrated to the Russell Islands for one year at age twenty-three, category 20–29 was scored one point; if the same person visited again for two years at age thirty-three, category 30–39 was scored two points, and so forth.

have resulted from the effects of malnutrition, if not starvation (Firth 1959:59).

The British government adds to pressures on the island's limited resources by declaring illegal or immoral certain of the traditional population controls. In precontact days, elder heads of families

TABLE 4  Tikopia Populations in Russell Islands and on Tikopia:
1964

| Age | Russell Islands | | | Tikopia | | |
|---|---|---|---|---|---|---|
| | Male | Female | Total (%) | Male | Female | Total (%) |
| 0–9 | 62 | 50 | 26 | 158 | 134 | 29 |
| 10–19 | 42 | 37 | 19 | 99 | 143 | 24 |
| 20–29 | 82 | 46 | 31 | 80 | 103 | 18 |
| 30–39 | 53 | 24 | 19 | 73 | 85 | 15 |
| 40–49 | 9 | 4 | 3 | 37 | 36 | 7 |
| 50 and over | 6 | 2 | 2 | 25 | 38 | 7 |
| TOTAL | 254 | 163 | 100 | 472 | 539 | 100 |

reduced the birth rate by discouraging young men from marrying. Coitus interruptus was practiced in an effort to reduce the number of pregnancies. Abortion was not common but did occur among unmarried females who hoped to avoid giving birth. Population growth was also checked by infanticide (burying the face of infants in the sand), by people being lost at sea, and by interisland warfare (Firth 1936:373–374).

The internal pressures of population and scarce resources on Tikopia would themselves have been sufficient causes for the eventual mass movement of inhabitants to other areas, but the specific migration to the Russells is largely the result of encouragement given by the British government and Lever's plantations. The need for cheap labor is an attribute of the large-scale production of tropical crops on plantations (Courteney 1965:2–7; Myint 1965: 54). Since the indigenous population of the Russell Islands is neither sufficiently large nor willing to provide the necessary manpower to work Lever's estates, the company recruits outsiders. Thus Lever's plantations, with the government's cooperation, made special efforts to entice Tikopia to come to the Russells. Following the advice of Spillius, the company altered recruitment practices and improved working conditions on the estates, thus opening the way for Tikopia not accustomed to regimental labor to adjust to a new life (Spillius 1957). Lever allowed Tikopia recruiters and not outsiders to interview prospective workers on the island. As a result, only those the recruiters thought would be happy and productive on the plantations were selected. The Tikopia chiefs were also included in the selective process. This decision tended to stabilize the flow of migrants to and from the island, since the chiefs desire to maintain a balance in population between Tikopia and the Russells.[1] Segments of extended families may locate both at home and abroad at the same time, keeping up properties in the two locations. Finally, the company agreed to be flexible in assigning jobs on the plantations. Tikopia were thus able to organize into small groups of their own choosing and to cooperate in labor tasks following traditional patterns of work organization.

The government for its part stimulated emigration by recommending that Lever offer Tikopia free land in the Russells. Together the government and Lever's representatives met with Tikopia chiefs and other influential men of the island and agreed to send a reconnaissance group of six Tikopia, including one chief, to inspect areas for possible resettlement in the Russells. The Nukufero site was later chosen, and the government and Lever provided the initial migrant contingent with food, seed for planting gardens, tools, and supplies to begin village construction. The government and plantation management promised eventual relinquishment of legal rights of the land to the Tikopia, and the migrants were led to understand that the government would allow resettlers full autonomy in what Tikopia regarded as the normal run of village affairs.

The favorable conditions of emigration as seen by Tikopia have continued over the past two decades, and in 1964, at the time of this investigation, 417 Tikopia people were residing in the Russells. In that same year, the number living on Tikopia was reduced to 1,011, or approximately 58 percent of the figure reported to have been on the island in 1952.

Tikopia in the Russells live in two plantation labor compounds, Semata and Pepesala, and in Nukufero village on Pavuvu Island (map 12). Pavuvu and neighboring Banika Island are the main land bodies of the Russell group, which also includes a number of smaller, low-lying islets. Banika Island is more developed than Pavuvu: European management and the main Melanesian labor force number approximately a thousand in residence, and there is a store, an elementary school, a small hospital, an airstrip, and a police station. Pavuvu is the larger of the two islands, but with the exception of 3,700 acres of coconut estates, it is covered throughout with thick tropical forest. Tikopia constitute the main population on the island and are charged with sole responsibility for

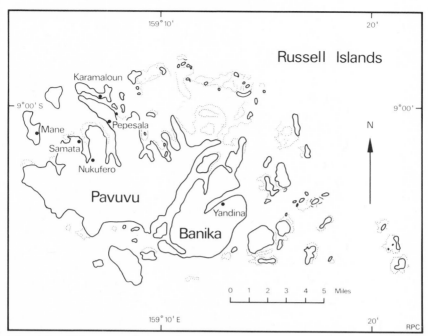

Map 12.   Tikopia settlements in the Russell Islands.

maintaining Lever's estates in the area.[2] Contacts with the small Melanesian settlements on Mane and Karamaloun Islands are infrequent, and migrants generally leave the resettlement only for special reasons—to receive medical attention, purchase items in the store, or make travel connections on Banika. On the other hand, the Tikopia form a tightly knit society, and communication between Nukufero and the labor compounds is easily maintained by close physical proximity. Nukufero village, built and developed by the Tikopia alone, is the hub of activity with thatch houses, a church and mission school with three elementary grades, a dispensary, and surrounding gardens. Migrants residing in the labor compounds own or have access to houses and land in the village.

Thus Tikopia in the Russell Islands have their own village, which is politically and socially autonomous. Contact with Europeans and Melanesians is periodic and minimal. Even the work on Lever's plantations is organized almost wholly by Tikopia themselves. The Tikopia, in other words, are more or less left to run their own affairs as they see fit. Given these facts, a curious feature

of the resettled community is the continual and explicit stress that
residents place on their ethnic uniqueness and on the maintenance
of their traditions in their interaction with one another. It is common in both public and private meetings to hear people harangu-
ing one another about maintaining Tikopia 'custom'. The extent
to which people consciously pursue this subject is curious for several reasons. One would think that since Tikopia interact almost
exclusively with one another in the village they would simply assume the relevance of their ethnic identity and talk about whatever is current at the moment. Their harping on the maintenance
of custom would be more understandable if there were Melanesians and Europeans constantly present and in contact with them,
but this has not been the case. There is no other ethnic group continually present to serve as a model for alternative life-styles.

It is obvious that the Tikopia are aware of their ethnic uniqueness and of the fact that they have an ancient tradition to maintain. Firth (1936) noted this long ago. Yet their continual reference to the subject raises several questions: Do the Tikopia believe
that, all other things being equal, they will lose or forget their
traditions without conscious safeguards? Do they really believe
that their traditions are in fact brittle? Do they fear the influence
of outsiders as powerfully subversive even with minimal contact?
Are there circumstances peculiar to the Nukufero situation that
pose a threat to the maintenance of Tikopia tradition?

The answers to these questions lie in the ways that Tikopia conceive of three things: themselves as an ethnic unit, their traditions,
and their situation in the Russell Islands. I shall demonstrate that
because of the ways in which Tikopia conceive of themselves as an
ethnic entity and their traditions, they perceive their situation in
the Russell Islands to be highly ambiguous. The continual ha-
ranguing about maintaining Tikopia custom can be seen as a response to the ambiguities with which they must live. I shall also
demonstrate that the major conflicts in the Nukufero community
are all manifestations of the ambiguities of their situation.

I shall demonstrate the nature of the ambiguity in the Nukufero
community and how it arises in the following way. First, I shall
describe the organization of the community, its relations with Lever's plantations and the colonial government, and its relationship
to Tikopia. Second, Tikopia ideas about their own ethnic characteristics and about their historical tradition will be presented. I

shall then relate these data to those presented in the previous section to show how ambiguity arises in the resettled community. In
other words, I shall show how Tikopia concepts of ethnicity and
tradition structure their perceptions of Nukufero. Finally, I shall
show how the ambiguity structures conflict in the community and
how the Tikopia attempt to resolve it.

## NUKUFERO

Nukufero village consists of approximately 200 acres of land near
the shore of an inlet of West Bay on Pavuvu Island. An advance
party of nineteen men, including a headman appointed by the four
Tikopia chiefs, began the work of clearing land, building houses,
and planting in May 1956. The advance party was joined
throughout 1956 and 1957 by other men from Tikopia and from
two other plantations on Pavuvu Island (Semata and Pepesala).
Once a communal sleeping house had been constructed, work on
gardens began.

Each resident chose his own garden plot in consultation with
the village headman and worked on it independently. Plots vary
from 2 to 8 acres in area. The major crops planted have been tapioca and sweet potatoes; taro, bananas, and breadfruit are of less
importance. This pattern contrasts with the Tikopia resource
base, in which taro, breadfruit, coconuts, bananas, cyrtosperma,
sago, and yams (in that order) were major crops (Firth 1939:65).
The reasons for this shift in emphasis seem to be that tapioca and
sweet potatoes require less trouble to cook and coconuts are already plentiful and are collected for use from plantation land
(with Lever's permission). With the exception of the first six
months after founding the village, Nukufero residents have been
able to subsist entirely on village resources.

The ownership and use of land in Nukufero more or less replicate that on Tikopia. Chiefs are the titular owners of the land on
Tikopia, and this is also ideally the case for the original land allotment (of 75 acres) in Nukufero, though the supplementary allotment of 125 acres seems to be owned by people other than chiefs.
The actual control of land both on Tikopia and in Nukufero is
vested in patrilineages. Although it has been mainly individuals
that work each land plot, plots are claimed for the individual's
lineage. Control and inheritance of plots follow the rules of patri-

lineal succession and inheritance that are characteristic of Tikopia. As on Tikopia, exploitation of land is carried on jointly by
people who are related as cognates or as friends. Such joint use is
more frequent in Nukufero than on Tikopia for two reasons. First,
newly arrived emigrants often have no agnates living in Nukufero,
so they stay with people to whom they are related cognatically, using their relatives' land until they can establish their own garden
plots. Second, the abundance of arable land in Nukufero relative
to the low population density allows each person more options in
land use than on Tikopia.

Once families began to emigrate to Nukufero, in 1957, family
dwellings replaced the communal residence house. By 1965 there
were thirty-one houses with several more under construction.
Households consisted mainly of nuclear families, often with a sibling or parent of either spouse (67 percent of the households).
Other households contained adult cognates or siblings or families
with one spouse dead or absent (see table 5). Their composition
reflects the structure of the Nukufero population in that the categories of kin with whom one would normally live on Tikopia are
often absent in Nukufero, necessitating various relationships in ar-

TABLE 5   Composition of Tikopia Households in Russell Islands
          and on Tikopia: 1964

| Composition | Russell Islands | | Tikopia | |
|---|---|---|---|---|
| | Number | % | Number | % |
| Married couple only | 6 | 7 | 7 | 3 |
| Nuclear family only | 29 | 34 | 79 | 29 |
| Nuclear family plus sibling(s) of spouse(s) | 8 | 9 | 26 | 10 |
| Nuclear family plus parent(s) of spouse(s) | 10 | 11 | 68 | 24 |
| Nuclear family plus sibling(s) and parent(s) of spouse(s) | 7 | 9 | 18 | 7 |
| Family with one spouse dead or absent | 3 | 3 | 27 | 10 |
| Other* | 24 | 27 | 45 | 17 |
| TOTAL | 87 | 100 | 270 | 100 |

*This category includes several kinds of households that are found only on Tikopia and
dormitory housing on plantations at Semata and Pepesala in the Russell Islands. A more detailed listing of household types and their distribution is presented in Larson (1966:72).

ranging residence (see Larson 1966:70–72). The household orga-nizes the daily activity of its members, such as work on Lever's plantations, work in the family's gardens, cleaning, cooking, and the like. As on Tikopia, the household is the major unit of econom-ic production and consumption. The location of households gen-erally follows the major paths traversing the village: houses tend to cluster in a line along the paths as on Tikopia (Firth 1939:50–51; Larson 1966:16).

By 1965, there were two schools in Nukufero. A boarding school for boys, built by students, teachers, and a few men in the village, drew its students—who numbered forty-four in 1965—from the plantations in Semata and Pepesala and from the village. The boarding school was staffed by three Tikopia, all of whom were trained in Melanesian mission schools. The headmaster, a 25-year-old man of high rank in a Tikopia clan, had been trained in a government teacher's college. The school has its own garden plots (worked by the students) from which the students' and staff's subsistence is drawn. The normal school day includes morning prayer and breakfast, followed by work in the gardens, morning instruction, the noon meal, physical education (usually soccer games or relay racing), garden work, evening prayer, the evening meal, and, finally, evening leisure and study. The curriculum in-cludes English, arithmetic, health, geography, and religion. The girls' school, which had just begun in 1965, had two Tikopia women as teachers; students came from the village and the Semata plantation for two hours each morning. Subjects taught were En-glish, arithmetic, and religion. Most instruction was conducted in English, though teachers used the Tikopia language to explicate difficult material.

The boys' school has played an important role in village affairs almost since its inception. The boys constitute a well-organized labor force that has participated in church construction, road con-struction, the laying out of a soccer field, feast preparations, and lending sundry aid to visiting dignitaries. The school headmaster, a talented teacher and organizer, exercised an influential position in Nukufero village affairs. His influence was based not only on his education and talent but also on his position as a religious leader of the village.

The political organization of Nukufero village represents signif-icant departures from but also continuities of Tikopian tradition.

While the four clan chiefs and their 'high-ranking kinsmen', the *maru*, wield political authority on Tikopia, a village headman, appointed by the chiefs and representing them, has charge of the affairs of Nukufero. He acts as an arbiter in community problems and is the Tikopia spokesman in relations with the outside. There have been three headmen since the founding of the village. A male from any of the four Tikopia clans, regardless of his traditional rank, is eligible for Nukufero headship, although experience with Europeans and Melanesians and an ability to speak Pidgin English or English are considered important assets for those aspiring to the position. The first and third headmen, for example, worked on ships that toured the protectorate, the first headman having traveled as far as New Zealand. The third headman had also worked a year as a domestic servant in a European home. Both men speak good Pidgin English. The second headman, in contrast, made few contacts with non-Tikopia and spoke little Pidgin English. His charisma and close kin relationship to a chief should have rendered him effective as a leader by traditional standards; instead he proved least competent of the headmen who served in Nukufero.

As indicated, the headman serves as a mediator, a link between the local community and the Solomon Islands. The headman, for example, met periodically with government officials in 1965 who, through visits to Nukufero and developing rapport with the Tikopia, hoped to change negative attitudes toward participation in a Russell Islands local council and payment of taxes to the council. The headman received his visitors, listening to their arguments and graciously providing them with special foods and drink, but refused to support the government's proposals. Such support would be irrelevant, he contended, because of his people's loyalty to the chiefs, their desire to maintain Tikopia traditions in the resettlement, and the counterarguments that would materialize if he were to try to convert them to the government's side. The headman met also with government representatives on San Cristobal to discuss representation of Tikopia Island in the local council of the Eastern District, but he advised the chiefs present at the meeting against participation.

The headman does cooperate with the government when functionaries come to Nukufero to dispense innoculations, check on the incidence of tuberculosis and other diseases, and advise on proper methods of garden cultivation. He may act as a host to the occasional European visitors who wish to observe Polynesian dances and ceremonies or to Lever's managers who consider it good policy to show token interest in the development of Nukufero. Any Melanesian wanting to trade in the village is expected to seek the headman's permission first.

The headman is responsible for allocating land to those Tikopia emigrants arriving in Nukufero or the labor compounds who own no property in the area. The Tikopia were given 200 acres on which to develop their village, and the usual procedure is for migrants to select the location themselves and later inform the headman of their choice. Since land is presently abundant, with sufficient area in the surrounding bush for expansion, the headman's approval of a site follows, and no Tikopia has had trouble settling where he wants.

The headman is responsible for supervising the construction of community facilities and keeping them in good repair. Such projects as laying footpaths with coral stones, removing overgrown weeds in the vicinity of the church, school, and houses, and repairing water lines are performed by volunteer labor from Nukufero and the labor compounds. The headman blows a conch shell each Wednesday afternoon, alerting adults and children to their half-day obligation, and a typical turnout brings together between twenty and forty people. The Tikopia take pride in the appearance of Nukufero and point to the success of their village work projects as an example of what is possible if they are left to their own devices.

Additional duties of the headman include the maintenance of law and order in the community. In this capacity, he is expected to function similarly to headmen representing local councils throughout the protectorate. In one case, a Nukufero headman imposed a fine on two intoxicated men who had been fighting in the plantation. The money was not turned over to the Russell Islands authorities but was given to men collecting for the Tikopia Development Fund. Serious crimes such as murder, rape, or assault are supposed to be reported to the police stationed on Banika Island. No crimes of this nature were said to have been committed in the resettlement, and jurisdiction over these matters is claimed to extend beyond the control of the headman. Given the detachment of the Tikopia from Russell Islands affairs, however, it is not certain whether a Tikopia alleged to have committed such a crime would have been reported to the authorities.

A group of men known as "the committee" functions as an additional political force in Nukufero. The committee, a loosely structured organization with no permanent membership, holds to no regular schedule, convening only when the need arises to resolve community problems. Any male wishing to participate on the committee may attend meetings, although the most active in deliberations in 1965 were the Nukufero headman, the foremen employed on the plantations, and individuals with formal education. These men formed the nucleus of recognized leadership, but none attempted to monopolize discussions, and no person presided as formal head of the committee.

Committee issues receive a thorough analysis, occasionally with strong rhetorical arguments backing various points of view, but in the end a consensus on action to be taken is generally reached. Topics coming before the group vary, but financial considerations were very important in 1965. The committee had decided that each wage-earning Tikopia should raise his annual contribution to the Tikopia Development Fund from A£3 to A£4. A group of educated Tikopia created the Fund in 1962, after the idea gained the approval of the chiefs. The Fund serves as a substitute for Russell Islands taxes. The Tikopia opposed taxation in 1965 but recognized the need for money to improve and expand community facilities at home and in the Russells. Initial expenditures from the fund would be used to build and staff a small dispensary on Tikopia and to buy additional supplies for the school in Nukufero. Only two men were said to have failed to pay into the fund, and the balance deposited in Honiara amounted to A£1,500.

The near unanimity of Tikopia financially supporting their own projects indicates their solidarity as an ethnic group. It follows that enforcement of committee decisions rarely becomes a problem. There were times when a designated person of the committee talked personally to dissident individuals, and a few people refused to pay any attention to committee programs of action. These people were the objects of private ridicule but were not subjected to overt sanctions to force them to conform. The minor disagreements with committee policies are insignificant since the community recognizes the legitimacy of the present leadership and programs developed by the committee reflect closely the sentiments of the majority.

The relationship between the Lever Company and Nukufero is both economic and social. The importance of the village to Lever cannot be underestimated, since one of the company's major prob-lems has been that of securing and maintaining a dependable la-bor force on its plantations. Without the Tikopia, Lever would have to rely almost exclusively on Malaitan laborers, who were rather restive during the 1960s. It was James Spillius who influ-enced the Lever Company to introduce drastic changes in its re-cruiting and work organization policies, thereby shaping the company's relationship with the villagers (Spillius 1957).

The company has used Tikopia persons to recruit laborers from the home island since the mid 1950s, following Spillius' advice. The recruiters select families whom they believe can best profit from wage work and educational opportunities and best adapt to conditions in the Russell Islands. Recruiters include the advice and consent of Tikopia chiefs in the selection process. Tikopia are also employed as foremen on the plantations, and they organize the work of planting, clearing underbrush, harvesting and husking coconuts, cutting the meat from the shell, transporting copra, and running the company's motor launch. Much of this work is done by small groups rather than by lone workers (formerly the com-pany policy), and jobs are rotated on a daily basis, cutting down on the boredom usually inherent in such work. Both men and women can be employed in some of these tasks, thereby increasing the labor force and also the incomes of village families.

Besides leasing 200 acres of land to the Tikopia, Lever also sup-plied them with seedlings, cuttings, and several experimental vari-eties of food plants. The management permits villagers to plant short-term crops in plantation groves and has granted them unlim-ited use of coconuts for drinking and cooking. Occasionally the company has petitioned the local government on behalf of the vil-lagers to get them supplies of sago thatch and other needed items. When the villagers built their church, the company supplied roofing material, milled timber, and cement at cost.

The European plantation manager has taken an active, if at times paternalistic, interest in the growth and welfare of the vil-lage. He has encouraged the founding of the village schools and church, and he was instrumental in forming a local soccer team which competed in league play on several islands. While he has not taken an active part in the internal affairs of the village, he has expressed his concerns about village education, economic growth, and morality to the headman. This man has been rather sensitive

to Tikopia interests in social contacts, being careful to show deference to visiting chiefs, the headman, and his foremen. The Tikopia, for their part, are particularly sensitive to the behavior of Europeans in personal relationships, and the care that the local
manager takes in cultivating personal relationships with villagers
is noted and appreciated (see Larson 1966:42–47).

The relationship between Tikopia and Nukufero is rather complex and involves a good deal of ambiguity. Tikopia characterize
the relationship by a deceptively simple statement: "Tikopia and
Nukufero are the same." Tikopia regarded the colonization at the
outset as a move to extend the home island's landholdings to the
Russell Islands, and they still believe this to be the case. The founding of a Tikopia village on Pavuvu Island was, then, simply a matter of replicating Tikopia social organization on newly acquired
land. The whole colonization scheme depended on the consent of
the Tikopia chiefs for its implementation, and the original grant of
land was under their titular ownership. This is, of course, true of
land on Tikopia. Political authority in the new colony, moreover,
is conceived to be ultimately in the hands of the chiefs, so that
disputes which cannot be settled by Nukufero villagers, for example, are referred to the chiefs and 'high-ranking clansmen' on
Tikopia (for examples, see Larson 1966:65). Ideally, then, "Tikopia and Nukufero are the same" means that Nukufero is Tikopia
replicated in miniature.

To even a casual observer, it is quite clear that Nukufero is not a
replica of Tikopia; the two communities are in many respects
quite different. The division of the Tikopia community into districts and the various kinds of district-oriented activity have not
been replicated in Nukufero. The chiefs are titular owners of only
some, but not all, of the land in Nukufero. Exchanges based on relations with chiefs are absent in Nukufero. Political organization,
and the social stratification on which it is based, is quite different
in the two communities.

To the migrants, the arrangements of plantation labor, kinship
relations, land tenure, community work, and frequent contact
with the home island are concrete manifestations of the Tikopia
culture abroad. Nukufero and the satellite plantation labor compounds represent extensions of Tikopia, but the resettlement situation being what it is, the entire Tikopia culture cannot be fully
replicated in the Russells. The reason is, basically, that a certain

measure of fluidity is necessary in confronting problems in the developmental stages of a new community and in responding to policies and directives of the protectorate government and Lever's plantations. The irrelevance of traditional rank in selecting headmen and the importance of overseas experience and ability to speak English or Pidgin English are examples of the recognition by Tikopia of the need for flexibility in the new situation.

There is, then, an implicit contradiction between the notions of the equivalence of Tikopia and Nukufero and flexibility to cope with contingency. This contradiction, theoretically, could make a difference in how people regard their situation. Whether the contradiction is important or trivial, attended to or ignored, perceived or not perceived, depends very much on how "equivalence" is perceived. If, for example, novel ways of coping with a new situation are perceived simply as alternative means for maintaining traditional relationships, then there need be no contradiction at all— "equivalence" would consist in maintaining a certain relationship rather than in how that relationship is maintained. If "equivalence" is perceived at the level of means (that is, specific ways of acting in a given situation), then the differences between the two communities become more important; "equivalence" and "flexibility" can pose a contradiction. I shall demonstrate that the latter possibility is in fact the case for Nukufero.

TIKOPIA ETHNICITY AND TRADITION

Tikopia have a well-developed image of themselves as a distinctive, unique people. Ethnic solidarity among Tikopia has been fully documented in the literature. The title of Firth's book, *We, the Tikopia*, deriving from the native expression *tatou nga Tikopia*, speaks to the keen sense of esprit de corps and respect for traditions. As Firth (1936:xv) describes it, [the expression] "is constantly on the lips of the people themselves [representing] that community of interests, that self-consciousness, that strongly marked individuality in physical appearance, dress, language, and custom which they prize so highly."

Pride in being a Tikopia has been sustained over the past four decades. At the core of present Tikopia culture is *arofa* 'love', a concept which embraces hospitality, generosity, respect for social status, and sensitivity to the opinions and feelings of others. 'Love' is a guide in social interaction wherein appropriate initiatives and responses in a variety of situations change according to the temperament, kinship relationship, and rank of individual participants. The value is expressed in one's contribution to the tasks at hand, performances seen not only as ends in themselves but also as obligations of group living. 'Love', in short, is believed to be peculiar to Tikopia life and lacking in other cultures.

Folklore and concepts of self lend further support to the idea of Tikopia ethnic superiority and prowess. Tikopia distinguish themselves from other groups as *faua kiri mero* 'brown skin people', *tau reka reka* 'handsome', *makeke* 'strong', and *fai fekau* 'hardworking'. A number of tales describe Tikopia courage and superiority in waging war against invaders of the home island. One myth tells of the original ancestors emerging from the land of Tikopia itself. Only later are immigrants said to have arrived from elsewhere in Polynesia and Melanesia.

The Tikopia concept of themselves inheres not only in their notion of 'love', the personal concern which people relate to one another, but also in their notions of 'tradition' and 'custom'. The Tikopia have objectified their patterned ways of doing things, their 'customs', in their concept of 'tradition'. Tradition is regarded as the entire body of customs that characterizes Tikopia and distinguishes it from other communities. Their concept of 'custom' is very much like the old anthropological concept of "culture trait" or "culture element" (e.g., Steward 1941, 1943; Stewart 1941). A custom may be an entire ceremony or any of its parts—a way of making artifacts, a way of inheriting property, and so forth. On Tikopia, for example, people periodically contribute labor to community projects as the need arises. In Nukufero, building and maintaining the village has required a more regular schedule of communal work, usually every Wednesday. One high-ranking man in Nukufero consistently refused to participate in this endeavor on the grounds that a regimented work week was contrary to Tikopia custom (Larson 1966:99). The Tikopia concept of tradition is, then, very much like the anthropological concept of a culture trait list.

The Tikopia distinguish themselves from other ethnic groups not only by their physiognomy and language but also in terms of differences in custom. Thus, for example, Tikopia contrast themselves with Melanesians on the basis of the latter's matrilineal transmission of property, lack of hereditary chieftainship, low status of women, and "unclean" personal habits. They interpret the Melanesians' emphasis on competitive exchange as greed and their treatment of women as contemptible, here evaluating customs in terms of their own concept of 'love'. The concept of tradition, therefore, serves the Tikopia both in defining themselves as a unique people and in contrasting themselves with other ethnic groups. Physiognomy, language, and customs are, for the Tikopia, the diacritica of ethnic identity.

The Tikopia insistence on maintaining physical and political separateness from other ethnic groups stems from at least two sources. One is their feeling of superiority and corresponding depreciation of other ethnic groups. For example, when it was suggested to the Tikopia chiefs that they join with Melanesians in a government council, the result was the following:

> In my preliminary conversation with the *Ariki* Tafua he expressed himself graciously, though patronizingly, on the subject of Melanesian politics. When I mentioned what the Government had in mind the atmosphere became more chilly. The chief maintained that the black men were numerically superior, they knew nothing of the customs of the Tikopia, and if any decisions were to be made they would favour their own kind. I was informed that if I was a friend of the Tikopia, I would tell the Government that it was not right to put them with the black man. [Cochrane 1969:4]

Second, the Tikopia believe they have a body of tradition to maintain, and such maintenance is most easily accomplished in relative isolation from outside interference.

Given the Tikopia definition of tradition and its maintenance, the statement that "Tikopia and Nukufero are the same" must inevitably assume the status of a fiction to the Tikopia in Nukufero. It is obvious to Tikopia adults that the list of customs that make up their tradition is far from complete in Nukufero. Moreover, most of the innovations that have replaced traditional customs cannot be said to have been forced on the Tikopia by outsiders. The Tikopia do live and work mainly in isolation from Melanesians and Europeans, and the latter have kept out of the internal affairs of the village and plantation communities. Yet the Tikopia insist that Nukufero is an extension of Tikopia and that they are simply replicating Tikopia tradition on an extension of Tikopia land. The contradiction between ideology and fact, which is made inevitable by the way in which tradition is defined, is not lost on the Tikopia. Their situation in Nukufero is ambiguous, and they are aware of the ambiguity. Is custom being maintained or is it not? This question is implicit in the continual harangues and admonitions to maintain Tikopia custom in Nukufero both in public and private conversations.

Adding to the ambiguity in the Tikopia social order in Nukufero is the question of the status of certain innovations. For example, the British colonial government has pressed the Tikopia in Nukufero to pay head taxes to the local government council, made up of Melanesian leaders. To avoid paying what they considered tribute to non-Tikopia leaders, the Tikopia created the Tikopia Development Fund as an alternative. Money is paid into the fund by annual assessment on all Tikopia adults in the Russell Islands. The money is used for community projects both on Tikopia and in Nukufero and is controlled by the 'committee' in Nukufero. The committee and the headman secured permission from the chiefs before starting the fund in 1962. They regarded this innovation not only as a way of getting around colonial government pressure but also as satisfying the government demands in a manner consistent with Tikopia identity and tradition. There is, then, a notion that one may be consistent with Tikopia tradition in one's innovations. What remains ambiguous is whether or not such consistency in innovation constitutes maintenance of tradition as does, say, replicating particular customs. This constitutes a paradox in which the very definition of tradition is at stake. As the question remains unresolved in Nukufero, the ambiguities raised by it persist.

Residents of Nukufero manage to live with the ambiguities of their situation, though their awareness of them is often expressed in their vociferous insistence on maintaining custom. But it is not only public harangues or the anthropologist's probing which makes these ambiguities apparent. They are manifested either explicitly or implicitly in every major conflict in Nukufero. These conflicts, some within the community and some between the community and outsiders, are examined in the next section.

### TRADITION, ETHNICITY, AND CONFLICT IN NUKUFERO

The most serious conflict in Nukufero concerns the constitution of political authority in the village as regards the headman vis-à-vis the men of traditional high rank on Tikopia. 'High-ranking clan' status is conferred on men who are closely related by patrilineal ties to a chief. An effective 'high-ranking man', by Tikopia standards, is one who articulates well at 'council' meetings and moves people to action. Most important, 'high-ranking men' act on behalf of the chiefs. However, since chiefs do not normally reside in the resettlement but have chosen headmen to represent them in their absence, 'high-ranking men' in the Russells have lost considerable power and prestige. On matters related to Nukufero development and relations with outsiders to the community, the chiefs prefer to rely on men with knowledge of the wider affairs of the Solomons, be they high ranking or commoners. The chiefs particularly oppose 'high-ranking men' who would undermine the new leadership for apparently personal reasons. In one case, a headman of low traditional rank had been appointed by 'high-ranking men' in Nukufero and later confirmed to the position by the chiefs on Tikopia. Following the confirmation, a 'high-ranking man', out of dislike for the headman, sought to have him dismissed and replaced by someone of high status. The man of high rank argued before a large gathering of the 'committee' that the headman was an egotist who was trying to amass personal power. Significantly, he buttressed his argument by stating that the headman was consolidating his own position by 'tearing down Tikopia tradition'. Although the community took no action on the matter, the headman felt compelled to return to Tikopia, where he was received warmly by the chiefs and reconfirmed to his position. The same 'high-ranking man' attempted a second time to oust the headman, failing in his argument this time before the chiefs themselves. Further animosity between this 'high-ranking man' and the headman led to an actual fight between the two. Most of the community blamed the former for this outbreak of aggression.

Disagreement between men of high rank and the new leadership may emerge for reasons other than personality conflicts. In one case, several 'high-ranking men' expressed resentment over a group of low-ranking men collecting money for the Tikopia Development Fund, complaining that such responsibility should fall on those of high rank. One 'high-ranking man' opposed the formality of community work projects instituted by the Nukufero headman on grounds that work in the village should be performed spontaneously, as on Tikopia where people volunteer labor without being

told. This 'high-ranking man' contended that the headman, in recruiting help, exceeded the authority invested in him by the chiefs,
and the chiefs themselves would not expect people to work on a
prescribed schedule.

The question of legitimate political authority in the Russells is
less a result of conflict between factions openly competing for
power than an unresolved ambiguity in the relevance of traditional rank to the supposed replica of Tikopia society in Nukufero.
That it is an ambiguous rather than a factional situation is demonstrated by the fact that the lines of controversy were not clearly
drawn. While there is no question that certain 'high-ranking men'
resented having authority vested in others, the grievances they expressed were directed only to specific issues and then stated in
private conversations with friends or others of high rank. As a
group, those of high rank did not constitute a loyal opposition;
outwardly, at least, they were leading spokesmen for maintaining
Tikopia identity in the resettlement. Still, the position of high-
ranking persons in the power structure was ambiguous both to
them and to the general community.[3]

The contingencies of resettlement have raised questions concerning not only the internal political order but also relations with
the protectorate government. The British have encouraged Tikopia and chiefs at home to support the traditional authority system,
recognizing that Tikopia are one of the few people in the Solomons
who have held onto their traditions. However, in an apparent
change of policy toward the migrants, the government sought to
involve Tikopia in the Russell Islands Local Council. Local government councils, established throughout most of the protectorate
but not on Tikopia, administer communication facilities, rural
health clinics, and schools. Except for headmen, who are appointed by the high commissioner, council representatives are
elected by the people. Headmen are responsible for carrying out
orders laid down by European district commissioners and ensuring compliance with council bylaws. Council revenues derive
mainly from a head tax levied against all males residing in the protectorate (BSIP 1965:7).

The government, by 1964, had urged Tikopia in the Russells to
elect representatives to the council and had imposed the requirement of local tax payment. The migrants, for their part, resisted
both representation and taxation, interpreting them as devices to
alienate them from the chiefs' authority and retractions of earlier

agreements reached at the outset of settlement in Nukufero. As indicated above, migrants were led to believe they would be allowed to maintain normal controls over the internal affairs of Nukufero; in the process of village development, they could see no immediate advantage in seeking community welfare through a council dominated by Melanesians. They recalled the early days of resettlement when native Russell Islanders refused to help clear the land and build houses; moreover, they regarded taxation in support of council activities as personal tribute to a Melanesian headman they knew only by reputation, held in little respect, and would mistrust with funds. As one Tikopia put it: "Why should we donate money to a government official? He is not a chief."

A year later, however, the government had apparently decided to take a harder line by imposing fines against six of the Nukufero community leaders and threatening incarceration for failure to meet the obligation. When the men continued to ignore the government demand and officials came to make the arrests, a substantial number of Tikopia submitted themselves for charges and custody, protesting that they should be arrested along with the leaders. At this point the authorities, seeing the difficulties involved in transporting the large number by small craft for arraignment on Banika Island, withdrew the charges (Firth 1969:355).

What is significant in this conflict is the solid response of the Tikopia community in its confrontation with the government, which the Tikopia knew had the power to jail them. The threat seemed somehow to foster a militant response rather than capitulation to the government's demands. This response becomes even more interesting when compared to another confrontation with outside authority, in this case with the Lever Company.

In 1964, Tikopia and workers throughout the Solomons joined in a strike against Lever's plantations. The demand made by the BSIP Ports and Copra Workers' Union was a wage increase for workers employed by Lever. The issue seemed clear enough, but to Tikopia the strike created a situation of ambiguity. While Tikopia would have happily accepted a pay raise, many of them who struck had been reluctant to join in the walkout because they mistrusted Melanesian union officials residing at headquarters in Honiara and, moreover, misunderstood the function of the union itself. Several believed that union officials were corrupt and regularly stole union funds to support families and friends. Others thought the strike had been called not to raise wages but simply to

halt all copra production because union officials and other Melanesian laborers were either too lazy to work or simply were raising
unnecessary trouble. Although Tikopia understood the walkout
was intended to bring workers more money, the exact amount
could not be stated. The union had demanded a flat 45 percent increase across the board—a raise, however, which no Tikopia fully
comprehended, since they knew little of percentages. To many the
strike was less an expression of grievance against Lever than a
time out in which to carry on traditional ceremonies. During the
week of the layoff, five weddings with great feasts and gift exchanges were held. This represents more than half the weddings
celebrated that year.

The ambiguities inherent in the strike, as perceived by Tikopia,
reflect also the status of the migrants as workers. The average
Tikopia earns the equivalent of around $25 a month. Such wages
do not draw him into full-time employment, since he sees no possibility of accumulating personal savings adequate for making substantial purchases (notwithstanding pay increases through collective bargaining and the strike). A Tikopia views plantation labor
not as a permanent job but as a periodic occupation enabling him
to earn a fixed sum of money with which to buy inexpensive com-
modities such as clothing, hand tools, and tobacco. The purchases
are consumed in the Russells or brought to Tikopia upon repatriation. A worker regards a return home as a welcome change from
routine plantation activity and a chance to enjoy the limited fruits
of his labor. A Tikopia is willing to accept a low wage because he
regards it not as compensation for an alternative full-time occupation but merely as a source of income supplemental to subsistence
activities carried out in the Russells and Tikopia.

The migrants, in other words, hardly represented a hard core of
militant strikers hoping in desperation to obtain an adequate wage
for survival. They did, however, support the strike until Lever
made the crucial decision to repatriate all striking migrants to
Tikopia. As the impact of this threat reached throughout the community, the back of the Tikopia phase of the strike was broken,
and workers returned to the plantations immediately. The moment of truth had arrived when the Tikopia realized they stood to
lose the land and possession of Nukufero.[4]

The Tikopia, to some extent, perceived both confrontations in
terms of their own interests as an ethnic group. The confrontation
with the government involved what Tikopia regarded as a threat

to their ethnic and political autonomy and to the traditions that define that ethnicity. To pay tribute to a Melanesian headman is to negate the authority of the chiefs and deny the traditional relationship between people and chiefs—not only is Tikopia tradition threatened, but so is the dictum that Tikopia and Nukufero are the same. The militant solidarity of the villagers can be seen not only as a show of determination to maintain their ethnic autonomy but also, and even more important, the integrity of the tradition that defines ethnicity. The very militancy of the display is highly symbolic of the Tikopia situation: all at once the ambiguity of the Nukufero situation disappeared in resolute action, almost ritual in its communicative form. The chiefs rule on Tikopia; Tikopia and Nukufero are the same; therefore the chiefs rule on Nukufero. The affirmation of this syllogism in the face of government sanction dwarfs the contingencies that require innovation and all its inherent ambiguities in one dramatic moment. For that moment and afterward, there is no ambiguity. Tikopia and Nukufero *are* the same.

The strike displays a pattern which is almost the reverse of the confrontation with the government. The Tikopia were aligned with other ethnic groups in a confrontation where issues were not very clear to the Tikopia. The leaders of the strike were Melanesians, none of whom was trusted by the Tikopia, and a raise in wages did not affect the Tikopia interests in the same way as that of other groups. The loss of their land, moreover, would have threatened their autonomy, forcing those remaining in the Russells to be totally dependent on Lever for subsistence. The uneasy alliance with Melanesians collapsed when the interests of Tikopia themselves were threatened. Moreover, rather than resolving ambiguity, the outcome of the strike served only to exacerbate it by adding a new dimension: the ambiguity as to whether or not the Tikopia would ever hold title to Nukufero and hence the insecurity over tenure on the land. It is perhaps significant that the strike occurred approximately a year before the confrontation between the Tikopia and the government.[5]

CONCLUSION

Tikopia define themselves in terms of distinctive physique, language, and, most important, a body of tradition unique to themselves. Because their tradition is composed of customs, regarded as ideal and behavioral elements, the failure to replicate the entire body of customs in the resettled community of Nukufero has given rise to a good deal of ambiguity concerning the kind of community Nukufero really is and therefore the kind of people the migrants really are. Since the migrants must deal with contingencies of resettlement in novel ways, such failures at replication of custom have been inevitable. The Tikopia are aware of this inevitability, and the efforts of some to innovate in a manner consistent with ideal Tikopia custom have introduced the possibility of redefining custom. This possibility in itself implies further ambiguity, however, in the meanings of custom and tradition.

The ambiguities implicit in such innovations as landholding (chiefs as opposed to others), the organization of communal activities, and political authority in one way or another underlie the major conflicts in the community. The internal conflict over political authority reflects ambiguity in the relevance of traditional rank to the resettled community. Confrontations with outside authorities have had to do with alignment of Tikopia with other ethnic groups as opposed to independence and isolation.

With the eventual departure of the British from the Solomon Islands and the growth of Solomon Island nationalism, we might well expect these ambiguities to be further exacerbated and the conflicts intensified, not only in Nukufero but also on Tikopia, as political independence for the protectorate becomes a reality. The Nukufero experience becomes crucial to all the Tikopia in light of this potentiality as a kind of experiment in adaptation to the inevitable increase in relationships with outsiders. The adaptations the Tikopia can make and the extent to which their social order and definition of themselves are jeopardized by the adaptations depend very much on the resolution of the present ambiguity as to what constitutes tradition and its maintenance.

NOTES

This study is based on fieldwork conducted in the Russell Islands and on Tikopia from June 1964 to August 1965. The research was supported by the University of Oregon on a grant from the National Science Foundation. Thanks are due H. G. Barnett, director of field research, and Michael D. Lieber for helpful suggestions on the writing of this chapter.

1. The involvement of chiefs in the selection of recruits is reported in a commu-

niqué dated 10 July 1956 and dispatched by the director of Lever's plantation to the senior assistant of native affairs: "In the past it has been the accepted practice that we recruit up to 70 men from Tikopia . . . , but it was only with great difficulty that [we] managed to obtain 30 of the required 70 men, and [the recruiter] states that the number one chief was very arrogant and did not wish him to have even these." Two of the chiefs stated explicitly in 1964 that they would limit the number of emigrants to no more than forty nuclear families. To exceed this number, they maintained, would reduce the population on Tikopia and seriously undermine community work projects, household maintenance, garden cultivation, and ceremonial activities. Labor recruits by practice seek permission from a chief to emigrate, and although a chief usually grants temporary leave of the island, the interchange checks against a hasty decision by someone who has not thought out the implications of a move.

2. A small number of Rennellese lived on the east shore of Pavuvu in 1964, but the lack of roads and the rugged interior made cross-island contact with the Tikopia infeasible, and no relationship between the two groups had developed. The Rennellese crossed a narrow channel to work Lever's estates on Banika.

3. The ambiguity of political control in the Russells has been produced not only by the replacement of those of high rank as an unchallenged leadership but also by the absence of the chiefs themselves. Although each chief had made at least one visit to Nukufero, and two had stayed over six months, they were regarded more as honored guests than as permanent residents in the relocation. As perceived by the migrants, the home of the chiefs is on Tikopia, where they are said to hold titular ownership of the island and ultimate control over the behavior of the inhabitants. In contrast, the rights and obligations of chiefs and the people in the Russells could not be stated with any precision. An arrangement among the migrants had been made in 1964 wherein 75 of the 200 acres of Nukufero would be deeded in the names of the chiefs, once the land was legally transferred from Lever to the Tikopia. Yet, while the chiefs were said to "own" the 75 acres with houses, gardens, school, and church located on the land, it was also said that chiefs would not intrude on the private rights of individuals and families who used these possessions. When asked about ultimate rights to the land, informants either could not answer the question or said the relationship of chiefs to the Nukufero site differed from that to Tikopia. True ownership, they maintained, resided with individuals and families in the Russells, unconditionally, whereas on Tikopia chiefs became involved in issues of property rights. It may be concluded, then, that land titled to chiefs would be symbolic in the people's minds of the ties between Tikopia and Nukufero.

4. It is worth repeating here that the government and Lever had promised the legal transfer of the land, but by 1964 title had not been put in the names of the migrants. The delay was attributed by the government to the absence of a qualified surveyor in the Solomons capable of demarcating accurate village boundaries. The government, in the meantime, had assured the Tikopia of the forthcoming title change, but the threat of repatriation by Lever brought

into bold relief the vulnerability and insecurity of the migrants' rights to land in the resettlement.

5. The government confrontation, however, brought Lever into the dispute. The company may have feared that a continued disagreement over tax payment would result in mass arrests or an exodus of Tikopia to the home island. Lever would suffer a loss of valuable manpower if the Pavuvu estates were stripped of the only work force on the island. The company decided to pay the fines imposed on the Nukufero leaders, and apparently convinced the migrants liable for taxes to honor their obligation. Lever would have been prepared to deduct the sum due from each worker and remit it to the government, but all Tikopia at this time are said to have submitted to the tax demand. It is conceivable, although not stated by informants, that Tikopia again felt the pressure of the company regarding rights to land, for at this point Lever still held a 999-year lease on the Nukufero site.

# 10

# THE EXPLOITATION OF AMBIGUITY: A NEW HEBRIDES CASE

*Robert Tonkinson*

Ambrym Island lies in the center of the New Hebrides chain about 100 miles north of the main island, Efate (map 13). Totaling approximately 160 square miles in area, Ambrym is dominated by two active volcanoes and a large surrounding ash plain that occupy the central area and divide the island into three habitable regions. The population (4,246 according to the 1967 census) clusters in the north (1,875), southwest (1,309), and southeast (1,062). This separation is reflected by linguistic and cultural differences, particularly between Southeast Ambrym and the other two areas.[1]

Both volcanoes are fairly active, and serious eruptions with lava flows have at times rendered parts of the island unsafe for habitation. Much more common than lava flows are ash-falls, which kill yam crops and, if prolonged, defoliate vegetation in affected areas. In 1950–1951, eleven months of heavy ash-falls ravaged the island, especially the southeast where all the vegetation was stripped bare.[2] By November 1951 the condominium government had evacuated the populations of both West and Southeast Ambrym.[3] The latter were hastily settled on the nearby island of Epi, only to be victimized weeks later by a disastrous hurricane.

Whereas most Southeast Ambrymese soon returned to their homeland and reestablished themselves there, the members of one village, Maat, resettled on Efate where their leaders had found

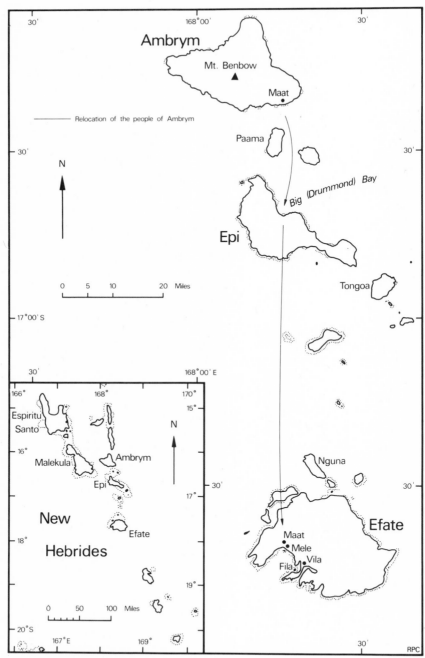

**Map 13.** Relocation from Ambrym to Efate.

Labels within the map:

Ambrym

Mt. Benbow

Maat

Relocation of the people of Ambrym

Paama

N

Big (Drummond) Bay

Epi

Tongoa

0 5 10 20 Miles

168°00'

30'

30'

30'

17°00' S

168°00' E

30'

Espiritu Santo

166°

168°

170°

15°

N

Malekula

Ambrym

16°

Epi

30'

17°

New

Efate

18°

Hebrides

Nguna

30'

Maat

Mele

Efate

Vila

Fila

0 50 100 Miles

19°

20°S

167°E

169°

30'

RPC

them employment and a village site, and this new Maat village became their permanent home. Their resettlement is the concern of this chapter.

The Maat villagers have extensive landholdings in Southeast Ambrym and abundant stands of coconuts. They have never renounced their land and coconut rights, and at any given time there are always a few of them visiting their homeland and living in the old village of Maat. Ambrym is an extremely fertile island; the ash soil is very easy to till, and it is possible for people to grow food there with little effort and to earn a cash income by cutting copra whenever they need money. Since the 1950–1951 eruptions, there have been no ash-falls severe enough to affect copra production or ruin gardens (apart from the delicate yam crops). Other Ambrymese and many outside observers find it difficult to understand why the people of Maat have chosen to remain on Efate, where they possess little land of their own, have insufficient coconuts to make copra, and must therefore work almost constantly— for European employers—while all this time their coconuts rot on Ambrym and their land there remains unworked.

Since each village in Southeast Ambrym as a social unit is part of a larger network of kinship, marriage, and economic ties, it is understandable that the removal of an entire village would disturb the network as a whole. Moreover, the fact that Maat land, its most important resource, remains but is unavailable for occupation by the other villages exacerbates an already disturbed situation. There is subtle pressure on the Maat people either to return to Ambrym or to make some definite disposition of their land, and the villagers are well aware of this. The persistence of the relocated community thus presents a paradox.

Given the apparent permanence of Maat Efate and the problems it engenders for both the villagers and their congeners, it is the persistence of the relocated community that demands explanation, both for the observer and for those involved. One possible explanation is that their successful adjustment to a new environment constitutes what the villagers regard as a major investment, a stake to be maintained. An alternative explanation is an economic one, of the kind usually suggested by government officials, which states that the relatively affluent life-style of the Maat Efate people is so attractive that they are unwilling to give it up. A third possibility is that there are crucial contrasts in the social orders of relocated and home villages, contrasts of sufficient significance to warrant a commitment by the villagers to their maintenance. The latter alternative assumes both sociocultural change and continuity whereas the others assume only change as an explanation of the persistence of the relocated community.

In this chapter each of the three alternative explanations is examined. It will be shown that the first alternative is not supported by available data, that the second involves faulty assumptions, and that only the third allows for an adequate explanation. In addition, it accounts for the nature of the paradox presented by the community's persistence and suggests resolutions of the paradox.

## MOBILITY, ETHNICITY, AND ADAPTATION

It is assumed that a major factor influencing the manner in which people cope with resettlement is their previous history of movement, particularly in terms of the perceptions and adaptive strategies that prior experience affords them. An examination of the history of mobility of the Maat community in relation to an account of their adaptation to Efate leads to three conclusions:

1. Maat people arrived on Efate with a set of adaptive strategies fully adequate to cope with the new physical and social environment.

2. Adaptation to Efate entailed no drastic changes.

3. Not only were Maat people able to replicate major features of their social order on Efate, but they were also able to replicate mobility patterns analogous to those they had practiced in Southeast Ambrym.

Maat, with a population of about 140 in 1950, was one of fourteen villages in Southeast Ambrym, a culture area in which there is a common language and a complex web of kinship-friendship ties linking members of different villages. Like the other villages, Maat was composed of a number of residentially contiguous patrilineages, united under a 'big name'. Residence was strongly patri-virilocal with a considerable amount of hamlet-village exogamy. The tendency for several hamlets to amalgamate was accelerated after the coming of Christianity, whose first influences date from about the early 1890s.[4] Traditionally, changes in the location of hamlets were common, occurring most often as a response to shifting patterns of slash and burn agriculture, intra- and interhamlet conflicts, problems with ancestral spirits, and sorcery scares.

There were well-established intervillage visiting patterns, since villagers had kinship and friendship links with some of the people in most other villages. Individuals or families sometimes made spontaneous, short-term visits to other villages, but these were rarely for more than two or three days at a time. Longer stays, exceeding a month, were rare and were most often prompted by some kind of conflict in the home village or when a family fled after a village sorcery scare.[5] The local schoolteacher-catechists who operated in every village, and to a lesser extent the village chiefs and their assistants, were the most mobile of the inhabitants. Any intervillage visiting that was other than purposeful was infrequent (with the exception of groups of young men who sometimes combined for hunting and sports) since anyone who wandered about aimlessly was likely to be suspected of having ulterior (sorcery) motives.

Traditionally, contacts with the rest of Ambrym and with neighboring islands were probably not strongly developed. There was some contact with Paama, a nearby island inhabited by people who speak a language related to that of Southeast Ambrym. However, Ambrym's notoriety as the home of the most powerful sorcery in the Group rule it out as a favored port of call for all but a few courageous Hebrideans from neighboring islands; besides, the perpetually rough seas and lack of anchorages in the southeast did not attract visitors.[6]

Contact with Europeans and resultant movements of Southeast Ambrymese outside their home area date from about the 1870s when recruiting vessels first called at Southeast Ambrym. During the following thirty or so years they took large numbers of ablebodied men to Queensland to work on sugar plantations as laborers, on contracts of at least three years.[7] The nine Maat men who are remembered as having gone were all repatriated safely to their homeland, complete with rifles, axes, cloth, and other trade goods.

The conversion of Southeast Ambrymese to Christianity, accomplished largely through the efforts of Hebridean evangelists, led to new kinds of movement by a small proportion of the local population. No European missionary ever lived in the southeast, but Maurice Frater, who was in charge of the nearby mission in North Paama, supervised both areas for nearly forty years after his arrival in 1900.[8] He trained schoolteacher-catechists (mostly Paamese at first) to teach in the schools he founded in both areas; then he began educating the most promising young Ambrymese at the mission boarding school in North Paama. Most of the brightest boys were later sent to Santo to attend a theological college (Tangoa Training Institute), which took students from all Presbyterian areas of the New Hebrides and gave them four years of general and religious education. After their return home, most of the eighteen Southeast Ambrymese men who attended the institute between 1913 and 1951 became the best teachers and most devoted evangelists in the southeast, where they exerted considerable influence and introduced important cultural innovations.

The kind of movement that involved the largest number of Southeast Ambrymese since the early 1900s was that of able-bodied men who were regularly recruited for plantation work on other islands—mostly Malekula, Santo, Efate, and Epi (map 13). For the Ambrymese this movement was prompted less by economic motives (except when volcanic activity or hurricanes destroyed their coconut crops) than by curiosity, a desire for a change of scene, or escape from conflicts or sorcery threats. Women and children rarely went, as the men were housed in large dormitories on plantations. They had little intercourse with non-Ambrymese coworkers or with villagers in surrounding areas—especially on Epi, which had a reputation for sorcery that was alleged to be even more virulent than their own.

During World War II, almost all able-bodied Southeast Ambrymese men were recruited to work at least one three-month contract for the Allied forces based on Efate. During this time they lived with Hebrideans from all over the Group and worked either in the town of Vila or in the surrounding Southwest Efate area. Some men served as many as five contracts. They were attracted by the wages, which were higher than those for plantation labor, and by the generosity of their Allied employers, who with their vast materiel were an exciting novelty.[9]

Another kind of movement was that of relocation, usually prompted by severe volcanic activity. An eruption in 1888 led to the abandonment of nine villages, and another in 1913 resulted in the evacuation of the people of Southeast Ambrym to Paama Island where they were billeted by the Paamese. As a result of this temporary resettlement, Southeast Ambrymese developed close ties of friendship and reciprocity that are still maintained with the Paamese. It is clear from available records and from informants' recall that hurricanes and ash-falls and the resultant destruction of food and crops and coconuts were sufficiently common to be an accepted part of life in Ambrym.[10]

The 1951 relocation differed from previous ones in several important ways. First, the prolonged ash-falls that precipitated the decision to evacuate the area were viewed as a crisis by the condominium government, not by the Ambrymese, who were accustomed to such phenomena and regarded them as inconveniences. Second, the decision to relocate was made by the administration, not by the Ambrymese. Third, the places selected for refuge were chosen because of their convenience for the administration, not the preferences and needs of the Ambrymese. The Ambrymese were reluctant to leave their homes, especially if this meant relocating on the allegedly sorcery-ridden island of Epi. The misgivings of the Ambrymese were confirmed when a hurricane struck Epi six weeks after the resettlement, killing forty-eight people and leveling the shelters of the refugees. Completely unsettled by the experience, the Ambrymese resolved to leave Epi as soon as possible, either by securing passage back to Ambrym (where the ash-falls had ceased) or by finding work on plantations elsewhere.

The fortunes of the Maat people diverged from those of their fellow Ambrymese shortly after the hurricane. Several of the village leaders, their most influential men, had been arrested on Ambrym the year before and sent to jail in Vila on fabricated charges of inciting Cargo Cult activity in their homeland. After their release from prison, the four men stayed on in the Vila area to work for local planters and later sent for their families from Ambrym, partly because of the difficulties caused there by the ash-falls.[11]

A local planter, already known to the villagers because he had operated trading vessels in the Ambrym area and had recruited laborers there, approached the village leaders with a proposal that would be mutually beneficial: he would give them land for a village site and some building materials if they would become his labor force and work exclusively for him on the several plantations he maintained in Southwest Efate. Knowing the deteriorating situation back on Ambrym and being aware that it would be at least three years before they could again earn cash from their coconuts there, the leaders agreed. They sent a messenger on a planter's boat with a letter instructing the Maat people to proceed en masse to Vila. On receipt of this message, the villagers were apparently unanimous in supporting the move: they could see the advantages of steady employment on Efate at a time when their homeland was unable to provide a source of cash; in addition, they were anxious to escape from the place they now associated with destruction. Thus the new settlement of Maat, 7 miles from the main town of Vila, came into being in mid-1952.[12]

For the men of the village, Southwest Efate was familiar territory, since they had previously worked there for the Allied forces and on several of the plantations in the area. The twenty-six Maat men who were born before 1935 had averaged almost three trips each to Efate before relocation, but only two of the women in this age category had been there before 1950. For the women, then, relocation involved movement to an area they had heard much about but had never seen. With a few exceptions, the only time women had left Ambrym previously was in response to some kind of crisis, such as the 1913 evacuation, or for the treatment of serious illness. So in this regard the relocations to Epi and then to Efate were no different because they too were prompted by crisis.

Their mobility before relocation inevitably brought Southeast Ambrymese into contact with other ethnic groups, with alien economic institutions, and, to a lesser extent, with officialdom. Because of the relative isolation of Southeast Ambrym, with its poor anchorages and its inhabitants' reputation as sorcerers, there has been little contact between Southeast Ambrym and the outside world. Apart from the occasional appearance of trading vessels seeking to recruit or repatriate laborers, periodic visits by missionaries and, rarely, district administrators were virtually the only other contacts with outsiders. Most interethnic contacts have occurred outside Ambrym.

The interaction between Southeast Ambrymese and members of other ethnic groups, with the exception of some Paamese, has been characterized by limited, highly context-specific contact involving narrowly defined roles and behavior. Roles such as those of employer-employee, clerk-customer, administrator-subject, coworker, and coreligionist define the entire range of contact before relocation.

Since men were the more mobile sex and women moved with the men only during temporary crises, it was mainly men who learned and assumed these roles. Their subsequent use of these roles provided the Southeast Ambrymese with the strategies necessary to cope outside their homeland. Thus, by the time of their relocation to Efate, the migrants already had the prerequisites for adaptation to their new social environment. Moreover, the families who were already living on Efate in 1951 constituted the leadership of the original Maat community. These people had already established contacts with plantation owners, the government, and coreligionists in order to provide the migrants with land, food, building materials, employment, and educational opportunities for their children by the time they arrived. Their adjustment to a peri-urban environment, in other words, required little of the migrants that was not already familiar to them.

Interethnic contacts since relocation reveal a strong continuity with those characterizing the period before the Maat people moved to Efate. Outside contacts still involve men much more than women, since the latter mostly stay in the village—as do the men when they are not working. Although outside contacts are certainly more frequent now, they are still fairly circumscribed and are limited to interaction that takes place away from the village, with the exception of coreligionist contacts described below. Contact with the administration remains minimal, and the Maat people are left to run their own internal affairs much as they were on Ambrym.

The relations between Southeast Ambrymese and other ethnic groups on Efate range from highly superficial to cordial. Maat people evince neither particular hostility nor enthusiasm toward any group other than the Paama people, with whom they have many friendship links. Maat people prefer to socialize with and marry other Southeast Ambrymese, but they do not appear to dwell on ethnic stereotypes. Their closest contacts have been with their neighbors, the inhabitants of Mele Village, which is the largest in the New Hebrides and is situated only a half-mile from Maat. Both villages are Presbyterian and share the same pastor and school facilities, located in Mele. Inhabitants of the two villages exchange visits for certain church services and social events such as dances and marriage feasts.

Apart from activities connected with the church, which sometimes take them to Vila and other peri-urban villages, Maat people are mainly interested in their own village relationships and in interaction with Southeast Ambrymese friends and relatives in the southwest Efate area and their homeland. Interethnic relations are neither stressed nor denounced, simply because they are not considered by the Maat people to be important.

The foregoing discussion should make clear that the patterns of mobility of the Maat people before relocation have been replicated in large part on Efate. Movement out of the village mainly involves males, and they leave for the same reason they did before relocation: to work. While in town they often shop, and they sometimes visit friends or relatives there. Women tend to remain at Maat, except for trips to the hospital and occasional shopping or visiting outings. Movement into the village by outsiders other than Southeast Ambrymese is rare and mainly involves vendors or coreligionists.

Only mobility connected with the homeland has undergone major change since relocation. Instead of spending temporary periods outside Ambrym, as was the case before relocation, Maat villagers now reside permanently on Efate and spend only temporary periods back on Ambrym, an average visit lasting a little more than seven months.[13] At any given time, then, Maat Ambrym has about ten to twenty inhabitants, and although the village population is small and fluctuating, it continues to function.

From the viewpoint of most remaining Southeast Ambrymese, the existence of Maat Efate makes visits to Vila a much more attractive proposition than in earlier times. People wanting to visit the town can expect to be accepted at Maat and to be offered lodging and hospitality there. Thus the population of Maat Efate always includes a small proportion of Southeast Ambrymese who are visiting from the homeland. They come for a variety of reasons and stay for periods ranging from a few weeks to a few years. Whether they choose to stay at Maat or with relatives who live closer to Vila, visiting Southeast Ambrymese generally spend some of their leisure time in the village, especially on weekends and for celebrations.

Friends and relatives from Southeast Ambrym form the largest category of outside visitors to Maat.[14] Maat villagers who visit Vila outside working hours interact mainly with other Southeast Ambrymese; women and children who visit town generally have informal contacts only with Southeast Ambrymese there. Friendships and visiting patterns indicate a strong preference among

Southeast Ambrymese for one another's company. The marked preference of Southeast Ambrymese for marriage with others who speak the same language has continued at Maat, and although the frequency of intermarriage with non-Southeast Ambrymese has increased since relocation, it is still not high. Despite a marked shortage of women in the village, very few Maat men have married girls from neighboring Efate villages.[15]

Adjustment of the Maat people to Efate does not appear to have been a difficult process. They have been able to replicate their village social structure with a minimum of ecological obstacles or interference from the outside. Back on Ambrym, the important boundaries beyond the family were the 'small name' (a named residential area of the village, most of whose male inhabitants claim membership in the same patrilineage), the village, and the culture area. Since relocation, the individual nuclear family boundary has grown more distinct as the unit becomes increasingly independent and self-sufficent, but the other significant boundaries are still the village and the culture area (that is, Southeast Ambrymese as opposed to outsiders).

CULTURAL CONTINUITY

In his detailed account of the Tolai of Matupit, a peri-urban village near Rabaul, New Britain, Epstein (1969:294) concedes that much of the evidence points to change; but he notes that "what gives the Tolai situation so much of its complexity, and, for the observer, its peculiar fascination, is the no less striking evidence of persistence and continuity. . . . Change and continuity represent two faces of a single coin, so that in any given context the one cannot be understood without at the same time specifying the nature of the other." These observations are relevant to the Maat situation. Following the important and dramatic changes that took place in Southeast Ambrymese culture during the first few decades after contact with Europeans, the whole pace of change slackened considerably, and by the time of the relocation the villagers of Southeast Ambrym had experienced at least thirty years of little change compared to the preceding period.[16]

In considering the persistence of Maat Efate it is more appropriate to talk of continuity than of change, because relocation involved, in most respects, adaptations or changes that were relatively minor and were handled by the villagers with a minimum of disturbance. Close similarities in climate, physiography, and vegetation between Ambrym and Efate enabled the villagers to establish a new settlement, make gardens, and cut copra with a minimum of conscious adjustment to altered conditions. Their adaptation was aided by the fact that their move to Efate was unanimously agreed upon and by their previous history of mobility. Change of location per se was not a new experience for these people, who traditionally abandoned their hamlets from time to time and rebuilt at new sites closer to their gardens. Also, the Vila area was well known to the men, and for many years after their resettlement they worked at jobs they had long since mastered: clearing and copra cutting. True, they had to cope with a new social environment beyond the village, but with Pidgin as the lingua franca and coreligionists as neighbors, communication with outsiders was not difficult for them.

A significant continuity was that relating to isolation and non-interference. The people were accustomed to isolation and little contact with outsiders while in Ambrym, and because there was little in the way of government assistance or interference, self-regulation was the normal state of affairs: they solved their own problems and settled their own disputes. This heritage of independence was very helpful to them after relocation, because the administration continued to ignore them. They have never been handicapped by feelings of dependence on outsiders, so in this important respect governmental laissez faire has been largely beneficial to their adaptation to Efate. The new location has so far been sufficiently isolated for the villagers to make their own decisions as to the level of interaction they desire with outsiders.[17]

The freedom of choice that the villagers have enjoyed since relocation appears to be another significant factor in the persistence of Maat Efate. They made the decision to build the new village; no contracts were signed, and no one could have prevented them from leaving Efate at any time. The option of returning to Ambrym always existed, and nothing was done, either by government officials or other outsiders, to prevent their return. Kiste (1968; 1972:92–93), in his study of the resettlement of the ex-Bikini Marshallese, tells of the reactions of these islanders to the news that a return to their homeland was impossible and how this belief led them to find many faults with their new location, while their home atoll came to be regarded as a kind of Elysium in retrospect. The Maat people, in contrast, maintained direct and indirect contact with Ambrym and thus had a reasonably accurate idea of conditions there. Those who felt homesick could, and often did, go back and stay as long as they desired; this liberty still exists, depending only on the availability of transportation and on individual inclination.

If Maat Efate is compared to the villages in Southeast Ambrym, it is clear that relocation has not in itself produced marked sociocultural changes. Demographically, Maat is notable for its rapid population growth and lower infant mortality rate than Southeast Ambrym villages (see Tonkinson 1968:67,252), but many of the other changes that have occurred at Maat have also taken place in Southeast Ambrym. In both places there is an increasing preoccupation with money-earning activities and a consequent decline in the amount of time spent at subsistence tasks; certain kinship observances have been relaxed, and certain taboos abandoned.

For Maat people, life in the new environment has not led to any rapid alteration in patterns of social relationships or in the operation of the kinship system. Nor have the people chosen to adopt radically different gardening methods or, until the 1970s, techniques of construction formerly unknown to them. Although more orderly in ground plan and more heavily vegetated with hedges, shrubs, and trees, Maat Efate is still a Southeast Ambrymese village, architecturally and culturally, and it more closely resembles a homeland village than it does any of its peri-urban neighbors.[18]

Despite a higher standard of living in their Efate environment, such are the continuities which link Maat to Ambrym that people can move from one place to the other with very few problems of adjustment. Maat people who visit Ambrym fit back into their old environment with ease. No drastic alterations in either diet or living conditions are entailed, and the same applies to Ambrymese visitors to Maat, who find themselves—within the village—in a social environment quite similar to the one they have just left. Differences do exist, of course, but they lie mainly in the realms of ideas and attitudes; Ambrymese, for instance, have no great enthusiasm for Maat or Efate, and they think their Maat relatives have lost their sense of values in choosing to remain away from Ambrym for so long. For their part, many Maat people feel that they are better Christians than their Ambrymese congeners and have more enlightened attitudes to such important questions as marriage arrangements and bridewealth. These differences are never aired openly between Maat people and Southeast Ambrymese, so relations between them remain amicable, to the advantage of all concerned.

### ECONOMIC RATIONALES FOR THE PERSISTENCE OF MAAT

Europeans, both inside and outside the administration, explain Maat's permanence in terms of what they see as the obvious advantages, economic and social, of living near Vila as compared to living on Ambrym. To an outside observer, the peri-urban environment of Maat affords its inhabitants advantages they could not possibly enjoy in the homeland. In support of this contention, outsiders cite the ready availability of wage labor in Southwest Efate, access to a wide range of material goods, proximity to the main administrative agencies and to excellent medical and educational facilities, the irresistible lure of the bright lights of Vila, the fact that the Maat people own their own land, the safety and predictability of life on Efate as compared to Ambrym with its active volcanoes, and so on. The worth of these assumptions will now be examined more closely.

The villagers have long been aware of certain economic advantages of their new location. Maat lies in a highly developed plantation area where the demand for labor has generally exceeded the supply, causing the villagers to be much sought after as copra cutters. Most villagers commute to and from work each day and have thus had time to devote to subsistence garden activities, which give them self-sufficiency in the native staples that still form the major part of their diet.[19] Understandably, they were opposed to the administration's suggestion that they move to the north side of the island, in 1954 and again in 1962, since this would have meant giving up an established village and gardens and leaving the area of greatest employment potential. This was especially true in 1962 because by this time some men had begun regular wage work in Vila, and others intended to do likewise. There were also the practical advantages of rent-free occupation of garden land and, on the plantations, a piecework payment rate that enabled them to work when and at what pace they liked, without supervision.

By about 1954 the coconut palms were again bearing on Ambrym and the main economic objection to the return of the Maat people to their homeland was removed, yet no one went back for more than a short visit. When asked to explain their reluctance to return home permanently, villagers give different reasons, all equally plausible. In discussing the advantages and disadvantages of the old and new locations, everyone can enumerate what they consider to be the good and bad points of both (see table 6). In some cases the same point is cited by different informants as a good feature of Ambrym as opposed to Efate, or vice versa; for example, an abundance of good food is often given as an advantage of both places.

According to the native advocate, an administration official who in 1954 reported that the Maat people intended to remain on

TABLE 6  Comparative Advantages of Maat Ambrym and Maat Efate

| Stated Advantages | Ambrym | Efate |
|---|---|---|
| One's own coconuts | x | |
| Plenty of good garden land | x | |
| Self-employment | x | |
| Better reef; more shellfish and fish | x | |
| More leisure time | x | |
| "You waste less money" | x | |
| No big hills | x | |
| Easily worked soil | x | |
| Bigger tubers | x | |
| More breadfruit | x | |
| More fowls | x | |
| Less malaria | x | |
| Abundance of bush and garden foods | x | x |
| Less sorcery | | x |
| Better facilities (educational, medical, etc.) | | x |
| Good water supply | | x |
| No ash-falls | | x |
| Fewer hurricanes | | x |
| More entertainment | | x |

Efate, the main reason given by the villagers was that Efate did not suffer from ash-falls or the risk of lava flows. This was no doubt a consideration, but the reason was probably based on the advocate's own assumptions, since the villagers rarely cite it when giving their opinions of the two locations. Many mention their reluctance to take their children away from the schools for fear of ruining their chances of a good education. They also talk of their unwillingness to abandon the village and gardens and thus waste all their hard work. The proximity of Maat to hospital facilities and to an excellent water supply (on Ambrym, water supply problems are commonplace) are also given by many informants as reasons why they remain on Efate.

Significantly, the attraction of living only a few miles from Vila is rarely given as an advantage of the Efate location. The lure of the town, as such, was never really a factor and it was not until about 1960 when hurricane damage caused a coconut shortage in Southwest Efate that men decided to seek work in Vila. Outside working hours, the only villagers who visit town are the young men, most of whom consider the bars, cinema, and nightclubs as worthwhile attractions but are often content to remain in the village, especially if a supply of liquor is assured. In fact, some informants stress that store goods and liquor are also available on Ambrym, as if to downplay this supposed advantage of being near Vila.

Economic rationales are markedly absent when villagers explain why they remain on Efate. All have stands of coconuts in the homeland, and most concede that they could work their own coconuts and make ample money, at their own pace, back on Ambrym. They complain that wage work in Vila ties them down to the job and that Efate is a place for work whereas Ambrym is a place for rest. Certainly, they are aware that they earn more money by working constantly, but they also know that they spend more than they would back on Ambrym and that some goods classed as luxuries on Ambrym are necessities on Efate. All are aware that they could get by comfortably on Ambrym with much less cash than they need in the new location and that they would be their own bosses back there, whereas on Efate they must work for outside employers at fixed rates. It must be concluded, then, that from the viewpoint of the Maat people economic rationales for their continuance on Efate are of little importance, as table 6 suggests.

## THE PARADOX OF PERMANENCY

Many villagers like to stress the comparative advantages of Ambrym, and many of them do in fact express a preference for their homeland. When asked why therefore they do not return permanently, they usually mention the lack of hospitals, poorer schools, water shortages, and so on, but many admit that their fear of sorcery is what inhibits them most from returning permanently to Southeast Ambrym. No matter what their level of commitment to Christianity, degree of sophistication, or educational background, the Maat people, almost to a person, firmly believe in the reality of sorcery, the existence of sorcerers, and their destructive capabilities and activities on Ambrym. Sorcery scares are endemic in their homeland, and fear of sorcery continues to be the greatest single determinant of the movement of people out of Ambrym.[20]

In Southeast Ambrym there are men who claim the ability to detect impending sorcery attacks on others. These men usually warn the people they have discerned to be potential victims, and the typical reaction of Ambrymese thus alerted is to lock themselves and their families in their houses and then take the first available boat off the island. They may stay away for months or even years, until they feel it is safe to return. Accounts of sorcery attacks, death attributed to poisoning and sorcery, near misses, and warnings of impending sorcery are being constantly communicated through and beyond Southeast Ambrym, and with each new letter or arrival from Ambrym, the news spreads throughout the Maat Efate community. It is not surprising that the Maat people are always most impressed by these stories and unhesitatingly accept them as absolute truth.

If villagers can give as many reasons for returning to Ambrym as for remaining on Efate, there is one feature of the village social order that appears to have tipped the balance in favor of Efate as a permanent home—the almost complete absence of sorcery in the new location. Informants often pointed out to me the large number of children at Maat, and they commented on the small number of deaths among their children since relocation, compared to the small number who survive on Ambrym.[21] It was surprising to discover that the Maat people do not attribute the different survival rate to their proximity to excellent medical services, of which they invariably make full use in cases of serious illness. As one informant put it, "On Ambrym the sorcerers always kill the small children; here, no sorcery, so lots of children." Thus the villagers have what is to them concrete proof of the murderous activities of sorcerers on Ambrym and a corresponding lack of sorcery in their village on Efate.

A significant feature of the relocation has been the lack of conflicts arising from land claims. As stated earlier, the villagers retained their land rights on Ambrym, and even after they had decided to remain permanently on Efate, there was little fear of land loss on Ambrym—there was always someone living in their old village, and the presence of such residents discouraged neighboring villagers from usurping Maat land. On Efate, the people at first owned none of the land they exploited for gardening, and the land they later purchased was registered and held communally in the village name. As a result, there have never been any disputes over boundaries, tree ownership, and so on, in marked contrast to what had apparently been the case on Ambrym before 1951. Thus relocation not only removed the Maat people from the threat of intervillage sorcery, but it also lessened the possibility of intravillage conflict and sorcery, much of which had allegedly stemmed from arguments over land and coconuts. The fact that on Ambrym sorcery was attributed almost entirely to males—in a male-dominated society with respect to descent, residence, and inheritance principles—suggests that quarrels over land, pigs, and coconuts probably brought about people's misfortunes. In this respect Maat Efate could be viewed as proof of such an assertion since there are no quarrels over these matters in the new location and there is no sorcery.

Once the people shifted to Efate, these disputes lost their potency and nothing in the new system of land tenure gave people the opportunity to revive them. It could perhaps be argued that relocation should have led to an increased incidence of alleged intravillage sorcery, once the blame for suspicious deaths could no longer be placed readily on people in other villages. Since 1952, however, only two Maat deaths have been widely attributed to sorcery poisoning, and in both cases the initial suspect was an outsider who lives in the village. It is for these reasons that the shift itself has been so important, because it has separated the people from their land, coconuts, and neighbors in other villages and thus from most of the conflict these engender.

It has been pointed out that movement out of the Ambrym community, for temporary but indefinite periods, was often the result of crises, which were of two main kinds: natural disasters (highly irregular in occurrence) and escape from victimization by sorcery (which apparently occurred quite regularly). Although the Maat resettlement was an outcome of a crisis, it should be remembered that the ash-falls that prompted the evacuation were not considered critical by the Maat people, who were opposed to leaving Ambrym if it meant relocation on Epi. Nor was the relocation a direct result of fear of sorcery; the initial reasons for staying on Efate were economic ones, and only later did the lack of sorcery in the new community come to be regarded as a major factor in the permanence of Maat Efate.

The absence of sorcery in Maat Efate represents a most important contrast with Ambrym, in that the homeland environment represents an ongoing context in which sorcery allegedly occurs whereas Maat Efate represents the context of a refuge outside the social system of Southeast Ambrym where a person can escape from the threat of sorcery as well as from other social obligations that are inevitably part of life in the homeland. It is precisely this situation, the contrast of homeland-sorcery and Efate-refuge, which generates paradox and ambiguity of at least two kinds.

The first paradox concerns the nature of the Maat Efate community, mainly the extent to which it corresponds to its Southeast Ambrymese counterparts. The Maat people have built what looks much like a Southeast Ambrymese village, and they have purchased some of the nearby land (using money contributed by themselves but with some assistance from their homeland congeners) so that they could carry on in the new location the same kind of subsistence gardening activities they practiced on Ambrym. The inhabitants view Maat essentially as an Ambrymese village, yet in one vital respect—the lack of sorcery—its social order differs from those of its Southeast Ambrymese counterparts. The ambiguity suggested by this difference resolves itself if sorcery is associated strictly with locale, but sorcery is obviously a relation, or the outcome of sets of relations, among people. In other words, locale may be used to symbolize the difference between the two areas, but it cannot account for the difference, so this contrast between Southeast Ambrym and Maat Efate remains somewhat paradoxical.

Another paradox, closely related to the first, concerns whether or not the Maat Efate community represents a permanent removal of an entire village from the homeland cultural milieu. Escape from sorcery in Ambrym, while common, has generally entailed temporary movement out of the homeland, yet the Maat villagers have shown no sign that they intend to return to Ambrym permanently. They have not, however, informed their Southeast Ambrymese congeners that they will never return, and some villagers periodically express their intention of returning permanently at some unspecified time in the future. At the moment, Maat Efate is the permanent home of the Maat villagers and Maat Ambrym is a place to stay while visiting Ambrym, but it is not inconceivable that the roles of the two villages could be reversed at some future time. Thus the twin set of ambiguities: Maat Efate is and is not an Ambrymese village; it is and is not a permanent resettlement.

These ambiguities merit further consideration for both substantive and theoretical reasons. Substantively, they affect the attitudes of the Southeast Ambrymese who remain in the homeland and thus the relations between them and their congeners in Maat Efate. Theoretically, the ambiguities and their resolution involve the process of cultural change and its relation to cultural continuity, not only in the Maat Efate community but also in comparison with other communities described in this volume.

Given a fear of sorcery as the major determinant of the Maat people's continued residence in Efate, it is reasonable to ask why the rest of the Southeast Ambrymese dared to return home in 1952 after the ash-falls had ceased. This question can be answered satisfactorily. For one thing, the refugees were more afraid of having sorcery worked on them by the people of Epi than they were of their own sorcerers. For another, despite the pervasiveness of real or imagined sorcery, few people live in constant fear of it. There are risky places (such as the deep bush, particularly when people must spend many days preparing new gardens there) and risky times (such as at night when sorcerers are said to be most active). Much of the time, however, people feel reasonably safe, provided they have done nothing to provoke a sorcery attack, go about their business openly, and take care never to expose themselves unnecessarily to the risk of attack.

In the case of the Maat people, it seems that they stayed away too long. They had time to think about all the alleged sorcery activities occurring back home, to hear the constant flow of stories concerning sorcery, and to inflate this fear into something stronger than it had ever been before they left Ambrym, until they literally reached the point of no return—or at least of no permanent return. If it is true that fear of sorcery has important social control functions, and that conflicts over land and coconuts invite the possibility of sorcery attacks on the participants, the few Maat people who do venture back to Ambrym from time to time should feel reasonably safe—provided they stay out of the bush and do not wander about alone at night—because they are no longer embroiled in conflicts of the kind just mentioned.

It is not clear at what stage after relocation the Maat people began to regard Maat Efate as a possible permanent home, but this point may well have coincided with their growing awareness of the absence of sorcery in the new village. Their perception of this contrast was no doubt due to the periodic influx of news from the homeland and of new arrivals who had fled Ambrym as a result of sorcery scares. The Maat people would then have realized that sorcery is not inevitable, but contingent. If they conceptualized this contingency in terms of location, then the homeland would have been seen as a milieu in which a certain set of relations leads to sorcery as an inevitable but to some extent unpredictable outcome. This perception would have become objectified in the contrast: homeland (sorcery and death) versus Maat Efate (life and well-being).

This positive evaluation of Maat in contrast with Ambrym was never perceived or shared by those who remained in Southeast Ambrym. The resident Southeast Ambrymese claim never to have understood the motivations of the Maat people in remaining on Efate while their coconuts rot in Ambrym and their valuable land there goes untilled. Typically, they characterize their congeners in Maat Efate as crazy for staying there and are convinced that Ambrym is a better place to live than Efate. The fact that the return of Maat people to Southeast Ambrym is sporadic and temporary could be taken by the Southeast Ambrymese to indicate a measure of noncommitment on the part of the Maat people toward their relatives in the homeland. The absence of practically an entire village suggests that links in the reciprocity network are being disrupted or at least attenuated. Moreover, to the extent that personal relationships are important above and beyond structural obliga-

tions, the continued absence of the Maat people becomes a con-
spicuous communication in and of itself. If this situation were not
somehow mitigated, it could easily lead to a permanent schism between the people of Maat and their Ambrymese congeners.

No such schism has occurred, however, in large part because of
the ambiguities inherent in the position of Maat Efate. First, some
of the money that was used to purchase land near the relocated
village was contributed by congeners in many Southeast Ambrymese villages; thus the new location is partly "theirs." This
ideal is supported by the fact that Southeast Ambrymese visitors to
Efate are welcome in Maat, are generally given hospitable treatment, and can stay as long as they desire. Second, men from Maat
go to Ambrym in search of brides and in return they give women
to Southeast Ambrymese men, most of whom then stay on at Maat
and live uxorilocally. Third, there has been continued communication between Maat and the homeland, with exchanges of
letters, messages, and visits, such that to a certain extent the Maat
people remain in the reciprocity network of the homeland and
thus fulfill many of their responsibilities to their relatives there.
Finally, the people of Maat still consider themselves to be ethnically Southeast Ambrymese and are unequivocal about this continuing identification with the homeland.

So, while the relocated village is strongly identified with Maat
Ambrym people, it is never exclusively so, since it is, ideally and
actually, a refuge for all Southeast Ambrymese who care to make
use of it. This ambiguity in Maat's status is a source of frustration
to the Southeast Ambrymese in the homeland in that they are not
being totally rejected but are instead in the position of tacit collu-
sion with the Maat Efate people. Thus they attempt to explain the
absence of the Maat people with statements such as "they must be
crazy" or "we can't understand them." In essence, this attitude
suggests that there must have been some mistake for which no one
is really responsible. Thus the Ambrymese perceive that the apparent rejection of them by the Maat people is not a deliberate response to something the Ambrymese have done or to what Southeast Ambrymese society is. The explanation that the Maat people
are crazy or do not understand implies that no one is responsible
for the current situation. Should some attribution of responsibility
arise, the result would inevitably be a serious rift in relations be-

tween the Maat people and their congeners in the homeland. As long as both sides retain an element of ambiguity in the situation and neither openly voices its objections to the other's choice of home location, the status quo will continue.

It may be productive to speculate on resolutions of this ambiguity for two reasons: one is that this speculation may produce testable hypotheses for research not only in this community but also in similar situations elsewhere; the other is that it may have comparative value—given the possible resolutions of this situation, would the outcomes resemble those discussed elsewhere in this volume?

At least three different kinds of resolution can be posited, and each entails some interesting theoretical implications. First, a schism could develop, although this possibility seems remote in the present circumstances. A serious rift implies a breakdown in communications and the likelihood that the Maat people would be forced to give up their land rights in Ambrym and the loss of Maat Efate as a refuge for visiting Ambrymese. None of these eventualities seems likely.

Second, it is possible that the Southeast Ambrymese as a whole, given time and further experience in Maat Efate and the world outside the homeland, will eventually redefine their own social microsystem. Given the many reasons for Ambrymese to visit Efate and stay at Maat, which include hospital care, visits to relatives, the negotiation of marriages, temporary wage work, holidays, and so on, as more and more people make the trip they will notice both the continuities and the differences between their homeland and Maat Efate. It should become apparent to them that Southeast Ambrym and Maat are really two different life-styles based on a similar pattern. They will notice that in their contacts with other ethnic groups, the latter perceive them as an ethnic entity regardless of whatever stylistic variations occur; and of course none of the Ambrymese themselves question their Southeast Ambrymese identity. Once the distinction between the relocated village and the homeland is seen as one of style, the identification of Southeast Ambrym's social order with Southeast Ambrym as a place will become much looser and will probably lose its symbolic force. The outcome may be a universalization of Southeast Ambrymese identity and social order such that they are seen as transcending a particular locale. Should this eventually be the case, sorcery will assume a position of central importance, since it is around the notion of a lack of sorcery that the Maat outlook crystallizes.

Consideration of sorcery, or the lack of it, leads to a third possibility. The Maat population will no doubt continue to grow rapidly through a combination of natural increase and immigration.[22] The village site itself is limited in size, and already there is a growing shortage of suitable garden land close to the village, so there is a possibility of eventual population pressure and overcrowding. In such a situation, lack of privacy and competition over women, jobs, garden land, and so on may lead to sorcery accusations and counteraccusations. This would be, then, the final replication of the Southeast Ambrym social order in Maat Efate. Such a development could lead to a movement back to Ambrym like the current one to Efate; the outcome could be a kind of equilibrium of population through reciprocal movement.

The implications of such a resolution are as follows. Sorcery is not necessarily or exclusively tied to conflicts over land and coconuts, but it could be regarded as a result of competition induced by population pressure; that is, it is a function of demographic structure at a given time. Thus the relations symbolized by sorcery would become universalized rather than remaining part of the concept of Southeast Ambrym's social order and being tied to the homeland locale.

Each of the foregoing possibilities for resolving the ambiguous position of Maat Efate has its parallel in other cases cited in this volume. The schism resolution is represented by the Southern Gilbertese situation (chapter 8) by a break between the home community and a break within the new community. The universalization of the social order through a "we, the people of . . . " idea is represented by the Kapinga (chapter 3) and the Rotumans (chapter 7). The third possibility, total replication of the relations that people are attempting to escape from, along with movements approximating an equilibrium, is precisely the Nukuoro case (chapter 4).

It appears normal in relocation situations that some kind of ideology about the old homeland evolves; generally the ideology emphasizes a kind of hindsight regarding what the former social system was all about. This ideology tends to reflect present concerns which interpret or reinterpret what was going on before relocation. In the Maat case, rather than a growing nostalgia for the good old days back on Ambrym, there arose among the people an increasing sense of relief at their good fortune in living in a place where the fear of sorcery could be kept to a minimum. Perhaps the Maat people are aware that in many respects they have the best of both worlds in their new location; perhaps they are merely using the sorcery as a convenient rationalization for not wanting to go back home and thus give up their new life. But, as table 6 indicates, they do appear to have a genuine preference for their homeland, although they feel it is not worth the risk to go back on a permanent basis. Efate will remain their home as long as their conception of Ambrym as a place riddled with sorcery continues unaltered.

## NOTES

This chapter is based on field research carried out on Efate and Ambrym, New Hebrides, from July 1966 to August 1967 and on Efate in July and August 1969. The earlier fieldwork was supported by the University of Oregon on a grant from the National Science Foundation; research in 1969 was undertaken while I was a Graduate Fellow of the University of British Columbia. I wish to thank H. G. Barnett, director of the Oregon-supported field research, and Michael Lieber, Joan Metge, Jean-Marc Philibert, and Murray Chapman for their helpful comments.

1. To date, the only detailed ethnographic information on Ambrym is that of Guiart (1951a:5–103; 1956a:217–225; 1956b:301–326).
2. Williams (1964:41–46) describes the volcanology of Ambrym and gives a list of recorded eruptions since 1774. He attributes the unusually heavy ash-falls in the southeast to the presence of high-altitude countercurrents to the prevailing southeast trade winds.
3. In 1906 the British and French took joint control of the New Hebrides. Since 1914 there have been, in effect, three main administrative organizations: British government, French government, and the joint administration. In each of the four main administrative districts, there are two resident district agents, one British and one French, who deal mainly with local matters and make regular tours of the islands under their joint supervision.
4. By the 1920s all Southeast Ambrymese were at least nominally Presbyterians.
5. Precise information on these intervillage movements was not obtained, since my stay in Southeast Ambrym was brief and this was not one of my major research concerns.
6. "The Group" refers to the New Hebrides, as it is commonly called by its English-speaking inhabitants. Robert Lane's South Pentecost informants attributed the alleged superiority of Ambrym's sorcery to the presence of active volcanoes on the island (Lane 1965:257).

7. Many Hebrideans were also taken to Fiji as plantation laborers, but no Maat men are remembered as having gone there. Unfortunately, I have no statistics on the approximate number of Ambrymese who were taken to Queensland; judging by the number who went from Maat, perhaps 150 to 200 men went from Southeast Ambrym.

8. Frater's book (1922) and magazine articles give the only published accounts of the early days of Christianity in Southeast Ambrym and Paama.

9. Worsley (1957:150) notes that "the large-scale activities of British and American forces in the New Hebrides, and rumours of events in the north, had powerful repercussions." As Worsley (1957) and Guiart (1951b: 86–88; 1956c) point out, these repercussions took the form of a recrudescence of Cargo Cult notions and activities, in most of which the Americans were hailed as the bringers of the millennium. Geslin (1956:245–285) discusses aspects of interaction between servicemen and Hebrideans in his description of the Allied presence in the New Hebrides during World War II.

10. In the postcontact era, however, these periodic setbacks became more serious in that people temporarily lost their only source of cash (copra), which their newly developed and increasing needs for European goods demanded. To continue to fulfill these needs they were thus forced to leave Southeast Ambrym and seek plantation work elsewhere to earn the necessary cash until their own coconuts were again ready for harvesting.

11. The leaders also remained on Efate because of an illegal banishment decree; two of them were forbidden to return to Ambrym for three years. This ruling was apparently imposed out of spite by the district agent, whose unjust treatment of the men in the court he convened in Southeast Ambrym later earned him the censure of the joint court, which reduced the original heavy sentences.

12. When Brookfield, Glick, and Hart (1969:116) took a census in the Southwest Efate area in June 1965, the nonvillage population of this area was 4,624, of whom 487 were on plantations or in schools located in the rural area; 1,491 were in the peri-urban areas around the town, and the balance were in the town itself. Of the latter, 2,786 were Hebrideans, 745 Europeans, 476 Metis and others, 305 Asians, and 303 people from other Pacific islands.

13. Between 1952 and 1967, over 75 percent of the adult population visited Southeast Ambrym; adult males made an average of almost three trips each, for an average duration of about seven months, and adult females made nearly two trips each and stayed for about seven and a half months at a time.

14. In May 1967 there were about 140 non-Maat Southeast Ambrymese living in the Southwest Efate area, and 18 percent of them were living at Maat.

15. In July 1969 the population of Maat consisted of 116 males and 85 females. Since about 1960 seven Maat girls have married outsiders; all had gone to work as housegirls in Vila, where the shortage of women is acute, and almost all married after becoming pregnant by men from other islands who were working in town. Marriage of Maat men with women from neighboring Efate villages dates from only 1972, when three such unions took place.

16. The reasons why their ritual life, their hierarchical grade system, and their whole "pig culture" should have collapsed so rapidly and completely in an

area as isolated from the mainstream of European pressures as Southeast Ambrym are unfortunately not known. The magnitude of this loss is surprising when one considers other parts of the same island. North Ambrym, with a history of much greater and more intensive contact with whites, still has several pagan villages which continue to exert considerable influence in the area.

17. Between 1970 and 1973, however, the unprecedented growth of Vila led to a rapid spread of suburbia, which has reached the environs of Maat; there are now whites living just across the road from the village. Increasing numbers of Maat men and women are being employed as laborers and domestics by these whites, so there is now a great deal more interaction, close to and even within Maat, between the villagers and outsiders. In one sense, land *has* become an issue at Maat, because of disputes over boundaries with newcomers whose properties adjoin village land. These were still being resolved when I left Maat in September 1973.

18. In the three years prior to 1973, however, the village almost doubled in area and now contains at least a dozen large, substantial cement and iron houses, several with louvered windows and store-bought doors, gutters, and so forth. These new buildings have given Maat much more of the look of an Efate village.

19. From Epstein's accounts (1963:182-215;1969) of the peri-urban Tolai community of Matupit on New Britain, there are many similarities to the Maat situation. In both places much of the labor force commutes each day, but the villagers are able to maintain subsistence activities as well. Both villages have many features of a peri-urban community, but they retain distinctive features of their own culture in terms of residential divisions, kinship structuring and marriage rules, language, and patterns of social interaction.

20. Excluding the people of Maat Efate, about 32 percent of the Southeast Ambrymese population was absent from the homeland in July 1973, and of these absentees only a very small proportion (7 percent, or 44/641) were children temporarily away at school. There has been no serious volcanic activity since 1951 and in only a few villages are there land shortages, so economic factors alone could not account for such a high absentee rate. I spent the months from June to September 1973 on Ambrym and Efate studying the connection between sorcery and emigration from Southeast Ambrym; this matter will be discussed in a forthcoming paper.

21. For a period of forty years prior to resettlement, 51 percent (57/111) of children born to women in Maat Ambrym died before reaching adulthood. This contrasts markedly to the 1952-1967 postrelocation period when only 15 percent (18/120) of their children died.

22. Between July 1969 and June 1973, Maat's population rose from 201 to 307 (the latter figure includes 53 Southeast Ambrymese visitors in temporary residence). According to the British District Agency in Vila, Maat is now the fastest-growing village in Southwest Efate. There is still adequate house and garden land, however, and the level of intravillage conflict does not appear to have risen as a result of this rapid population increase. Nor have sorcery accusations yet appeared as a feature of life in Maat.

# 11

# WHAT DID THE ERUPTION MEAN?

*Erik G. Schwimmer*

How should anthropologists study a nonrecurring event? It is obviously of interest only if it is paradigmatic of some social law. But what kind of law? The question has often been faced and, most of the time, one of two answers has been given. The literature on this question has recently been surveyed by J. Kingsley Garbett in an essay, "The Analysis of Social Situations" (1970).

Garbett defines a social situation as "a temporally and spatially bounded series of events abstracted by the observer from the ongoing flow of social life" (1970:215). He summarizes the two types of analysis that have been made as (1) depending on some concept of a typical actor as performer of roles and (2) depending on a concept of the typical actor as a manipulator, the limits of whose rationality are specified.

Neither of these methods accounts for the "social situation" discussed in this chapter—the eruption of Mount Lamington in the Northern District of Papua (map 14). I therefore turned to a semiotic approach based on methods developed by Lévi-Strauss (1960) and Barthes (1964b). Semiology, as defined by Saussure, is "a general science of signs." This science studies systems of signs according to methods which will be indicated in the course of this chapter. The term "semiotics" was introduced by Margaret Mead. If this method is to be applied to the study of nonrecurring events, the assumption is that such events are read by a social group as constituting a sign or system of signs.[1]

Such an assumption is legitimate in the case of the eruption of Mount Lamington. In the view of the great majority of my Orokaiva informants, the cataclysmic explosions in the mountain and related volcanic activity were utterances communicating a message. With unimportant exceptions to which I shall refer later, informants took what may be called a religious view of the eruption (Lévi-Strauss 1962:292). They invested with personal will what we would call forces of nature (van der Leeuw 1938:chap. 9). And not only did some Being cause the eruption, but he used it as a means of communication.

Whether it is expedient to study a cataclysm such as the eruption of Mount Lamington as a system of signs emitted by the mountain depends entirely on the quality of the insights that emerge. In this case, field inquiry showed the existence of at least four systems of thought on the significance of the disaster. The adherents of these systems each expressed a different world view consistent with their view of the eruption. The existence of such ideological differences within a single society reflects conflicts which occur not only on the level of discourse but also on that of social transactions.

Such data raise several questions that merit close examination. If all Orokaiva had placed the eruption within one logically consistent framework of meaning, we might believe that we had thus discovered *the* cognitive system of the Orokaiva. In the present case we find four ideologies and explanatory frameworks all generated by the same cognitive system, in the same way that different players may use a variety of strategies while competing with one another in the same game. It then becomes our task to reconstruct this cognitive system and account for a system of interrelated ideologies generated by a sequence of events as interpreted by the cognitive system.

Another question is whether ideological discourse about the cause of the eruption deals with all or some or any of the basic conflicts identified in the society by ethnographic study and analysis. My data, dealing with the period 1951–1966, suggest that Orokaiva ideological discourse was rather selective in the conflicts with which it concerned itself. The conflicts between tribalism and regionalism and between denial and acceptance of the partnership with European power are fully canvassed, but conflicts arising out of the relocation of refugees after the eruption and conflicts concerning land tenure are not reflected in ideological discourse related to the disaster. How can we explain this selectiveness?

We may finally ask: To what extent have signs communicated by the eruption become an integral part of the Orokaiva system of thought in 1966? To what extent do they appear in the rhetoric expressing current ideologies? To what extent has the eruption generated these ideologies? How do cognitive systems adapt themselves to far-reaching events (such as the establishment of Australian authority) which call into question the traditional rationale for behavior? In short, the Orokaiva data lead us to an exploration of the dynamics of non-Western thought.

The factual material presented here corresponds closely to the preoccupations agreed on by the contributors to this volume. I commence with the presentation of some background data, emphasizing institutional, transactional, and ecological factors. The semiotic analysis that follows is focused on crisis behavior. The analysis will bring to light conflicts in two areas which are of special concern in comparative study of exile and migration in Oceania: the macrosystem/microsystem relationship and the maintenance of ethnic boundaries.

My discussion of land tenure conflicts, ignored in the ideological discourse under examination, will deal with the cultural meaning of spatial movement and the significance of land at various levels of culture. It will be demonstrated that although land tenure does not figure in ideological discourse about the eruption directly, it is integrated into ideological discourse indirectly.

The use of semiotics in anthropological analysis is at an early stage of development. Among the well-known pioneers in America are Bateson (1935, 1951), Mead (1964), Sebeok (1970), and sources such as E. T. Hall, Alfred Hayes, and Weston LaBarre. In this chapter, I have relied a great deal on the work of Lévi-Strauss (especially 1958, 1960, 1962), whose semiotics forms an integral part of his structural comparative method.

Semiotics has inevitably drawn extensively on linguistic concepts, since linguists have traditionally engaged in sophisticated analyses of symbols. The present chapter owes a debt to Saussure, to Hjelmslev, and especially to Barthes (1964a, 1964b). I would agree, nonetheless, with Sebeok's contention (1970) that semiotics is not merely concerned with a "secondary language" but is an independent discipline for decoding sign systems which are often not at all linguistic.

Among the concepts drawn from linguistics is the notion of a "sign" composed of a signifier and a signified. While many linguists do not concern themselves with the signified (which they tend to relegate to the realm of psychology), in semiotics the relationship between signifier and signified is the chief object of study. We may put this differently (with Hjelmslev and Barthes) by saying that a sign has a level of expression and a level of content. Furthermore we may distinguish, at each of these levels, between form and substance. Semiotics differs from linguistics in that the signifiers often do a great deal more than just signify something. For instance: the eruption of Mount Lamington did a great deal more than emit an utterance; it emitted enough substance to change the landscape of the entire district.

Semioticians argue that whatever object we use to serve our needs and whatever object affects our destiny obtains a semantic value, becomes a sign. Wearing a raincoat not only protects; it also signifies some fact about the weather. In Papua, wearing a banana leaf signifies that it is actually raining; wearing a raincoat may mean no more than that it is likely to rain. Barthes speaks, in this connection, of "functional signs": on the level of expression, the form has semantic value but the substance is utilitarian, going beyond signification.

Our concern in this chapter is to describe the frameworks of meaning attached to the eruption of Mount Lamington. Therefore we are dealing with what Barthes has termed complex semiotic systems. To show why this is so, let us first consider the primary sign system. Hjelmslev (1963) represents a sign by the formula ERC, where E is the level of expression, C the level of content, and R the relation between the two. To give a semiotic example, in the Road Code the level of expression (E) is made up of the colored signals and the level of content (C) is a set of orders given to drivers of motor vehicles. The relationship (R) between the lights and the orders arises out of a system of legally sanctioned conventions. The total sign is ERC.[2] Here the level of expression (E) is made up of volcanic phenomena and the devastation they caused. At the level of content (C), informants explain that the anger of the mountain or of God is demonstrated by geophysical phenomena. But several other questions at once present themselves: Why was the mountain or why was God angry? To discuss this question we need a metalanguage in which we can define terms such as "anger," "Sumbiripa (the mythical master of Mt. Lamington)" and "God." Hjelmslev and Barthes call this a "denotative system": the level of content (C) is made up of a second system of signification (ERC).

There is another system of signification, called a "connotative system," which has been studied far less than metalanguages but is of great importance in semiotics. For instance, wearing a raincoat and wearing a banana leaf do not, for a Papuan, have the same connotation. Wearing a banana leaf connotes that one is a simple villager; when a Papuan wears a raincoat, it connotes that he is going to town or for some other reason wishes to emphasize his familiarity with European custom. A connotative system is a system (ERC) whose level of expression (E) is itself made up of a full system of signification.[3]

Differences in the signifier which are insignificant in the primary system (a raincoat and a banana leaf both protect against rain; there is no difference on the level of content) become significant in the connotative system as signaling differences in social position. Connotative systems are frequently used in the art of persuasion. If one wishes to persuade another person to choose one alternative over another, a frequent technique is to invoke an appealing ideology by the use of appropriate rhetoric. Thus an advertiser may evoke in the reader's mind an image of a desirable way of life and then persuade him, by a clever use of analogies, that a product he wishes to sell opens a way to this mode of life.

The difference between systems of connotation and denotation is not always easy to mark in the material analysed in this essay. For instance, discourse about the eruption not infrequently served the purpose of proving that one tribe was better than another, that white power will disappear, that white man's science is the road to Papuan salvation. Could one seriously maintain that the meaning of the eruption lay in propositions of this kind? One may rightly say that those who put forward such propositions, while ostensibly explaining the eruption, were in actual fact using a rhetorical device to promote their own ideology. On the other hand it is impossible to go far in the analysis of Orokaiva or Yega metalanguages without ending up with a construction of the type just quoted.

What Lévi-Strauss demonstrated for primitive thought in general applies in large measure to the thought of the Orokaiva: metalanguages are constructed in such a manner that associations between signs provide causal explanations. Hence, in a purely formal sense, there may actually be no "level of content" in Orokaiva discourse, but only an endless chain linking different signifiers together by principles of association.[4] Thus every metalanguage among the Orokaiva is reducible to systems of connotation.

In the circumstances it may be argued that the distinction made by Hjelmslev and Barthes between systems of connotation and denotation ought to be abandoned. I think, however, that it has some utility in distinguishing phases of the Orokaiva thought system— that is, a phase where the main concern seems to be explanation and a phase where the main concern is rhetorical and ideological.

In this chapter, I have applied semiotics in the context of the anthropology of development. I shall deal with several hierarchically ordered systems. The largest is the regional colonial macrosystem, comprising on the one hand the Papuans of the Northern District and on the other the colonial power foci, administration and mission.[5] Below this is the tribal level, consisting of an Orokaiva and a Yega cognitive system. In the Orokaiva system, several subtribal systems exist in opposition to one another. Two of these, the Waseta-Isivita and the Sangara system, are considered in this chapter. As each person is at the same time a member of a subtribe, a tribe, and the regional communication system, each person has access to, and potentially draws upon, a plurality of systems of thought, so that contradictions normally exist between the various views held by the same person within the context of different systems.

Environmental circumstances act on these various semiotic systems not by creating them but rather by changing the emphases placed on some of the available systems at the expense of others. Thus cultural changes become apparent as changes in the emphases placed on alternatives present in semiotic systems. This raises a problem of obscurantism. Since the evidence for a semiotic system is made up, in the first instance, of informants' statements, it may reflect no more than a "conscious model" of the system while highly important aspects may be suppressed for ideological reasons. For instance, if the evacuees desired a "new age," why were they so anxious to return home where they could no longer be instructed in its practices? The answer seems to lie in the land tenure problem, discussed later, which was reflecting fundamental structural changes in the society. But why was this problem passed over in silence in all the statements about the "new age" recorded for the period immediately after the eruption? The answer to this question may be mere speculation, but it is clear that by excluding land tenure from our analysis, we shall become the victims of our informants' own mystifications, which is all the more regrettable since, by 1966, Orokaiva ideologists had recognized the importance of the land tenure problem for the setting up of the "new age." Our final analysis is therefore based on an unconscious model which includes this factor.

## THE EVENT AND ITS SETTING

On 21 January 1951, Mount Lamington, a mountain situated in the Northern District of Papua, was torn apart by what is technically known as a Pelean eruption. A paroxysmal explosion burst from the crater and produced a *nuée ardente* which completely devastated a surrounding area of 68 square miles (Taylor 1958:7).[6] Almost 4,000 people, mostly belonging to the Orokaiva-speaking group of tribes of the Northern District, were killed. The word "Orokaiva" is used here to designate speakers of the Orokaiva language, resident in an area roughly coinciding with the Popondetta, Sohe Popondetta, and Saiho census divisions (see map 14).[7] This area comprises the foothills of Mount Lamington and the alluvial plains to the north and east. The area is rather homogenous in culture, and dialect differences are minor. Destruction in this inner zone of devastation was almost complete. A further 22 square miles were partially devastated, and it was from this area that some 3,000 inhabitants were able to save themselves by running away from the *nuée ardente*. The population of the Mount Lamington foothills, within a radius of at least 10 miles from the crater, fled from their villages as the explosion threw stones over all the area, destroyed the administrative center at Higaturu, and blotted out the light of the sun.

It was at this point that the administration of the Territory of Papua intervened. Australian authorities sent in supplies for the

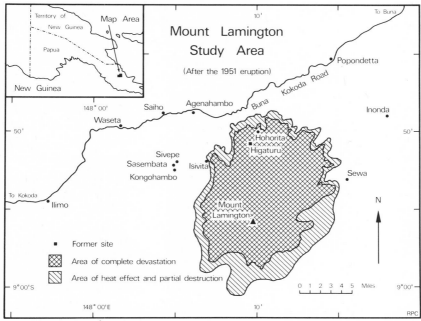

Map 14. Mount Lamington, Papua.

survivors, established camps to house them, and set up a volcanological observation post. Acting on technical advice that further
explosions were to be expected, the administration at once
restricted access to a fairly wide area surrounding the crater, thus
forbidding most of the fugitives to return to their homes. It was at
this stage also that the administration called in two anthropologists, Felix Keesing and Cyril Belshaw, for advice on what should
be done with the now homeless population.[7] Shortly after the two
anthropologists left the scene in May 1951, volcanological studies
indicated that the active, paroxysmal stage of activity of Mount
Lamington had ceased and hence that a large part of the restricted
area could be resettled. In March 1953, it was possible to reduce
the restricted area still further, to a circle of 2 miles surrounding
the crater. As a result of these events, virtually all arable land in
the district was in use when I visited in 1966–1967. There were no
displaced communities in the proper sense of the word. There had
been movements of villages from the crater area to consolidated
settlements in the vicinity of paved roads, but here convenience

rather than security was the main motive. Villagers were able to use the land they had occupied before the eruption.

The Orokaiva case was therefore anomalous in a comparative study of community displacement. There was no new physical or social environment to which the Orokaiva had to adapt. There was, however, a very traumatic experience and a temporary displacement. Moreover, the eruption did permanently change some significant geographic features of the district: the network of roads, village sizes, village locations in relation to paved roads, the location of the administrative center and institutions like the hospital and mission. As these facts have been fully covered in my earlier report, in this chapter I treat them briefly and then turn to a somewhat broader but related question: How does a cataclysmic event such as this eruption (and the temporary relocations that followed) affect the structure of Orokaiva society?[8]

My research included three intensive studies of single villages. The relocated village on which the fullest data were collected was Sivepe, situated 7 miles from the crater, on fertile, well-watered, well-drained volcanic loam, with a population density of 180 persons per square mile. Like all the villages west of the crater, Sivepe suffered hardly any casualties but the people fled in panic and were accommodated in the evacuation camp at Ilimo, a few miles west of Kumusi River near the road to Kokoda. They stayed at the camp until May, after which two of the local clan groups returned home while the third was relocated in one of the large villages established along the main Buna–Kokoda road after the eruption.[9] This third clan group returned to Sivepe early in 1952. Sivepe was rebuilt less than 1 mile from the old site. The most important immediate consequence of the eruption, as far as Sivepe was concerned, was the establishment of a large mission complex at Sasembata, 1 mile away. With the assistance of surrounding villages, the mission built a large school, a large church, and a hospital. One reason for this development was the establishment, by the government, of a large village for victims of the eruption. This was built at Kongohambo (maximum population 900), a quarter mile from the mission station. The mission services remained after the Kongohambo evacuees had returned to their own areas shortly after 1953.

For Sivepe, therefore, the eruption led directly to two highly important event sequences: first at the evacuation camp; later in relation to the mission station. The government had demonstrated in the most tangible way that it accepted broad responsibility for the people's welfare in a time of crisis and would act with great generosity in such circumstances. The mission, which likewise had established close relations with the people of Ilimo, had subsequently remained to develop those relations.

As a control group for the study, I used the small village of Inonda, 12 miles from the crater and outside the restricted zone. Inonda differed from Sivepe in that its population was never evacuated or relocated. It continued to use its own land. The comparison of Sivepe and Inonda thus provides a measure of the effects of actual relocation as distinct from other experiences the two villages had in common. In Inonda only one-fifth of the land is arable; none of it is as fertile as the volcanic loam of the Mount Lamington foothills; rainfall is lower than in Sivepe and so distributed that lengthy droughts are not uncommon. Drainage is inferior while population density is only ten persons per square mile.

Inonda acted as host for the population of Sewa village who fled their homes on the morning of the eruption. Among the fugitives was a mission teacher who set up a school in Inonda. When he was later transferred to another district, Inonda pleaded fervently and successfully to get him back. Today Sunday services are given by a lay preacher and children attend a mission school several miles away which teaches up to grade two.[10] Interaction with government and mission authorities was far less intensive at Inonda than at Sasembata.

The third village I studied was Hohorita (population 348), 7 miles from the volcano, with soil largely similar to Sivepe's, good rainfall, good drainage, and a population density of 135 persons per square mile. Hohorita is made up of the survivors of the Sangara tribe, once 4,000 strong, which was almost entirely wiped out by the eruption. The survivors were evacuated to camps along the coast and then allowed to return to the boundary of the restricted area, where they built a village called Irihambo. They were ordered to leave this village some years later (as it was situated on crown land intended for the settlement of Australian ex-servicemen) and then established Hohorita in 1957–1959. The Hohorita people, like other relocated groups, had had intensive contact with government and mission personnel. An unusually large number entered skilled occupations, partly because the San-

gara lived close to a large mission station which offered educational facilities until it was wiped out by the disaster. Afterward,
the mission took a special interest in their welfare.

What distinguished the relocated villages from the others was
not greater contact with European-dominated institutions. On the
contrary, it would seem that contact with such institutions was
probably most frequent among the male residents of Inonda, who
were much engaged in wage labor; such contact was least frequent in Sivepe, with Hohorita holding an intermediate position.
Nor could it be said that economic prosperity, in the sense of
money income, was correlated with relocation. On the contrary,
the average income was higher in Inonda than in Sivepe or
Hohorita.

In summary, the major outcomes of the eruption and relocation
have been the following: first, the administrative center Higaturu,
situated on the mountain, was destroyed and replaced by Popondetta, which lies on the alluvial plain to the north, thus shifting the
center of Australian influence away from the relocated villages.
This detracted from rather than contributed to development of the
relocation areas and placed the administrative center at some
distance from the areas of greatest population density. However,
the relocated villages were provided with subsidiary centers of
Australian influence such as the hospital in Saiho and the mission
stations at Sasembata, Isivita, Agenahambo, and Hohorita. In addition, a number of large villages (with populations of 250 to 500)
came into being along the main road between Popondetta and
Kokoda at a distance of 6 miles or more from the crater; these villages were made up of groups previously domiciled in small bush
villages.

The government prefers these large villages because they make
it possible to introduce such Western social institutions as schooling, water supplies, road construction, and health clinics more
conveniently. The eruption offered the government a good opportunity to establish large villages. The population of the bush settlement had abandoned the area, and by the time the population was
allowed to return, the villages were no longer habitable because of
eruption damage and subsequent neglect. In this sense the eruption offered an opportunity for speeding up development programs. One might also argue that social development among the
Sangara survivors was accelerated when the entire older genera-

tion perished in the eruption and the survivors were therefore not fully instructed in traditional religious knowledge. Innovation proceeded without the resistance an older generation might have offered had it survived. I have argued elsewhere that this absence of the elders led to striking changes in the Sangara perception of the world (Schwimmer 1969:70–71).

If we compare relocated villages such as Hohorita and Sivepe with villages touched less by the disaster, such as Inonda on the alluvial plains, we notice that the former villages are larger, display more of the innovations advocated by the government, have a higher level of school education, and have responded more to government-sponsored schemes such as coffee growing. In my detailed report (Schwimmer 1969), I was inclined to ascribe such differences to the effect of close contact and guidance during the period immediately following the eruption, but such an explanation should be treated with caution.

The differences are probably due largely to ecological factors described in the report. Inonda land provides more animal foods; it is slightly closer to wage employment and markets; the climate is less suitable for cash crops than in Sivepe. The population, due to its sparseness, is relatively deficient in health and educational services. Hence the conditions for cooperation with government programs were less favorable than at Sivepe. Furthermore, the observed differences may also be due to historical factors. While coastal and foothill areas had been missionized and in contact with the administration for many years, the intervening Sauaha groups including Inonda were defeated and sustained heavy losses in the warfare of the early postcontact period. They subsequently remained aloof from white contacts. After the Japanese occupation, some of their men were hanged by the Australians for having acted as collaborators.[11] Hostile feelings are still an impediment to the acceptance of government and mission programs.

Such social consequences of the Mount Lamington eruption do not in themselves lead readily to illuminating anthropological generalizations. The actions of government and mission immediately after the eruption greatly relieved the distress of the population, but we cannot establish that these actions, directly and specifically, led to major social changes. One might therefore be inclined to view the eruption of Mount Lamington as lacking serious anthropological interest, yet such a view would greatly

limit the relevance and power of anthropological study. A cataclysm of such awesome proportions must obviously have had psychological as well as social effects on Orokaiva individuals since
the same cataclysm was, after all, experienced in one form or another by everybody. If a culturally homogeneous group has any intellectual facility in the development of common symbols and the
transformation of its symbol system, then it is reasonable to suppose that the eruption would have social effects of this less tangible
kind.

The Mount Lamington eruption, viewed in this way, offers a
case history of theoretical importance. Where the immediate
cause of relocation is a natural disaster, we are dealing with contingency in its purest form: an event no sociological (or psychological) theory could possibly predict. Can such an event change the
structure of a people's symbolic thought? If it can, then this would
cast doubt on any claim that cultural systems are determinate, as
they could be changed at any time by unpredictable contingencies. The question whether the content of the symbol systems and
social systems of specific cultures is determinate has been raised
throughout the work of Lévi-Strauss. Determinacy may be found,
however, in the processes of human thought as we seek to comprehend an event, however unpredictable. If our method of understanding humans is the analysis of symbolic thought, then the
study of unpredictable contingencies is important in revealing the
genesis of symbolic thought.

EXPLANATIONS OF THE DISASTER

I showed in an earlier work that Mount Lamington has long had a
central position in the Orokaiva world order (Schwimmer 1969:
5–6). In fact, the Orokaiva regard Mount Lamington as the center
of the cosmos. It is the place where, in Orokaiva myth, death, warfare, and fire originated. Many of the transforming deities who are
said to have established the rituals and social customs of the
Orokaiva came from the crater of this mountain. The division of
the populations of the Northern District into tribes or language
groups supposedly occurred at the same place. The mountain is
called Sumbiripa Kanekari, 'the separation of Sumbiripa', after
the myth in which the mountain opened up and split into several
unscalable crags. Sumbiripa was hunting on the mountain with

his wife; the two were separated and found themselves on different crags. Sumbiripa became the first man to die, the master of the mountain within which he has since dwelt together with all Oro- kaiva who died subsequently.[12]

The myth explained the shape of the mountain as it was before the eruption. The crags are not there today because they were blown apart by the eruption. The myth also explained the rum- bling of the mountain and the smoke that issued from it long be- fore the eruption of 1951. Such phenomena were regarded as signs sent by Sumbiripa. Ritual prohibitions limited access to the area close to the crater as there was a belief that Sumbiripa, if dis- turbed, would be angry. There was also a great fear of the dead who were supposedly dwelling in the mountain. It is believed that the dead wander about the countryside, where they may attack humans. Sumbiripa is dangerous, even if he does not erupt, be- cause he can send out his ghosts to cause misfortune among men. The myth about Sumbiripa Kanekari hints at the possibility of an earlier eruption by the account it gives of the origin of the crags existing before 1951.

The sociological importance of the eruption lies largely in the explanations of the event developed afterward by the survivors. These explanations are related to the situation of Orokaiva society in 1951. Here we must distinguish between the situation as it ap- peared to the Orokaiva individual or to small refugee groups and the collective situation of the Orokaiva tribes as they collectively perceived it, in terms of the basic forces shaping their social life at that period. We may follow Burridge (1960) in identifying these basic forces with the colonial government, planters and traders, the mission, and relations within and between tribal groups.

Immediately after the eruption, the situation for individuals and small groups was dominated by fear of the mountain, grief for dead relatives, and anguish at separation from the land. The situa- tion was influenced, moreover, by abrupt changes in social orga- nization. The Sangara fugitives mostly fled alone or in very small groups, leaving behind their numerous dead; the Sasembata fugi- tives mostly fled in village groups led by their village constables. While the disaster made the Sangara leaderless, in Sasembata it merely reduced dependence on traditional leaders at the gain of the village constables whose responsibility was greatly increased. Village constables were members of village communities appointed by the administration to enforce regulations concerning law and order, works and amenities. They were not necessarily 'big men', customary feast-givers or, military commanders.[13] At Ilimo they at once became the leaders of all operations (food distribution, house building, visits to the home village), as these involved dealings with the Europeans in control of the rescue and supplies.

These organizational changes, individual fears, grief, anguish, and the increased dependence on village constables and white authorities were certainly reflected in the explanations given of the eruptions. But these explanations took account also of far broader cultural issues, in fact of the total postcontact experience common to the population of the Northern District.

The Orokaiva explanations of the disaster to be considered here certainly cannot be understood except in the context of the total Orokaiva cognitive system. Any Orokaiva explanation places the eruption within a logically consistent framework of meaning, but it is only one of several possible frameworks that might, successively or even simultaneously, be constructed out of the Orokaiva cognitive system. I propose, in the present section, to construct a model of the various systems of connotation and the relations between them. Systems of denotation are briefly referred to here but explored in more detail in the following section.

One obvious line of explanation of the eruption was to ascribe it to the anger of Sumbiripa. Many Orokaiva actually explained the disaster in this way at the time it happened, as may be seen from the evidence of Tomlin (1951), Benson (1955a, 1955b), and Schwimmer (1969:69ff.). The anger of Sumbiripa, as supposedly expressed in the eruption of Mount Lamington, was explained by Orokaiva by various disrespectful acts against the mountain. Grenades had been thrown near the crater during the war. Afterward, the Orokaiva began to acquire guns for hunting on the mountain. Such were the acts quoted to me in Hohorita and Sivepe as arousing Sumbiripa's anger. The eruption was regarded by informants as an unprecedented event. The question arose in the Orokaiva mind why such an event should occur just then, when it had never happened before. The anger of Sumbiripa had always been feared, but no sinister meaning had been attached to the rumblings and smoke signals, and, moreover, revenge had always been mediated through 'ghosts'. The new form of punishment could be explained only with reference to a quite novel form of infringement of the taboo—a far more offensive infringement than had ever happened before. Just what made grenades and guns so offensive?

This question may be answered on several levels. The first of these is a purely ritual level. Of all the novel activities in which the Orokaiva engaged near the mountain, the ones that were singled out as significant stood out by making a sharp, loud, and dangerous noise. Now there are many ritual contexts where the Orokaiva use silence as a sign of respect and noise as a sign of disrespect. Hence the Orokaiva were ritually consistent when they told me it was the noise of the hunters' guns that angered Sumbiripa. But hunting rifles have a further symbolic significance that should be taken into account. I was told that game on the mountain was plentiful until the guns were introduced but that today hardly any game is left because the guns killed it all. In this instance the Orokaiva were giving a very reasonable explanation of a drop in game population which was probably real enough. In fact everybody uses guns today or wants to use them, as they are effective for hunting. But they are also sinister—that is, their effectiveness is known to be too great to allow the game population to survive.

The young men who took up the use of hunting rifles between the end of World War II and the time of the eruption were bold innovators and at the same time they were considered slightly wicked in abandoning traditional hunting methods. This is implied by informants who account for the eruption by the anger of Sumbiripa. They are thinking of the breakdown of the old order by the adoption of European innovations, Sumbiripa representing the potency of the old order. They argue that if only the young men had not started to use hunting rifles, the disaster would not have happened. The young men would never have dared to make such a din close to the crater if their respect for the spirits had not been undermined by newfangled doctrines.

The explanation of the disaster considered here resembles all other recorded explanations in one fundamental respect: it is not merely the application of a traditional rule to a new event but it generates a new rule, justifies the rule in the light of empirical evidence, and can be comprehended only in the framework of an ideology which in turn was generated by contemporary events. The starting point of all the explanations is the activity of white officials, missionaries, and traders among the Orokaiva and the innovations they have brought. Those who blame the eruption on the anger of Sumbiripa regard these innovations as potentially disastrous. They argue that the eruption has proved their point; it has fortified them in their ideology. Furthermore, they have established the rule that people should not shoot on the mountain. Before the eruption this was not, to my knowledge, clearly formulated as a ritual prohibition. Today it is clearly stated though generally disregarded for reasons we shall soon learn. In justification of the rule, it should be noted that it is supported by some very cogent evidence from Sivepe villagers. It is a fact that while the eruption killed nearly all the Sangara it killed very few people of Isivita and the Sasembata districts, even though they live equally close to the crater. It is also a fact that while the Sangara had many hunting rifles in the late 1940s, the Isivita and the Sasembata districts then had few or none. I was told that Sumbiripa gave two signs just before the eruption. To the Isivita people and those of Sasembata district he made a sign of blue fire, which meant they would be saved. To the Sangara people he gave a sign of red fire, which meant they would all die.

We note that this way of explaining the disaster is concerned with a precontact social macrosystem comprising two allied groups, the Sasembata and Isivita, and their traditional enemies, the Sangara. It is not concerned with the contemporary macrosystem which is the system of relations holding between Papuans, the government, and the mission. Neither the government nor the mission enters into the explanation. Furthermore, the explanation emphasizes the tribal boundary between the Sangara people and those designated as the Waseta tribe by Williams (1940).[14] It is, in fact, the opposition between Sangara and Waseta that is stressed by this explanation.

It is precisely this opposition that makes clear the strategic and manipulative nature of the argument. Waseta are using the occasion of the eruption to score a point against their old rivals and enemies the Sangara, who deserved to be punished as retribution for earlier acts of war. The explanation ignores the fact that ninety-two Waseta also were killed in the disaster.

At this point we recognize the explanation as part of a connotative system. Any reasonable explanation of the disaster would account for all the deaths. The division of the dead into tribal or ethnic groups is logically insignificant. In a connotative system, significance is assigned to this distinction for the purpose of stating some ideology.

Barthes (1964a) points out that in a connotative system the level of expression is "rhetoric" and the level of content is "ideology." This seems to describe the pattern accurately enough. The present explanation may be reduced to a rhetoric or moralistic vilification expressing a tribalist Waseta ideology. The rhetorical aspect is clear because in actual fact both tribes hunted on the mountain though only one was hit seriously by the disaster.

I now turn to a second explanation which deals with Orokaiva, though we have very few data on its currency among them. The explanation is contained in a report (undated but probably written shortly after the eruption) from Fred Kleekham, district agricultural officer, Popondetta, in which he describes a mission-sponsored "Christian Cooperative." This cooperative flourished among the Yega at that time where, in Kleekham's opinion, it "did indeed become a cult." Kleekham reports that members of the cult refused to have their rice hulled or bought by the government and that this was due to "some mystical element . . . involved in rice marketing." He continues:

> I think that more influential than the thought that Europeans would leave Papua as a result of cooperatives was the belief that the formation of and participation in cooperatives would—magically or mystically—in short time raise the native to the status of the European in all respects. . . . I am sure that this movement owed much to hanging of Orokaivas judged responsible for the murder of missionaries and the former officer in charge of the coffee project.
>
> It is interesting to recall that one group was prepared to do *anything* under European guidance to get money. Their message was "show us how to get the money to buy the guns." Later the Lamington eruption which obliterated the government station at Higaturu was regarded by many as payback for the hangings.

There is no evidence that this explanation of the disaster was ever held by any Orokaiva. It is more than probable that this explanation is that of the Yega, who are traditional exchange partners of the Orokaiva and enemies of the Sangara. It is among the Yega that Kleekham worked, and I am inclined to believe that the Yega widely accepted the views he reported. This would fit the facts as we know them. Certainly we should not expect the Orokaiva to explain the disaster by a theory which accounts only for

the death of the 45 Europeans on the mountain but not at all for
the death of 4,000 Orokaiva and the destruction of hundreds of
villages. It is far easier to understand such an explanation coming
from the Yega, traditional enemies of the Sangara tribe, whose
own losses through the disaster were very small. There is indeed
no reason why the Yega should have been grief-stricken by the
eruption at all. They were involved in an anti-European cult according to which the death of the administration personnel at Higaturu was thought nothing less than a divine blessing, while the
misfortunes of the Sangara may well have been a further source of
satisfaction. The Sangara survivors, who were quartered in an
evacuation camp in Yega territory from February to April 1951,
felt most uncomfortable there and very frightened that they too
would be killed off by their old enemies through poisoning, sorcery, or other mischief.

The data do not enable us to say with certainty whether or not,
in the Yega explanation, the eruption was actually caused by the
anger of Sumbiripa. Benson (1955a, 1955b) describes the general
atmosphere among the Yega immediately after the eruption, and
from his account one gathers that the Yega, like the Orokaiva tra-
ditionalists, believed Sumbiripa was responsible, though he was
credited with somewhat different motives. Kleekham is undoubtedly right that the public execution of the so-called collaborators,
conducted by the Australian army in a spectacular and rather
gruesome manner, caused much resentment among the various
tribes of the Northern District. The Yega cooperatives of the late
1940s, described in some detail by Dakeyne (1966) and discussed
in Schwimmer (1969:86–89), were led by two Anglican clergy-
men, Benson and Clint. They must therefore have believed that
power would come to them through the intervention of the Christian God. Though the precise significance they attached to the
eruption is not known, the context suggests that they must have
regarded it as a sign that supernatural forces were working in
their favor or at any rate against their enemies.

The metalanguage used in the Yega explanation is that of a millenarian cooperative cult, arising in response to what was regarded as oppression and commercial exploitation. The eruption established a rule that supernatural agencies punish white people who
hang Papuans. In justification of the rule, there was again cogent
empirical evidence. Most of the forty-five Australian victims of the

eruption met their fate on the very same spot (Higaturu) where the executions took place some years earlier.

I include the Yega explanation in this study because it influenced the total regional communication system from which the Orokaiva derive their basic concepts. What is this regional system? It is certainly not a postcontact introduction, yet it has a very different significance now as compared to the last century.

Williams (1940, n.d.) shows that the external boundaries of the human race, as defined in Orokaiva myths, take in most of the population of the Northern District of Papua but do not extend beyond the Northern District. Internal boundaries drawn in the myths separate this population into a number of mutually hostile language groups, each specializing in the production or supply of certain distinctive products. It was an integral part of Orokaiva social thought to hold that permanent peace was impossible between the groups thus separated, although a truce was occasionally established and trade and intermarriage were regular occurrences. In this respect, the Cargo Cults of the early postcontact period (the Baigona Cult in 1912 and the Taro Cult in 1914) marked a radical innovation. The chief social message, especially of the Taro Cult, was that villages and tribes hitherto divided by strife should be united in brotherhood. The cult taught that the traditional tribal boundaries should be disregarded and all Papuans of the region were one people. This idea started in the coastal region but soon spread from there to Orokaiva territory (see Chinnery and Haddon 1917; Williams 1928).

At the time of the eruption, the coastal people were again involved in a millennial movement, the Christian Cooperative, which was spreading throughout the Orokaiva tribes. While tribal boundaries were a source of anxiety in all the evacuation camps (though the anxiety was more acute among Sangara relocated on the coast than among Orokaiva relocated at Ilimo), the possibility of a further development of the Christian Cooperative was still open, and this would have involved general acceptance of the Yega explanation of the disaster.

Comparing the Orokaiva and Yega explanations, we note that the cause of the eruption in both cases is the anger of Sumbiripa, although the Yega explanation is not entirely explicit on this point. Furthermore, both explanations take a rather negative view of European power—one by ignoring it, the other by making it the ob-

ject of the wrath of the mountain. There are, however, two interesting differences. The first is that in the Orokaiva explanation we
find an opposition between two tribes (Waseta innocent; Sangara
guilty). In the Yega explanation we find an opposition between
ethnic groups (Papuans of the Northern District innocent; Europeans guilty). This classing together of the Papuans of an entire
region is a departure from traditional tribalism. It reflects an
ideology aimed at maximizing indigenous power by the establishment of an intertribal regional coalition.

The second difference lies in the role of Sumbiripa (or whoever
the angry deity was) in the two explanations. In the Orokaiva version, the transgression was against the sacred domain of Sumbiripa and thus of a familiar traditional type. In the Yega version,
the punishing God assumes a strangely political role in taking the
side of the Papuans against their enemies, the whites. The crime of
the whites admittedly took place near the mountain, though not in
the sacred domain. Sumbiripa was never, in any other context, described as a general defender or avenger in support of "his" people. Indeed he seems to be playing a somewhat Jehovah-like role in
this tale. We are here in the sphere of the Cargo Cults or millennial
movements rather than in that of traditional Melanesian religion.

Meanwhile no mention is made of the 3,500 Sangara who died
in the disaster. This would have weakened the argument, for any
reference to the Sangara victims might have suggested that they
too were worthy of punishment. Though the Yega probably do
think so, it would not have been expedient to say so when an intertribal alliance was contemplated. Here we are obviously closer to
ideological rhetoric than to philosophical speculation.

The third explanation of the disaster is the one that has attracted the most attention by previous writers. Belshaw, who met
Orokaiva survivors a few weeks after the eruption, records the following observations (1951:242):

> Some people said that this was God's visitation because they had
> disobeyed the Bishop's instructions to build new churches. Others said
> that God had punished them because they had not helped the Allies
> sufficiently during the war and because some of them betrayed mis-
> sionaries to the Japanese. [Others again mentioned] lack of coopera-
> tion in Mission and Government plans for development. . . . This
> sense of guilt is a most important factor in resettlement attitudes.

Keesing (1952:18) agrees with this summary, adding that the eruption resulted in "strong feelings of insecurity and even of guilt in their retrospective look at the pre-eruption way of life."

A great deal of evidence supports Belshaw and Keesing in their suggestion that in 1951 the Orokaiva ascribed the eruption to the anger of the Christian God and thought they had brought this anger on themselves by various transgressions. Orokaiva informants reported that this view of the eruption was widely current at Ilimo evacuation camp. It is reflected in a song about the eruption which is still sung by Sivepe youth. This song declares the omnipotence of God and man's absolute dependence on him. It also attests to a wholly Christian eschatology: the abode of the dead is Heaven, where the living will later meet their brothers who died in the eruption. The song admits the guilt of the dead ('our brothers on earth had many temptations'), but the strongest emphasis is on the suffering of the living through the loss of their 'brothers'. Unlike Job, the singer is far too polite to contend with God and criticize his actions. He does not openly and clearly identify God as the author of his sufferings, but God's responsibility is subtly implied.

The rationale of this explanation is not obvious. Quite clearly those who believe that God and not Sumbiripa was responsible for the disaster have some belief in Christianity. In response to contact with the white man they have developed an ideology supporting the work of the missions. But how do they explain the eruption? It seems very clear that in 1951 many explained it as retribution for their lack of respect for the Christian God. But Orokaiva Christians interviewed in 1966 and 1967 rejected this explanation as resting on a misunderstanding of the nature of God. Father Albert, who composed the song referred to above, was one of those questioned. He said that many of those who died in the eruption were little children. He did not think God would punish the innocent along with the guilty. On the other hand, he did ascribe a divine purpose to the eruption. Father Albert said the Orokaiva used to have no idea of the end of the world; this notion was taught by Christianity. After the disaster the people discussed it a great deal: when they saw the sky darken and people dying from the blast, they thought the end of the world had come. God had shown them what the end would be like. In other words,

Father Albert thought that God sent the eruption as a sign. Orokaiva Christians would generally agree with this view, though none of those interviewed formulated it so clearly.

From the viewpoint of this study, the question whether the Orokaiva considered the eruption as a punishment or as a sign is perhaps not a crucial one. In either case, whoever believes that God was responsible must also believe that a dire fate awaits anyone who fails in his obligations to the mission.

Comparing the three explanations surveyed so far, we note that the Christian explanation, like the Yega one and unlike the Waseta version, attached no significance to tribal divisions. God (like the Sumbiripa of the Yega) makes no distinction between tribes, but he does distinguish between the disobedient Papuans of the region and the administrators and missionaries these Papuans failed to obey. The former are guilty but not the latter.

Christian and Yega theories are opposed as to who is the guilty party. Indeed, the Christian explanation omits all reference to European deaths on the mountain, just as the Yega version suppressed the fact of the Sangara victims. The reason is no doubt the same: rhetoric demands that one should not in the same breath advocate a coalition with the white power bearers and admit that the latter suffered many deaths in circumstances implying their guilt.

With regard to connotations, all three systems differentiate between either tribes or ethnic groups that fell victim to the disaster, even though such differentiation is insignificant for explanatory purposes. If we use a minus sign to designate the social groups classed as guilty and a plus sign for the groups classed as innocent (though in fact the latter, too, suffered serious losses), we find:

|             | Victims |         |          |
| ----------- | ------- | ------- | -------- |
| Explanation | Waseta  | Sangara | European |
| Waseta      | +       | −       | omitted  |
| Yega        | +       | +       | −        |
| Christian   | −       | −       | +        |

I shall briefly mention a fourth system, though the explanation it contained was put forward by a small minority and was but feebly believed. Several Orokaiva close to the mission maintain nowadays that the eruption was due solely to geophysical causes. The mission authorites put forward this explanation to counter criticism from white planters and public servants that the church, by preaching that the eruption was due to God's wrath, is pursuing obscurantist and reprehensible power politics. Orokaiva informants who adopted the geophysical explanation said that before the eruption they did not know about volcanoes but have now learned from the white man that a volcano operates according to certain natural laws.[15]

There is no magico-religious Orokaiva metalanguage in which this explanation can be expressed. On the other hand, its connotation is clear. The explanation marks an informant as highly educated, free of superstition, and a good friend of the whites (including the anthropologist). The explanation connotes that magico-religious theories are old-fashioned and geophysical theories are modern. It divides the social universe into old-fashioned people (whose views have become irrelevant) and modern people (who include the Europeans and a Papuan elite who befriend them). Such a division vitiates the regional unity envisaged by the Yega and Christian explanations.

The connotations of the four explanations I have presented can thus be expressed in a simple model based on two highly significant oppositions which arise in the macrosystem of the Northern District and in the changing system of ethnic boundary maintenance.[16] The first opposition is between refusal and acceptance of a relation of positive reciprocity with Europeans. The second opposition is between tribalism and ideologies envisaging the unity of the Papuan tribes of the region.

| | Explanation | | | |
| --- | --- | --- | --- | --- |
| Connotation | Waseta | Yega | Christian | Geophysical |
| Rejection (−)/acceptance (+) of Europeans | − | − | + | + |
| Absence (−)/presence (+) of regionalism | − | + | + | − |

ANALYSIS OF THE METALANGUAGES

Our next task is to analyze the evidence for Orokaiva systems of thought in which notions like 'the anger of Sumbiripa' and 'the anger of God' become fully comprehensible. We shall soon find that instead of timeless constructs of primitive philosophers we are occupied with a series of historical events both before and after the eruption, all of which became signs much in the same way as the eruption; the explanation will take the form of the tracing of associations between these signs. There are, however, some stable principles governing these connections. We turn to these first.

I have argued elsewhere that the social structure of the Orokaiva is characterized by a weak patrilineality with small corporate groups but that exchange transactions between these groups are, in many respects, highly structured (Schwimmer 1970a, n.d.). These exchanges follow rules which are justified by an elaborate system of thought arising out of the principle that gift making is the source of social potency and exchange is the measure of that potency. Such a system, by its very nature, makes no assumptions about the permanency of social associations, as it is only the success of exchange transactions that allows associations (outside the small corporate groups) to endure. Decisions about the upkeep of particular associations are of necessity determined by criteria of allocation. According to Orokaiva ideas, associations go through alternating periods of positive reciprocity (friendship) and negative reciprocity (war). Whereas in Western thought permanence is considered normal and quarrels a deviation from the norm, the Orokaiva do not envisage either friendship or enmity as permanent states but rather as alternating temporary states.

The implication of this philosophy for social relations (and this includes Orokaiva-white relations) is that they never are what a Westerner would call "friendly" or "hostile." It would be more correct to say that at any given time they may be going through a positive (friendly) or negative (hostile) cycle. Movements from positive to negative cycles tend to be gradual, since in the Orokaiva view social relations tend to deteriorate constantly, little by little, until they become hostile. On the other hand, movements from negative to positive cycles tend to be highly dramatic and ritualized—usually through reconciliation feasts and gifts. In relations with Europeans, reconciliations are harder to effect since there is no commensality between the ethnic groups.

If it is natural for social relations to deteriorate constantly and gradually, it is still possible to decide that one will allow an association to deteriorate before one takes active steps to restore it. Such a choice is determined by many factors: intrinsic attraction felt toward the exchange partner, fear of the trouble he might cause, instrumental benefits he has to offer, the importance of the partner in the total exchange network, and so on.

Anger, in this Orokaiva philosophy, is a normal attitude toward a partner with whom one stands, for the time being, in a relation of negative reciprocity. An exchange of injuries takes place until peace is made by the offer of an appropriate gift and feast. The anger of Sumbiripa does not completely fall into this pattern because here the exchange relationship is somewhat limited in scope. Sumbiripa's gift to man is the safe confinement of the dead, whereas man's gift is merely the avoidance of any disturbance of Sumbiripa's mountain. Man mediates the relationship by sending his dead to Sumbiripa; Sumbiripa mediates it by emitting his usually innocuous rumbling. Before 1951, Sumbiripa was not known by Orokaiva to have ever erupted. Hunting on the mountain and similar infractions were believed to have broken the exchange relationship and thus aroused Sumbiripa to a just reprisal.

Sumbiripa's anger was righteous not only because he was a god. In the framework of Orokaiva thought, serious anger is normally regarded as righteous, at least among persons standing in a regular exchange relationship. If anger expresses itself in verbal abuse or physical violence it is not serious, but it becomes so if misfortunes occur because of sorcery imputed to the person who is wronged. The successful magical expression of anger proves that anger to be well founded. A man may of course decide to use countermagic, and if that works the anger is no longer serious. If countermagic does not work, a man must be ready to acknowledge his fault and make reparations.

In such a dispute it is of course relevant which side has broken a rule, but the rules are most often debatable. In the end nothing is considered worse than to have made another person seriously angry. Prudence demands that seriously angry persons should be mollified, unless their kinship and physical distance is such that they can be defined as enemies. But even between enemies, a time comes when anger is shown by magical and other misfortunes to become inexpedient.

Self-accusation and self-inflicted injury are a regular part of this system. In order to make peace a person must define himself as the transgressor (Schwimmer 1970a, n.d.), as the Papuans did in the 'anger of God' explanation. Self-injury is a regular strategic weapon, since the person who cuts down his own tree to injure himself shows anger about a hostile act perpetrated by some unnamed person. He thus makes a claim for community sympathy and possible restitution (Williams 1940). Self-accusation is a form of self-injury and therefore at once places an obligation on the *sufferer* of the supposed original injury. In this sense an acknowledgment of guilt by Orokaiva would place some obligation on Sumbiripa or God to forgive them. Thus we can never ignore the transactional element in what is manifestly a sincere state of contrition.

It is far more complicated to explain the anger of the Christian God, and people's belief in it, than to explain the anger of Sumbiripa. At the time of the eruption, few Orokaiva had been baptized, whereas it was precisely in Sangara territory that the mission was well established and had many adherents. Most of the persons who thought they had been punished by God were actually still pagan, which strictly should have put them out of reach of his wrath. We need to reconstruct as best we can what kind of exchange relationship was deemed to exist in 1951.

We can appraise this only if we consider briefly the total system of relationships of the Orokaiva within the colonial macrosystem, namely the social unit comprising Orokaiva, mission, government, and traders. Theories about the punishment of God referred not only to Orokaiva neglect of the mission but also neglect of instructions and advice given by the government. The traders were never mentioned.

One common characteristic of government and mission is that both institutions believe they are the Papuans' benefactors and say so on many occasions. In particular, it is on these supposed benefits that they base any moral claims they make on the Orokaiva. When the eruption occurred it was therefore reasonable, from the Orokaiva viewpoint, to conclude that their slowness in satisfying the claims of government and mission had aroused in them great anger and that God, who manifestly was looking after the white authorities, acted as agent of the punishment.

In exchange relations it is a fixed policy to satisfy the claims of important partners first and be much slower about the others. The fact that the whites, in spite of their immense wealth, had a fairly low partnership ranking is not difficult to explain. If we glance at the kind of interaction typical of the years 1900 to 1950, we find that the European exchange partner did not have a great deal to offer the Orokaiva, because not even money was essential. Conversely, the fear of the trouble the white man might cause was not so great as one might suppose. Certainly, there were horrifying stories about what the white man might do if angered, but the Orokaiva had since learned some simple rules telling them how such anger could be most conveniently evaded.

Until World War II, the relationship between the Orokaiva and the government followed this general pattern almost entirely. The government made the regulations and the Orokaiva did the unavoidable minimum. World War II began to change the pattern of this partnership. Australian and American soldiers moved into the Northern District to drive out the Japanese. They camped in the bush, they shared their food with the Orokaiva, they accepted Orokaiva hospitality, they generously distributed what supplies they had to spare. The white soldier, unlike the civilian, lived in a style much closer to what the Orokaiva consider human. He laughed and joked in the presence of the Orokaiva; he put on no colonial pretense.

After the war, the Australian government changed its policy in the territory, suppressing corporal punishment of employees, emphasizing economic development in the villages, improving schooling, introducing local self-government on a limited scale (and later political representation in the House of Assembly), offering Papuans jobs of some responsibility, and discontinuing the type of village policing that made all reforms dependent on the enforcement of regulations. The village constables, whose job was in practice confined to reporting infractions of the regulations, were replaced by elected officials (local government councillors) who are indoctrinators rather than policemen. They harangue the people with a diffuse message covering a wide area of social and economic development. They seek to secure acceptance for new ideas, so that people will genuinely believe in the usefulness of changes they are making.

When I visited the Orokaiva in 1966–1967, I found a great deal of ideological discussion, the key concept being *iji eha* ('the new day, the new age')—a new way of life based on the economics of coffee growing and wage earning, the social amenities of improved villages, school education, Christianity, avoidance of violence, and, generally, cooperation with the mission and administration. I was amazed to see how closely the councillors' harangues and other speechmaking in the villages corresponded to official policies. Many of the advocated ideas were not being put into practice, but generally the transition seemed rather smooth. There were conflicts between the Orokaiva and their mentors, in some instances irreconcilable ones, but it seemed that consideration of these conflicts was being deferred because there was evidence of steady improvement, as long as coffee prices would only keep rising.

Informants, when asked when the 'new age' had started, all replied that it was after the Japanese were driven out. The eruption was never mentioned as the beginning of the 'new age'. It was after the war that the money economy became important and men began to take jobs outside the village for protracted periods. It was then that money became a necessary part of bridewealth so that, as an initiatory ritual, every young man had to have earned some. It was after the war that village improvement started seriously, as the history of individual Orokaiva villages shows.

The eruption of Mount Lamington in 1951 came a few years after these beginnings, at a time when the impact of money was not yet great, though the government and mission had had time to communicate the new order they sought to establish and to press for changes the Orokaiva were not too ready to accept. The eruption strengthened the message. On the transactional level, there was the large-scale help offered by the Europeans after the eruption. This was done in the most dramatic way possible, by planes dropping their riches in great abundance shortly after the disaster. Certainly such a massive display of concern in a moment of need did much to enhance the image of Europeans as desirable exchange partners. This display was followed by the organization of the camps and by the widespread introduction, especially at Ilimo Camp, of activities that were symbolic of the 'new age'.

Daily church services were conducted, all children were given regular schooling, adults were educated in a number of new agricultural and technical skills, good medical services were provided, and regular food and clothing distributions continued. New ideas on housing, village layouts, and women's handicrafts, lectures on how trade goods are manufactured in Australia, the presence of a strong development-oriented and numerous European staff—all these elements must have amazed the Orokaiva villager of 1951, whose contact with this aspect of European culture heretofore had been rather slight. The impact of these intensive programs should not be overestimated, however. For people whose world had been shattered by disaster and relocation, adult education was, according to administrators involved in the program, hardly a major concern. Belshaw (1951) expressed the view that the villagers would agree to almost any reform in their villages, as long as they would be allowed to leave Ilimo quickly and return to their land.

Nonetheless, the terms of the exchange relationship between administration and mission on the one hand and the Orokaiva on the other had become a great deal clearer and more profound. The Australians had made gifts and had stated what they wanted from the Orokaiva in detailed, explicit terms. Furthermore, this had been done under the shadow of a calamity which was interpreted by the mission as a sign of God, if not God's punishment, indicating the dangers of not satisfying the Orokaiva's new exchange partners.

The administration has leveled much criticism against the mission for promulgating the theory that the eruption was a visitation of the wrath of God. Numerous instances are quoted of ecclesiastical blackmail: the bishop allegedly threatened to blow up the mountain a second time unless he was obeyed. The bishop denies these allegations and claims to have discouraged the belief that the eruption was a divine punishment of the (largely unbaptized) Orokaiva. He said it was the Orokaiva themselves who had this idea of retribution.

To explain the Orokaiva idea of the anger of God found in the preceding pages, I have brought together a somewhat haphazard collection of signs which make no sense if arranged in a synchronic pattern. They are a sequence of transactions which took place within the colonial macrosystem and were selected on no other grounds than that they were commonly invoked by Orokaiva in discourse about the 'new age'. Soldiers on punitive expeditions, physical punishment at the plantations, the warm exchange relations with Allied troops, the local government councils viewed as a gift from the whites to the Papuans—all these are random selections from history and owe their place in the analysis of the metalanguage to the fact that the Orokaiva commonly used them to signify the opposition 'old order/new age'.

Earlier in this section, I explained the idea of the 'anger of Sumbiripa' in terms of a simple transactional sequence. The 'anger of God' can be similarly explained, though here the sequence is more complex. As a general device for constructing metalanguages, transactional sequences are of course wholly inadequate. I have, however, indicated that in the Orokaiva cognitive system God is classified as an exchange partner (though more powerful than all other possible partners).

The eruption thus becomes one of a sequence of signs which express the development of the exchange partnership with God. Similarly, in other explanatory systems, the eruption becomes part of a sequence of exchanges with Sumbiripa. It follows from this argument that the eruption changed the relationship with God or Sumbiripa, in the sense that a sign of such magnitude provoked a response. While the sign may have existed as such only in the minds of the Orokaiva, the response was on the level of real social, economic, political, and religious behavior. The general form of Orokaiva metalanguages, as exemplified in the case of the eruption, is sketched in figure 1.

EXPLANATIONS AND THE COGNITIVE SYSTEM

We have now surveyed the four explanations given of the eruption of Mount Lamington. In my discussion of the denotative systems, I concentrated on two of them: the anger of Sumbiripa and the anger of God. I did not specifically discuss the geophysical explanation because it was too summary for analysis, nor did I analyze the Yega explanation further because of the uncertainty about the agent of vengeance. We have seen that the four explanations were, in each case, not only a psychological response to calamity and a philosophical exercise but also expressed ideologies essentially unconnected with the eruption and that, in this respect, discourse about the eruption was actually rhetoric used to express the ideology.

The coexistence of four such ideologies in the same society poses obvious questions about their interrelations. Were they held by separate groups who did not communicate? Did they reflect divisions within the society? Furthermore, a formal problem arises: as these four explanatory systems all arise in one, fairly homogeneous society, are they in a sense cognate and do they display features of homology? On the basis of Orokaiva data, it may be possible to construct a higher-level system which accounts for all the explanations taken together.

Let us first survey the relationships between the explanatory systems on the social level. They do not logically contradict one another: they can be and are held simultaneously by the same people. There is no need to believe that the eruption was caused *either* by God *or* by Sumbiripa nor that the intended victims were *either* Orokaiva *or* Europeans. My informants did not seem to view God and Sumbiripa as wholly distinct. Whether one ascribed the eruption to one or the other depended on the context of the discourse. Most Orokaiva do connect the death of European public servants and army personnel at Higaturu with the hangings that occurred after the war. They believe that these Europeans acted wrongly and that God punished them. But at the same time they believe that the eruption was a sign of God's anger toward the Orokaiva who had not followed the laws of the Church of England.

One cannot, therefore, gauge the relative strength of the three ideologies by counting what proportion of a sample of Orokaiva informants subscribes to one or another of the three explanations. One can, however, evaluate the general effect of each of the three ideologies. The belief that Sumbiripa caused the eruption had only the mildest historical consequences—merely the reinforcement of a hunting taboo. The belief that the mountain erupted to punish Europeans might have become historically important if the mystical Yega cooperative movement had grown to a major millennial cult, but this did not happen. In fact, the Yega cooperatives went into a decline after 1951, owing to crop failure, the departure of its advisors, and governmental opposition in the form of economic and legal obstacles.

None of these reasons would have sufficed to kill the movement had there been, in the 1950s, a strong opposition to the administration of the Northern District. There is, however, no evidence of this. On the contrary there was, between 1951 and 1967, steadily increasing support for the ideologies advocated by government and mission. In this context the theory blaming the eruption on previous noncooperation by Orokaiva obtains some historical significance. It would be absurd to suggest that the increased support can actually be explained by the existence of the Orokaiva theory about the eruption. On the other hand, this support is now undoubtedly more powerfully motivated than if the eruption had

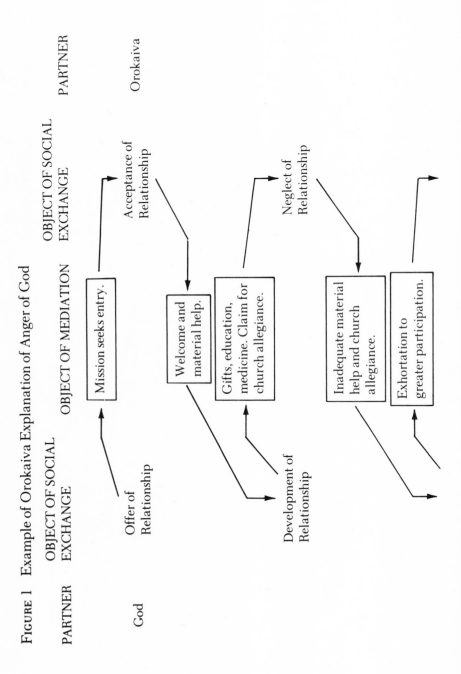

FIGURE 1   Example of Orokaiva Explanation of Anger of God

PARTNER    OBJECT OF SOCIAL    OBJECT OF MEDIATION    OBJECT OF SOCIAL    PARTNER
           EXCHANGE                                   EXCHANGE

God                                                                      Orokaiva

                                          Mission seeks entry.    Acceptance of
                                                                  Relationship

Offer of
Relationship

                                          Welcome and
                                          material help.

                                          Gifts, education,
                                          medicine. Claim for
                                          church allegiance.      Neglect of
                                                                  Relationship
Development of
Relationship

                                          Inadequate material
                                          help and church
                                          allegiance.

                                          Exhortation to
                                          greater participation.

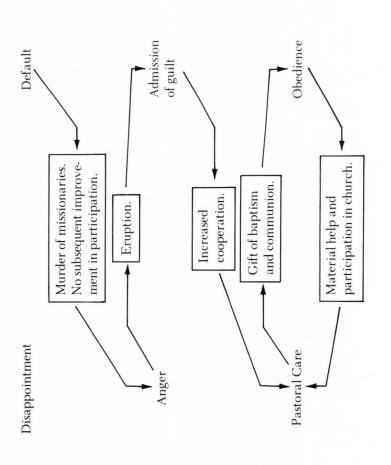

Disappointment

Default

Murder of missionaries. No subsequent improvement in participation.

Anger

Eruption.

Admission of guilt

Increased cooperation.

Gift of baptism and communion.

Obedience

Pastoral Care

Material help and participation in church.

never occurred. The vast increase in the number of baptisms indicates a significant development in the pattern of transactions in
the exchange relations with the new god.

The effect should not, however, be overestimated, as the environment and the socioeconomic situation did not change significantly immediately after the eruption. No socioeconomic transformation occurred because of the eruption or the belief that the
eruption itself was divine retribution for noncooperation with the
government. On the other hand, significant social, political, and
economic changes did happen within ten years or so of the eruption; and when these changes occurred, they were interpreted in a
manner consistent with the Christian explanation of the eruption.

Let us now consider the relationship between the various explanations on the religiophilosophical level. Perhaps the best
starting point for our analysis is our apperception that the three
religious explanations have to do with political strategies—that is,
with the maximization of power. It may be enlightening to look at
these strategies in terms of the Orokaiva's own general ideas about
power. The Orokaiva word for 'power' is *ivo*, a mana-like concept
envisaging 'power' as derived from spirits and bringing success in
difficult ventures by overcoming misfortune, obstacles, and enemies. Misfortunes are explained by 'power' coming from a hostile
source—for instance, from one's human or spirit exchange partner
during a cycle of negative reciprocity.

The first of these three explanations postulates the existence of a
negative exchange cycle with Sumbiripa, so that the people's
'power' depends on placating Sumbiripa and avoiding his anger in
the future. The second explanation postulates that, in fact, the
disaster was a restoration of the 'power' of the Papuans, as it
punished Europeans who hanged Orokaiva ambushers. The third
explanation, however, raises some difficulties. The restoration of
'power' here seems to depend on obedience which must be shown
to the mission and the government.

This question of obedience is perhaps more one of degree than
of essence. Students of religion (such as van der Leeuw 1938) distinguish between relations of "manipulation" and "obedience"
which may exist between man and the gods. In this sense the relations with Orokaiva deities, including Sumbiripa, would tend to
be manipulative. On the other hand, the relationship with the
Christian deity involves far greater and far more diffuse demands,

so that the room for manipulation becomes greatly reduced. Furthermore, the church teaches a doctrine of obedience, which the Orokaiva nominally accept.

Taken at its face value, this would imply that the Orokaiva are satisfied to subordinate themselves to mission and government and do not consider themselves capable of serious competition with white authority. Such a notion of 'power'—that is, that it depends on obedience to white foreigners—has no rational basis in Orokaiva thought, since the bearer of 'power' cannot be subordinate to human power but only to spirit power. There are thus only two reasonable possibilities: either the ideology which made the eruption into a punishment by the Christian God denies the possibility that the Orokaiva henceforth can have 'power', or that ideology must make some distinction between, on the one hand, God and the principle of rightful authority (which should be obeyed on the pain of dire penalties) and, on the other hand, the existing ecclesiastical and political power bearers (who need not be regarded as having perpetual rightful authority). The position taken by Orokaiva informants on this question is not in the least ambiguous.

The Orokaiva are willing to obey the present power bearers, but only on the ground that they feel unready at present to assume power themselves. They regard the existing relationship as temporary. They are able to state this openly, since the Australian administration claims to prepare the way for early autonomy and optional independence. On the surface, there appears to be no acute political conflict.

In fact, however, the 'new age' ideology is fiercely competitive. The activities it advocates are perceived by Orokaiva as leading to a balance of power between the Europeans and themselves. The strong interest in schooling, savings clubs, coffee production, village improvement, wage labor, and so forth was explained time and again by the argument that these activities would ultimately place Papuans on the same level as Europeans and would remove the power differential. It was explained that in the 'new age' one no longer kills and eats the enemy because victory must now be achieved by different means. The reforms advocated by mission and government are perceived as the first weapons in the armory needed for victory. Victory, however, should not be understood here in the European sense, where it implies a permanent defeat of the enemy, but rather in the Papuan sense, where one contends with exchange partners in an inconclusive tug-of-war and the strength of the opponents is approximately equal. Victory, in other words, is the establishment of an equal rather than an unequal relationship.

Given this view of the European-Orokaiva relationship, it is difficult to distinguish between millenarian and gradualist ideologies among the Orokaiva. They are all, in a sense, millenarian, even though they advocate full collaboration with both mission and government. From the more objective view I have taken here, the three Orokaiva ideologies present at the time of the eruption all convey the same message. They are all concerned with the restoration of what the Orokaiva call 'power', which always implies some form of power balance between themselves and their colonial masters.

### IDEOLOGY, POWER, AND LAND

As we have seen, all Orokaiva discourse about the eruption can be reduced to one basic theme: competition for power between Papuans and Europeans. I have not surveyed administration discourse about the eruption in the same detail, but it is safe to say that, apart from the mechanics of relief, the administration was likewise concerned with one central ideological theme, namely socioeconomic development. Our structural analysis would hardly be adequate unless we considered the relation between these two ideologies, not only in abstract terms but also in the framework of concrete events.

During the period immediately after the disaster, the administration planned to make the evacuation camps the beginning of permanent relocation under conditions where socioeconomic development throughout the region could be accelerated (Belshaw 1951; Keesing 1952; Plant 1951). While this relocation was being planned, the evacuees were adamant that they wished to go home as soon as possible (Belshaw 1951; Kaad, personal communication). That the administration gave in to the evacuees should not be regarded as a Papuan demonstration of their own power but rather as a necessary response to practical problems facing Orokaiva as swidden agriculturists lacking a secure system of individual, unencumbered landholding. The circumstances of the closing of the evacuation camp provide an interesting case study in the relation between administration and Papuan ideologies.

Several frightening explosions and floods occurred in February and early March 1951. These vindicated the administration's restricted area policy, which kept the mountain slopes out of bounds. But after the period of acute volcanic phenomena was over, Orokaiva pressure on Mr. Kaad, administrator of the Ilimo Camp, grew steadily. The opening up of restricted areas began as early as April 1951, so that the population of Ilimo began to decline sharply in that month—from 2,000 to about 1,000. It declined to 500 before the camp was closed in May. Although the speed of resettlement did not actually conflict with administration policy, Kaad freely admits that the pace was forced by Orokaiva pressure.

This speedy return to the land was prompted largely by fears which rapidly began to overshadow the Sasembata villagers' fear of the mountain. In part, these fears were religious. Separation from the land meant separation from ancestral spirits who were left altogether untended when the whole community lost access to the land. Proper birth rites and ritual care for infants became impossible, as was ritual care for the dead, for both must be performed on the taro field associated with certain deceased consanguines. On the sociojural level, the migration of an entire agnatic group was dangerous since it could activate residual rights over land which were held by other agnatic groups.

It is likely that the same anguish about separation from the land would have been felt by most swidden agriculturists in the same circumstances. Such anguish cannot be fully explained by the religious and jural system prevailing in one culture alone. My purpose in this chapter, however, is more limited. It is to relate Orokaiva ideas about the eruption to Orokaiva ideas about land and spatial movement.

These ideas are part of the structural patterns to which I referred above: the weakness of corporate groups and the emphasis on the exchange system (see also Rimoldi 1966; Schwimmer 1970a, n.d.). At least half the land in Sivepe and nearly all the land in Inonda is occupied by persons other than the agnatic corporation acknowledged to be the "original" owners. Occupation of such land arises mainly out of use rights granted by these owners to nonagnates. In practice such use rights often become hereditary within the user's agnatic group. Although the use rights were, at first, mostly granted as an act of friendship, occupation may continue even when positive reciprocity is no longer well maintained between owner and user and the owner would like to find pretexts for recovering the land.

It is a clear rule that land reverts to the owner as part of his residual rights as soon as the user ceases to occupy it. Hence departure, even by individuals, at once raises a problem of maintaining control over use-right land. An individual does not leave his land for more than a few days without appointing some person to look after it. This person may be an agnatic or uterine kinsman or an affine whose wife is consanguine to owner or user. Men taking jobs outside the village regularly resort to the appointment of a caretaker for their land. This practice has not only ritual but also legal implications. The caretaker will fight other claims to the land, if only because he himself has become the occupier and the legal beneficiary of its products. If the original occupier stays away too long and his social position in the village is not strong, he may have trouble recovering his land from the caretaker upon his return. This is a risk arising in many cases of labor migration, uxorilocal marriage, adoption, or departures prompted by personal conflicts.

Interviews I conducted in 1966 and 1967 showed that the evacuees at Ilimo were extremely fearful for the safety of their land. The danger they feared most was the activating of residual rights by persons whose agnatic group had at one time been associated with their land.[17] Community relocation, by its very nature, leaves nobody behind to look after the land. It thus creates a legal vacuum that is ordinarily absent in migrations of individuals and small groups. Any individual who sneaked out of Ilimo and settled on a coveted piece of land to which he had some residual rights would be hard to dislodge under the conditions of Pax Australiana because the Australians, so far, have been able to maintain law and order without the benefit of land registration.

The fears about losing the land which explain much of the tension at Ilimo Camp are a direct consequence of conflicts implicit in Orokaiva social structure. The institution of land borrowing, the retention of residual rights over several generations, and the consequent multiplicity of rights and claims over land parcels are directly related to the small size of corporate groups and the dependence on the exchange system for the creation of larger solidarity networks. In a culture where warfare was endemic, these larger networks were indispensable in order for the traditional land tenure system, with its emphasis on multiple rights, to be socially adaptive under precontact conditions.

The 'new age' ideology, as expounded in 1966–1967, does not ignore these basic conflicts but incorporates them in the notion that multiple ownership belongs to the 'past age' whereas sole tenure is the modern ideal. There is strong support today for administration moves to establish a system of sole titles and to abolish the institution of multiple rights. Cash cropping has emphasized the need for such a change. In practice most Orokaiva today plant cash crops on patrimony land rather than on land on which there are invocable claims of residual rights.[18]

The movement toward individual landholding did not start in the Northern District until the mid-1950s, when there was a government-inspired attempt to have landholding titles issued by the Higaturu Local Government Council (see Crocombe and Hogbin 1963). I am not aware of any organized attempt to reform the system of Orokaiva land titles at or before the time of the eruption of Mount Lamington. If such reform is being introduced into the 'new age' ideology today, this must be credited to indoctrination mediated through members of the local government council.

We have seen that, at Ilimo, the traditional land tenure system was the basic cause of a conflict which strongly affected the course of the administration's resettlement policy. The officer in charge of the camp perceived two main purposes: to keep the people safe from the volcano and to rehabilitate them afterward in villages which would have a more modern life-style. As we have seen, the Orokaiva accepted both these objectives as desirable and benevolent. On the other hand, there was a difference in the importance that Orokaiva and administration attached to an early return to the home villages. The administration might have preferred a longer period of evacuation for the sake of safety from the volcano and also for the sake of its program of community education. They met, however, with a restlessness which made them hasten the disbanding of the camp. The same restlessness induced the Orokaiva to agree quickly to some programs of resettlement, not because these programs appealed to them very much but because agreement would hasten their return to the land. European administrators, accustomed to secure forms of land tenure in their own culture, could not fully share the Orokaiva anxiety about losing their land.

This conflict between people and administration was settled amicably. It did, however, emphasize the fundamental difference between Orokaiva and European perceptions of the crisis. For the Orokaiva, it was the relatives—the holders of residual rights to land—who were viewed as the greatest danger, whereas the volcano was soon considered less dangerous. For the European, the relatives were not perceived as dangerous, as it was imagined they could somehow be controlled by the legal weapons available to centralized government. On the other hand, the danger of the volcano was viewed far more gravely, for the Europeans knew of no way to control future eruptions.

Both sides had a strong case in this disagreement. The Orokaiva had a strong case because the Europeans had no institutions that could have protected them against encroachments on their land. There was (and is) no adequate registry. The administration's case rested on its logical consistency with the development ideology it was trying to inculcate. The traditional Orokaiva land tenure system is incompatible with development because it impedes spatial movement and the traditional extended exchange network lacks the flexibility of a market system. Modernization depends on the creation of large corporate groups with well-defined systems of rights and obligations, instead of the subtle but essentially unstable web of warfare, diplomacy, affinity, and friendship. The 'new age' ideology of 1951, though fortified by the experience of the eruption, did not envisage modernization in this basic sense, while in 1966–1967 the implications of the 'new age' for land tenure and the kinship system were just being discovered.

This analysis of the 'new age' ideology indicates that it is related only loosely to social and economic development. It arises directly out of political competition between the Orokaiva, the mission, and the government. Whenever new techniques appear to the Orokaiva to serve this power struggle, their adoption is advocated. We have seen that a traumatic event such as the eruption of Mount Lamington, when it became the subject of Orokaiva philosophizing, was at once put at the service of this competitive struggle. Even when obedience to ecclesiastical and administrative rules is advocated by the ideology—and when the dire conse-

quences of disobedience are stressed by the ideology—such an attitude is viewed by Orokaiva not as part of a permanent new order
but as a temporary expedient, a ploy in the power struggle.

Reform is advocated in terms of such strategy. Over the last fifteen years we have seen that the Orokaiva have begun to accept
the idea of converting land titles to sole tenure, as well as the inevitable consequences of such conversion for kinship organization. Such changes are explained in ideological terms as a necessary part of the competitive struggle against Europeans. The fact
that Europeans view the same move as serving the cause of social
and economic development is almost a coincidence.

Perhaps the most important practical conclusion we can draw
about the genesis of cognitive structures has to do with the nature
of power competition between Orokaiva and the administration.
It is often supposed that development and political competition
are separate processes in conflict with one another. The case in
question shows that the Orokaiva view both aspects as part of an
ongoing exchange relationship. It will have been noticed that in
political debate Papuans, especially those in the villages, are reluctant to seek immediate political independence from Australia,
even though tensions clearly exist. The point here is that they like
to see the exchange relationships with their Australian partners
continue, even though they wish to improve greatly their own position in that relationship. It may be, of course, that this attitude
will change later. In the exchange relationship their own very considerable prestation is their subordination to foreign authority. In
return they are receiving educational benefits which they value
highly—not, fundamentally, because these benefits increase their
private incomes but rather because they maximize Orokaiva power in the exchange relationship.

In addition, the material presented here may have theoretical
implications with regard to the genesis and dynamics of cognitive
structures. We must distinguish here between macro- and microprocesses. For the purpose of the discussion, I have assumed that
the Orokaiva world view, with its notions of exchange and power,
remained unchanged between 1951 and 1966. This assumption
was convenient for the analysis, but it must be qualified. In 1966 I
was given geophysical explanations of the eruption as well as
magico-religious ones, and the former (though feebly held by a
small elite) do prefigure a basic structural change in the Orokaiva

cognitive system. For the most part, however, I was concerned with microprocesses, such as the simultaneous development of explanatory systems based respectively on a tribal, Cargo Cult, and church-administration ideology. None of these ideologies was generated by the eruption, but the eruption was treated as a sign within the context of each of these ideologies, with a different interpretation in each case.

The eruption became a sign because it took its place in a series of ongoing transactions with supernatural beings. As such it had the effect of changing the relationships with these beings in regard to both duties and expectations. The eruption differed from other such signs mainly by its cataclysmic character and its unequivocal demonstration of power. The fact that different interpretations evolved is not an accident but mirrors an ongoing debate within the society. The evidence suggests that cognitive structures do not change by a process of unilineal development but by a process of internal differentiation opening up a dialectic between ideologies opposed to one another along the axes of basic social conflicts. In the Orokaiva case these axes were tribalism/regionalism and denial/acceptance of the partnership with European power. If opposition exists along these two axes, four systems are theoretically possible—namely, tribalism + denial, tribalism + acceptance, regionalism + denial, and regionalism + acceptance. As we have seen, each of these four combinations was found in actuality. The four Orokaiva theories thus form a well-structured whole, and together they express contemporary Orokaiva social reality. The structural changes that were taking place in the period 1951 to 1966 did not come out overtly in discourse but had been recognized and given meaning in terms of the ideologies in 1966.

NOTES

I acknowledge with gratitude financial help received from the Displaced Communities Project, the Canada Council, and the Killam Foundation in the preparation of this chapter. I thank Michael Lieber for his valuable comments on the original draft, which stimulated me to clarify and expand my arguments, and Sandra Wallman for her comments and criticisms. My wife, Ziska Schwimmer, gave valuable assistance in the interviewing of female informants in the sample communities. This chapter was written before independence for New Guinea became a reality.

1. In the Mount Lamington case, the institutional approach would produce results somewhat similar to Lessa's in his excellent paper "The Social Effects of Typhoon Ophelia (1960) on Ulithi" (1964). The major innovations over the last thirty years were due not to the eruption but to the Japanese invasion, the subsequent expulsion of the Japanese by Allied forces, the introduction of large-scale cash cropping, increased urban migration, and the development of officially supported indigenous political institutions.

   The exchange theory approach of Blau and Barth has been followed to some extent in the present essay, but as Garbett (170:225) remarks in the essay already referred to: "Unless one wants to treat situations as simply another kind of 'small group' in an extra-laboratory setting for the testing of propositions from exchange theory, one's findings have to be related to, and set in, a wider context presumably studied by other methods."

2. For semiological discussion on the Road Code, see Lévi-Strauss (1958:chap. 5) and Leach (1970:chap. 2).

3. As an illustration of connotative systems, Barthes (1964a) analyzes a full-color advertisement for grated cheese, spaghetti, and tomato paste and shows that the items in the picture are so displayed as to connote all the delights of a carefree life in sunny Italy where foods are sweet, fresh, unadulterated, and perfect in appearance.

4. The relationship between signifier and signified suggested here may not be peculiar to "the savage mind" but universal, as is suggested by Lacan (1966: 493–528).

5. One of the first useful studies of regional colonial macrosystems known to me in New Guinea ethnography is Burridge (1960), which indicates clearly the modalities of conflict and alliance in the Papuan–administration–missionary triangle. Extremely important also is Fredrik Barth's work on polyethnic systems (1969) and on forms of regional organization in New Guinea (1971).

6. The term "Pelean eruption" is applied to the type that occurred at Mount Pelée (St. Pierre, Martinique) in 1902. A large mass of ash is projected rapidly into the stratosphere to form an expanding mushroom-shaped cloud. The base of the column begins to expand rapidly as clouds of incandescent ash (the *nuée ardente*) avalanche down the slopes. The *nuée ardente* is lethal because of sudden damage to the respiratory system caused by inhaling hot (200°F) dust.

7. The reports written by these two scholars (Belshaw 1951; Keesing 1952) led to the inclusion of the case of the Mount Lamington Orokaiva in the project directed by H. G. Barnett and entitled "A Comparative Study of Cultural Change and Stability in Displaced Communities" (1961).

8. Here and throughout this essay I use the term "structure" in the sense of Lévi-Strauss (1958:chap. 15).

9. I have used British terminology in most of this essay as it seems hazardous to adopt American terms in a British-French conceptual framework. Where I use clan, American anthrolopologists would usually write "sib." The term "local clan group" refers to a coresident segment of a dispersed clan (or sib). A full discussion may be found in Schwimmer (1970a).

10. Compare this with the school at Sasembata, which teaches to grade six.
11. A small band of Orokaiva captured European fugitives, including male and female missionaries, and handed them over to the Japanese. The members of this band came from the area east of Mount Lamington inhabited by what Williams called the Sauaha tribe.
12. Though the Sumbiripa cycle of myths was not noted by Williams, I feel confident it existed prior to 1951, partly on evidence given in Schwimmer (1969) and partly on the evidence of a myth recorded in Belshaw (1951).
13. For sources on Orokaiva leadership, see Reay (1953) and Schwimmer (1967).
14. The term "Waseta tribe" used by Williams is perhaps unfortunate, as I demonstrated elsewhere (Schwimmer 1969:49–53). It is used here for the sake of convenience to group together the people from the Waseta area, all of whom were quartered at Ilimo evacuation camp. The name "Waseta" is not used as a tribal name by Orokaiva; it denotes no more than the village where Williams happened to do his fieldwork.
15. See also Waddell and Krinks (1968:16, fn. 3). In the final section of this chapter, I argue that the geophysical explanation is important for anthropological analysis, since it foreshadows structural change in the Orokaiva cognitive system.
16. These two oppositions are, as I understand it, singled out for detailed study in most of the chapters in this comparative volume. Unfortunately, a more detailed discussion is impossible in this chapter. Transactions between government and people during the relocation process have been described fully in Schwimmer (1969), including the massive administration intervention in the evacuation camps, the changes of location of government and mission centers after the eruption, and the gradual widening of the scope of government and mission activities. In my earlier report, I also referred in detail to the manner in which the relation between whites and Papuans is mediated by Papuan mission teachers, village constables, and other functionaries. On an ideological level the entire 'new age' rhetoric discussed in this chapter may be regarded as a form of mediation between microsystem and macrosystem.

    With regard to boundary maintenance, empirical evidence is available in my earlier report about the relations between the evacuees and the people among whom they lived. At Ilimo something akin to traditional friendly host-guest relations were established. I stress in the present essay the ambiguity of the boundary maintenance patterns. There is an ideology advocating unity and there is increasing evidence of common action, especially in the context of formal organizations set up under the influence of administration and mission, while individual webs of intertribal relationships tend to become denser as a result of migration associated with schooling, employment, and so forth. At the same time, tribalism is still the underlying principle in most transactional contexts.
17. This does not contradict my earlier statement (1969:66) that there was a brief period when the evacuees feared the government would take their land. Kaad reported to me that this fear existed, and I do not doubt it. In

1966–1967, however, this fear was not mentioned to me by informants, whereas I often heard of their worries about the danger that relatives from other villages might take their land, goods, and chattels.

18. On the average, an Orokaiva derives approximately half his land from patrilineal inheritance. In accordance with British terminology, I have called this "patrimony land." The other half comes from a variety of sources, mostly from uterine kin.

# 12

# CONCLUSION: THE RESETTLED COMMUNITY AND ITS CONTEXT

*Michael D. Lieber*

It is evident from the preceding chapters that the circumstances surrounding movement of a community or part of it from one place to another vary. There is a difference between the kind of movement that has resulted in enclaves of Rotumans in Suva and the kind of movement that has resulted in Bikinians living on Kili. We ought to have a terminology that reflects these differences.

I suggest the following terms for referring to population movements and their effects as they are reported in this volume. "Resettlement" refers to a process by which a number of culturally homogeneous people from one locale come to live together in a different locale. To the extent that people form an identifiable community—identifiable to themselves as well as the observer—we can describe it as a resettled community. Except for the Nukuoro, all the groups described here are resettled communities.

We can distinguish two types of resettled communities on the basis of the processes by which communities come to be resettled: planned movement of a group of people, whose destination is determined by some outside agency, and movement undertaken by individuals without the intervention of an outside agency. The first process is here termed "relocation"; the second is "migration".[1] According to these definitions, Bikinians, Banabans, Southwest Islanders, Southern Gilbertese, Ambrymese on Epi, Kapingamarangi homesteaders in Metalanimwh on Ponape, and Tikopia live in relocated communities. The Rotumans, the Kapingamarangi in Porakiet, and the Ambrymese on Efate are migrant communities.[2] The Orokaiva, who migrated because of the eruption, resettled in their homeland after about a year, and we shall see that they resemble a relocated community more than a migrant one. The Nukuoro, who have migrated to Ponape, form no community at all.

Once these distinctions have been made, the question naturally arises: Must the two processes of resettlement somehow yield categorically different results? From the data reported in the previous chapters, the answer is: It depends. Murray Chapman made this fact clear to the participants in the symposium that resulted in this volume. The nature of this contingency constitutes Chapman's crucial contribution to the symposium and to this volume. He pointed out that the patterns of mobility of a community only makes sense (to us or to the community) in terms of some larger system of which the community is a part. His discussion of community mobility forced us to focus our attention on the levels of the larger system in which movements of people occur: the neighborhood, the village, the district, the island, the colonial territory. Each type of resettlement—relocation or migration—can make a difference in the history of a community insofar as it implies that a certain relationship exists between the community and the larger system.

## THE CONTEXT OF COMMUNITY MOBILITY

Movements of people always occur as part of a relationship between persons, groups of persons, or categories of persons. These relationships occur at various levels of the social system. A woman might go to a neighboring village to visit her mother, for example, or a chief from an outer-island village might go to a port town to negotiate with colonial officials. These two movements not only involve different relationships, but they also imply relationships that make sense at different levels of the social system. Social systems that form the contexts of movement can themselves have very different structures, and these differences are associated with differences in the nature and regularity of movements of persons within the systems. The foregoing chapters amply illustrate this point.

Robert McKnight has demonstrated that in precontact Palau,

resettlement was common: Palauans had institutionalized methods for dealing with immigrants in the villages where they appeared. In addition to the occasional canoeload of castaways, warfare sometimes dislocated entire villages or districts: "Villages and districts defeated in war fled to friendly communities and were sometimes absorbed by the villages that received them and the abandoned lands divided by the victorious villages" (Kaneshiro 1958:301). This is highly reminiscent of the New Guinea Highlands system described by Watson (1970), where resettlement is a recurring feature as a result of warfare and the competition between political factions within villages. When a victorious village drives a defeated village from its territory, the losers flee to villages where they have kin, affines, and friends. The process of resettlement in the new village is much as McKnight has described it for precontact Palau. The immigrants are integrated into the host village under the authority of a village 'big man', beginning a transformation of the immigrants' identity that usually culminates in a merging of the emigrants' identity with that of their hosts in two or three generations.

Despite differences of structure at the village and lower levels of the intervillage system, New Guinea Highlands societies and the Palauan social system are similar in some fundamental respects. In the New Guinea Highlands, relations between villages are competitive; intervillage relations are expressed through warfare and alliance, as well as through economic reciprocity; resettlement is a constant feature of the system. The position of a village in relation to other villages is not fixed but varies with time as competitive relations are played out. Thus, when we look at the larger set of relations in a multivillage district, the ordering of relations at time A is different than it is at a later time B. It is possible that at time B, one or more villages present at time A will no longer exist. The state of the larger (district) system at any given time depends totally on the states of the relationships among the component villages of the system at the time. Erik Schwimmer has shown in chapter 11 that these relationships fluctuate between hostility and alliance.

Palauan villages, like their New Guinea counterparts, functioned as discrete units in political relations. Even so, each village was part of a confederation, and the villages of a confederation were ranked from highest to lowest. The highest-ranking village of a confederation controlled political activity for all the lower-ranking villages, especially decisions concerning the making of war and peace. According to McKnight (1960), the ranking village could and did engineer armed conflict between villages within its own confederation. Thus there is evidence of intraconfederation competition among villages, although this was not ideally the norm. The four large confederations that made up the larger Palauan social system continually competed with one another for rank. Villages within a confederation fought as a unit and were represented as units within the confederation. Palauan political relations appear to have been more highly ordered than those of the New Guinea Highlands; confederations were permanent and internally ranked on Palau whereas there were no stable confederations in the Highlands, where villages were unranked and inter-village relations were constantly in a state of flux. Like the New Guinea Highlands, however, relationships between Palauan confederations did vary with time. The state of the entire Palauan system at any given time is an outcome of the competitive relationships between confederations. This outcome is not predetermined by any higher level of organization. Furthermore, each village, whatever its position in a confederation, is a social and cultural unit in terms of political relations; its identity is maintained within its confederation and in its relationships with villages of other confederations, especially in its role as a military unit. Immigrants to a village represent both a resource and a danger. They can add to the fighting strength of the village and to the esoteric knowledge of its political leaders; but until their commitment to the village is assured, they represent a danger. Significantly, in neither New Guinea nor Palau are there migrant communities: migrants either return to their old village or are absorbed by the host village.

Colonial systems show a much different structure than that of the New Guinea Highlands or of precontact Palau. The colonial system is characterized by a hierarchy in which local communities, villages, and districts are under the control of a politically and militarily powerful group. This group is itself organized, and its organization bears little resemblance to that of the local communities it controls. The colonial system contains components of different orders with a suprasystem (a high-level organization that controls and coordinates the subsystems) whose organization is different from the subsystems it controls. It is a differentiated, hierarchically organized system in contrast to the New Guinea and Palau systems, whose largest local components are not constrained by any sort of suprasystem. It is in the hierarchical social system that we find relocation, relocated communities, and migrant communities. Relocation is not restricted to colonial systems, however; it becomes possible in any society that has the requisite organization to conceive of and implement it. Moreover, the character of migration in the Palau–New Guinea Highlands type of system is sharply different from that of migration in the colonial system.

Migration, like relocation, is closely geared to the needs of the higher orders of the colonial system such as administrative agencies, commercial organizations, and missions. This point is clearly illustrated by the Rotumans, Kapinga, and Ambrymese on Efate, all of whom have migrated to those islands where wages or cash for services are readily available. Members of all three groups were recruited at one time or another by commercial organizations, missions, or administrative agencies. Relocation provides even clearer examples of how mobility within colonial systems contributes importantly to their maintenance. The Southwest Islanders, for example, constituted a problem for the German administration on Palau: expensive shipping was necessary to service the atolls. The typhoon of 1905 offered a pretext for solving the problem by relocating the islanders. The Tikopia situation parallels that of the Southwest Islanders in that a natural disaster offered the administrative agencies and a commercial organization an opportunity to solve two problems at once: servicing the isolated island and recruiting needed labor by reducing the population. The Ambrymese relocation took place under similar circumstances, although the magnitude of the natural disaster that prompted it was perceived differently by the administration than by the Ambrymese. The worst disaster, a typhoon, occurred once the Ambrymese had been moved to Epi; the commercial interests were quick to take advantage of it by recruiting the Ambrymese as laborers. The experiences of the Southern Gilbertese and the Kapingamarangi homesteaders, like that of the Ambrymese, illustrate what happens when relocation is a function of the colonial administration's perception of an impending emergency—in these two cases, overpopulation. Also involved in the relocation plans for these two groups were government programs that called for ethnic integration of larger administrative districts.

The relocations of the Bikinians and the Banabans clearly were prompted wholly by the interests of the colonial hierarchy. Bikini was used for bomb testing and Ocean Island was exploited for its phosphate resources. At first appearance, the Orokaiva situation seems to differ from the others in that relocation was only temporary and people returned to their home territories little more than a year after the eruption. But the location and internal arrangements of the new villages and, subsequently, their economic organization reflect a new relationship with the colonial administration. As happened in the Tikopia, Ambrymese, and Kapinga cases, the administration was quick to take advantage of a natural disaster to implement its own plans for the affected people. The Orokaiva did not simply return to living in their old villages just as they did before the eruption. After their return to their home territory, the Orokaiva constituted a resettled community comparable to the Bikinians and Ambrymese.

The differing structure of the two types of social macrosystems discussed here have another implication for movement and its consequences: the maintenance of ethnic boundaries (see Barth 1969). The Palau–New Guinea Highlands type of social system is an ethnic boundary-dissolving system vis-à-vis the emigrants. Because of the kinds of factors that provoke resettlement within the Palau–New Guinea system, return is at best problematical for the emigrants. If they are to remain in the new community, the maintenance of their ethnic boundary poses serious difficulties for themselves and their hosts. In communities where personal identity and rank depend on land rights, attendant kinship connections, and demonstrable commitment to coresident villagers, the maintenance of ethnic identity by resettled people denies them permanent access to these. Although the immigrants may be under the aegis of a 'big man' at the outset, 'big men' do not live forever, nor are they politically powerful forever. The favor of a 'big man' or a chief does not really offer dependable access over the long run to village resources. Meanwhile, their hosts might want them to remain in the village for any number of reasons: to provide fighting strength, labor, special knowledge, or marriage partners. If the immigrants' continued presence is deemed important to their hosts, then the maintenance of their ethnic boundary is likely to be regarded as diluting any permanent commitment and posing a threat to their hosts or at least some considerable faction of the host community (Watson 1970:116–117). Intermarriage with the

hosts, and the consequent incorporation of children into the inheritance system, often initiates the process of boundary dissolution. The dissolution of ethnic boundaries of migrant groups seems
to be complete within about three generations both in precontact
Palau and the New Guinea Highlands.

Colonizers create ethnic boundary-maintaining systems by first
imposing peace on the subject peoples. Although a colonial regime
may act for humanitarian reasons, it is also true that local warfare
interferes with profitable commercial operations. Labor recruitment and the maintenance of a labor force require relatively stable island populations with a modicum of mobility. These populations both supply labor and consume manufactured goods. Thus
suppression of warfare within its territories is always one of the
first programs of a colonial regime. In Oceania, accomplishment
of this objective made intervillage and interisland travel a much
less risky affair than it had been in precolonial days. The elimination of warfare might not end interethnic hostility, but it does
allow a resettling group to maintain itself as a community by preventing subjugation, or the threat of it, by surrounding groups.
Given the need of a colonial government to maintain a flow of personnel within its territories for such purposes as labor recruitment,
mission work, education, and so forth, the protection of emigrants, including resettling groups, is ensured. Ethnic boundaries
are effectively frozen as a result. This is not to say that individuals
or families of one group might not be absorbed by another through
marriage or other means. Barth (1969) has shown that there can
be a flow of people back and forth between one ethnic group and
another that does not in any way obliterate the boundary between
the groups.

The role of missions in the maintenance of ethnic boundaries
must be emphasized. Although colonial regimes have the power to
enforce peaceful relations among subject ethnic groups, missions
typically form contexts in which peaceful and cooperative interaction is both possible and desirable. The context is legitimized by a
consistently stated ideology that makes it possible to play down
ethnicity, replacing its unifying role with that of membership in a
congregation (and opposition to other religious sects). Even the
missions can be forced to recognize ethnicity in their programs,
however. Periodic services in the Rotuman language on Fiji and
the growth of ethnic congregations among resettled communities

on Ponape are examples of such recognition (Lieber 1968b:135–137). Even in these instances, the contexts in which ethnicity is recognized emphasize its distinctiveness only as part of the larger whole that is the church. In other words, the church is an environment in which interethnic interaction occurs in an atmosphere of safety; ethnic boundary maintenance poses no threat in that context. By contrast, commercial interests can use ethnicity to stimulate competition, as in the gold mines in Vatukoula, where management encourages competition between Rotumans and Fijians in order to increase production.

Whether the different processes of resettlement yield categorically different results, then, depends in the first instance on the structure of the larger intercommunity system in which the movement takes place. Although migration can lead to the resettlement of all or part of a community in a nonhierarchical system (such as that on Palau), there are no permanent migrant communities in such a system. Permanent migrant communities are to be found in the more differentiated, hierarchical systems such as states and colonial regimes, which typically act to ensure the maintenance of ethnic boundaries. Relocation is peculiar to this latter type of social system.

In addition to the structure of the system in which movement takes place, the structure of the relationship between the moving group and the larger system also determines the consequences of the movement, whether it is a migration or a relocation. This point is amply illustrated in the foregoing chapters. The decision to relocate is always part of an asymmetrical relationship between some superordinate government agency and a local community. The decision can range from forced relocation, such as the resettlement of Ponapeans on Saipan after the Sokehs rebellion against the Germans (Bascom 1950), to a series of delicate negotiations that result in a joint decision, such as occurred in the Tikopia resettlement. It is obvious that the colonial administration has the upper hand in such negotiations, because at the very least it usually must fund and provision the resettlement program. Moreover, the administrative agency, at the very least, controls the alternative sites to which the emigrants can move. It thereby controls the ecological-demographic environment to which the community must adapt.

Despite the power differential in the relationship, forced migration is rare; some sort of negotiation almost always occurs in the relocation situation. This is extremely important, because the content of the negotiations includes not only the decision to move and the details of implementing the decision, but also the nature of the relationship between the colonial administration and the community (though it is rarely discussed explicitly). It is this latter aspect of the negotiation process that can prove significant for the future of the relocated community. The Bikinian relocation is an obvious example. The history of that community can be seen, from one point of view, as a series of negotiations between the Bikinians and the U.S. Trust Territory administration whereby Bikinians have sought, with some success, to persuade the administration to adopt their view of the relationship. Once this was accomplished, the focus of negotiations shifted to attempts to get the administration to act in accordance with this point of view. The Banabans and the Orokaiva have similarly attempted to persuade their respective administrations to accept their view of the relationship, but the outcomes have been different. Unlike the Bikinians, Tikopia negotiated to prevent the colonial administration from becoming involved in their internal affairs and to keep Nukufero as isolated as possible from other communities. The Southern Gilbertese situation seems to have been somewhere between these two extremes—that is, between asking the administration to take responsibility for the support of the community and asking it to ignore the community.

The difference between the relocated Southern Gilbertese and the other relocated communities is the result of two factors. First, the relationship between the community and the administration was worked out in detail before the actual resettlement. The new community was to have exactly the same relationship to the administration as the communities from which the emigrants came. Second, the major problem of the emigrants was an internal one: the formation of a community by people who had not lived together previously. The administration could do nothing to solve this problem.

The difference in the outcomes of the relationships between the Bikinians, Banabans, Orokaiva, and their respective colonial administrations raises a problem complementary to that of the structures of larger social systems. Although the structure of the colonial system can make certain processes (such as negotiation) inevitable, the outcomes of the negotiations still depend heavily on who the colonialists happen to be. The notable success of the Bikinians in gaining concessions from the Trust Territory administration, as opposed to the frustrations of the Banabans who attempted to do the same, might have depended less on their relative negotiating skills than on the fact that Bikinians were dealing with Americans while the Banabans were dealing with British (Barnett 1953:93). Until anthropologists begin to study seriously the different sorts of colonialists, we shall not be in a position to test this idea.

Migrant communities differ from relocated communities in two important and related respects. First, the migration process does not require nor does it usually involve negotiation between the migrants and the colonial administration. In every case presented in this volume, the formation of a migrant community begins with a very small enclave of migrants. They provide a nucleus around which growth occurs as later migrants come to join their families, obtain wage work, and so forth. Community formation is neither a conscious goal nor a particular problem for the migrants or the colonial administration, at least at the outset. Second, migrant communities have a different relationship with the colonial administration and the colonial system as a whole than do relocated communities.

Relocated communities almost always constitute administrative units within the colonial system. The extent to which the community is willing to allow the administration to involve itself in community affairs and the extent to which the administration is willing to be involved in the community's affairs vary according to the actual negotiations between the community and the administration. We have seen that the range is from dependency (Bikini) to noninvolvement (Tikopia). In either situation, however, the community has a special position within the administrative hierarchy; there is a directness of communication between the community and administration that bypasses the usual hierarchy from local community to district legislative body to the various levels of colonial bureaucracy. The administration, for its part, has a stake in the outcome of the relocation because the expense and effort have to be justified by whatever agency planned and undertook the program. Moreover, the outcome (or some image of an outcome) of the program can be crucial to administrators whose careers are at stake. What the relocated community makes of this relationship may largely determine its subsequent history. For one thing, the relationship outlines the parameters of adaptation for the community. The Bikinians, for example, sought to establish a relationship of dependency on the Trust Territory administration from the outset of their settlement on Kili. The size, quality, and availability of taro land were far less crucial to their adaptation than were the form and location of Kili's shoreline and harbor. What mattered was whether boats could land supplies from administration ships, not how much taro could be grown (see Barnett 1953:88–89).

Migrant communities have no special relationship of this kind with the colonial administration. By and large, they do not constitute administrative units within the colonial administration or the colonial system: their status as ethnic communities is relevant to the administration, if at all, only for census purposes. The administration can ignore their existence, as is true of the Ambrymese on Efate, or it can actively resist attempts by the community to establish itself as an administrative entity, as has been the experience of the Kapinga in Porakiet. Migrant communities' invisibility within the administrative hierarchy does not mean they have no place in the colonial system, however. If they are not seen by the administration as communities, they are at least seen as ethnic groups both by the administration and by their neighbors. The Rotumans and Kapinga provide examples of this: their status as "Polynesians" in non-Polynesian areas gives them, as individuals, certain privileges such as administrative jobs and career advancement. Porakiet, for example, has been the administration's showplace on Ponape for tourists.

In the absence of any direct relationship with the colonial administration, the parameters of adaptation for the migrant community are set by lower levels of the colonial system: specific ecological conditions and relations with neighboring communities, commercial organizations, and missions. Commercial interests and missions are, of course, important in the adaptation of relocated communities, as the Tikopia, Southern Gilbertese, Banaban, and Orokaiva examples attest. Nevertheless, the relationships between these organizations and relocated communities appear to be different from the relationships between the same organizations and migrant communities. The differences can be attributed to the structures of the colonial systems in question. The British, Australian, and Japanese colonial administrations have been far more involved with commercial organizations and missions than have the Americans in Micronesia. Relationships of the Orokaiva to the Australian administration, and of the Banabans, Tikopia, and Southern Gilbertese (since 1963) to the British administration, have necessarily involved them as communities, with commercial interests operating with the sanction of the administration. In each case, involvement of the community with local commercial interests has been an important part of what has been negotiated in the community-administration relationship.

Involvement of the relocated communities with missions has also depended on the relationship between administration and mission. Education as well as medical care in the Mount Lamington area has been delegated to the missions by the administration. Schwimmer demonstrates that Orokaiva contact with the missions did not become intensive until after the eruption; this is the point at which negotiation with the administration becomes meaningful. In the British colonies only education has been controlled largely by missions. By contrast, the American administration has kept education and medical care within the administrative sphere, with missions providing these services to only a small proportion of the population. In short, the extent to which relocated communities have been involved with commercial interests and missions has been largely a function of the relationship between the community and the colonial administration. Thus the constraints on the relationship between these communities and commercial and mission interests have been political as well as economic.

Migrant communities, like relocated communities, face the problem of recreating an infrastructure. In every case in this volume, the infrastructure has evolved as the community has evolved. Beginning with a few individuals or families who are later joined by relatives and friends, the community infrastructure develops by gradual accretion as more facilities are needed for more people. Moreover, friends and relatives who join the enclave obtain such things as wage work through those who already hold jobs. Two of the migrant communities have developed more or less permanent ties with commercial operations; these ties parallel the relationship between Tikopia and Lever to some extent. The Ambrymese acquired land from a local planter in exchange for labor, and the Rotumans at Vatukoula are housed and fed by the mining firm for which they work. In both instances, the company has developed a relationship with the community, but the relationship is somewhat different in each case. Ambrymese, when they are acquiring land for their community, negotiate as representatives of a community. The planter is interested in the Ambrymese as a community only in that their settlement and stability ensure a dependable labor supply. Other than land and its products, the planter furnishes no other facilities of an infrastructure. Moreover, not all wage earners in the community work for him. By contrast, the Rotuman community at Vatukoula is to a great extent an artifact of company policies that provide Rotumans with *en bloc* housing and stimulate competition between Rotumans and Fijians for the purpose of increasing production. In neither case has the colonial administration played a role in developing and sanctioning the relationship. The constraints on the relationships are purely economic.

Except for the situation of the Rotuman community at Vatukoula, relations between commercial interests (or missions) and the migrant communities seem to be institution–individual or institution–interest group, rather than institution–community. Although the missions can be forced to recognize ethnicity, they tend to deal with individuals and families rather than with the community in their day-to-day educational, medical, and ritual activities. Thus, for missions, ethnicity is largely a matter of ethnic categories.

Interethnic relations seem to be far more important in the adaptation of migrant communities than in the adaptation of relocated communities. In every case in this volume (with the exception of Rotumans at Vatukoula), migrant communities have been forced to depend on reciprocity with neighboring groups in order to secure access to at least some of the resources crucial to the creation of a community infrastructure.[3] On the other hand, not one of the relocated communities described here has had to depend on its neighbors for its infrastructure, at least for as long as it maintained its relationship, as a community, with the colonial administration.

There is, then, a significant difference between relocated and migrant communities. The different processes of resettlement do yield different processes of community formation, owing to differences in the relationship between the community and the colonial macrosystem of which it is part. These differences include the relations between the community and the colonial administration, relations between the community and other agencies such as businesses and missions, and relations between the community and other ethnic groups. The differences between the positions of relocated and migrant communities within the colonial system determine different adaptive strategies, and these are, in turn, broadly determined by the different levels of the system within which the community has to operate. Yet, given these differences, the crucial question posed by Homer Barnett remains: Can a knowledge of these differences, plus specific knowledge of the relationship between the social macrosystem and microsystem, allow us to predict what type of stability or change to expect in the organization of the microsystem and the way people in the community conceptualize themselves and their surroundings?

## THE CONTEXT OF CHANGE IN RESETTLED COMMUNITIES

A comparison of the Nukuoro and Kapingamarangi resettlements answers Barnett's question firmly in the negative. Given the same relations with the same colonial administration and roughly the same amount of land in the same location, the two attempts at resettlement have yielded entirely different results. Prediction of change and stability in social organization and culture is impossible if we know only the relationship between the community and the social macrosystem of which it is part. It is also clear from this comparison, as Vern Carroll so succinctly points out, that stability and change in social organization cannot be separated from stability and change in culture. Both the Nukuoro and the Kapingamarangi have replicated their cultures on Ponape; because of this, the Nukuoro community falls apart whereas the Kapinga community does not. The Rotuman data afford a similar comparison. Only one of the four enclaves of Rotumans in Fiji replicates anything similar to the community organization of the home island. The question raised by the Howards and by the Nukuoro and Kapinga data is a fundamental one for social science: What does it take to make a community?

Throughout this volume the concept of community has been

used mainly as a sociological construct—namely, as a coresident group of persons with some sort of formal organization. The contrast between the Nukuoro and Kapinga on Ponape suggests that using this definition might be foolhardy. A human community is, clearly, more than just a sociopolitical unit. It is also a complex unit within the culture of its members. Exactly how complex it can be, especially to its own members, is clear in Martin Silverman's account of the Banaban meeting.

Living together in some organized fashion is not merely a sociological fact; it is a cultural fact as well. Living together *means* something to people. The meaning of living together depends on people's living together in a particular way, not just any way at all. The meaning of living together includes the definition of the relationships within which individual careers are played out, relationships such as those of kinsmen, affines, friends, rivals, neighbors, and colleagues. It must also include definitions of the social settings in which the relationships take place and the premises that make the relationships and their settings either vital or negligible, comfortable or dangerous. Sociological arrangements of people— or, more properly, people's models of their sociological arrangements—express these meanings. These models inevitably act as constraints on the formation of a resettling community.

The Howards confront the question of community formation for the Rotumans, outlining cultural, sociological, ecological, and demographic variables as the important parameters. The Howards go on to ask whether the importance of each variable differs with the particular community or whether one variable structures the relevance of the others in every case. The data presented in the preceding chapters all point to the Howards' second alternative as having comparative validity. Although the meaning of living together can be expected to vary from one community to another, the relationship between the meaning of living together (the cultural variable) and the sociological, ecological, and demographic variables will be roughly the same in every case. The magnitude of the constraints on the replication (or formation) of a community that are exercised by sociological, ecological, and demographic variables will vary as a function of the cultural variable. The premises that structure people's perceptions of living together will make specific demographic or sociological or ecological problems more critical or less critical to the formation of a community. The contrast between the Nukuoro and Kapinga resettlements clearly illustrates this point.

Carroll has shown that for the Nukuoro, the anxiety and mistrust with which they regard their social relationships can be expressed in two alternative ways: by constant "scanning" of one another and testing of their relationships or by total dissociation (see Carroll 1970). The nucleated village settlement pattern can be seen as an expression of the need for constant scanning, and one's prolonged absence from the village (without having left the island) quickly raises queries from one's fellows. The Nukuoro, consequently, find it exceedingly difficult to form cooperative groups, even kin groups, for any purpose. Land, for example, is held on an individual basis. By contrast, the Kapinga regard social relationships as normally solidary; hostility and mistrust are temporary problems that will eventually be dealt with successfully by the parties concerned. They are group oriented, and most land on the atoll is held by kin groups. Cooperative labor is typical of Kapinga daily life, including fishing, house and canoe construction and repair, and bridge and pier construction. Although borrowing and lending have a decidely pejorative evaluation on Nukuoro, the Kapinga define these actions as essential to being human. The nucleated village settlement pattern on Kapingamarangi and in Porakiet expresses the Kapinga perception of social interaction as solidary and satisfying. This becomes quite clear when contrasted with the Kapinga homestead program in which more than seventy people were relocated to Metalanimwh on Ponape between 1955 and 1956. Homestead land was allocated in two areas—thirty-four of the sixty homesteads near the lagoon and the other sixteen 5 miles inland. The inland homesteads had many more productive food plants growing on them at the outset then did the homesteads near the lagoon. The inland homesteads were dispersed in such a way that people working on them had to live in isolated hamlets. All but two of the sixteen homesteads are continually vacant, and the inhabitants of the other two spend about half their time in Porakiet. Given the Kapinga cultural model of living together, residential dispersal was an insuperable barrier to communication. On the other hand, although the residence pattern of the Nukuoro makes concentration impossible, as Carroll has shown, the pattern here means something different than in the Kapinga case: it is the Nukuoro replication of their model of living together.

Given the opportunity to choose, Nukuoro elect to live apart from one another. From the point of view of the Nukuoro, there is neither cultural nor social change; there is only change in the frequency of adoption of an arrangement that is already present in the cultural system. The residential dispersion and the consequent lack of strong ties between households and the lack of enough productive land to support a large population make community formation impossible. The antecedent condition that accounts for these demographic and sociological factors is clearly the Nukuoro premises defining the meaning of living together. By contrast, the Kapinga, with an allotment of usable land only half the size of that originally granted to the Nukuoro, have formed a community in Porakiet whose population almost equals that of the atoll. Given Kapinga premises about living together, the lack of productive land was a problem requiring innovative adaptive strategies, but it was never a problem with respect to forming a community.

The Howards state that the Rotumans appear to be in an intermediate position between the Nukuoro and the Kapinga, because they neither coalesce nor fall apart as a community. As a sociological statement, this is clearly true. Yet a comparison of residence patterns and group stability of the Rotuman enclaves on Fiji and on Rotuma itself reveals that the enclaves on Fiji have replicated traditional Rotuman premises that define living together and the social arrangements that express these premises. In so doing, Rotumans on Fiji have formed (what are from their point of view) four communities. On Rotuma, there is much movement of families from one house and from one district to another. As personal relationships in one neighborhood become strained or explosive, members of one or more households simply move to another house where they have residence rights. With this sort of mobility, the population of a neighborhood is fluid (Howard 1970). Thus it is hardly inevitable that one will see any particular person at any given time, except as required by ceremonial obligations. Participation in social relationships on Rotuma occurs in various contexts, including those of the household, the neighborhood, the descent group, the district, the church, and the island. The multiplicity of options each person has in descent group membership, land rights, residence, and various voluntary associations means there is no fixed set of relationships that demands permanent commitment and participation.

What is significant about the Rotuman enclaves in Lautoka,

Levuka, and Suva is that they do provide a variety of contexts for social interaction and participation much like those on Rotuma (household, ceremonial, recreational, occupational, religious) while maintaining the fluidity that characterizes relationships on Rotuma. Religious services in the Rotuman language, Rotuman clubs, weddings, funerals, visiting, and interhousehold reciprocity are all contexts of interaction that symbolize community. These have all been replicated, along with the expectation that the participation of any given person in any of them will not be uniform over time.

Although Vatukoula is the only coresident Rotuman enclave, it is the mining company rather than the Rotumans who created the possibility of coresidence. The location and allocation of housing are not decided by Rotumans but by company bureaucrats. Although coresident households, neighborhood relations, Rotuman-language church services, and some political structures characteristic of the home island are replicated at Vatukoula, the residential fluidity and multiplicity of options that characterize Rotuma and other Rotuman enclaves on Fiji are clearly lacking. Older relatives who are an economic liability, for instance, might be forced to leave. Rotumans at Vatukoula have a community that partially replicates the Rotuman model; Rotumans in Lautoka, Levuka, and Suva also have communities, and these also partially replicate the Rotuman model, but in a different way. In other words, the issue is not why Rotumans replicate a community at Vatukoula and not elsewhere, but why they replicate their community in a different way at Vatukoula than in Suva, Levuka, and Lautoka. Demographic and sociological contraints on community formation take on a different character in this context. Residential dispersion, for example, poses a serious barrier to the formation of a coresident community, especially in Suva, which is already crowded. However, the spread of the Rotuman population does not form any serious barrier to communication among Rotumans in Suva. Moreover, the residential dispersion of Rotumans found in Lautoka, Levuka, and Suva maintains the spatial and communicational fluidity that is traditional in Rotuman social relationships. The fact that a Rotuman in Suva can obtain almost anything that he or she needs without going outside of the ethnic group suggests that despite a lack of a stable, coresident Rotuman settlement, there is in fact a Rotuman community in Suva, at least from a Rotuman point of view.

The Howards' argument for the relevance to the formation of ethnic consciousness of an opposing ethnic group takes on a new significance in the argument presented here. In Vatukoula, it might well be the presence of Fijians and the intense rivalry between them and the Rotumans that allows the Rotuman rigidity of residence and association to be maintained without tearing the Rotuman community apart. When personal relations become strained, Rotumans cannot get away from one another without giving up their jobs. Competition between the two ethnic groups, in other words, compensates for the lack of fluidity in the Rotuman community at Vatukoula. The Howards note that this intense competition seems not to be apparent elsewhere on Fiji; they point out, for example, the common phenomenon of reciprocity between Rotuman and Fijian households in the other enclaves.

The Southern Gilbertese provide the clearest example of what it takes to form a community. Unlike the other resettled communities described in this volume, this community consists of people who had not lived together previously. The formal organization of the community had been worked out before relocation. Districts, political organization, spatial arrangements of houses and horticultural areas, and the like were all mapped out before the move. The administration provided building materials, seedlings, cuttings, and basic subsistence needs during the period of initial settlement. In addition to mobilizing the large amount of labor needed to lay out the village, construct houses, and clear and plant land, the essential problem for the Southern Gilbertese was that of creating the social relationships that make a community. Various organizational modes were tested during the period of early settlement in order to establish these personal relationships. When the first wedding was performed in the community, the parents of the couple invited the entire community to the wedding feast (Knudson 1965). In the Southern Gilberts, wedding guests are normally restricted to kinsmen of the couple. The father of the groom, who was also the chief magistrate of the community, used a kinship model of the community in deciding to issue the invitation. It is this kind of testing that finally leads to the solution of the problem of organization.

In attempting to organize the work of clearing and planting on Sydney Island, two alternative modes of organization were suggested: a single work group of community men working on each family's land in turn, or each household working only its own land. This problem became a major issue, as each alternative implied a different conception of community relations and each had its own adherents. Both positions were based on traditional, though different, norms of Gilbertese culture. Communal organization of work projects is traditional in the Gilberts, although this was rarely applied to the clearing and planting of privately held land. Although the model of organization was an established one, its proposed application was novel. Moreover, the proposal ran counter to the axiom that a person's land is his own and those without rights of ownership or usufruct have no right to make decisions concerning its disposition. Both sides in the dispute held fast to their positions, and the tension finally erupted into a permanent schism between the two groups of settlers. It was this schism that finally organized the community.

The ideological nature of the schism is demonstrated by the fact that although the settlers were all Protestants at the outset, one of the groups converted wholesale to Catholicism after the split. In other words, the schism was given religious legitimization (see Berger 1969). That the schism is a permanent and necessary feature of the community as a whole is demonstrated by the fact that when the second relocation (to Ghizo Island) occurred, both groups moved (although not at the same time) and maintained their spatial separation in the new locale. The ideological dispute articulates two different but related conceptions of community based on different levels of norm of the same cultural system. In this sense, the Southern Gilbertese community affords another demonstration of Schwimmer's point that a culture is not a monolithic entity. The same event or issue can be the subject of different ideologies. These ideologies, in turn, can become political weapons, as the two Gilbertese ideologies were.

The schism plays the same role in the Southern Gilbertese community that opposing ethnic groups play in the Rotuman community at Vatukoula and in the Southwest Islanders' community on Palau. The presence of a competing or hostile ethnic group promotes solidarity within the Rotuman and Southwest Islanders' communities in the face of divisive factors. In the Southern Gilbertese resettlement, where the community solidarity that results from long histories of personal relationships is absent, opposing groups provide one another with a basis for permanent solidary relations—members of each group are united in their opposition to the other group. The principle of solidarity through opposition to some out-group is the same in all three cases.

The limiting case for our hypothesis regarding the relationship among ecological, demographic, sociological, and cultural variables is that of the Bikinians on Rongerik. The atoll was simply too small and too unproductive to support the Bikinian population. The communal system of allocating labor and distributing food, traditionally used for organizing feasts, was employed at first only as a temporary expedient and then as the only available means of preventing famine. Even this tactic was inadequate for coping with the low productivity of the atoll's resources.

The food shortages on Kili contrast with the situation on Rongerik. The coconut and taro resources might have been adequate for the community's needs had they been carefully cultivated and exploited. The Kili food shortage was to a great extent the result of political conflict within the community: any land allocation proposal provoked conflict between those who held land on Bikini as headmen and those who wanted land (and its attendant headman status) of their own. The communual allocation of labor on Kili failed to provide the incentive for careful cultivation that was furnished by land division. At the same time, the community's strategy of maintaining a dependency on the Trust Territory administration would have been ill-served by a comfortable adaptation to life on Kili. In other words, the food shortage was in great measure a result of a compromise made to avoid conflict within the community. It also became a political weapon in the struggle between the community and the colonial administration. Kili's ecosystem had little to do with the food shortage.

If cultural premises that define living together give shape to the demographic, sociological, and (within limits) ecological problems for the resettled community, then we must explain an apparent paradox. In each of the resettlements just described, the process of replicating the social relationships that are structured by those premises leads to change in the relationships. The paradox disappears, however, if the change is examined at the relevant level of the cultural system. We can distinguish three levels of the cultural system at which change occurs (hereafter referred to as levels of change) in the communities described in this volume. First, there is change in life-style—alterations in the way people allocate their time and resources. These alterations correspond to the learning of new skills and subsistence activities (and the novel application of old skills) and the adopting of new roles and relationships in order to adjust to a new ecological and social context. The first level of change can be seen in all the communities described here. Wage labor and the use of money for subsistence purposes, with their implications for the allocation of time and resources, can be seen in all but the first Southern Gilbertese resettlement. The adoption of new skills, new types of entertainment, and new plants and planting techniques is common to all the atoll populations that moved to high islands. The learning of new roles for interethnic relations is common to all the resettled communities. So, for example, a Kapinga man on Ponape who has a full-time job may be absent from his community for eight or more hours a day, five or six days a week, whereas his atoll congener would not. The time that the wage earner can spend with his family and friends has changed in a patterned way. Moreover, if he is required to wear a shirt and slacks to work, he has to invest more money in clothes than would a man who does not hold a job.

The second level of change involves the way people organize their social relationships with one another within the community. Organizational change can be seen as an outcome of the implementation of new strategies for deciding and acting. Although this sort of change is well exemplified below, what needs to be clarified at the outset of the discussion is the distinction of life-style and social organizational changes as different *levels* of change. The distinction implies that life-style, particularly the way people organize their time, energy, and other personal resources, is somehow embedded in the larger context of how people in a community organize their personal relationships with one another. We have seen, for example, that the Kapinga in Porakiet have undergone many changes in life-style without much change in the way people organize their social relations within the community. We have also seen that many of the changes in life-style constitute strategies for securing resources from outside the community; these resources flow back into the community as goods and services that people bring to their relationships with one another. The changes in life-style, therefore, preserve the social organization of the community, as has been well illustrated in chapter 3. Moreover, it is the way that community social relations are organized that gives shape to its life-style changes; who learns which new skills and in what contexts is determined as much by the community's rules for assigning roles as by the opportunities to learn the new skills. Thus, for example, it is no accident that Kapinga men hold full-time wage work in Porakiet nor that women in the community control the expenditure of money. The traditional domain of Kapinga men is at the peripheries of the village (outer islets, the lagoon, the reef), bringing back to the village the means of subsistence. Women are traditionally responsible for scheduling meals, planning the amount of food needed, and timing its collection. It is the women in Porakiet who do the shopping, even though it may require a trip to town to do so. This constitutes a life-style change for women, but not a social organizational change. If, on the other hand, Kapinga men went to town to do the shopping (or routinely did it on the way home from work), this would constitute a social organizational change; specifically, the change would be one in the organization of male and female roles.

People's models of their community's social organization follow logically from premises that define persons, categories of persons, relationships between persons and categories, and the settings in which these relationships occur—premises defining the meaning of living together (as a kind of shorthand). These premises form the cultural context in which people's models of their community's social organization are nested. Thus the premises that define the meaning of living together are of a higher logical order than models of social organization that follow from them; the relation between them corresponds to that of a class and its members (Bateson 1972:279–308). Change in the premises defining the meaning of living together constitutes the third level of change discussed here. In the hypothetical case of the Kapinga man doing the grocery shopping, the social organizational change in male and female roles would lead us to infer that there has also been a change in the premises defining males and females. We would want to test this inference by looking for other changes in the distribution of responsibilities by sex. If there were such changes, and they all had a similar pattern—men taking over responsibilities formerly assigned to women—we would be justified in describing the changes as having occurred both at the second level (of social organization) and at the third level (of premises defining the meaning of living together). As we shall see, change at the level of social organization often conserves higher-level premises defining living together, but social organizational changes can also be a condition for change at the higher level of premises.

The second level of change is evident in the Nukuoro, Rotuman, Southern Gilbertese, Orokaiva, and Bikinian communities. We have already seen that living in dispersed, noninteracting households is one way of expressing Nukuoro premises of living together. For the Rotumans on Fiji, the incorporation of Fijians into household reciprocity relations and the formation of Rotuman clubs implement Rotuman assumptions about the maintenance of their social relations with one another and their personal mobility within these relations. In the Southern Gilbertese situation, schism and its religious expression stem from two different levels of meaning inherent in traditional patterns of landholding and labor allocation.

The Orokaiva resettlement is another clear illustration of change at a lower level that follows from and conserves a higher level of premise. In this case, the Orokaiva view of the colonial administration as a trading partner in the traditional sense, that is, as an equal in an exchange relation, structures (or restructures) not only the Orokaiva political stance vis-à-vis the administration but also their external and internal economic relations. The change from subsistence farming to growing coffee for cash is, from the Orokaiva point of view, an economic strategy to strengthen their competitive position with the administration. Coffee and cash replace the traditional articles of exchange without changing the way the Orokaiva perceive the structure of the trading-partner relationship. This strategy, however, induces other kinds of change. Joint ownership of land and the complex fabric of ownership and use rights traditional in Orokaiva subsistence farming make stable cash cropping difficult. These land tenure practices gradually gave way to fee-simple ownership. This complex set of changes in social organization is symbolized by the 'new age' ideology; yet Schwimmer shows that underlying this ideology is a very traditional set of premises about interethnic relations. The ideology and its associated economic practices are expressions of these premises at the levels of social organization and life-style.

The Bikinian resettlement offers an even more dramatic example of organizational change. Bikinian social organization appears to have undergone a spectacular transformation in a 25-year peri-

od. Matrilineages have ceased to function as landholding social
units and what appear to be cognatically organized groups are
taking their place. But has there really been a fundamental change
in the process of replication of the community's structure? Clearly
the answer is no. Bikinians continue to assume that prestige, influence, and authority are outcomes of the responsibility a person
can assume for the destinies of others. They continue to assume
that ownership of land, through which one provides the resources
that maintain others in a dependent relationship, is the where-
withal to demonstrate one's ability to handle responsibility. If the
political organization of the Bikinians is viewed as a game—a
competition for high rank according to prestige and authority—
then responsibility for a group of kinsmen continues to be the
criterion of eligibility to play the game. What has changed are the
criteria for deciding who is a legitimate dependent and how
authority is to be transferred from one generation to the next.
These changes are not entirely new, however, because use rights
over land were distributed cognatically on Bikini and patrifilial
inheritance of land was already a traditional strategy of land
transfer (when one could get away with it). As in the Nukuoro
situation, the change in Bikinian social organization is one in
which an alternative that is initially one of low incidence becomes
more or less standard practice in a new social context.

The role that the social macrosystem plays in changes at this
level, whether it is the colonial administration, other colonial
agents, or other ethnic groups, is far from clear. Certainly, we cannot talk about "causes." In no case is there any evidence that the
changes described here are caused by policies, decisions, or actions of groups with whom the resettled communities are in contact. Nor can we categorically state that change at this level is the
result of adaptation to the new environment. For the Rotumans on
Fiji, it does seem clear that their relations with Fijians and their
formation of Rotuman organizations are a response to demographic problems—finding housing and maintaining households
and communication with other Rotumans in a crowded urban
area. To this extent, these changes are adaptations; but it is not at
all clear that there is no available alternative, such as arranging *en
bloc* housing in a section of Suva.[4] In the Orokaiva case, the
changes described by Schwimmer are adaptations to a relationship with the colonial administration. Given the Orokaiva deci-

sion to establish a "trade partnership" with the administration, the adaptations are necessary ones. Yet Schwimmer demonstrates that the decision to establish the relationship was not a necessary one and that the Orokaiva have not adopted all the programs and policies required by the administration. The stability of the relationship depends on each party being able to maintain its own perceptions of the relationship; this, in turn, depends on each side ignoring a good deal of evidence that would contradict its view of the relationship.

The failure of the Nukuoro on Ponape to articulate any organization above the household level, the formation of the Southern Gilbertese community through schism, and the transformation of Bikinian corporate kin groups are only indirectly related to the environments in which these communities resettled. For the Southern Gilbertese and Bikinian communities, neither the specific locale and its ecosystem nor the relationship between the community and the colonial system have any effect on the organizational changes that followed resettlement. What is crucial in both situations is that the settlement is a new one and that certain organizational decisions were not made before resettlement. In effect, not having considered how labor was to be allocated on Sydney and how land was to be distributed on Kili before moving subsequently provided an opportunity for differences of opinion on these questions to be expressed. It was a new ball game in both communities. People had an opportunity to shape the community to their own advantage in a manner that would have been impossible on their home islands. The colonial administration provided the opportunity by carrying out the resettlement; otherwise its role in the changes was negligible. The physical and social environment played a slightly more important role in the change in Nukuoro organization. The possibility of wage work, acquisition of homestead land, and marriage with spouses of other ethnic groups on Ponape afforded the Nukuoro the opportunity to live independently of one another.

Maintaining the premises that define the meaning of living together can necessitate change at some lower level of the social system; however, the premises themselves can change. This is the case in the Tikopia, Ambrymese, Kapinga, Banaban, and Southern Gilbertese communities. In each instance, premises about what living together means become a basis of more or less conscious controversy regarding issues that demand action by the entire community.

The controversies in the Tikopia, Ambrymese, and Kapinga communities involve the relationship between the resettled and the home communities. In the Tikopia resettlement, various adjustments had to be made to a new ecosystem, to the relationship with Lever Company, and to the need for concerted action on community projects in the absence of the chiefs. These adjustments required innovative responses by the Tikopia. Changes in work schedules and tasks, uses of cash, and the organization of decision making were necessary in Nukufero. These were changes in life-style and community organization. The fact that these adaptive changes were both necessary and successful made them even more problematic to the Tikopia, who had created a new community with the conscious intent of exactly replicating their social system on the Tikopia model. Given the manner in which they conceptualize their system—as an assemblage of customs, units of behavior, and organization—complete replication was impossible under the circumstances. Thus it is the very necessity of these adjustments that makes them problematic from the perspective of Tikopia custom. The conflict between necessity and custom has permeated discussion and decision making in the community, finally calling the concept of custom itself into question. As Eric Larson points out, some villagers began to ask whether it was possible to preserve the spirit of custom without exactly duplicating its details. This question, which has not been resolved, is crucial for the community; it represents a change in the idea of custom for all the villagers. The change is one of differentiation of levels—between intent and practice, between ideals and strategies for implementing them.

The ramifications of this change in the concept of custom are wide for two reasons. First, the change opens the way to numerous strategies for living together. Second, differentiating the concept of custom into the levels of ideals and strategies for implementing them makes possible the conscious evaluation of new strategies in terms of how they affect other ideals inherent in other customs. Moreover, by making the level of ideals explicit, conscious evaluation and discussion at that level (and possibilities for further change at that level) become possible, as we have already seen in Martin Silverman's description of the Banaban meeting. Under these conditions, the phrase "Tikopia and Nukufero are the same" acquires a new order of complexity through the differentiation of the levels at which they are the same (or different). Yet even a change in the idea of custom does not call into question the still higher-level premise that there is a uniquely Tikopia order of thinking and acting. The change does, however, make possible conscious reflection on what that order really is.

In the Ambrymese community on Efate, changes in both life-style and community organization underlie a change in high-order premises. An initial shortage of land and a consequent need for cash for subsistence, combined with the availability of wage work, had two important results. First, the Ambrymese established relationships with a local planter, securing jobs and, later on, land by lease and sale. Second, the resettled Ambrymese were unable to replicate traditional land tenure patterns. Wage labor restructured the villagers' life-styles, especially the time spent in the village. More important, exchanging labor for grants of land required a well-organized community effort. This effort is connected with the impossibility of replicating traditional land tenure practices on Efate.

Traditional land tenure practices were inapplicable on Efate, initially because there was too little land and later because the land that was acquired belonged to the village as a whole rather than to individuals. Although the failure to replicate traditional land tenure practices is common to all the migrant communities discussed in this volume, this fact is crucial here because land disputes so often result in sorcery allegations on Ambrym. From the beginning of the resettlement, a major source of conflict was absent. In this respect, Maat Efate is comparable to the Southern Gilbertese and Bikinian situations; it too was a new ball game. Many fewer deaths were attributed to sorcery in Maat Efate. For the villagers this was salutary enough but it also changed mobility patterns in a decisive way. Sorcery scares on Ambrym resulted in a periodic exodus of people, especially males, out of the village for periods of up to several years. The bargaining power of the villagers on Efate that enabled them to secure land from the commercial planter in exchange for their labor depended on a stable population of males in the village. Not only are the need for a stable work force and the absence of sorcery mutually reinforcing, but the stable village population and lack of potentially homicidal conflict allow the villagers to explore, in a way that would have been impossible on Ambrym, potentials for community action that are already inherent in their social system.

The permanence of the Maat Efate community became a continuing issue as people on Ambrym exerted constant pressure on their relatives on Efate to return or at least to clarify their status with regard to land rights on Ambrym. The studied ambiguity of the Efate villagers only sharpened this pressure. This issue articulated for the Efate villagers the differences between the two communities as they examined their commitments to each. Although the details of this series of changes might not have been apparent to Efate villagers, the net result certainly was. They have evolved two models of their own social system; although the presence or absence of sorcery has been the stated difference between the models, it was not the only one. Sorcery has implications for how each community works. In other words, sorcery became a metaphor for the two different models of the Maat community as the implication became clear to the villagers that sorcery is an outcome of certain social contexts. Maat Ambrym villagers are not unaware of the two competing models of the community, as was demonstrated by their efforts to defend their own version.

The relationship between Maat Efate and its immediate environment is important at the lower levels of change. The ecological-demographic problems of land shortage for the villagers and labor shortage for the commercial planter make possible the exchange of land for labor. It is the willingness of the planter to negotiate land transfers for a reliable labor force that makes it both possible and necessary for Maat Efate villagers to act as a corporate community in the negotiations. The disappearance of sorcery from the village cannot be regarded as inevitable just because one major source of conflict was eliminated. The necessity for corporate community action constrains divisive activity such as sorcery. Once such a positive feedback relationship begins, it is self-reinforcing, at least insofar as the elimination of intracommunity sorcery is concerned (Maruyama 1963).

In Porakiet, changes in life-style and the organization of relations with the home atoll of Kapingamarangi generated a series of issues that called into question the definitions of 'Kapinga person' and 'community'. The gradual growth of a core of permanent residents committed to careers on Ponape, and distinguishing themselves from transient residents, resulted in a differentiation of atoll and Porakiet life-styles. The differentiation is reflected in organizational changes in the relationship between the two communities. Porakiet had been a colony of the atoll under the authority of the atoll chief, but by the early 1960s it was recognized by residents of both communities as politically independent from the atoll. These changes left the relationship between the two communities and its future ambiguous in two ways: To whom did the land in Porakiet belong? And to what extent were members of one community financially responsible for major projects conducted in the other?

When housing improvement loans became available to Ponape residents through a local cooperative, some of the permanent residents in Porakiet sought to secure loans. To do so required that they put up land as collateral. This would have necessitated a land division of the village, which was proposed at a village meeting. Relations with persons and agencies outside the village (which normally generate resources for personal relationships within the community) are characteristic of the Ponape life-style of the Kapinga. Kapinga interest in housing loans in no way diverges from this pattern, yet its implication for the relationship between the atoll and Porakiet—that village land should belong to a few families—contradicted the notion that Porakiet was a place for all Kapinga people. The relationship between the village and its context generated this issue, and its resolution involved redefining that relationship.

The issue of the financial and moral responsibility of Porakiet residents for major projects on the atoll and, later, the issue of the responsibility of Kapinga homesteaders for major projects in Porakiet are intercommunity issues. To resolve them, the concepts of 'Kapinga person' and 'community' were invoked, discussed, and redefined. As we have seen in chapter 3, the definition of community that eventually resolved these issues was, in effect, a redefinition of the context of the community. The redefinition of 'Kapinga person' and 'community' involved a recognition of the larger geographical and social system within which people who define themselves as Kapinga live together. The redefinition of these concepts interpreted the facts of the geographical and political separation of the Kapinga communities while preserving premises about personhood and responsibility at a still higher level.

The Kapinga, Tikopia, and Ambrymese cases have fundamental similarities. In all three communities, systematic changes in life-style and organization distinguish the home community from the resettled community in a manner recognizable to members of both. This distinction, combined with the commitment of people in the resettled community to its maintenance, renders the relationship between the paired communities ambiguous. The ambiguity comes to the fore unavoidably when people's commitment to the home island is somehow called into question. The question of commitment is brought about by specific issues in each case. The resolution of the ambiguity involves change at the level of premises that define a specific concept—community in the Kapinga and Ambrymese cases and custom in the Tikopia case. In each case, redefinition involves a symbolic differentiation at the level of premise that interprets the differentiation of the life-style, organization, and demography of the home island and resettled community. In the Kapinga and Tikopia situations, the change of the premise is one in which the crucial symbol is differentiated into higher and lower levels of abstraction. In the Ambrymese case, the differentiation is between models of Ambrymese community. In all three cases, the symbolic differentiation redefines the community as part of a universe larger than that of the home island.

The Banaban resettlement was preceded by several decades of change on Ocean Island involving both life-style and community organization. These changes resulted in the relationship between the Banabans and the commercial phosphate firm mining Ocean Island. This relationship altered the infrastructure of Banaban daily life. Electricity, running water, machines, and conveniences of various sorts provided by the mining company were part of Banaban daily life on Ocean Island by World War II. Moreover, conversion to Christianity eroded a ritual system that had organized the relations between kinship, the ecosystem, economics, and locale on Ocean Island. Although the resettled Banabans were able to replicate their land tenure patterns and many patterns of personal relations, interest in replicating a traditional system was qualified by conflict over the specific content of that system; people no longer knew what it was. The Banaban dilemma was based on the close connection between what they decided to do about themselves and their relations with colonial authority and commercial interests.

Resettlement on Rambi necessitated making decisions about land distribution and land use, house and road construction, settlement pattern, public utilities, and so forth, all of which implied that there be models of organization on the basis of which these decisions could be made and implemented. Unlike the other communities described in this volume, the Banabans were in the position of having to invent, test, and refine their organizational models rather than being able to replicate comprehensive, existing models. This process, which Silverman calls "testing out," is essentially a matter of survival for the community from the beginning of the resettlement. The Banabans develop organizational forms around which to structure activity; they test the forms by deciding, acting, interpreting the consequences of their actions, and modifying the original construction on the basis of their experience. This process is illustrated in chapter 6.

To decide how royalty money from Ocean Island land was to be distributed, the relationships between land and people, between various categories of people, and between government and people were discussed at great length. Categories of people, especially, were the subjects of examination and definition (or redefinition); relations between the categories, such as workers and farmers, workers and old people, were scrutinized in order to identify how the social order forced the victimization of some people by others. The Banabans are trying to arrive at some clear picture of a human order within which sensible action maintains justice in social relationships. But in the conscious examination of these categories and the relations among them, the categories and their relations have been subjected to change. The results of any decision based on this examination and redefinition are necessarily fed back into the next decision. Given that this process is both continual and necessary for the survival of the community, change in the premises defining living together is inevitable.

Change in Southern Gilbertese premises that define living together stemmed from the attempt to reconstitute the traditional communal meetinghouse. Traditionally, seating areas in the meetinghouse were ranked according to membership in a landowning kin group (Lundsgaarde and Silverman 1972). To resolve the heated conflicts over which families would get which seating areas, the emigrants agreed to designate all seating areas as of equal rank. Although the agreement avoided the short-term problem of squabbling over which family would get which seat, it also reduced the channels through which prestige aspirations could be expressed. The traditional basis of rank in Gilbertese communities is a historical relationship between kinship and land. This relationship could not exist on Sydney and Gardner Islands because the land had no history that was meaningful to settlers and because the reconstitution of the meetinghouse divorced rank from land and kinship. In terms of rank, which was a traditional mode of organizing the relations between persons and between families, the land on Sydney and Gardner Islands had neither a history nor a future. Thus, unlike the Banaban and the Tikopia situations, the home island and the new island could not be metaphors for each other. The meaning of real property as a set of relations among persons had been irrevocably changed and the symbolic connections of land to relations among families severed. This implies either that the assumption that families are ranked had changed or that this assumption would have to be realized by a different strategy. In fact, this implication is a major reason for the decision by the Southern Gilbertese community to request a second relocation.

Although the organization of the Southern Gilbertese community offered few channels for the expression of prestige aspirations, the world outside the community had no such apparent limitations. The experience of community members working and living off the island demonstrated that relations within the larger colonial system offered a variety of options for accumulating personal resources that could be brought to relations within the community. The decision to request a second relocation was a community decision made after much discussion. The reason given for the request—that life on Sydney Island, although comfortable, provided no opportunities for "advancement"—has two implications. First, the reasoning implies that although the relationship among land, kinship, and rank had changed, the assumption that persons and families are differentiated by rank had not. Expressions of rank shift from relations based on resources held in the community to relations based on resources acquired from the larger social context of the community. Second, the symbolic connection between community and place had been severed, in that one no longer necessarily implied the other. Moreover, this connection had been severed in several other contexts, both as part of the relocation plan and as an adaptive exigency.

A particular place in the meetinghouse no longer had any connection to the relations between persons or between families; also, it was no longer connected to particular places on the island, that is, to specific parcels of land owned by specific families. The ordering of relations between persons and families, therefore, no longer had any necessary connection with place on the island. Moreover, as an adaptive necessity, the places from which emigrants come are largely irrelevant to the formation of relationships with others in the new Southern Gilbertese community. To the extent that these ethnic differences are allowed to become relevant to everyday interaction, the formation of a single, solidary community becomes that much more difficult. This is one reason for requiring the emigrants to renounce all rights to land and rank on their home islands. To the extent that place of origin and place on the new island have become irrelevant to the organization of social relationships, the problems of forming a new community have become largely those of establishing predictable personal relationships. Once established, therefore, the community is portable. Unlike the atoll model, in which the community is identified in terms of a particular place (the island), the new community is not identified in these terms. The decision to relocate a second time clearly implies the portability of the community and its irrelevance to a particular place in any terms other than instrumental ones.

For the Tikopia, Kapinga, Ambrymese, Banabans, and Southern Gilbertese, it is clear that change in the premises defining living together is preceded by and in some way depends on changes of a lower order. These lower-order changes are of two kinds—lifestyle and organization of social relationships. In all five cases, both types of change are designed to cope with specific problems. All these changes are the result of trial and error. People become committed to certain patterns of change because of their success in meeting adaptive needs, be it adaptation to a new ecological and social environment, as is seen with the Kapinga, Ambrymese, Tikopia, and Banabans, or adaptation to strangers who comprise the community, as in the case of the Southern Gilbertese. At these levels of change, the relationship between the community and its larger social and ecological context is important in every instance.

It is not unusual that changes in life-style and social organization in communities might ultimately contradict people's expectations of one another, expectations based on experience and unconscious assumptions about their relationships on their home islands. Ambrymese have reason to expect that a certain number of children will die each year as a result of sorcery. Kapinga have reason to expect help from other Kapinga when their community undertakes large and expensive projects. Tikopia have reason to expect that persons of high rank will be preeminent in making community decisions. Yet sorcery is virtually absent from the Maat Efate community, whose organization has changed in order to deal with outside agencies. The Kapinga distinguish themselves as members of different, politically autonomous communities. The Tikopia realize that those in the best position to make decisions for the Nukufero community are those with the most experience in dealing with commercial and colonial agencies.

It is neither necessary nor inevitable that such contradictions will become manifest to people in the community. The premises that people hold about themselves and their relationships are, more often than not, highly abstract and unconscious. The expectations of behavior and attitude that follow from these premises are not always met on their home islands even in the best of circumstances. Even when expectations are constantly contradicted by experience, people can ignore the contradictions or fail to see them for what they are, as is illustrated by the contradiction between personal and status relations on Kapingamarangi Atoll described in chapter 3. Change in the higher-order premises that define the meaning of living together, in other words, does not automatically follow a certain accumulation of change at lower levels of life-style and organization. Change at the level of premise is not dynamic in any sense of that term, nor is it the result of "impact" or "forces" or any other such metaphors that anthropologists are wont to borrow from physics. Contradictions are a matter of human perception, of the ordering of information that people have about themselves and the contexts they act in.

When decisions that must be made by a community hinge on resolving the contradictions between experience and expectations following from highly abstract premises, the contradictions become apparent and unavoidable. The context of making decisions about specific issues is the crucial condition of change in higher-order premises in all five communities. In the Banaban, Kapinga, and Tikopia communities, people explicitly discussed and redefined premises about living together. In the controversy over specific issues, the premises were consciously articulated and examined before being redefined. People moved from the issue to the premise and back to the issue in order to decide on a course of action. As Silverman points out, the decision on a specific course of action concretizes the change at the higher order. In the Ambrymese and Southern Gilbertese communities, the implication for the higher-level premise, rather than the premise itself, is under discussion. We can infer the change at the higher level from the manner in which people discuss the implications and the decisions they make about them.

The particular issues that bring about discussion, decision, and action in each community serve two important purposes. First, as has been pointed out already, such issues direct attention to the existence of a contradiction that makes explicit either a higher-level premise or its implications; the resolution of the contradiction involves changing the premise. Second, resolutions of these issues are moments in the history of the community during which past decisions and adaptive strategies, community organization, people's expectations of one another, and the premises on which their expectations are based are teased apart, examined, and pulled back together in order to reach sensible decisions. The issues thus serve as focal points around which people in the community organize their experience of change and articulate their own history in relation to current community needs.

## THE PROBLEM OF PREDICTION, AND PROGRAMMING RESETTLEMENT

Given the levels of the cultural system at which change occurs and the processes by which change occurs at each level, the problem of predicting change must be differentiated accordingly. Prediction at the lower levels, especially of life-style, seems to be possible, but not necessarily easy. For example, one could predict that given the Orokaiva decision to grow coffee as a cash crop, changes in economic organization, land tenure practices, and kin relationships must follow. Given the Bikinian decision to allocate land by household, certain changes in political organization and the structure of corporate kin groups were likely. Given an initial shortage of food-producing plants in Porakiet and the Kapinga need for cash, certain changes in Kapinga economic activity, and thus in life-style, must follow. But the nature of the givens in each of these examples constitutes a major problem. In the case of the Kapinga, knowing the structure of the Japanese colonial system on Ponape, the skills of Kapinga as fishermen, and the distribution of plant resources on Ponape allows a fair prediction of Kapinga adaptive strategies and their consequences for how the Kapinga allocate their time and resources. One does not need to know much about Kapinga culture in order to make such a prediction. In the Oro-kaiva case, we are dealing with an entirely different sort of given. First, the decision to grow coffee is an outcome of a decision to es-tablish a relationship with the colonial government; this decision is an outcome of a "contingency in its purest form," as Schwim-mer has demonstrated. Moreover, unless one sees the structure of the Orokaiva-administration relationship from the Orokaiva point of view, predictions of change based on the idea that the Orokaiva have "accepted" government programs must prove false. In the Bikinian case, allocating land by household was one of three possi-ble arrangements; the organizational implications of each de-pended on Bikinian assumptions about power, responsibility, and land and on political conflict and its resolution within the com-munity. Nothing in the relationship between the community and the administration or in the relationship between the community and the Kili ecosystem would lead us to expect that land distribu-tion would even be a problem to the Bikinians.

Prediction of change at the higher levels of a culture might be theoretically possible if we had adequate ethnographic accounts of social and cultural changes attendant on resettlement and a thorough ethnographic analysis for each community of the pre-mises that structure people's perceptions of themselves and their environment. In practical terms such prediction is impossible. More often than not, discovery of the premises of the culture under consideration comes precisely through analysis of the very sorts of change we are trying to predict. Moreover, in the analysis of higher-order changes, we are dealing with the types of contingen-cies that Schwimmer's analysis copes with, although they are not all so dramatic as a volcanic eruption. The specific issues that form the crucial context of change described here are, by and large, contingencies. One could hardly assert, for example, that the proposal for a land division of Porakiet and the request for an assessment of villagers for roofing materials for the atoll church would be inevitable issues in the Kapinga community on Ponape.

Given the history of the Kapinga settlement on Ponape, one can understand why these issues were important in changing Kapinga concepts of ethnicity and community, but prediction in such a case is out of the question.

The severe limitations on our ability to predict change in resettlement situations can give little comfort to governmental and other agencies contemplating relocation schemes. In the best of circumstances, adjustments to a new locale are not easy, nor are all the variables affecting it readily apparent. The provision by the responsible agency of adequate living and subsistence facilities for the emigrants, difficult enough to procure, is only the first step. What is adequate initially may not be sufficient subsequently, as we have seen in the Southern Gilbertese case. Natural population increase or higher aspirations may render the relocated community's facilities inadequate in a relatively short time. It can only be considered a lucky coincidence for the Southern Gilbertese that their decision to request a second relocation came at a time when the British administration was looking for ways to integrate its Gilbert and Ellice Island Colony with its Solomon Island Colony as a prelude to emancipation of both. Kapinga homesteaders relocated in Metalanimwh on Ponape were not so lucky; nor were the Bikinians relocated on Rongerik. One of the two tracts of land allocated to the Kapinga had very few productive trees growing on it. Even with the input of labor required to provide subsistence for the homesteaders, it would have taken two or three years for most of the homesteaders to produce an adequate food supply. The administration had agreed to provide food for only the first year of the program. By the end of the second year, all but seven of the homesteads had been abandoned.

Even when adequate subsistence and living facilities are assured—and what appears adequate to the administration may not be adequate for the emigrants, as we have seen in the Bikinian case —the administration has very little control over the relations between the resettled group and other ethnic groups who may be their neighbors. It can, of course, try to provide an area for resettlement that is isolated from other groups. It can also ensure that the relocated group is not annihilated by its neighbors. Other than these strategies, the relocating agency can do little to ensure even cordial interethnic relations. The idea that interethnic integration can be effected by political programming, strategic resettlements, and propaganda has become popular among colonial regimes in Oceania. The program of dissolution of ethnic boundaries (what McKnight calls "ethnocide") within a system whose very presence serves to maintain, if not to freeze, such boundaries is both contradictory and naive.

On the whole, the migrant communities' adjustments to their physical and social environments have been more stable and less conflict-ridden (both internally and externally) than have those of the relocated communities. This difference owes to the difference between the resettlement processes and to the fact that migrant communities have fewer variables affecting their adjustments. Migrants settling in a new location tend to be few in number, and their immediate problems are food and housing. Relations with neighbors, learning new skills, and assimilating new roles are adaptive responses acquired on the way to ensuring adequate subsistence. The early migrant enclaves tend to be organized by households and relationships between households; that is, kinship relations are the major organizational tools of migrant enclaves, at least until the enclave grows to the point where some higher level of organization is necessary to maintain it. Such problems are dealt with as they arise—for example, the Ambrymese organization of the community in their dealings with commercial firms and the Kapinga's political reorganization of Porakiet to maintain order and initiate work projects for a growing population. The growth of the community at every stage is geared to the problems that arise in the new environment. The structure of the community is the result of a series of decisions (and their ramifications), informed by their culture, as the need for collective action arises. The migrant community, in other words, is the result of an evolutionary process. Throughout the period of establishment and growth, we have seen that the migrant communities manage quite well without the aid of, or often the notice of, the colonial administration. Moreover, the demands of maintaining a relationship with the administration are not present to complicate the various issues with which the communities must deal.

The relocated community, by contrast, has to cope with the necessities of housing, subsistence, community organization, and the relationship with the administration simultaneously and immediately. Miscalculations regarding the environment (physical or social) by the administration or the community will be felt quickly.

The Bikinians' famine on Rongerik and the Southwest Islanders' position as an instant pariah group are good examples of oversight. Rectifying such errors (if that is possible) can be costly both to the community and to the administration, as U.S. Trust Territory officials have learned, and as the British government, now facing a huge lawsuit by the Banabans, may well learn. The extent to which the problems of community organization are connected with the community's relationship to the administration will make the problems of both more complicated. The Banaban relocation and its aftermath furnish a good example of this, especially in contrast to the Tikopia, whose community in the Russell Islands has developed without much interference from the administration.

It should be apparent at this point that with all the possibilities of oversight and miscalculation inherent in planning a relocation, a critical variable that need not be left to chance is the relationship between the community and the administration. This variable is at once abstract and intensely practical. Besides all the many details of the move and the establishment of the community that have to be worked out and agreed on, the details—and, more important, the form—of the relationship between the parties must be clear to both. Each side needs to know what the other believes the relationship to be, as well as what the other expects by way of concession, compliance, and action in the future. Usually, all these matters are under negotiation, but such negotiations are implicit and fraught with ambiguity rather than explicit and clear. Perhaps the best model of clarity in this volume is the Southern Gilbertese relationship with the British administration. With all their other problems, including creating a community from a collection of strangers, if the Southern Gilbertese community's relationship with the administration had been ambiguous, the resettlement probably would have been impossible. In contrast, the Bikinians' relationship with the Trust Territory at the outset was a model of ambiguity.

It is obvious from the data presented here that ambiguity in the relationship between the relocated community and the administration can be exploited by both sides, despite the vast difference of political and economic power between them. The exploitation of the Banabans by the British and the skill and success by which Bikinians gain concessions from the U.S. Trust Territory exemplify this point. Administrations might have an initial advantage in negotiating with their subject populations, but with a more sympathetic and effective international press, with a highly critical coalition of Third World nations making its presence felt in the United Nations, and with various other organizations, such as public interest law firms, willing to take up the cause of an exploited community, the initial advantage can be quickly neutralized.

Working out the relationship between a community and a colonial administration is a delicate process subject to misunderstanding in the best of circumstances and intentions—especially when the negotiating parties have different cultures and each party's view of the other, as well as of their relationship, is vague at best. Added to this problem is that of different modes of communication in which proper deference, for example, might be construed as agreement. It is clear that some skilled third party, an interpreter familiar with both cultures, is necessary in such negotiations. But the interpreter's relationship to each party needs to be at least as clear as the relationship between the negotiating parties. Social scientists have played these roles, but anthropologists in particular have become very sensitive about the ethical implications of their roles in negotiations between colonizers and colonized.

Monitoring the progress of the establishment of a new community is also extremely important. There are at least two ways in which this can be done. One way is for periodic surveys to be conducted by the responsible agency, but this approach has several drawbacks. There is a tendency for administrators to be overly optimistic about the progress of the community, and this is understandable. Administrators planning and carrying out a relocation have personal stakes in its success. Failure of the program (or the image of failure) can damage their careers. There is a tendency to gloss over problems in making reports to superiors. One corrective measure is to have representatives from another agency take part in the surveys. This has its own drawback, however, as it opens up the possibility of complicating the situation with interagency politics. A second monitoring strategy is to assign an administrative representative to the community for as long as it takes the community to establish itself or even on a permanent basis.[5] This was the strategy used in the Southern Gilbertese relocation (Knudson 1965). The British colonial agent participated in the establishment of the community, acting as coordinator and troubleshooter with the colonial office. The community's needs were communicated to the office headquarters on the spot rather than going unreported until they developed into crises, as happened with the Bikinians on Rongerik. This strategy has its own drawbacks, however, for it opens up the possibility that the administrator might become a pawn in community factional struggles, as seems to have happened on Rambi Island. But if the administration's positions and policies are clear to begin with, this sort of thing is far less likely to occur.

CONCLUSION

The resettlement of communities is an occurrence ancient in human history, although the study of such communities is recent. Comparative study of relocated communities was initiated by Homer Barnett, director of the Pacific Displaced Communities Project. The project was designed to study and compare twelve resettled communities in Oceania, six of which are reported in this volume. The project grew out of Barnett's theories of the process of culture change, specifically his theory of innovation as the basis of all culture change (Barnett 1953).

A culture, like any other viable system, must have the capacity for change. The process of innovation within a society, which Barnett has described, analyzed, and illustrated in detail, generates the variability within a community's culture that represents its capacity for change. Individual persons innovate, whereas the framework of community organization, belief, and interpersonal relations constrain innovative activity. A change in the physical, social, or geographical context of a community is necessarily a change in the constraints on innovative activity. Therefore, according to Barnett (1961), resettled communities are natural laboratories for the study of culture change.

Barnett's design for collecting field data (see the appendix to this volume) was ordered in terms of variables that influence change and stability. The variables are subdivided into those external to the community and those internal. These variables, which are seen as a set of constraints that either induce or inhibit innovative activity, correspond to variables of the macrosystem or the microsystem. On the basis of the comparative issues discussed in this volume, the outline of cultural variables in the appendix will afford anyone studying resettled communities in the future an extremely valuable guide for the collection of essential data.

The communities described here vary widely in terms of the circumstances of resettlement, their new environments, the relationships they have with the colonial system, and the specific changes they have undergone. Some are migrant communities; others have been relocated. Some communities resettle because of crisis; others do not. Some communities consist of the entire population of the home island; others comprise only part of the home island population. Two of the relocated communities consist of members of more than one ethnic group. It is regarding problems of community formation, the maintenance of and the changes in cultural systems, and the relations between the community and its context that comparison is most fruitful.

Resettled communities are phenomena of complex, hierarchically ordered social systems such as state and colonial systems. In these social systems, retention of ethnic identity is possible in a context of mobility of communities (or parts of communities). We have distinguished two processes of resettlement: migration and relocation. Also, we have determined that there are significant differences between migrant and relocated communities. First, the position of each type of community within the colonial (or state) system is different. Relocated communities are administrative units within the colonial system; they have ongoing administrative and political ties to the administration, its agencies, and nongovernmental institutions connected with the administration. Relocated communities negotiate with these agencies as a community. Adaptations that relocated communities make to their new contexts depend heavily on these negotiations. Migrant communities are not administrative units within the colonial system and are rarely in a position to negotiate as communities with colonial agencies. The adaptation of a migrant community depends largely on the relationships that community members, as individuals, are able to establish with the lower echelons of the colonial system— missions, commercial firms, and members of other ethnic groups.

The differences in position of migrant and relocated communities within the colonial system result in different processes of adaptation for each type of community. Migrant communities develop gradually through accretion of newcomers to a small core of emigrants. Ties of kinship and friendship are the major organizational modes at the outset. Newcomers are socialized to the new environment by older emigrants, who procure jobs and other aid for them and introduce them to other individuals and institutions outside the community. Kinship and friendship give way to other modes of organization when the population reaches a size that makes this organization inadequate for coping with issues affecting the entire population, as is seen in the formation of a council in Porakiet and the election of a headman in the Rotuman community at Vatukoula. These higher-level organizational modes, usually adaptations of home island models, serve primarily to deal with intracommunity problems, although they may also represent the community to the outside, as in the Maat Efate group's negotiating for land.

Relocated communities have different adaptive problems: a substantial population is transferred to a new locale in a relatively short time and must create its infrastructure immediately. Moreover, problems of recreating a social organization that is adequate for coping with the new locale arise simultaneously with those of housing and feeding the population. In every case, the adjustment of the relocated community requires a heavy initial dependence on administrative or other agencies charged with responsibility for the community (for example, Lever Company in the Tikopia case and the missions in the Orokaiva case). At the outset, negotiation with the administration is crucial to the survival of the community. Moreover, the negotiations set a pattern for the relationship between the community and the administration following the initial resettlement. Also, in every case, the problems of initial settlement release a tremendous amount of innovative activity in both subsistence and organizational spheres. This innovative activity includes the adaptation of old practices to new contexts, such as the Bikinians' use of communal organization of labor and food distribution on Rongerik and Kili, and the introduction of new practices, such as coffee growing by the Orokaiva and the 'council' in Nukufero. Of course, this trial and error process of "testing out" is characteristic of both migrant and relocated communities, but it is more visible in relocated communities because of the immediacy and complexity of adaptive problems and the relatively short time people have to develop solutions. It should be noted here that Barnett not only predicts that the rate of innovative activity will rise sharply in such situations, but he also accurately predicts the form the activity will take; this has been called "testing out" and ethnographically described in detail by Silverman (Barnett 1953: 80–89; Silverman 1971). Finally, relocated communities are far

less dependent for their maintenance on relations with other ethnic groups than are the migrant communities.

For both migrant and relocated communities, the problem of
community formation is ultimately the same. It is a problem of recreating a set of relationships among people in a new context. Of
all the variables listed in the appendix to this volume and discussed above, the one that is most crucial to the formation of a
community is the culture with which it starts its new settlement.
In a community's culture, the information people have about
themselves and their environment, along with the structuring of
perceptions of the ecosystem and of people and organizations outside the community, come together in a more or less coherent system of premises. The adaptive problems of a community are structured as much by the community's perceptions of itself and its
relations as by the "objective" facts these perceptions interpret
(and which are transformed into what the community considers
facts). Geographical spread of population, available land, the
presence of other ethnic groups, and the nature of colonial agents
become problems or nonproblems in community formation according to what it means to live together in that community.
These meanings are the assumptions people have about their relationships with one another; they are the (largely) unconscious
premises that define people, relationships between people, and
community. Because these assumptions define living together,
they must also define what constitutes the problems of living together, as we have seen in the data presented here. Resettlement
presents a host of novel problems to a community; much of a community's innovative activity replicates in novel ways the assumptions about living together. New skills, artifacts, and statuses are
transformed into socially meaningful activities as they become resources or means of access to resources to bring to relations within
the community.

Finally, the systemic nature of change in both the cultures of
the resettled communities and the colonial systems of which they
are part is the same. The structure of the colonial system might require that its subject peoples be mobile, especially when large-
scale administrative projects and commercial operations require
large labor forces. Resettlement is one way of securing labor. In
general, as Chapman pointed out to participants in the relocation
symposium, the maintenance of the colonial system might require

more or less constant changes in its constituent populations. In every instance reported in this volume, resettlement has contributed in some important way to the maintenance of the colonial system. We see exactly the same principle operating in the resettled community (or the microsystem): maintaining the higher orders of a system often involves changes at the lower orders. This was true of the Nukuoro, Bikinians, Rotumans, Southern Gilbertese, and Orokaiva. We can add to this list the Banaban, Kapinga, and Tikopia instances of change in higher-order premises. For the Kapinga, change in the concept of community conserves the concepts of personhood and responsibility (Lieber 1974:91–92). For the Banabans, concepts of 'farmer', 'worker', and other roles and relationships between those roles are subjected to change in such a manner that each is still consistent with the higher-order concepts of land and freedom. When the Tikopia concept of custom begins to change, the premise that underlies it—that there is a distinctive order that is uniquely Tikopia—remains unquestioned. This type of change is an evolutionary process that is typical of viable systems, whether they are cultural or biological.

## NOTES

I would like to acknowledge the generosity of Homer Barnett, Vern Carroll, David Schneider, and Martin Silverman, who provided valuable criticisms and suggestions on earlier drafts of this chapter.

1. This use of the term "relocation" in no way departs from its normal usage. Ambiguity is introduced when the definition of the term is expanded to include migration.
2. The maps in this volume differentiate each kind of community with the label "relocation" for the relocated communities and "movement" for the migrant communities.
3. By "infrastructure" I mean those resources necessary to maintain the community, such as locally produced foods, access to land, materials for construction, techniques of production, and so forth.
4. Alan Howard, in a personal note, reports that the Rotumans in Suva are now seriously discussing the possibility of arranging *en bloc* housing.
5. Ideally, the representative would be defined as a community advocate (and would not be punished by the administration for acting as such). The community advocate should also be replaceable if the community believes that the advocate is not adequately representing its interests.

# APPENDIX:

## FIELD GUIDE TO THE COLLECTION OF DATA ON VARIABLES INFLUENCING CHANGE AND STABILITY IN RESETTLED COMMUNITIES

INTRODUCTION

The outline presented here is a slightly modified version of the Outline of Cultural Variables used as a guide to collecting field data on resettled communities by members of the Project for the Study of Cultural Change and Stability in Displaced Communities in Oceania. The modifications have been mainly editorial ones to make the outline more readable. The original version can be found in Larson (1966:179–182).

The outline lists the major categories of variables influencing change and stability in resettled communities under "external" (macrosystem) variables and "internal" (microsystem) variables. Under each major category are listed specific variables. None of these should be taken to be exhaustive of the category but rather as examples of what one might encounter in the field. Under the category "topography" (I.B.2 in the outline), for example, one might find that mountains make a difference in the adaptation of a resettled atoll community living on a high island, although that variable is not listed in the outline. Under the category "addition and loss of members" (II.F), one might find, when collecting data on mobility in the community, that ship passenger lists are available so that detailed information on movement of people to and from the relocated community can be used as a basis for questioning informants and establishing demographic patterns. Although this variable is not listed under the category, the specific variables that are listed do suggest collection of such information if it is available. That specific variables listed are suggestions and examples is indicated by the frequent inclusion of "et cetera."

In a situation in which part of an island community had been resettled and the field researcher had access to both the resettled and the home communities, researchers in Homer Barnett's project found it useful to employ the outline to collect comparable sets of data from both communities. As a field procedure, this helped highlight areas of change as well as those of stability in both communities.

THE OUTLINE

I. External influences: variables outside the community
  A. Circumstances contributing to the decision to resettle
    1. Initiating conditions
      a. Environmental variables
        (1) Land shortage
        (2) Drought
        (3) Volcanic eruption
        (4) Isolation, etc.
      b. Social variables
        (1) Factionalism within the community
        (2) Economic depression (as in the 1930s and after World War II), etc.
    2. Source of the suggestion to resettle
      a. Government or other colonial agency
      b. Native leaders
      c. Examples of other communities that have been removed, etc.
    3. The decision to resettle
      a. Participation in the decision
        (1) Total community (e.g., in a formal meeting)
        (2) Native council
        (3) Individual families, etc.
      b. The procedure of resettlement
        (1) Presentation of the argument for resettlement
        (2) Advance inspection of the new location
        (3) Emergency evacuation, etc.

    c. Community attitudes toward the necessity of resettle-
       ment

      (1) Differences of opinion (if any) between individuals or
          categories of persons

         (a) Men as contrasted with women

         (b) Young as contrasted with old

         (c) Leaders as contrasted with nonleaders

         (d) Government officials as contrasted with community
            leaders

         (e) Educated as contrasted with parochial

         (f) More prosperous as contrasted with less prosperous

      (2) Differences of opinion (if any) between earlier and
          later emigrants

         (a) At the time of removal

         (b) After the community has been established

         (c) After the initiating crisis (if any) has passed

B. Physical variables affecting change and stability

  1. Climate—effect of temperature, storms, seasonal fluctua-
    tions, etc., on

    a. Clothing, housing, etc.

    b. Subsistence activities

    c. Contacts with outsiders, etc.

  2. Topography—effect of the new area's size, its relief, beach
    area, streams, water table, reefs, etc., on

    a. Village ground plan, paths, roads, etc.

    b. Location of farmland, groves, etc.

    c. Subsistence activities

    d. Internal communication, communication with outsiders,
      etc.

  3. Strategic resouces—effect of their kind and location on

    a. Availability and exploitation of local products for food,
      construction, or commerce

  4. Location with respect to other islands, affecting

    a. Visiting patterns

    b. Wage labor

    c. Commercial development

    d. Acculturation, etc.

C. Social variables affecting change and stability

  1. Opportunity for contact (before and after resettlement)
    with outsiders

    a. Identity of the outsiders—Americans, British, etc.

    b. Status and role of the outsiders
       (1) Colonial agents—administrators, armed forces, trad-
          ers, employers, missionaries, tourists, etc.
       (2) Natives of other islands—ships' crews, mission person-
          nel, people on the way to other islands, etc.
    c. Differences within the community with respect to oppor-
      tunities for contact with outsiders
       (1) Men as contrasted with women—do women in the
          community, for example, have a chance to meet Brit-
          ish women and men?
       (2) Young as contrasted with old
       (3) Chiefs as contrasted with commoners
       (4) Spokesmen, etc.—do only leaders of the community,
          for example, have appreciable contact with outsiders?
2. Kind and amount of contact by persons in the community
  (young, old, men, women, etc.) with outsiders
    a. Daily, periodic, planned, casual, incidental, impersonal,
      commercial, etc.
    b. Marriage with outsiders
       (1) Frequency of occurrence
       (2) Rights and obligations with respect to affinal kinsmen
          —economic cooperation, coresidence, etc.
    c. Friendship with outsiders
       (1) "Trade partnerships"
       (2) Adoption of individuals or whole families by outsid-
          ers, etc.
3. Locale of contact with outsiders—inside or outside the village
4. Initiators of contact—community members or outsiders
5. Different reactions to categories of outsiders
    a. Americans as contrasted with British
    b. Europeans as contrasted with indigenous neighbors
    c. Traders as contrasted with missionaries, etc.
6. Attitudes toward neighbors
    a. Hostile
    b. Suspicious
    c. Aloof
    d. Superior
    e. Inferior, etc.
7. Attitudes of neighbors toward the emigrants
    a. Hospitable

b. Resentful

c. Contemptous, etc.

8. Group self-image

  a. Mistreated

  b. Unlucky

  c. Indomitable

  d. Pioneers

  e. Failures

  f. Representatives of their people, etc.

9. Acculturation within the community

  a. Learning new skills from outsiders

  b. Accepting outsiders' customs—food, house types, etc.

  c. Involvement with outsiders socially through

    (1) Church activity

    (2) Employment or commercial enterprise

    (3) Entertainment—bars, theaters, etc.

    (4) Accepting favors

10. Impact of resettlement on community organization with respect to

  a. Leadership

  b. Interpersonal relations, including those among kinsmen

  c. Work groups, including labor for village benefit

  d. Social and recreational groups and the occasions when they actively function

  e. Religious activities

  f. Cooperatives and other commercial enterprises

  g. Individualism and independence of primary kin groups

  h. Temporary procedures and patterns of behavior (said to replace traditional behavior until the community is well established)

D. Contact with congeners

1. Category of contact

  a. Contact before resettlement (e.g., Gilbertese and Ellice Islanders living and working together on Ocean Island, Tarawa, and Canton, etc.)

  b. Contact between the resettled community and the homeland (e.g., Tikopia in the Russell Islands)

  c. Contact between two relocated communities (e.g., Southern Gilbertese on Sydney and Gardner Islands)

2. Kind and frequency of contact

  a. Correspondence and visiting

b. Return to the homeland

c. New emigrants joining the resettled community

d. Schooling for children, etc.

3. Encouragement of contact (or the lack of it)

a. By government policy

b. By community leaders in the relocated and the home communities

4. Contact with congeners as it influences morale in the resettled community

a. Homesickness

b. Maintenance of identification with the homeland and its customs

c. Severance with tradition

d. Pride as pioneers

e. Dissatisfaction or self-justification resulting from comparison with others

f. Fear of losing land or other rights and privileges at home

E. Disease

1. The community as a carrier of disease

2. The community as a victim of unfamiliar disease

3. The community's perception of the new location as healthy or unhealthy

F. Government welfare efforts*

1. Resettlement plans and their implementation

a. Reasons for choosing the site for resettlement

b. Procedure of resettlement

(1) Government supervision (e.g., a resettlement officer)—assistance in removal from home island, in constructing the new village, etc.

(2) Reconnaissance party to survey the site for resettlement

(3) Advance work party to clear land, construct temporary houses, etc.

(4) Waves of emigrants or total community arriving at one time

---

\* In all instances attempt to determine the extent of government efforts to adapt measures to traditions of the community, to plan measures in consultation with community leaders, and whether a procedure or an innovation was proposed by a government agent or by a person in the community.

(5) Initial living arrangements for the settlers

c. Relation of settlers to the homeland

    (1) Maintenance of rights to land and position with expectations of eventual return to the homeland

    (2) Renunciation of land rights and foreclosure of possibility for return

    (3) Payment for expropriated homeland by the government

    (4) Income from produce of the homeland (e.g., royalty money for phosphate on Ocean Island)

d. Traditional value placed on land ownership

    (1) Basis of social control and prestige

    (2) Secondary to use rights, fishing rights, and other forms of property

e. Land tenure in the new location

    (1) Government policy regulating land tenure as opposed to land tenure being left up to the community to decide

    (2) Type of ownership

        (a) Communal

        (b) Individual

        (c) Kin group, etc.

    (3) System of allocating land plots

        (a) Individual choice

        (b) Drawing lots

        (c) Priorities of selection, etc.

    (4) Unit of allocation

        (a) To individuals

        (b) To families

        (c) To descent groups, etc.

    (5) Temporary or permanent assignment of land

    (6) Land survey, formal registration of allocated plots, etc.

f. Duration of relocation

    (1) Effect of duration on the adjustment of emigrants—do younger members of the community, for example, want to go back to the homeland of their parents?

g. Number of relocations

h. Actual or alleged governmental encouragement of hopes to

    (1) Return to the homeland

    (2) Resettle a second or third time

    2. Health measures
       a. Provision of dispensaries, hospital services, medical aides, drugs, etc.
       b. Public health programs—mosquito control, innoculations, latrines, sanitation regulations, etc.
    3. Economic assistance
       a. Issues of food in the initial (or other) stages of the resettled community's development
       b. Issues of cuttings and seeds, tools, etc.
       c. Advice and assistance by experts on
         (1) Agricultural development
         (2) Fishing techniques
         (3) Commercial development, including rewards (or lack of them) for clearing land, planting certain crops (such as cacao), etc.
    4. Education
       a. Extent to which it is available
         (1) Inside or outside the village
         (2) Day school, boarding school, etc.
         (3) Curriculum—language, subjects, vocational, etc.
       b. Extent to which it is required
         (1) Compulsory or voluntary
         (2) Age requirements
         (3) Standardization of curriculum
       c. Sponsorship, such as by government or by church
       d. Teachers
         (1) Ethnic affiliation, family status (if relevant) of teachers
         (2) Source of training, pay
         (3) Language of instruction
       e. Provision of school buildings, supplies, educational materials
       f. Attitudes toward education
       g. Literature available in the language read
    5. Attitudes toward the government
G. Mission welfare efforts
    1. Consider all items listed under government welfare efforts that are relevant
    2. Provision of resources for members of the community
       a. Recreation

      b. Community projects—health programs, house improvement, etc.
   3. Provision and training of pastors
      a. Ethnic identity of pastors
      b. Religious affiliation of pastors
      c. Relationship of the pastor to the community
         (1) Teacher-preacher combination
         (2) Pastor's identification with the community
         (3) Pastor's role and position—is he, for example, a strong political voice in the community?
         (4) Community support of the pastor (material or other)
         (5) Change in religious affiliation with resettlement (e.g., Southern Gilbertese Protestants in Titiana)
 H. Selection of emigrants
   1. Nonselection: all members of the community resettled
   2. Selection by government based on
      a. Quotas for age, sex, state of health, skills, etc.
      b. Family status, political position in the community, etc.
      c. Economic status on the home island
   3. Self-selection by community members
      a. Criteria for deciding who can emigrate
      b. Reasons for emigrating
         (1) Joining friends or relatives
         (2) Seeking jobs, adventure, etc.
         (3) Factionalism or deteriorating relationships on the home island
II. Internal influences: variables within the resettled community
 A. Size and distribution of the resettled community
   1. Concentrated in a single village
   2. Segmented into two or more villages
   3. Dispersed in individual homesteads or hamlets
   4. Attitudes toward integration with neighbors
 B. Socioeconomic variables
   1. Distribution within the community of
      a. Age, sex, marital status, dependents
      b. Division of labor
      c. Occupational skills (and money income)
      d. Available mates
      e. Available manpower for community needs
      f. Education

C. Homogeneity of background of community members
    1. All from one island or from more than one island
    2. All from one village or region of the same island or from different villages or regions
    3. Differences within the community
      a. Dialects, traditional histories, etc.
      b. Affiliation with groups outside the community, such as different churches
D. Degree of acculturation at the time of resettlement
    1. Abandonment of precontact indigenous customs because of government or church regulation, etc.
    2. Adoption of foreign customs
      a. Dress, house types, tools, etc.
      b. Skills, wage work, use of money
      c. Formal education, bilingualism, etc.
      d. Reasons for adopting new customs
E. Familiarity with the new homeland before resettlement
    1. Limited to reconnaissance by community representatives
    2. Known from visits before resettlement (e.g., through travel, work, etc.)
    3. Known by tradition or hearsay
F. Addition and loss of members
    1. Births and deaths
    2. Continuing emigration (including repatriation) because of
      a. Reuniting families, joining friends
      b. Securing heirs, wage work, or education
      c. Land shortages, labor opportunities
      d. Government regulation or policy (e.g., conscription of labor by Japanese in Micronesia)
    3. Community segmentation
    4. Intermarriage, adoption, friendship
    5. Residence in urban centers, on plantations, etc.
G. Key persons who have had a significant influence on the course of events in the resettled community
    1. Native and nonnative residents of the community (such as Gallagher on Sydney Island or *you*, the anthropologist)
    2. Social isolates, marginal individuals, "troublemakers," etc.
H. Factionalism, whether actual or incipient, with regard to
    1. Religious or political activity
    2. Ethnic affiliation

    3. Generational factionalism, etc.

I. Adherence to tradition

    1. Actual as opposed to alleged observance of tradition

       a. Informants' descriptions as contrasted with anthropologist's observations

       b. Informants' reasons for deviating from tradition

    2. Constraints influencing maintenance or nonmaintenance of traditional practices

       a. Training of young people

       b. Position of and respect for elders in the community

       c. Obligations of individuals (and their possibilities of fulfillment) to kinsmen and community

       d. Ease of escape from community obligations

       e. Sensitivity to the opinions of friends and relatives on the home island

       f. Formal mechanisms of reward and punishment

          (1) Councils, committees, courts, police, etc.

          (2) Positions of prestige (e.g., within the village polity or local church)

J. Esprit de corps as defined by Linton (1936:92–94)

# REFERENCES

Alkire, William H.
  1972  *An Introduction to the Peoples and Cultures of Micronesia.*
         McCaleb Module no. 18, Addison-Wesley Publications in An-
         thropology. Reading, Massachusetts: Addison-Wesley.

Althusser, Louis
  1969  *For Marx.* New York: Vintage Books.

Barnett, Homer G.
  1953  *Innovation: The Basis of Culture Change.* New York:
         McGraw-Hill.
  1961  "A comparative study of cultural change and stability in
         displaced communities." Grant application to the National
         Science Foundation.

Barth, Fredrik
  1966  *Models of Social Organization.* Royal Anthropological Insti-
         tute of Great Britain and Ireland, Occasional Paper no. 23.
         London: Royal Anthropological Institute.
  1969  "Introduction." In *Ethnic Groups and Boundaries: The Or-
         ganization of Cultural Difference*, edited by Fredrik Barth.
         Boston: Little, Brown.
  1971  "Tribes and intertribal relations in the Fly headwaters."
         *Oceania* 41:171–191.

Barthes, Roland
  1964a "Rhetorique de l'image." *Communications* 4:40–51.

1964b "Elements de semeiology." *Communications* 4:91–144.

Bascom, William
1950 "Ponape: the tradition of retaliation." *Far Eastern Quarterly* 10:56–62.

Bateson, Gregory
1935 "Culture contact and schismogenesis." *Man* 35:178–183. Reprinted 1972 in *Steps to an Ecology of Mind*, by Gregory Bateson. New York: Ballantine Books.
1951 "Information, codification and metacommunication." In *Communication: The Social Matrix of Psychiatry*, by Jurgen Reusch and Gregory Bateson. New York: Norton.
1967 "Cybernetic explanation." *American Behavioral Scientist* 10:29–32. Reprinted 1972 in *Steps to an Ecology of Mind*, by Gregory Bateson. New York: Ballantine Books.
1972 *Steps to an Ecology of Mind*. New York: Ballantine Books.

Belshaw, Cyril S.
1951 "Social consequences of the Mount Lamington eruption." *Oceania* 21:241–252.

Benson, Canon James
1955a "The Bapa Saga and the brothers Ambo." *The Anglican* (Melbourne), 4 March 1955, p. 6.
1955b "Kirikiri and Gatara." *The Anglican* (Melbourne), 18 March 1955, p. 6.

Berger, Peter
1969 *The Sacred Canopy*. New York: Doubleday.

Black, Max
1962 "Metaphor." In *Models and Metaphors*, by Max Black. Ithaca: Cornell University Press.

Blau, Peter
1964 *Exchange and Power in Social Life*. New York: Wiley.

British Solomon Island Publications (BSIP)
1965 *Facts about the British Solomon Islands Protectorate*. Honiara: Information Service, BSIP.

Brookfield, H. C., Paula Glick, and Doreen Hart
1969 "Melanesian Mélange: the market at Vila, New Hebrides." In *Pacific Market Places*, edited by H. C. Brookfield. Canberra: Australian National University Press.

Burke, Kenneth
1957 *The Philosophy of Literary Form*. Rev. ed. New York: Vintage Books.
1962 *A Grammar of Motives and A Rhetoric of Motives*. Cleveland: Meridian Books.

Burridge, Kennelm O. L.
  1960   *Mambu: A Melanesian Millennium*. London: Methuen.
  1969   *New Heaven, New Earth*. Oxford: Basil Blackwell.
Carroll, Vern
  1966   "Nukuoro kinship." Ph.D. dissertation, University of Chicago. (Copies available from the University of Chicago Photoduplication Service.)
  1970   "Adoption on Nukuoro." In *Adoption in Eastern Oceania*, edited by Vern Carroll. ASAO Monograph no. 1. Honolulu: University of Hawaii Press.
  1975a  "The demography of communities." In *Pacific Atoll Populations*, edited by Vern Carroll. ASAO Monograph no. 3. Honolulu: University Press of Hawaii.
  1975b  "The population of Nukuoro in historical perspective." In *Pacific Atoll Populations*, edited by Vern Carroll. ASAO Monograph no. 3. Honolulu: University Press of Hawaii.
Catala, Rene L. A.
  1957   *Report on the Gilbert and Ellice Islands: Some Aspects of Human Ecology*. Atoll Research Bulletin no. 59. Washington, D.C.: Pacific Science Board, National Academy of Sciences—National Research Council.
Chinnery, E. W. P. and A. C. Haddon
  1917   "Five new religious cults in British New Guinea." *Hibbert Journal* 15:448–463.
Cochrane, D. G.
  1969   "Racialism in the Pacific: a descriptive analysis." *Oceania* 40:1–12.
Courteney, P. P.
  1965   *Plantation Agriculture*. New York: Praeger.
Crocombe, Ronald G. and G. R. Hogbin
  1963   *Land, Work, and Productivity at Inonda*. Canberra and Port Moresby: Australian National University, New Guinea Research Unit Bulletin no. 2.
Dakeyne, R. B.
  1966   "Cooperatives at Yega." In *Orokaiva Papers*. Canberra and Port Moresby: Australian National University, New Guinea Research Unit Bulletin no. 13, pp. 53–68.
Drucker, Phillip
  1950   "The ex-Bikini occupants of Kili Island." Unpublished report to the High Commissioner of the U.S. Trust Territory of the Pacific Islands. (Copy located in the Trust Territory files at Headquarters, Saipan; 67 pp.)

Dumont, Louis
    1970    *Homo Hierarchicus.* Chicago: University of Chicago Press.
Elbert, Samuel H.
    1949    "Uta-matua and other tales of Kapingamarangi." *Journal of American Folklore* 62:240–246.
Emory, Kenneth
    1965    *Kapingamarangi: Social and Religious Life of a Polynesian Atoll.* Bernice P. Bishop Museum Bulletin 228. Honolulu: Bernice P. Bishop Museum.
Epstein, A. L.
    1963    "The economy of modern Matupit." *Oceania* 33:182–215.
    1969    *Matupit: Land, Politics and Change among the Tolai of New Britain.* Berkeley: University of California Press.
Fiji Legislative Council
    1922    *Fiji Census, 1921.* Legislative Council Paper no. 2. Suva: S. Bach, Government Printer.
Firth, Raymond
    1931    "A Native voyage to Rennell." *Oceania* 2:179–190.
    1936    *We, the Tikopia.* Boston: Beacon Paperback Press.
    1939    *Primitive Polynesian Economy.* London: George Routledge and Sons.
    1954    "Anuta and Tikopia: symbiotic elements in social organization." *Journal of Polynesian Society* 63:87–131.
    1959    *Social Change in Tikopia.* London: Allen and Unwin.
    1969    "Extraterritoriality and the Tikopia chiefs." *Man* 4:354–378.
Francis, E. K.
    1947    "The nature of the ethnic group." *American Journal of Sociology* 52:393–400.
Frater, M.
    1922    *Midst Volcanic Fires.* London: J. Clarke.
Gallie, W. B.
    1962    "Essentially contested concepts." In *The Importance of Language,* edited by Max Black. Englewood Cliffs, New Jersey: Prentice-Hall (Spectrum Books).
Garbett, J. Kingsley
    1970    "The analysis of social situations." *Man* 5:214–227.
Geertz, Clifford
    1964    "Ideology as a cultural system." In *Ideology and Discontent,* edited by David Apter. New York: Free Press.
    1965    *The Social History of an Indonesian Town.* Cambridge: M.I.T. Press.

1966    "Religion as a cultural system." In *Anthropological Approaches to the Study of Religion*, edited by Michael Banton. ASA Monograph no. 3. London: Tavistock Publications.

Geslin, Y.
1956    "Les Américains aux Nouvelles-Hébrides." *Journal de la Société des Océanistes* 12:245–285.

Goffman, Erving
1963    *Stigma*. Englewood Cliffs, New Jersey: Prentice-Hall.

Goodenough, Ward H.
1955    "A problem in Malayo-Polynesian social organization." *American Anthropologist* 57:71–83.
1963    *Cooperation in Change: An Anthropological Approach to Community Development*. New York: Russell Sage Foundation.

Grimble, Arthur
1921    "From birth to death in the Gilbert Islands." *Journal of the Royal Anthropological Institute* 51:25–54.

Guiart, Jean
1951a    "Sociétés, rituels et mythes du Nord-Ambrym (Nouvelles-Hébrides)." *Journal de la Société des Océanistes* 7:5–103.
1951b    "Forerunners of Melanesian nationalism." *Oceania* 22:81–90.
1956a    "Unité culturelle et variations locales dans le centre nord des Nouvelles-Hébrides." *Journal de la Société des Océanistes* 12:217–225.
1956b    "Système de parenté et organization matrimoniale à Ambrym." *Journal de la Société des Océanistes* 12:301–326.
1956c    *Un Siècle et demi de Contacts Culturels à Tanna (Nouvelle-Hébrides)*. Paris: Société des Océanistes.

Harding, Thomas G.
1971    "Wage labor and cash cropping: the economic adaptation of New Guinea copra producers." *Oceania* 41:192–200.

Hilder, Brett
1961    *Navigator in the South Seas*. London: Percival Marshall and Company.

Hiller, E. T.
1947    *Social Relations and Structures*. New York: Harper and Brothers.

Hines, Neal O.
1962    *Proving Ground: An Account of the Radiobiological Studies in the Pacific, 1946–1961*. Seattle: University of Washington Press.

Hjelmslev, L.
  1963    *Prolegomena to a Theory of Language.* Madison: University of Wisconsin Press.

Hobbs, William
  1923    *Cruises along the Byways of the Pacific.* London: Stratford Company.

Homans, George C.
  1961    *Social Behavior: Its Elementary Forms.* London: Routledge and Kegan Paul.

Howard, Alan
  1961    "Rotuma as a hinterland community." *Journal of the Polynesian Society* 70:272–299.
  1963a   "Conservatism and non-traditional leadership in Rotuma." *Journal of the Polynesian Society* 72:65–77.
  1963b   "Land, activity systems, and decision-making models in Rotuma." *Ethnology* 2:407–440.
  1964    "Land tenure and social change in Rotuma." *Journal of the Polynesian Society* 73:26–52.
  1970    *Learning to be Rotuman.* New York: Teachers College Press, Columbia University.

Howard, Alan and Irwin Howard
  1964    "Pre-marital sex and social control among the Rotumans." *American Anthropologist* 66:266–283.

Kaneshiro, Shigeru
  1958    "Land tenure in the Palau Islands." In *Land Tenure Patterns: Trust Territory of the Pacific Islands*, vol. 1, edited by John de Young. Guam: Office of the High Commissioner, U.S. Trust Territory of the Pacific Islands.

Keesing, Felix M.
  1952    "Papuan Orokaiva vs. Mount Lamington: cultural shock and its aftermath." *Human Organization* 2(1):16–22.

Kiste, Robert C.
  1968    *Kili Island: A Study of the Relocation of the Ex-Bikini Marshallese.* Eugene: University of Oregon, Department of Anthropology.
  1972    "Relocation and technological change in Micronesia." In *Technology and Social Change*, edited by H. R. Bernard and P. Pelto. New York: Macmillan.
  1974    *The Bikinians: A Study in Forced Migration.* Menlo Park, California: Cummings.

Kleekham, Fred
  n.d.    Unpublished, untitled manuscript available in the New Guinea Research Unit Library in Port Moresby, New Guinea.

Knudson, Kenneth
  1965    *Titiana: A Gilbertese Community in the Solomon Islands.*
          Eugene: University of Oregon, Department of Anthropology.
  1970    "Resource fluctuation, productivity, and social organization
          on Micronesian coral atolls." Ph.D. dissertation, University
          of Oregon. (Available from University Microfilms, Ann Ar-
          bor, Michigan.)

Lacan, Jacques
  1966    *Écrits.* Paris: Seuil.

Lambert, Bernd
  1966    "The economic activities of a Gilbertese chief." In *Political
          Anthropology*, edited by Marc J. Swartz, Victor W. Turner,
          and Arthur Tuden. Chicago: Aldine.

Lane, Robert B.
  1965    "The Melanesians of South Pentacost, New Hebrides." In
          *Gods, Ghosts and Men in Melanesia*, edited by Peter Law-
          rence and Mervin J. Meggitt. Melbourne: Oxford University
          Press.

Larson, Eric
  1966    *Nukufero: A Tikopian Colony in the Russell Islands.* Eugene:
          University of Oregon, Department of Anthropology.

Laxton, P. B.
  1951    "Nikumaroro." *Journal of the Polynesian Society* 60:134–
          159.

Leach, Edmund
  1954    *Political Systems of Highland Burma.* Boston: Beacon Press.
  1970    *Lévi-Strauss.* New York: Viking.

Lessa, William A.
  1964    "The social effects of typhoon Ophelia (1960) on Ulithi."
          *Micronesica* 1:1–47.

Lévi-Strauss, Claude
  1958    *Anthropologie Structurale.* Paris: Plon.
  1960    Leçon Inaugurale. Paris: College de France.
  1962    *La Pensée Sauvage.* Paris: Plon.
  1966    *The Savage Mind.* Chicago: University of Chicago Press.

Lieber, Michael D.
  1968a   "The nature of the relationship between kinship and land
          tenure on Kapingamarangi Atoll." Ph.D. dissertation, Uni-
          versity of Pittsburgh. (Available from University Microfilms,
          Ann Arbor, Michigan.)
  1968b   *Porakiet: A Kapingamarangi Colony on Ponape.* Eugene:
          University of Oregon, Department of Anthropology.

1972 "Person, role, and relationship on Kapingamarangi." Paper presented at the 73rd annual meeting of the American Anthropological Association. Toronto, Canada. (Available from the author.)

1974 "Land tenure on Kapingamarangi." In *Land Tenure in Oceania*, edited by Henry P. Lundsgaarde. ASAO Monograph no. 2. Honolulu: University Press of Hawaii.

Linton, Ralph
1936 *The Study of Man*. New York: Appleton-Century.

Lundsgaarde, Henry P.
1966 *Cultural Adaptation in the Southern Gilbert Islands*. Eugene: University of Oregon, Department of Anthropology.
n.d. *Social Change in the Southern Gilbert Islands*. Eugene: University of Oregon, Department of Anthropology.

Lundsgaarde, Henry P. and Martin G. Silverman
1972 "Category and group in Gilbertese kinship: an updating of Goodenough's analysis." *Ethnology* 11:95–110.

Luomala, Katharine
1965 "Humorous narratives about individual resistance to food distribution customs in Tabiteuea, Gilbert Islands." *Journal of American Folklore* 78:28–45.

MacKenzie, Boyd
1961 Memorandum to the District Administrator, Marshall Islands. (Copy located in the files at district headquarters, Majuro, Marshall Islands.)

Mair, Lucy
1965 "How small scale societies change." In *Penguin Survey of the Social Sciences 1965*. Baltimore: Penguin Books.

Mao Tse-tung
1965 "On contradiction." In *Selected Works of Mao Tse-tung*, vol. 1. Peking: Foreign Languages Press.

Markwith, Carl
1946 "Farewell to Bikini." *National Geographic* 90(1):97–116.

Maruyama, Magoroh
1963 "The second cybernetics: deviation-amplifying mutual causal processes." *American Scientist* 51:164–179.

Mason, Leonard
1947 "Economic organization of the Marshall Islanders." *Economic Survey of Micronesia*. U.S. Commercial Company Report no. 9. (Available in microfilm from the Library of Congress.)
1954 "Relocation of the Bikini Marshallese." Ph.D. dissertation,

Yale University. (Available from University Microfilms, Ann Arbor, Michigan.)

1958    "Kili community in transition." *South Pacific Bulletin* 8(2): 32–35.

Maude, H. C. and H. E. Maude

1931    "Adoption in the Gilbert Islands." *Journal of the Polynesian Society* 40:225–235.

Maude, H. E.

1950    "The co-operative movement in the Gilbert and Ellice Islands." *Proceedings of the Seventh Pacific Science Congress* 7:63–76.

1952    "The colonization of the Phoenix Islands." *Journal of the Polynesian Society* 61:62–89.

1960    "The evolution of local government in the Gilbert Islands: an historical reconstruction." Unpublished manuscript, courtesy of the author.

1961    "Post-Spanish discoveries in the Central Pacific." *Journal of the Polynesian Society* 70:67–111.

1963    *Evolution of the Gilbertese Boti: An Ethnohistorical Interpretation.* Polynesian Society Memoir 35. Wellington: The Polynesian Society. (Originally published as a supplement to *Journal of the Polynesian Society* 72:[1] 1963.)

1967    "The swords of Gabriel: a study in participant history." *Journal of Pacific History* 2:113–136.

McArthur, Norma

1958    *Report on the Census of the Population, 1956.* Fijian Legislative Council Paper no. 9. Suva: Government Press.

McArthur, Norma and J. F. Yaxley

1968    *Condominium of the New Hebrides: A Report on the First Census of the Population, 1967.* Sydney: Government Printer.

McKnight, Robert K.

1960    "Competition in Palau." Ph.D. dissertation, Ohio State University. (Available from University Microfilms, Ann Arbor, Michigan.)

Mead, Margaret

1964    "The study of the total communication process." In *Approaches to Semiotics,* edited by Thomas Sebiok. The Hague: Mouton.

Meade, Lt. (jg.) Herbert C.

1946    "Operation Crossroads: resettlement of the Bikini population." Unpublished report on administration of the military government for the month of March by the Island Commander, Kwajalein, to the Commander, Marianas. Copy available from R. C. Kiste.

*Micronesian Independent* (Majuro)
1975a   "Bikinians may win yet," 6(32):1–2.
1975b   "Bikinians filing case in Hawaii federal court," 6(35):10.

Murphy, Robert F. and Julian H. Steward
1956   "Tappers and trappers: parallel processes in acculturation." *Economic Development and Cultural Change* 4:335–353.

Myint, Hla
1965   *The Economics of the Developing Countries.* New York: Praeger.

Nathan Associates, Inc., Robert R.
1966   *Economic Development Plan for Micronesia.* Prepared for the High Commissioner of the Trust Territory of the Pacific Islands. Washington, D.C.: Robert R. Nathan Associates. Mimeographed.

Peacock, James L.
1968   *Rites of Modernization.* Chicago: University of Chicago Press.

Plant, H. T.
1951   "Reestablishment of the Isivita villages." Unpublished manuscript. (Copy available in the New Guinea Research Unit Library.)

Reay, Marie
1953   "Social control among the Orokaiva." *Oceania* 24:110–118.

Richards, Lt. Comdr. Dorothy E.
1957   *United States Naval Administration of the Trust Territory of the Pacific Islands.* Vol. 3. Washington, D.C.: U.S. Government Printing Office.

Riesenberg, Saul H.
1954   "Report on visit to Kili." Unpublished report to the High Commissioner of the U.S. Trust Territory of the Pacific Islands. (Copy located in the files of the Trust Territory Headquarters, Saipan, Marianas Islands.)

Rimoldi, Max
1966   *Land Tenure and Land Use among the Mount Lamington Orokaiva.* Canberra and Port Moresby: Australian National University, New Guinea Research Unit Bulletin no. 11.

Sahlins, Marshall D.
1957   "Land use and the extended family in Moala, Fiji." *American Anthropologist* 59:449–462.

1965    "On the sociology of primitive exchange." In *The Relevance of Models for Social Anthropology*, edited by Michael Banton. ASA Monograph 1. London: Tavistock Publications.

1968    *Tribesmen*. Englewood Cliffs, New Jersey: Prentice-Hall.

Sahlins, Marshall D. and Elman R. Service
1960    *Evolution and Culture*. Ann Arbor: University of Michigan Press.

Schneider, David M.
1968    *American Kinship: A Cultural Account*. Englewood Cliffs, New Jersey: Prentice-Hall.

Schneider, Harold
1970    *The Wahi Wyanturi: Economics in an African Society*. Viking Fund Publications in Anthropology, no. 48. Chicago: Aldine.

Schwimmer, Erik G.
1967    "Modern Orokaiva leadership." *Journal of the Papua New Guinea Society* 1(1):52–60.

1969    *Cultural Consequences of a Volcanic Eruption Experienced by the Mount Lamington Orokaiva*. Eugene: University of Oregon, Department of Anthropology.

1970a   "Alternance de l'échange restreint et de l'échange generalise dans le système matrimoniale Orokaiva." *L'Homme* 10(4):5–34.

1970b   *The Ideology of Exchange*. Paris: Laboratoire d'Anthropologie Sociale. Mimeographed.

n.d.    "Exchange in the social structure of the Orokaiva: a study of the traditional and emergent ideologies in the Northern District of Papua." (Unpublished manuscript; copy available from the author.)

Sebeok, Thomas A.
1970    "Is a comparative semiotics possible?" In *Échanges et Communications*, edited by Jean Pouillon and Pierre Maranda. The Hague: Mouton.

Service, Elman R.
1962    *Primitive Social Organization*. New York: Random House.

Sharp, Lauriston
1952    "Steel axes for stone age Australians." In *Human Problems in Technological Change*, edited by Edward H. Spicer. New York: Russell Sage Foundation.

Silverman, Martin G.
1969    "Maximize your options: a study in symbols, values, and

social structure." In *Forms of Symbolic Action*, edited by Robert F. Spencer. Proceedings of the 1969 Annual Spring Meeting, American Ethnological Society. Seattle: University of Washington Press.

1971    *Disconcerting Issue: Meaning and Struggle in a Resettled Pacific Community*. Chicago: University of Chicago Press.

Spillius, James
1957    "Polynesian experiment: Tikopia islanders as plantation labour." *Progress* 46–47:91–96.

Spoehr, Alexander
1949    *Majuro: A Village in the Marshall Islands*. Fieldiana: Anthropology, vol. 39. Chicago: Chicago Natural History Museum.

Steward, Julian H.
1941    *Culture Element Distributions XIII: Nevada Shoshoni*. University of California Anthropological Records, vol. 4, no. 2. Berkeley: University of California Press.

1943    *Culture Element Distributions XXIII: Northern and Gosiute Shoshoni*. University of California Anthropological Records, vol. 8, no. 3. Berkeley: University of California Press.

1955    *Theory of Culture Change*. Urbana: University of Illinois Press.

Stewart, Omer
1941    *Culture Element Distributions XIV: Northern Paiute*. University of California Anthropological Records, vol. 4, no. 3. Berkeley: University of California Press.

Taylor, G. A.
1958    *The 1951 Eruption of Mount Lamington*. Canberra: Department of National Development, Bureau of Mineral Resources, Geology and Geophysics Bulletin no. 38.

Tobin, Jack
1954    "Kili journal." Unpublished report. (Copy located in the files of the district headquarters, Majuro, Marshall Islands, U.S. Trust Territory of the Pacific Islands.)

1958    "Land tenure in the Marshall Islands." In *Land Tenure Patterns: Trust Territory of the Pacific Islands*, vol. 1, edited by John de Young. Guam: Office of the High Commissioner, U.S. Trust Territory of the Pacific Islands.

Tomlin, J. W. S.
1951    *Awakening: A History of the New Guinea Mission*. London: Fulham Press.

Tonkinson, Robert
1968    *Maat Village, Efate: A Relocated Community in the New*

*Hebrides*. Eugene: University of Oregon, Department of Anthropology.

Turbott, I. G.
1954 "Portulaca—a specialty in the diet of the Gilbertese in the Phoenix Islands, Central Pacific." *Journal of the Polynesian Society* 63:77–85.

Turner, Victor
1957 *Schism and Continuity in an African Society*. Manchester: Manchester University Press.
1970 *The Forest of Symbols*. Ithaca: Cornell University Press (paperback edition).

U.S. Department of State
1968 *Bulletin*, vol. 54, no. 1525. Washington, D.C.: U.S. Government Printing Office.

U.S. Trust Territory of the Pacific Islands (TTPI)
1974 *Highlights*. A newsletter. 15 February 1974.

van der Leeuw, G.
1938 *Religion in Essence and Manifestation*. London: Allen and Unwin.

Waddell, E. W. and P. A. Krinks
1968 *The Organization of Production and Distribution among the Orokaiva*. Canberra and Port Moresby: Australian National University, New Guinea Research Unit Bulletin no. 24.

Watson, James B.
1970 "Society as organized flow." *Southwestern Journal of Anthropology* 26:107–124.

Watson, Richard A. and Patty Jo Watson
1969 *Man and Nature*. New York: Harcourt, Brace and World.

Wiens, Herold J.
1962 *Atoll Environment and Ecology*. New Haven: Yale University Press.

Williams, C. E. F.
1964 "Vulcanology." In *Progress Report of the Geological Survey for the Period 1959–1962*. New Hebrides: British Government Service.

Williams, F. E.
1928 *Orokaiva Magic*. London: Oxford University Press.
1940 *Orokaiva Society*. London: Oxford University Press.
n.d. Unpublished manuscripts. (Copies located in Sydney, Australia, Mitchell Library, envelope 48.)

Worsley, Peter
1957 *The Trumpet Shall Sound*. London: McGibbon and Kee.

Zwart, F. H. A. G.
  1968    *Report on the Census of the Population, 1966.* Fijian Legis-
          lative Council Paper no. 9. Suva: Government Press.

# CONTRIBUTORS

VERN CARROLL is professor of anthropology at the University of Michigan. He attended Yale University, where he received a B.A. in 1959 and an M.A. in 1963; Cambridge University, where he received a B.A. in 1961 and an M.A. in 1966; and the University of Chicago, where he received his Ph.D. in 1966. His field research took him to Nukuoro Atoll in the Eastern Caroline Islands for thirty months between 1963 and 1966 and in 1967.

ALAN HOWARD is professor of anthropology at the University of Hawaii. He received his Ph.D. from Stanford University in 1962. He conducted field research on Rotuma and among Rotumans on Fiji from 1959 through 1961 and among contemporary Hawaiians from 1965 through 1968.

IRWIN HOWARD is associate professor of linguistics at the University of Hawaii. He received his Ph.D. from Massachusetts Institute of Technology in 1972. He conducted field research on Rotuma and among Rotumans on Fiji during 1960 and 1961 and on the Polynesian outlier, Takuu, in 1964.

ROBERT C. KISTE is associate professor of anthropology at the University of Minnesota. He received his B.A. from Indiana University in 1961 and his Ph.D. from the University of Oregon in

1967. He conducted field research on Kili Island and on Kwajalein Atoll in the Marshall Islands during 1963 and 1964 and in 1969 and 1973.

KENNETH E. KNUDSON is associate professor of anthropology at the University of Nevada, Reno. He received his B.S. from the University of Washington in 1956 and his Ph.D. from the University of Oregon in 1970. He conducted field research in New Mexico in 1961, on Ghizo Island in the Solomon Islands during 1961 and 1962 and again in 1975, in Norway in 1972 and 1974, and in Galveston, Texas, in 1974. He was chairman of the department of anthropology at the University of Nevada, Reno, from 1971 to 1973.

ERIC H. LARSON is a member of the faculty in anthropology at The Evergreen State College in Olympia, Washington. He received his B.A. from San Jose State College in 1956 and his Ph.D. from the University of Oregon in 1966. He conducted field research in Colombia, South America, in 1963 and on Pavuvu (Russell Islands) and Tikopia (Solomon Islands) during 1964 and 1965. He was an assistant professor in anthropology at the University of Connecticut before joining the faculty at The Evergreen State College.

MICHAEL D. LIEBER is associate professor of anthropology at the University of Illinois at Chicago Circle. He received his B.A. from Trinity College in 1960 and his Ph.D. from the University of Pittsburgh in 1968. He conducted field research on Ponape and Kapingamarangi in the Eastern Caroline Islands during 1965 and 1966 and has since compiled a lexicon of the Kapingamarangi language.

ROBERT K. McKNIGHT is professor of anthropology at California State University at Hayward. He received his B.A. from Miami University of Ohio in 1951, his M.A. from Ohio State University in 1954, and his Ph.D. from Ohio State University in 1960. He was district anthropologist for Palau in the U.S. Trust Territory of the Pacific Islands from 1958 to 1963, during which time he conducted extensive field research. He was the community development officer for the Trust Territory from 1963 to 1965. After leaving the Trust Territory, he was a visiting associate professor in anthropology at the University of Wisconsin in 1965 and 1966.

ERIK G. SCHWIMMER is professor of anthropology at the University of Laval, Quebec. He received his M.A. from the University of Wellington in 1949 and his Ph.D. from the University of British Columbia in 1970. He conducted field research among the Maori in New Zealand for sixteen months from 1960 to 1961 and among the Orokaiva at Sivepe in New Guinea for eighteen months from 1966 to 1967 and again in 1970 and 1973.

MARTIN G. SILVERMAN has been associate professor of anthropology at the University of Western Ontario since 1973. From 1966 to 1973 he taught at Princeton University and was Visiting Fellow in Pacific and Southeast Asian history at Australian National University during 1973 and 1974. He received his B.A. from Harvard University in 1960, his M.A. from the University of Chicago in 1964, and his Ph.D. from the University of Chicago in 1966. He was a Fulbright scholar at Australian National University in 1960 and 1961 and conducted research on Rambi Island, Fiji, for eighteen months in 1961 and in 1964 and 1965.

ROBERT TONKINSON is assistant professor of anthropology at the University of Oregon. He received his B.A. from the University of Western Australia in 1962, his M.A. from the same institution in 1966, and his Ph.D. from the University of British Columbia in 1972. He conducted field research in aboriginal Australia for a total of thirty-two months between 1962 and 1974. He also conducted field research in the New Hebrides on Efate and on Ambrym in 1966–1967, 1969, and again in 1973. He was a Visiting Fellow in anthropology at Australian National University from 1973 through 1975.

# ☃ PRODUCTION NOTES

The text of this book has been designed by Roger J. Eggers and typeset on the Unified Composing System by the design and production staff of The University Press of Hawaii.

The text and display typeface is California.

Offset presswork and binding is the work of Vail-Ballou Press. Text paper is Glatfelter P & S Offset, basis 55.